HUMPHREY NEWTON (1466–1536)
AN EARLY TUDOR GENTLEMAN

HUMPHREY NEWTON (1466–1536)
AN EARLY TUDOR GENTLEMAN

Deborah Youngs

THE BOYDELL PRESS

© Deborah Youngs 2008

All rights reserved. Except as permitted under current legislation
no part of this work may be photocopied, stored in a retrieval system,
published, performed in public, adapted, broadcast,
transmitted, recorded or reproduced in any form or by any means,
without the prior permission of the copyright owner

The right of Deborah Youngs to be identified as
the author of this work has been asserted in accordance with
sections 77 and 78 of the Copyright, Designs and Patents Act 1988

First published 2008
The Boydell Press, Woodbridge

ISBN 978–1–84383–395–6

The Boydell Press is an imprint of Boydell & Brewer Ltd
PO Box 9, Woodbridge, Suffolk IP12 3DF, UK
and of Boydell & Brewer Inc.
668 Mt Hope Avenue, Rochester, NY 14620, USA
website: www.boydellandbrewer.com

A CIP record for this book is available
from the British Library

This publication is printed on acid-free paper

Printed in Great Britain by
CPI Antony Rowe, Chippenham, Wiltshire

Contents

Illustrations	vi
Acknowledgements	ix
Abbreviations	xi
1. Introduction	1
2. The Newton Family	10
3. Humphrey and the Law	41
4. Land and Lordship	69
5. Beliefs	106
6. Lifestyle	143
7. Writer	177
8. Humphrey: The Man and his World	201
Appendices	
1. Timeline of key events during Humphrey Newton's life 1466–1536	213
2. Bodleian Library, MS Latin Miscellaneous c.66	215
Bibliography	219
Index	249

Lists of illustrations

Plates are between pages 148 and 149

1. Arms of the Newton family quartering the Mainwaring of Peover at Wilmslow parish church
2. Page from the Newton accounts. Bodleian Library, University of Oxford, MS Latin Misc.c.66, fo. 45v
3. The sacred heart. Bodleian Library, University of Oxford, MS Latin Misc. c. 66, fo. 129v
4. The tombs of Humphrey and Ellen Newton, Wilmslow parish church. Photo: Conway Library, The Courtauld Institute of Art, London.
5. The tomb of Humphrey Newton, Wilmslow parish church. Photo: Conway Library, The Courtauld Institute of Art, London
6. Sketch of a quadrant and secular lyrics. Bodleian Library, University of Oxford, MS Latin. Misc.c.66, fo. 94v
7. St Veronica and the vernicle. Bodleian Library, University of Oxford, MS Latin Misc.c.66, fo. 106v
8. Sketch of a harp. Bodleian Library, University of Oxford, MS Latin Misc. c.66, fo. 8v

Figures

1.	Genealogy of the Newton family	12
2.	The Newton chapel	130

Maps

1.	Humphrey's landholdings and stewardships in their regional context	xii
2.	The Newton estate in its locality	70

For Alex

Acknowledgements

It is over a decade and a half since I first alighted on Humphrey Newton's manuscript in the Bodleian Library in 1992. While my own historical interests have broadened and changed since then, the belief that Humphrey deserved a book-length study has never waned. I would, therefore, like to express my gratitude to Boydell and Brewer, and particularly to Caroline Palmer, for the support and encouragement given to this project when I decided, finally in 2005–6, to act on this belief. I am equally grateful to the AHRC and the Marc Fitch Fund for their financial support of this project, and in the assistance of the very kind and helpful staff at the National and local record offices where Humphrey's documentary remains lie. I would especially like to thank Mrs C.J.C. Legh of Adlington Hall, near Macclesfield, for her kind permission to access the Legh of Adlington Archive.

The 1990s were an exciting time to begin researching the late medieval gentry, and I benefited from the stimulating papers and conversations of numerous historians and literary scholars. My warmest memories belong to the annual Fifteenth Century conferences, the 'M6 seminars' and the 'Gentry Culture' colloquiums jointly-hosted by Keele and York universities. My thanks extend to all participants, but Peter Fleming, Simon Harris, Carol Meale, Nicholas Orme, Nigel Saul and Tim Thornton deserve special mention for the help and interest they gave my work. It was particularly fortuitous on my part that I spent my postgraduate years and early career in the inspirational company of Ralph Griffiths, Philip Morgan and Colin Richmond. I have profited greatly from their continuing support and indispensable advice; they have taught me to remember the humanity in history. Ralph Griffiths and Philip Morgan have also been kind enough to cast their critical eyes over a number of chapters of this book and I am similarly grateful to Michael Bennett, Rhianydd Biebrach, Julia Boffey, Maureen Jurkowski, Jane Laughton, Raluca Radulescu and to the two anonymous readers of the manuscript. All have improved this work by sharpening my thinking and pointing out errors; any faults that remain can be my responsibility alone.

While keen academic minds have helped shape my ideas, it has been the wider support of family, friends and colleagues that has brought the project to fruition. My trips to London were facilitated by the 'lifts' and kind hospitality of Colin and Jennie Marsh. At Swansea I received encouragement from Leighton, Louise, Ifor Rowlands and John Spurr. My family have offered their continued support too, in their own inimitable ways. My parents will be pleased with the book's publication and I hope it will finally remind them that the subject was called Humphrey rather than Herbert (Dad). Of all, however, my greatest debt is to Alex, as he himself knows far too well. He has acted as sounding-board, copy-editor, computer technician and emotional prop throughout this project. I owe him everything: the dedication could go to no other.

My final acknowledgement is the hardest to write. A week after I sent the manuscript to the publishers, my dearest friend, James Thomas, unexpectedly died, tragically young. It is of great sadness to me that he cannot see the publication of this book. My one, small, consolation is that I had time to thank him personally for his ever-present, ever-generous support. I will be forever in his debt.

Abbreviations

BL	British Library
Bodl	Bodleian Library
Canterbury Tales	All quotations taken from L.D. Benson (ed) *The Riverside Chaucer* (3rd edn., Oxford, 1988)
CPR	*Calendar of patent rolls*
CRO	Cheshire Record Office (Cheshire and Chester Archives and Local Studies)
CS	*Chetham Society*
DKR	*Annual Reports of the deputy keeper of the public records* (London, 1840)
EETS	Early English Text Society
HMC	Historical Manuscripts Commission
JRUL	John Rylands University Library, Manchester
KUL	Keele University Library
LP	*Letters and papers, foreign and domestic, of the reign of Henry VIII, 1509–47*, eds. J.S. Brewer, J. Gairdner and R.H. Brodie (London, 1862–1910)
NIMEV	*NIMEV: A new index of Middle English Verse*, eds. Julia Boffey and A.S.G. Edwards (British Library: London, 2005)
NUL	Nottingham University Library
Ormerod, *Chester*	George Ormrod, *The history of the county palatine and city of Chester*, 2nd edn, rev. and enlarged by Thomas Helsby (3 vols, London, 1882)
PMLA	*Publications of the Modern Language Association of America*
RSLC	*Record Society of Lancashire and Cheshire*
THSLC	*Transactions of the Historic Society of Lancashire and Cheshire*
TLCAS	*Transactions of the Lancashire and Cheshire Antiquarian Society*
TNA: PRO	The National Archives, Public Record Office, London
TRHS	*Transactions of the Royal Historical Society*
VCH	*Victoria County History*

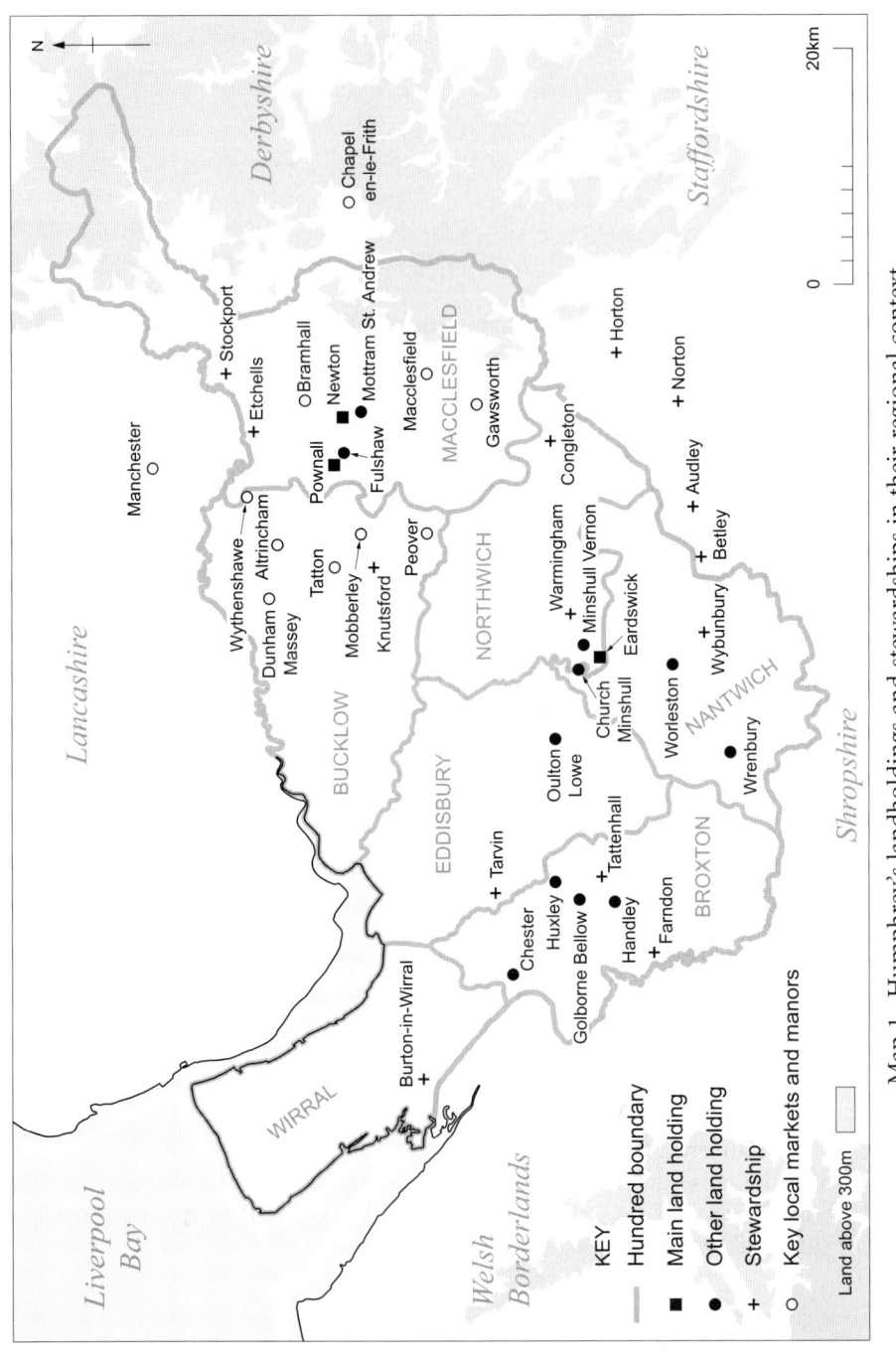

Map 1. Humphrey's landholdings and stewardships in their regional context
Map by Anne Leaver

1

Introduction

On 8 December 1499, Humphrey Newton walked around the grounds of his estate in Newton, Cheshire, accompanied by Thomas Cross, a local builder. Crosse was to construct the new fulling mill at Newton and had already supplied Humphrey with an estimate for the work. As Humphrey's estate was to provide the raw materials, the two men spent some time pinpointing the trees suitable for the building project. Around a dozen were to be felled, and Humphrey made careful note of their location and their purpose. He appears to have been a man with a keen eye for trees and, in a spare page in his notebook, he sketched the form of a tall tree, which he then made home to a parrot, high up in its branches, and a hovering osprey. It was also the resting place of a bird about which Humphrey seemed a little unsure: he wrote around the drawing 'crow or egle'. The hooked beak and talons can only suggest a bird of prey, but perhaps Humphrey had some other query in mind that was beyond his limited artistic skills.[1]

It is such details that fascinate the historian and which identify a person. Individuals often reveal themselves in the flash of an eye, a laugh, a gesture or a desire. With these images we glimpse the subject of this book, Humphrey Newton of Newton and Pownall (1466–1536). He seems an energetic and observant man, practical and yet creative. Moving from the fragments and the particular to a picture of the whole, however, is far from easy. It is not a straightforward process in any period or for anyone. When musing on her biography of Roger Fry, Virginia Woolf wrote to her niece: 'Do you think it possible to write a life of anyone? I doubt it; because people are all over the place.'[2] For fifteenth- and sixteenth-century English society, this is often literally true. Sources bearing the name of Humphrey Newton may presently be found in Chester, Keele, London, Manchester, Nottingham, Oxford, Sheffield and Wilmslow. Drawing together the elements of his life will therefore involve piecing together scattered fragments. The challenge of the historical evidence, both qualitatively and quantitatively, is inevitable in studying someone who lived at the close of the Middle Ages. Personal records were not produced by large sections of the population and substantial archives survive mainly for England's wealthiest, most powerful and best educated. This has meant

---

[1] Bodl, MS Lat. Misc.c.66, fos 31ar, 95v.
[2] The letter to Angelica Bell (written 1935) can be found in Hermione Lee, *Virginia Woolf*, p. 667.

that studies of late medieval individuals have generally focused on royalty, nobility, significant religious characters and key literary figures like Chaucer and Lydgate. While the rise of gender history has sought to shift the focus away from great men contributing to great events, even here the biographical focus largely remains on extraordinary women: on queens, wealthy noblewomen and Margery Kempe. 'Ordinariness' in itself rarely generated contemporary comment and consequently a trace in the records; it does not always attract the historian's eye.

Humphrey Newton, by contrast, was not famous or infamous in his time. The vast majority in early Tudor England – including his home county of Cheshire – would not have recognised his name. Historical study has hardly redressed the balance. He has no place in the *Oxford Dictionary of National Biography*, and few know of his tomb, which lies alongside that of his wife in the parish church of Wilmslow. This book is not about a person of whom many will hitherto have heard. And that is the point. Its intention is to examine an individual who was neither singled out as unusual in his own time, nor someone whom later history books consider marginalised. This means that Humphrey Newton may offer a rare and valuable insight into late medieval and early Tudor English society.

On the other hand, Humphrey was not a man whom historians consider to have been of average income or power in his day. His contemporaries regularly called him 'gentleman' and, towards the end of his life, he achieved recognition as an esquire. For modern historians, this means that Humphrey belonged to a section of society conventionally labelled 'the gentry': the lesser landowners located between the yeomanry and the peerage, and encompassing, by the late fifteenth century, the categories of knight, esquire and gentleman. Who the gentry were at any one time, in any one county or country, has generated lengthy discussions, especially in attempting to identify those at the lower reaches of this social group. There were various routes to becoming a gentleman: the acquisition of land with rights of lordship; the blood of traceable ancestry; and royal and seignorial service.[3] In recent years additional weight has been placed on cultural identification through lifestyle and a shared outlook on life. In other words, contemporaries themselves would have recognised those whom they considered to be of gentle status – like Humphrey Newton – by the cut of their clothing, the size of their households, their leisure pursuits and their privileges.[4] What this helped to

---

[3] For thorough surveys of the historiography on defining the gentry see Carpenter, *Locality and polity*, ch. 3 and Coss, *The origins*, ch. 1. Good discussions of the range of criteria can be found in Morgan, 'The individual style'; Pugh, 'The magnates, knights and gentry'; Heal and Holmes, *The gentry*, pp. 7–19; Maddern, 'Gentility'; and Keen, *Origins*, esp. chs 5 and 7.

[4] For example, Dyer, *Making a living*, pp. 340–1; Morgan, 'Ranks of society', pp. 73–5; Radulescu and Truelove (eds) *Gentry culture*. Humphrey's qualifications for gentility will be discussed throughout the book.

create was a collective identity with a marked sense of social difference. To be judged a gentleman ultimately meant an acceptance by social equals together with deference accorded by those below.[5] It was the gentry who formed the backbone of late medieval society, their social and political power assigning them notable roles in the governance of local communities. Their number in fifteenth-century England has been estimated at between 6,000 and 9,000, perhaps closer to 6,000 by 1500. In short, Humphrey Newton belonged to a section of society comprising less than two per cent of the total English population.[6]

As a group, the gentry received detailed attention in many historical studies written in the 1980s and 1990s. In these years the county study dominated, with a focus on the knights and esquires.[7] In addition, few extended studies of the individual medieval gentleman have been produced since Colin Richmond's seminal work, *John Hopton*, in 1981.[8] Some might say that there are good reasons for this state of affairs. For Christine Carpenter a better understanding of the gentry emerges less from a focus on individuals and more from an examination of the 'fundamental beliefs and attitudes that informed their [the gentry's] political life'.[9] There is also the patent obstacle that, while there is no shortage of records about the gentry, these are overwhelmingly formal and impersonal, and generated by their landed interests: title deeds, estate accounts, court records and the like. There is a marked lack of surviving personal evidence that would enable the researcher to penetrate private and mental worlds. Outside the well-known letter collections of Paston, Plumpton, Stonor, and Armburgh, there are few opportunities to listen to the gentry's authentic voices.[10]

Happily Humphrey Newton is one of those fortunate voices because he has left us a comparatively rich amount of material. His landed status generated some of the expected public documents (such as his inquisition *post mortem*), while the frequency with which landowners went to the law to defend or challenge boundaries has resulted in several court records relating to him. That he and his family shared gentle society's desire for memorialisation led to the construction of two tombs in Wilmslow parish church, which can still be seen in the north chapel. Rather less expectedly, there is a thirty-two-page

---

[5] Given-Wilson, *English nobility*, p. ix; Maddern, 'Gentility', p. 26; Coss, *The origins*, pp. 9–11.
[6] Pugh, 'The magnates, knights and gentry', p. 97; Given-Wilson, *English nobility*, p. 69; Carpenter, *The Wars of the Roses*, p. 45; Britnell, *The closing of the Middle Ages?*, p. 190.
[7] For example, Acheson, *A gentry community*; Bennett, *Community*; Carpenter, *Locality and polity*; Fleming, 'Gentry of Kent'; Payling, *Political society*; Saul, *Knights and esquires*; Wright, *Derbyshire gentry*.
[8] Richmond, *John Hopton*. But see Moreton, *The Townshends*, and Swabey, *Medieval gentlewoman*.
[9] Carpenter, *Locality and polity*, p. 8.
[10] Acheson, *A gentry community*, p. 2: 'the gentry have been silent about themselves and their concerns; there have been too few voices to hear'.

cartulary (a collection of deeds and charters), which Humphrey's eldest son, William, transcribed in the mid-sixteenth century.[11] Although a handful of deeds relate to William's time, much of the material dates to Humphrey's lordship. Internal evidence, along with several extant deeds, suggests that the cartulary was a part-transcription of one or more earlier documents written by Humphrey himself.[12] No extensive, consolidated 'Newton archive' has survived, but the cartulary indicates that the Newtons, in common with other gentry families across England, were self-conscious preservers of their charters and supporting documents. Like other cartularies, the aim of the Newton manuscript was to record deeds relevant to the owner's landholdings and, amongst other things, it is invaluable in charting a major local land dispute in which the Newtons became embroiled during the first half of the sixteenth century. It is unusual to have such a cartulary surviving for a secular lord and it may well have been this dispute which prompted William's transcription.[13]

Above all, it is the survival of a commonplace book, compiled by Humphrey some time between the 1490s and the 1520s, which provides the most exciting and unique information upon which this study is based.[14] Such books are exceptional survivals today: no other miscellany written by a gentleman from early Tudor Cheshire, or indeed the North West, is known. The 129 folios that comprise the book demonstrate the range of Humphrey's literary skills and the breadth of his interests: pages are filled with estate accounts, legal documents, land deeds, genealogies, prayers, charms, astrological charts, medical recipes, prophecies, literary extracts and love lyrics (a number of

[11] BL, Add MS 42134A. It is evident that leaves have been lost from the original manuscript. The lacunae are noted in the transcription made in the nineteenth century by the Cheshire antiquarian J.P. Earwaker; this is Add MS 42134B. As is to be expected, the core of the cartulary is a collection of land deeds systematically arranged according to place/property. Additional material includes several genealogies, two rentals and a poem. The manuscript has received little attention since the nineteenth century, and the fullest description and discussion may still be found in Noyes, 'Some notices of the family of Newton', pp. 312–42.

[12] For example, two deeds now in the Bromley Davenport collection at the John Rylands University Library, Manchester (JRUL), reveal that William transcribed not only the documents, but Humphrey's annotations too: JRUL, Bromley Davenport, 'Newton' deeds nos 1 and 5. Other folios in the cartulary appear to have been copied straight out of Humphrey's commonplace book (for which see n. 16).

[13] Davies, *Medieval Cartularies*, lists 1185 cartularies belonging to religious houses and 169 owned by laymen. For preservation as a characteristic of the gentry, see Morgan, 'Making the English gentry', p. 23.

[14] Bodl, MS Lat. Misc.c.66. A summary of contents can be found in HMC's second report, *Reports on manuscripts in various collections*, pp. 80–1. The book is mainly of paper and in a variety of stocks and sizes. As a guide, the majority of the pages can be considered as just slightly bigger than A4 size, around 300mm x 220mm. It was written in English and Latin, with a little law French. The overall condition of the manuscript is fair to good, though some parts are badly faded and corners have succumbed to mice, damp and general wear and tear. For summary of contents see Appendix 2 below.

which are his personal compositions). There are some quite uncommon finds. There are estate accounts and dealings with servants, which are rarely found for a small gentry estate. A Middle English vision of the afterlife survives uniquely in the commonplace book, and is one of only four known examples of vernacular otherworld visions to date to the fifteenth century.[15] Yet, overall, it is very much a notebook, bitty, laconic, sometimes inscrutable, and all the more interesting for that. Those qualities explain the book's treatment since the sixteenth century. It has not been ignored, but the tendency has been to mine the document for information rather than study it in the round. Sixteenth- and seventeenth-century antiquarians poured over its genealogies, nineteenth-century manuscript editors were interested in its courtesy treatises, and twentieth-century literary scholars have discussed its courtly love lyrics.[16] In contrast, the present book considers the manuscript and its author as a whole. A detailed discussion of the manuscript's form will be found in Chapter 7, and readers wishing to view Humphrey with its structure in mind may wish to turn first to that section. The preceding chapters will make full use of the book's contents, placing Humphrey's writings in the context of other material illuminating his life and interests. What will be seen throughout is the extraordinary personal detail that the commonplace book contains, and the way that its survival allows a more intimate picture of an English gentleman than could otherwise be achieved.

The main aim of this study is to produce a biography of an early Tudor gentleman, as far as it is possible. Like much of medieval history, what survives for the man are clusters of information. The evidence focuses on Humphrey's 'middle' years; we know little of his early and later life, and we know more about his time at Newton than about the years he spent at Pownall. There are no letters, diaries or autobiography, which modern biographers might expect. However, the personal nature of the commonplace book means that, as Charles Moreton found when reading Roger Townshend's fifteenth-century notebook, Humphrey's 'character filters through' in his writings.[17] The major advantage in studying Humphrey is that he can be viewed as a multi-dimensional figure: the following chapters place him in the context of his family, the law, landownership, religion and cultural interests. While these topics are frequently assigned a place in county studies of the gentry, it is unusual to be able to analyse the different dimensions of the same individual, especially one who stood below the nobility. This is particularly the case with Humphrey's cultural interests, influences and achievements. Chapter 6 focuses on his lifestyle and Chapter 7 discusses his role as a writer, while throughout this study his literary skills and reading material feature prominently. Humphrey was

---

[15] For discussion see pp. 117–18 below.
[16] Bodl, MS Lat. Misc.c.66, fo. 1; CRO, CR 63/1/93/8; Furnivall (ed.), *The babees book*; Robbins, 'The poems of Humfrey Newton esquire', pp. 249–81. For a recent study that does consider the whole manuscript, see Hanna, 'Humphrey Newton'.
[17] Moreton, *The Townshends*, p. 18.

living during a period of improving literacy rates and greater availability of books; he was eleven years old when Caxton established the first publishing house in England in 1476. In considering Humphrey's preferences, similarities and contrasts will be drawn with contemporary readers and writers in order to assess the degree to which he was following current trends. Living his adult life largely during the reigns of the early Tudors, Henry VII and VIII, Humphrey bridges a traditional historical divide between the medieval and early modern eras, and in focusing on the viewpoint of such an individual, this study addresses certain current questions concerning pre-Reformation religious beliefs and practices, land management and gentry culture during a period of considerable change.

Two important components of this analysis are location and social status. The gentry have long been seen as rooted in their locality: county studies are predicated on the need to understand the gentry in their own communities. Close examination of the gentry's associations and preoccupations have continually served to underline what Eric Acheson has declared to be 'the triumph of localism in the gentry's business dealings'.[18] It is vital, therefore, that Humphrey Newton is placed in the context of the area in which he was born, raised, wielded authority and won his reputation. He lived in the parishes of Prestbury and Wilmslow, within the hundred of Macclesfield in the county of Chester. The hundred and the county have been well served by historians, especially in relation to the late medieval political community.[19] They suggest, on the one hand, that Humphrey had not been fortunate in the location of his birth. The backdrop to Michael Bennett's study of the fourteenth-century North West is an area remote, sparsely populated, poor and economically under-developed. Its distance from the main centres of power and population discouraged the establishment of noble households and resulted in meagre cultural patronage. While others have tempered this view,[20] and economic development occurred in the later fifteenth century, notably associated with the port of Chester, Humphrey was not living in one of the most developed or wealthiest regions of England. On the other hand, he lived in an area which had once produced the famous *Sir Gawain and the Green Knight* and which possessed a rich political culture. Cheshire was a county palatinate with its own system of government, council, courts and administration. Tim Thornton, in particular, has championed the vitality of these structures of late medieval Cheshire. Such distinctive privileges may have had a downside for an aspiring gentleman: the offices of JP and MP, common routes to advancement elsewhere in England, were not introduced

---

[18] Acheson, *A gentry community*, pp. 85–7. Moreton, 'A social gulf?' and id., *The Townshends*, p. 196.
[19] For example, Bennett, *Community*; Booth, *The financial administration of the lordship*; Morgan, *War and society*; Clayton; *The administration of the county palatine*; Thornton, *Cheshire*; Tonkinson, *Macclesfield*.
[20] Booth, *The financial administration of the lordship*, p. 5.

to the county until after Humphrey's death. Yet the Cheshire gentry were both numerous – 'the seed plot of gentilite', as one Elizabethan writer called the county – and powerful. Studies by Bennett, Thornton and Dorothy Clayton have emphasised the importance and dominance of the gentry in Cheshire and the relative weakness of noble influence.[21]

In employing examples from Cheshire, this book will both place Humphrey in his local context and draw attention to an area currently poorly represented in historical discussions of religious beliefs or economic developments compared with other regions (such as in East Anglia and the West Midlands). The private world of Cheshire's gentry is almost unknown. Nevertheless, early Tudor England was not an agglomeration of insular enclaves: England had been the most centralised political state in the British Isles for several centuries. Culturally the fifteenth-century ruling elites were far more Anglocentric than they had been a century earlier: they spoke and wrote in English, and read a growing corpus of English historical writing and English poetry. This book, then, will not be a parochial study, but one that assesses the relative impact of international, national and local trends on a gentleman and his family.

It is also important to consider Humphrey in relation to his fellow landowners both in Cheshire and elsewhere in England. Recent studies have emphasised not only the collective interests of the gentry, but also the commonality between the nobility and gentry during the fifteenth century. For Kate Mertes, the aristocracy (both nobility and gentry) should be seen as a culture, 'a complex web of habits, traditions, relationships, behaviours, assumptions and beliefs'.[22] The culture of the gentry, however, has not always been assessed positively. It has been described as a 'pale reflection' and a 'watered-down version' of nobility, as Chapter 6 indicates.[23]

Yet, at the same time, distinctions have been drawn within the gentry which bear on a study of Humphrey Newton. Among early modern studies, a threefold division of the gentry into lower, middling and upper has been made.[24] Among late medieval county studies – such as those of Derbyshire, Gloucestershire, Kent, Nottinghamshire and Cheshire – the division has been into two: an elite group of greater or county gentry and a lesser group of parish gentry. The greater gentry comprised knights and some esquires, the number varying between county and period. For fifteenth-century Derbyshire, Susan Wright identified fifty-two among her total of 212 gentry families which could be considered county gentry. Nigel Saul identified fifty such families in four-

---

21 Bennett, *Community*, especially chs 5 and 10; Clayton, *The administration of the county palatine*, ch. 4 (quotation on the 'seed plot' found on p. 132); Thornton, *Cheshire*, ch. 1 and *passim*; Given-Wilson, *The English nobility*, p. 72, for comparisons.
22 Mertes, 'Aristocracy', p. 42; Coss, *The origins*, p. 11; Carpenter, 'England: the nobility and the gentry', pp. 266–7.
23 Harriss, *Shaping the nation*, p. 140; Coss 'An age of deference', p. 41.
24 Heal and Holmes, *The gentry*, p. 15.

teenth-century Gloucestershire, while Simon Payling identified only about a dozen for Nottinghamshire. In Payling's study, his elite group of greater gentry were those wealthy families who dominated the county, performing to some degree the role of magnates in Nottinghamshire, a county which lacked a strong noble presence. Thornton's directly comparable study of Cheshire, 1480–1560, argues along similar lines: the county was dominated by an elite group of thirty to fifty families which possessed most of the county's wealth, led the county's men to war and were active in its administration.[25] Below this elite, the lesser gentry comprised the poorer esquires, the gentlemen and some lawyers and merchants – in other words, the vast majority of the gentry.

The differences between these knights and esquires, on the one hand, and the gentlemen, on the other, have been described as amounting to an 'enormous gulf'[26] and an 'economic chasm'.[27] Distinctions have been made in terms of gradations of wealth, patterns of landholding, social connections, business dealings, office holding, religious practices and cultural outlook. The county gentry, for instance, were more likely to own property in several areas and hold franchises such as view of frankpledge; the parish gentry had more localised landed interests with no franchises. The county gentry dominated the key offices of the shire, such as those of sheriff and JP; the parish gentry were more likely to be tax collectors and jurors. Ultimately it was the county gentry who formed the main political community of the shire: in Cheshire the elite families provided the military and administrative authority in the shire.[28] In society at large the two groups are seen as having their own distinct circles, with very little social mixing between them. The county gentry tended to marry one another and use one another as witnesses and feoffees in their deeds. Whereas the county gentry may have mixed with the baronage, the minor gentry more often consorted with those living in the immediate vicinity of their estates.[29]

While this construct of the greater and lesser gentry makes some useful distinctions, and the latter have not been entirely overlooked in gentry studies, it has been the case that the lesser gentry have rarely received extensive coverage. This is where a study of Humphrey Newton is of great import. Humphrey was not one of his county's major worthies; there is nothing to suggest he was ever close to achieving knightly status. His fourteenth-century ancestors are minor figures in the Cheshire studies of Bennett and Tonkinson,

---

[25] Wright, *Derbyshire gentry*, pp. 5–6; Saul, *Knights and esquires*, p. 34; Fleming, 'Charity', pp. 36–7; Payling, *Political society*, ch. 1; Thornton, *Cheshire*, p. 29; Given-Wilson, *The English nobility*, p. 71.
[26] Wright, *Derbyshire gentry*, p. 6.
[27] Acheson, *A gentry community*, p. 43.
[28] Summaries to be found in Given-Wilson, *The English nobility*, pp. 73–4, and Harriss, *Shaping the nation*, p. 140; Thornton, *Cheshire*, pp. 24–5.
[29] For example, Payling, *Political society*, p. 86; Ormrod, *Political life*, p. 47.

and, more significantly, the Newtons are absent from Thornton's list of the major families in Cheshire in 1480–1560.[30] That is not to say that Humphrey was on the very margins of gentility, where the parish gentry merged with the elite of the village peasantry. As the chapters on his family and estate demonstrate, his status as a gentleman was recognised in local society. But by moving the focus away from the county elite, greater light is shed on the provincial gentleman, enabling Carpenter's question to be turned into a statement: 'there was more to the life of a lesser landowner in the late Middle Ages than discussion with neighbours over the price of pigs.'[31]

While Humphrey was not among the elite of Cheshire, he had aspirations. If the fifteenth century is turning out to be less of an 'age of ambition' than was once thought, it still boasts a number of success stories.[32] Those who rose into the ranks of the gentry include, for example, the families of Paston and Townshend in East Anglia, and the Kebells in Leicestershire.[33] Humphrey's story may lack their dramatic trajectories, but he did markedly improve his family's position in society. The present study examines his upward social mobility in terms of the routes he took – marriage, land acquisition and development, lordship and seigniorial service. It considers the lifestyle he followed as he fashioned an image for himself which he believed was consonant with his status. The gentry as a whole was a competitive and status-conscious group; social position needed to be constantly negotiated and asserted.[34] Humphrey's commonplace book offers a valuable insight into the micro-processes and tactics of social advancement.

There is much that remains a mystery about Humphrey Newton, and entries in his commonplace book often raise more questions than they answer. How did he know Lady Jane Delamere of Aldermaston, Berkshire? What was the play he watched in 1499? Why did he buy a piece of marble in the early sixteenth century, and was it the stone or the cloth?[35] Even if these questions must be left tantalisingly unanswered, Humphrey's writings allow us to construct a clearer and more nuanced picture of a section of society which rarely emerges from the background of historical discourse. This book recovers the individuality of a remarkable man who strode out one December day at the turn of the fifteenth century to survey his Cheshire estate.

---

[30] Bennett, *Community*, pp. 232, 234; Tonkinson, *Macclesfield*, pp. 20, 71; Thornton, *Cheshire*, table 1, pp. 30–1.
[31] Carpenter, 'Who ruled the Midlands?', p. 9.
[32] Du Boulay, *An age of ambition*; Maddern, 'Social mobility'; Harriss, *Shaping the nation*, p. 142.
[33] Richmond, *The Paston family in the fifteenth century*; Moreton, *The Townshends*; Ives, *The common lawyers*.
[34] Maddern, 'Gentility', p. 31.
[35] Bodl, MS Lat. Misc.c.66, fos 29v, 59av, 61r.

2

The Newton Family

Humphrey's commonplace book opens with a list of his Newton ancestors and the growing number of his children. Past, present and future are represented, neatly demonstrating what Kate Mertes has described as the 'abstract devotion to the perpetuation of the name' found among aristocratic families.[1] It is appropriate to introduce Humphrey through his kin because he saw himself as one link in a genealogical chain, stretching over centuries. Through his ancestors – his bloodline – Humphrey was able show his gentle origins. He fulfilled the criterion voiced by medieval writers like the fifteenth-century Burgundian Olivier de la Marche who wrote that 'the gentleman [*gentil homme*] is he who of old springs from gentlemen and gentlewomen.'[2] At the same time, the family was the fundamental political, social and economic unit of early Tudor England.[3] As a result of inheritance and marriage, Humphrey became the head of families located first at Newton and subsequently at Pownall. Both properties were legally under his management and he was responsible for the welfare and actions of the dependents – his wife, children and servants – residing there. He needed to ensure harmony; he needed to try and maintain the integrity of the Newton estate, while simultaneously creating new alliances; and he needed to secure the future of the family. In focusing on Humphrey's blood relations and lineage, this chapter considers his role as head of the Newton family and the legacy he left it.

The Ancestors

We must begin with the earliest Newtons. The late medieval gentry sought knowledge of their ancestors in order to establish their blood line, to proclaim important connections and to make claim to land. Humphrey was well aware that his own identity and position in life were connected to the past, and as a consequence he made his own genealogical searches through family papers.[4] When he looked back over his findings, he would have seen few of the attributes that graced the more significant lines of medieval England. There

---

[1] Mertes, 'Aristocracy', p. 46.
[2] Keen, *Chivalry*, p. 150. Keen, *Origins*, p. 106.
[3] Fleming, *Family and household*; James, *Family*, pp. 19–21.
[4] Marsh, '"I see by sizt of evidence"'; Radulescu, *The gentry context*, p. 68.

was no Conquest origin, no knighthoods, no one of great political importance or even regional fame that ever headed the household. Yet his ancestry did have two very important characteristics: the family had always been freeholders, and it could be traced back in the male line for over two centuries. It had also achieved a gradual improvement in wealth and status throughout that period. No wastrel ancestor or over-indulgent father had led the family close to ruin by dissipating its modest fortunes.

Who, then, were the Newtons? According to Humphrey's researches, the origins of the Newton family lay in the late twelfth century with an obscure family named Hoppehall, holders of a third of the Newton estate.[5] Their gradual land expansion in the area prompted an early landmark in the family history: the match of place and name. When William Hoppehall became known as William de Newton in the early thirteenth century, the identification acknowledged a major landholder in the area.[6] The family's tenure of the vill of Newton, however, had to await the next century as the intervening years saw the estate pass through the hands of the Hyde and Davenport families. It was in 1302 that Thomas Newton, a descendant of William Newton, married Sybil Davenport, the daughter of Thomas Davenport of Davenport (*fl.* 1260–1320). The Newton estate was Sybil's dowry.[7]

Despite the fourteenth century's reputation as a century of crisis and missed generations, the Newton family appears to have continued successfully in the male line. Humphrey recorded that Thomas was succeeded by his son and his grandson, both named Richard, and both, apparently, were still living in the 1390s.[8] Marriage again brought the family benefits, though this time they were confined to broadening connections. The younger Richard made two advantageous marriages. The first was to Sybil, daughter of William Downes of Worth (*fl.* 1341–5), an important landholder in the Macclesfield hundred, and therefore an indication of the growing status of the Newton

---

5   BL, Add MS 42134A, fo. 8. Hoppehall in all likelihood derives from the place name 'Hephales' or Hepal, in Torkington (near Macclesfield). The name appears sporadically in thirteenth- and fourteenth-century court records: for example, Stewart-Brown (ed.) *Chester county court rolls*, pp. 214, 224.
6   Presumably because William had received grants of land in Newton from Thomas de Norbury (living 1173) and Richard de Aldford (d. 1213): JRUL, Bromley Davenport, 'Newton by Mottram', no. 9; CRO, CR63/1/45/6. See BL, Add MS 42134, fo. 8v and Bodl, MS Lat. Misc.c.66, fo. 101b for a 'descent' of the Newton estate from Hoppehall, through Hyde and Davenport, to the Newtons. For the value placed on the name see Morgan, 'Ranks of society', p. 74 and, id., 'Making the English gentry', p. 24.
7   The marriage settlement no longer exists but later copies can be found in the Newton cartulary (BL, Add MS 42134A, fo. 18) and JRUL, Bromley Davenport 'Newton by Mottram', no. 3.
8   Humphrey's genealogy only allows for two generations following Thomas in the fourteenth century, which would suggest suspiciously long lives for both Richards. While I have doubts concerning the accuracy of Humphrey's research, no evidence survives to settle the issue. What matters here, at least, is Humphrey's own interpretation of his genealogy.

Figure 1. Genealogy of the Newton family

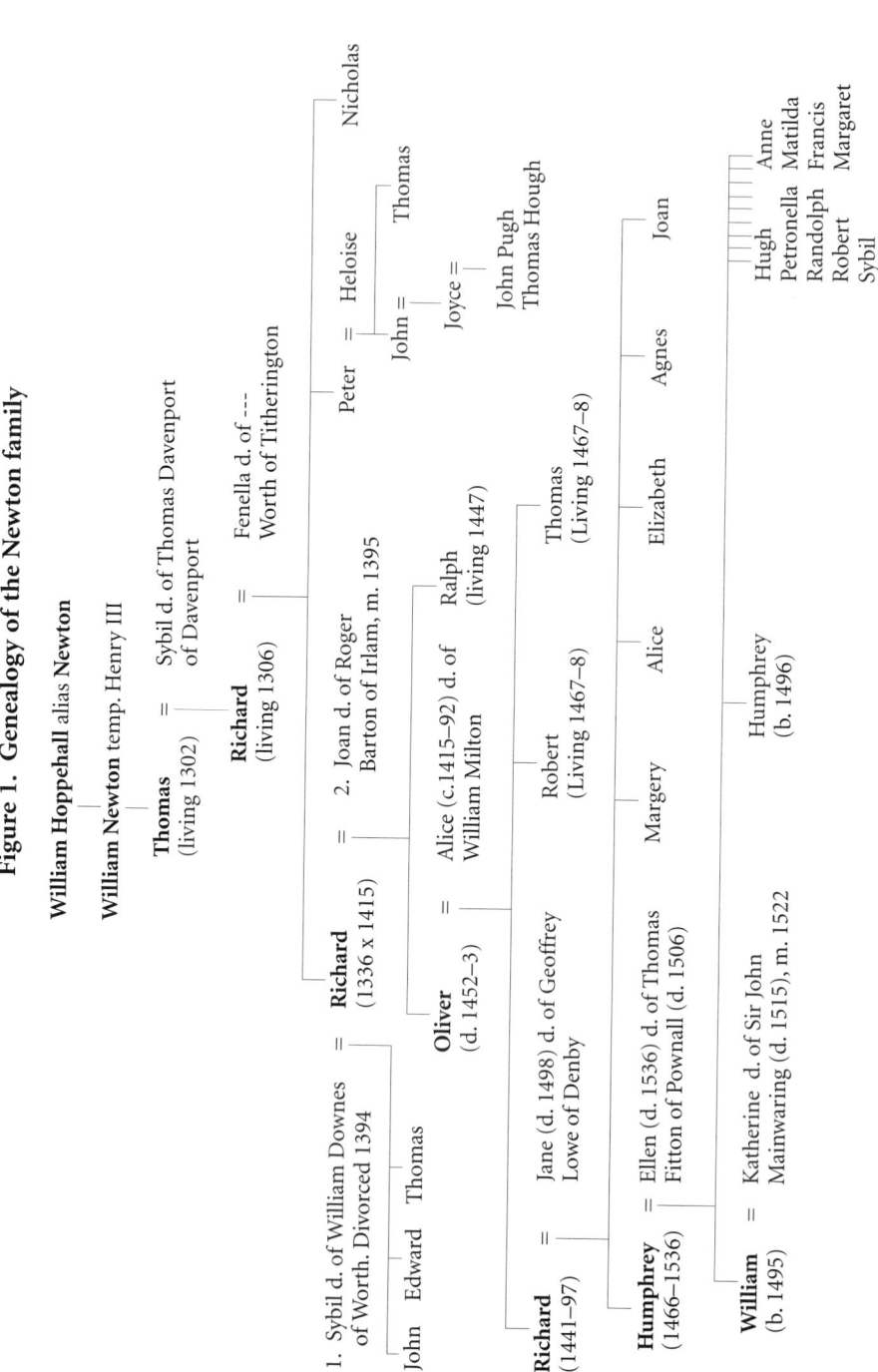

William Hoppehall alias **Newton**

William Newton temp. Henry III

Thomas (living 1302) = Sybil d. of Thomas Davenport of Davenport

Richard (living 1306) = Fenella d. of --- Worth of Titherington

Peter = Heloise; Nicholas

John = Joyce; Thomas

John Pugh; Thomas Hough

Richard (1336 x 1415) = 2. Joan d. of Roger Barton of Irlam, m. 1395

1. Sybil d. of William Downes of Worth. Divorced 1394
   - John
   - Edward
   - Thomas

Oliver (d. 1452–3) = Alice (c.1415–92) d. of William Milton

Ralph (living 1447)

Robert (Living 1467–8); Thomas (Living 1467–8)

Richard (1441–97) = Jane (d. 1498) d. of Geoffrey Lowe of Denby

Margery; Alice; Elizabeth; Agnes; Joan

Humphrey (1466–1536) = Ellen (d. 1536) d. of Thomas Fitton of Pownall (d. 1506)

William (b. 1495) = Katherine d. of Sir John Mainwaring (d. 1515), m. 1522

Humphrey (b. 1496)

Hugh; Anne; Petronella; Matilda; Randolph; Francis; Robert; Margaret; Sybil

family.⁹ Despite the birth of three children, however, the couple divorced in 1394 on grounds of consanguinity. It is interesting that in recording this information, Humphrey felt it necessary to suggest that the separation was painful: 'howbeit they were sorie to depart but that the lawe at those days would not suffer them'.¹⁰ Perhaps he was quoting family tradition, but it might have reflected his own unease at divorce, either on moral grounds or because it was an example of family disunity. A rather different perspective is offered by Richard Newton senior, who seems unlikely to have felt remorse at his daughter-in-law's departing. A poem he wrote in the 1390s included the lines 'Sebott [i.e. Sybil] with her loude cry/ she wakens me so early/ that under of the day/ that I noe sleepe may'. Richard junior's speedy remarriage in 1395 may further suggest that any sorrow was brief, but most probably reflected his need to provide legitimate heirs. Like any sensible landholder concerned with the preservation of the estate, he made sure that neither Sybil nor her children could make claim to land: in 1395 they were made to sign away their rights to the Newton property.¹¹ Richard's remarriage was to Joan Barton, whom Humphrey described as the daughter of Roger Barton from the distinguished Lancashire family at Irlam. If that were the case, it is possible that the divorce was obtained chiefly in order to cement a relationship with this influential family.¹² At least two sons, Oliver and Ralph, were born to the second marriage before Richard Newton died in the first quarter of the fifteenth century. His widow lived into the 1440s, hinting at a large age gap between them. Joan's survival caused several problems because her dowager status prevented the full Newton estate descending to her son Oliver. The matter was put to arbitration, and this second case of family discord, and its resolution, was carefully recorded and archived at Newton.¹³

It comes as no surprise that information on Humphrey's early ancestors is sparse for the modern researcher. What needs to be underlined, however, is that Humphrey himself knew little more. In common with other late medieval gentry, such as his contemporaries in Warwickshire, he had problems in compiling and verifying the family's early descent.¹⁴ The gaps are shown in the genealogy that opens the commonplace book. The lone name of William Newton – no dates, or wife – begins the list. Thereafter, the information gradually increases: an approximate date of death for Thomas Newton; the family

---

9   Booth, *The financial administration of the lordship*, p. 103.
10 Information on the divorce, including a copy of the divorce paper from the officials of the archdeacon of Chester, is recorded in the cartulary, BL, Add MS 42134A, fos 21r–22r.
11 Ibid., fos 20r, 21v. A full transcription of the poem can be found on p. 196 below.
12 Bodl, MS Lat. Misc.c.66, fo. 1r. Roger Barton has not been fully identified, but was clearly not of the main line. One possibility is the Roger Barton mentioned in the Black Prince's *Register* in 1359 (*Register of Edward the Black Prince*, III. p. 365). Another is the Roger Barton 'of Clutton', who is mentioned in 1363 in a recognizance alongside Robert son of William Newton: TNA: PRO, Ches 2/45, m. 1d.
13 BL, Add MS 42134A, fos 23–24.
14 Carpenter, *Locality and polity*, pp. 246–7.

of Richard senior's wife (though not her name); and the names of Richard junior's wives. What is also missing, and is something to which Humphrey never alludes, is the family's involvement in warfare, an important route for social advancement in thirteenth- and fourteenth-century Cheshire. The county's strong military reputation, with its ability to produce fine men-at-arms and archers, was put to considerable use during royal campaigns. At the beginning of Edward I's Welsh campaign in 1277 a corps of 100 archers was selected from the Macclesfield hundred and served during the entire war. Macclesfield men, including several members of the Newton family, were again on call in the mid-fourteenth century when the Black Prince, as earl of Chester, used the area as 'a major recruiting ground' for the Anglo-French wars.[15] As with many Cheshire families, it was Richard II's intention of turning his earldom into a 'bastion of royal power' that brought the Newtons wider attention. One of the watches or division of bodyguards established by Richard in 1397 was filled with men from Macclesfield. In that year, Richard, son of Thomas Newton, was among the early recruits and was granted livery of the Crown with 6*d* a day for life. Similarly, Richard, son of Richard Newton, was retained by the king in 1399 and made the fateful expedition with him to Ireland.[16]

Did Humphrey know of his ancestors' military skills? Would it have mattered to him if he had? It could be assumed so, because we have been led to believe that the gentry of the relatively demilitarised society of early Tudor England were keen to make a connection to a military past. Maurice Keen has written how 'They loved to find in their pedigrees ... ancestors who had come with the Conqueror, or who had played their part on crusade or in the great wars in France of the preceding age'.[17] Humphrey, however, did not share this love: he highlighted no soldiers in his family tree. It might be because, while military service extended the Newton family's connections and provided a regular income, it does not appear to have given them any long-lasting rewards such as land, certainly not when compared with marriage alliances.

An absence of military information might also have sprung from the type of sources Humphrey had to hand: he relied heavily on local land deeds, and would not have had access to the royal administration and noble household records available to later historians. The approximate dates which Humphrey used for Thomas and the two Richards concur with three dated title deeds of the Newton estate.[18] The Newton archive appears well-kept, but was small and limited, and Humphrey had to hunt around neighbouring archives at

---

[15] *John of Gaunt's Register 1379–83*, 1, no. 698, p. 225. Morgan, *War and society*, especially ch. 1; Hewitt, *Medieval Cheshire*, p. 157; Bennett, *Community*, p. 168.
[16] TNA: PRO, CHES 2/71, m. 40, CHES 2/72, m. 3d. TNA: PRO, E101/42/10, m. 2. For further details see Bennett, '*Sir Gawain and the Green Knight*', pp. 67–71. For the involvement of the two Richards in suits at Macclesfield courts, 1376x88, see Tonkinson, *Macclesfield*, pp. 20, 71.
[17] Keen, *Origins*, p. 10 (see also p. 99).
[18] BL, Add MS 42134A, fos 18r, 19.

Adlington Dunham Massey, Trafford and Handforth Hall, among others, to gather much of his genealogical information.[19] His notes reveal the problems in trying to compile genealogies, yet what he wanted to achieve was a serviceable, not a comprehensive, family tree. There is no attempt to romanticise his ancestors, and he did not follow the path of the Townshend family of Norfolk, whose history, Charles Moreton concluded, 'is clouded in obscurity and downright invention'.[20] For Humphrey, tracing ancestors meant finding evidence for continuity, principally through the male line, and specifically in relation to a particular location or property; his searches meant that he could demonstrate an uninterrupted Newton male line for over two centuries.

Not everyone was convinced by Humphrey's handiwork. In many villages and townships across England, rumours, which had the potential to question a neighbour's honour, abounded concerning many families' backgrounds. Humphrey himself recorded stories, often scurrilous, of local gentry origins, and he was not immune to them.[21] Humphrey's neighbours were not exercised in quite the same way about the origins of the Newton family as were those who felt the Paston family of Norfolk were less than honest about their ancestry.[22] Nor did Humphrey face the task of William Dutton of Denbigh who, in 1432, set out with the help of nineteen prominent Cheshire gentry to convince his fellow townsfolk that he was not Welsh.[23] However, the limited documentation available ensured that alternative theories about the Newton family's origins circulated in Humphrey's neighbourhood. One theory held that the Newtons were descended from the Davenport of Davenport family and that Thomas Newton had changed his name from Thomas Davenport. The story particularly exercised Humphrey who refuted the notion with his reading of local deeds:

> Howbeit it hath been said that the anncestor of Neutone should be called Davenport of Neuton of right notwithstanding. I cannot perceyve that by no writing that ever there was any of the name of Damport that in his stile caled himself Davenport of Neuton, and this is of truth longe tyme or ever any of the Davenport hadd any interest in Neuton.

Ever the careful researcher, Humphrey located examples of Thomas Davenport and Thomas Newton appearing in the same deed, and wrote forcefully that both William Newton and Thomas Newton 'have been so named tyme out of minde as freeholders in the same [Newton]'.[24] Yet whatever he may have declared publicly, he harboured some doubts about his information. Under-

---

[19] Marsh, '"I see by sizt of evidence"', particularly pp. 81–5.
[20] Moreton, *The Townshends*, p. 5. See Morgan, 'Making the English gentry', p. 25 for gentlemen who shared Humphrey's view.
[21] Maddern, 'Honour among the Pastons', pp. 362, 364; Marsh, '"I see by sizt of evidence"', p. 84.
[22] Richmond, *The Paston family in the fifteenth century*, ch. 1.
[23] Armitage and Rylands (eds) *Pedigrees made at the visitation of Cheshire*, p. 91.
[24] BL, Add MS 42134A, fos 18v–19r, 20v. Puntuation added.

neath a drawing of the descent of the Newton estate, Humphrey wrote: 'this Thomas Neuton must needs have these lands as cousin to William Neuton by gift of marriage of Thomas Davenport daughter and heir or else said Thomas Davenport changed his name to Neuton'.[25] Nor was the pragmatic Humphrey committed to his main argument: 'howbeit if there were any advantage it might bee said there name was changed'.[26] Again the link between the family and the holding was the key. In the interests of continuity, the Newtons were willing to accept the name change.

Humphrey was on firmer ground when it came to his grandfather. The recurrence of plague during the fifteenth century meant that Humphrey, like many other English men and women, never knew his paternal grandfather.[27] Nevertheless, his knowledge of Oliver Newton (born after 1395) was more detailed than that of any of his earlier ancestors, and presumably came from first-hand sources. He knew that Oliver had died of the plague in London in 1452–3 and was buried at St Andrew's, Holborn. With a concern for measurements that was characteristic of him, Humphrey noted the exact position of the grave: it was in the churchyard about four feet from the porch on the north side. It is a description that suggests a personal visit. It also means that, despite being a plague victim, Oliver's resting place had evidently been recorded, marked even.[28] A death in London suggests a man on business, perhaps 'of' business. One possibility is that he was a lawyer, given that Holborn was the location of the Inns of Court, and St Andrew's was regarded as the local church of the Inns of Court and Chancery with a long tradition of members being buried there.[29] That his widow would marry a prominent lawyer – Laurence Lowe of Denby, Derbyshire – less than a year after Oliver's death may suggest some prior contact with the profession. Oliver is not known to have held any prominent administrative positions in Cheshire, but his name appears among a list of 500 or so freeholders, gentlemen and knights for Cheshire that was penned in 1445. Dorothy Clayton believes that this was a list of all those eligible for jury service and hence a roll-call of the Cheshire gentry.[30]

The Newtons' inclusion on the list owed much to Oliver Newton, for it was under his stewardship that the family experienced its greatest upturn in fortune since the securing of Newton in 1302. Again it was the product of a good marriage, and one that brought the twin benefits of land and ancestry. In 1428–9 Oliver married Alice, daughter and co-heiress of William de Milton, who held land in western Cheshire; and co-heiress of Thomas de Crewe of Sond, in line to inherit an estate scattered through western and

---

[25] Ibid., fos 8v–9r.
[26] Ibid., fo. 18v.
[27] Rosenthal, 'When did you last see your grandfather?' for examples of those who did and those who did not.
[28] Bodl, MS Lat. Misc.c.66, fo. 1r.
[29] Barron and Roscoe, 'The medieval church of St Andrew's', p. 50.
[30] CRO, ZCR 63/1/7. Clayton, *The administration of the county palatine*, p. 135.

mid-Cheshire. Alice was the youngest of three daughters, being thirteen at the death of Thomas de Crewe in 1428–9.[31] Oliver, therefore, had married her shortly after she had become an heiress and only a year after she had achieved the canonical age of marriage (twelve years). His swift action and his potential gain probably lay behind a fine of £4 which he was required to pay in 1431 for the marriage; Alice and her sisters were by then wards of the king. In that year Alice reached sixteen – her age of majority recorded in a 'proof of age' – and a writ was granted to Oliver and Alice for the division of a messuage and lands in Grafton into three parts. These scattered lands did not amount to a coherent estate, but they provided the Newtons with a useful annual rent.[32]

What made the Milton connection doubly important was the ancestry it offered. Alice was said to be a descendant of Pagan, one of the illegitimate daughters of Hugh Cyfeiliog, the fifth earl of Chester (1153–81). Not surprisingly for a man lacking illustrious relatives, Humphrey was keen to display his comital connections. He reconstructed the Milton family tree beginning with the earls of Chester and ending with Humphrey and his children. Interestingly, he did not begin the genealogy with Hugh of Cyfeiliog but with Leofric, the last earl of Chester before the Norman Conquest.[33] Perhaps it was an attempt to outdo those families claiming a Conquest foundation. It may also be an indication of regional pride. There was continuing and widespread regard for the earls in fifteenth-century Cheshire, with figures like Ranulph III – William Langland's 'Ranulf, earl of Chester' – retaining what Tim Thornton considers a 'remarkable reputation'. Genealogies of the earls were popular and Humphrey transcribed three such lists into his commonplace book.[34] Humphrey never tried to conceal the illegitimacy of the Milton line. It may have been too well known; the seventeenth-century writer Sir Peter Leycester drew attention to a deed where Pagan is described as 'filius bastardus Hugonis comitis Cestriae'. The opportunity to display a connection with the earls of Chester probably made illegitimacy a minor blemish.[35]

As he was growing up Humphrey could look over his lineage and see a family which had always comprised freeholders and which was recognisably gentle by the mid-fifteenth century. There had been land gains, good local

---

31 BL, Add 6032, fos 45v, 46r–v. Together, the Milton and Crewe lands lay in Aston, Broxton, Chester, Churton, Handley, Huxley, Grafton, Milneton, Nantwich and Woreston.
32 TNA: PRO, CHES 2/101 m. 2; CHES 3/36/5; CHES 2/103 m. 1. Comprising lands and rents in Chester, Golbourne Bellow, Handley (Cleyley and Milneton Hall) and Huxley. See Map 1.
33 Bodl, MS Lat.Misc.c.66, fo. 63v; BL, Add MS42134A, fo. 2r.
34 Thornton, *Cheshire*, pp. 42–4. For Humphrey's lists see pp. 165–6 below.
35 Leycester, *Historical antiquities*, p. 134. For a seventeenth-century case where the legitimacy of another of Cyfeiliog's daughters, Amicia, did matter, see the famous dispute between Sir Thomas Mainwaring of Over Peover and Sir Peter Leycester: Beamont (ed.) *Tracts written in the controversy respecting the legitimacy of Amicia*. Sir Simon d'Ewes's effort to prove descent from one of the illegitimate daughters of Earl Hugh Lupas can be found in BL, Harley 2187, fo. 150r.

connections created or reinforced through marriage, and a link made with the earls of Chester. In his grandfather's day, the Newtons were among the 500 major families in Cheshire. Yet they were clearly nowhere near the top fifty, and theirs was not a name to reckon with in Cheshire. Humphrey had a reasonable start in life, but he also needed the ambition to exploit the opportunities and improve the family's fortunes.

Humphrey Newton

Humphrey was born on 3 October 1466. His parents, who must have carefully noted his birthdate, were Richard Newton (1441–1497), the eldest son and heir of Oliver Newton, and Jane Lowe (d. 1498) from the Lowe family of Denby, Derbyshire. They suffered no divorce or early death; they shared over thirty years of marriage and were alive to see the births of their first two grandchildren. It would seem that in general they brought stability rather than change to the Newton household. Richard Newton appears to have been useful to the county and to neighbouring gentry, but is not regularly found in the records.[36] He was not a keen jury man, and Clayton has calculated that he was sworn on civil juries eleven times (1473–1482), was involved in one recognizance, three mainprizes, and was only rarely empanelled on grand juries and gaol delivery juries. In 1494 (at the age of fifty-three) he obtained an exemption from serving on juries of assize and holding the positions of coroner, bailiff and subsidy collector.[37] The one highlight came in 1476 when he was chosen as a collector of subsidy (or mise) for Macclesfield hundred. The collection of the mise was Cheshire's most important commission and it reflects well on Richard that he was selected alongside the county elite of Sir Edward Fitton of Gawsworth, John Arderne and Hugh Davenport of Henbury.[38] Overall, he appears more a consolidator of Newton wealth and position rather than someone who augmented them, but he at least fulfilled the most important task of passing on his patrimony to a son.

Humphrey had no surviving brothers, but shared his childhood with at least five sisters: Margery, Alice, Elizabeth, Agnes and Joan.[39] Nothing is known of Humphrey's early years in terms of how and where he played, who his friends were, or how he was educated. Yet, almost from the beginning, his status as heir drew him into the world of gentry land deals. In 1467, before he was able to walk, Humphrey was made one of the twelve feoffees of his father for all his lands and tenements in Newton.[40] Among the other feoffees were Richard's step-father Laurence Lowe of Denby, and Richard's two

[36] For example, as a feoffee in the late 1490s (CRO, ZCR 63/1/43), and an arbitrator in 1496 (CRO, DAR H/67/1).
[37] TNA: PRO, CHES 29/194, m. 5.
[38] Clayton, *The administration of the county palatine*, pp. 195, 200–2, 240.
[39] BL, Harley MS 1535, fo. 223r.
[40] BL, Add MS 42134A, fo. 25.

brothers, Robert and Thomas. It may well have been Humphrey's recent birth, and his survival of his first year, that prompted the enfeoffment. It was not the only deed in which Humphrey appeared with his father and his Lowe relatives. In 1472 (at the age of five) Humphrey was enfeoffed, alongside his father, with the lands of Laurence's younger brother, Thomas Lowe of Alderwasley.[41] In 1487 Richard and Humphrey Newton were among the feoffees in a number of Laurence's Derbyshire lands, including those in Ashbourne, Fenton and Sturton; and, at around the same time, father and son were named as remainder men for the Denby estate.[42] Prior to his inheritance, Humphrey never appears in a land deed without his father: he is always labelled Richard's son and heir. Even during his twenties, Humphrey had not achieved full social and political identity as an adult.

These deeds show the young Humphrey firmly among his Lowe family relatives. As mentioned above, the association had begun back in 1452–3, when the recently widowed Alice Newton married Laurence Lowe, an aspiring Derbyshire lawyer.[43] With the Newton heir, Richard, being only eleven at the time of his father's death, Lawrence took distant control of running the estate during the minority. In the 1450s he commissioned a rental of Newton; in 1452–3 he was party to a new division of the Milton and Crewe inheritance; he attempted to resolve a boundary dispute between the Newtons and their neighbours; and he presumably had a guiding hand in arranging Richard Newton's marriage to a Lowe.[44] The Newton/Lowe relationship carried on through the generations, and illustrates how family ties could develop into friendship and an important reciprocal relationship.[45] Humphrey remained a feoffee for Laurence during the rest of the latter's life. His decision to transcribe an epitaph to Laurence Lowe (who was dead by 1491) into his commonplace book perhaps hints at a strong respect.[46] Humphrey also stayed in close contact with Laurence's sons – his own uncles – Humphrey and Ottiwell. In 1490, for example, Humphrey and Ottiwell Lowe and Richard and Humphrey Newton were feoffees and witnesses in the deeds of William Rode of Congleton.[47] It is possible, given that his name was unique among the Newtons, that Humphrey was named after Laurence's heir, Humphrey Lowe, who took over running the estate on his father's death. Meanwhile, Ottiwell

---

41 BL, Add MS 6666, fo. 47v.
42 Sheffield Archives ACM/DD/23; Garratt and Rawcliffe (eds) *Derbyshire Feet of Fines*, no. 1135. TNA: PRO, C1/535/13; Bodl, MS Lat. Misc.c.66, fo. 55r; BL, Add MS 42134A, fo. 28r.
43 BL, Add MS 6032, fo. 32v. No children are recorded for the union. Alice was nearly forty when she married Lowe and her three sons Richard, Robert and Thomas all have Newton surnames: BL, Add MS 42134A, fo. 25.
44 Bodl, MS Lat. Misc.c.66, fo. 24v; BL, Add MS 6031 fo. 32v; see pp. 71 n.7, 96 below. Richard's father-in-law has yet to be positively identified.
45 For comparisons: Maddern, '"Best trusted friends"', p. 112.
46 Bodl, MS Lat. Misc.c. 66, fo. 18r.
47 BL, Harley MS 2077, fo. 43.

followed his father's career in the law, and as local land deeds style him 'lerned in the law' he presumably received his education at an Inn of Court.[48] It seems rather telling that Humphrey chose to doodle Ottiwell Lowe's name in his commonplace book (the only name he scribbled other than his own); it intimates a valued relative, perhaps a close friend. Humphrey certainly placed his trust in his Lowe uncles, because he enfeoffed both in his lands in Newton and Pownall.[49] Such contact is in sharp contrast to relations with his Newton uncles who play no recorded role in Humphrey's adult life.

Being brought up within the Lowe family circle would have given Humphrey a particular perspective on life. It drew him into a social world that at its highest levels included the political elite of fifteenth-century England.[50] In the years following his marriage to Alice Newton, Laurence Lowe became a highly successful lawyer, and his clients are an impressive roll-call of England's powerful in the 1460s and 70s. In 1461 he was retained by Henry, Lord Grey of Codnor (the head of the baronial family of Derbyshire); he subsequently moved into the service of the king's brother, George, duke of Clarence, before being retained as one of the learned council of William, Lord Hastings, in 1474.[51] His list of formal positions includes acting as JP for Derbyshire in 1472–3 and as burgess and recorder of Nottingham in 1480.[52] Profits of law were invested in land. By leasing and extensive purchasing, Lowe built up an agglomeration of Derbyshire holdings in Offcote, Underwood, Ashbourne and Coldeaton, with his main holding and residence at the manor of Denby (comprising forty messuages, twenty tofts and around 600 acres of land, meadow, woodland and heath).[53] Land was not the only way to make a mark and Lowe made his presence felt in Denby by securing a permanent priest for the chapel of Denby to administer the sacraments.[54] The young Humphrey Newton would have heard of and observed these successes; he would also have known about the struggles. Lowe had problems in holding the lands, a predicament he shared with many rapid social climbers. Laurence was an ambitious man, an *arriviste* who provoked several disagreements in Derbyshire landed society. Court records refer to broken promises, houses being

---

[48] JRUL, Jodrell 34a, 38b. Baker, 'The English legal profession', p. 17.

[49] Doodles are in Bodl, MS Lat. Misc.c.66, fos 95v, 122v. Enfeoffments are found in CRO, DVE/MX/10 and TNA: PRO, CHES 29/221 m. 7.

[50] Lawson Lowe, 'Some account of the family of Lowe', p. 158.

[51] See the letter from Clarence to Lowe in NUL, Mi C.5b; Dunham (ed.) *Lord Hastings' indentured retainers*, p. 119; Wright, *Derbyshire gentry*, pp. 26–7, 79, 105, 250, 252.

[52] *Records of the Borough of Nottingham*: vol. II, pp. 302, 419, and vol. III, pp. 233, 266. *CPR*, 1485–94, I, p. 180.

[53] His purchases were largely secured through his connections with Lord Grey of Codnor, who held a large part of the town; a small portion came from his first marriage to the heiress of the Rossells of Derby: Noble (ed.) *History and gazetteer of the county of Derby*, II, part I, p. 366 and Wright, *Derbyshire gentry*, p. 27. See the case brought to chancery by Lord Grey accusing Lowe of reneging on the promised purchase price for the manor of Denby: TNA: PRO, C1/95/42.

[54] BL, Add MS 6666, fo. 96v.

burnt and his family and servants being threatened.[55] The fragility of the Lowe position would eventually force Humphrey Lowe to sell family lands and engage in a series of disputes concerning Denby; in 1499 Coldeaton was sold for £88 13s 4d.[56]

We do not know what conversations Humphrey engaged in with his Lowe relatives, but they may well have influenced his early upbringing. Like them and like his grandfather and father, Humphrey sought the benefits of a career in service, the profits of law (see Chapter 3) and, chiefly, the fortunes of a good marriage.

Marriage: Humphrey and Ellen

Marriage was crucial to the fortunes of gentry families. It was a means of consolidating power, transferring family assets and acquiring important connections, and was ultimately the key to social advancement; it could even be 'the method by which a poor man became rich without effort'.[57] The history of the Newton family is one of gains made through successful alliances: virtually all Humphrey's inheritance had come *via* this route. In addition, marriage would provide Humphrey with the means to establish a new family unit and mark his development from a dependent son to the head of a household. Full financial independence would have to await his inheritance, but becoming a husband and father brought him the new roles of protector and provider.

For gentry families seeing marriage as a route to social advancement, the principal goal was to secure an heiress. Being an heir himself, Humphrey was in the ideal position to succeed, although he only managed a co-heiress.[58] On 7 April 1490, at the age of twenty-three, he married Ellen Fitton, the elder daughter and co-heiress of Thomas Fitton of Pownall esquire (*c.*1441–1506). The marriage ceremony did not take place in the parish churches of Prestbury or Wilmslow – the parishes of the Newton and Pownall estates respectively – but at Handley church in the parish of Tattenhall (western Cheshire) where

---

[55] For example, NUL. Mi D 1690. Wright, *Derbyshire gentry*, p. 120. Cf. Harriss, 'The dimension of politics', p. 3.

[56] Wright, *Derbyshire gentry*, p. 26. Petitions to Chancery reveal the Lowe family's disputes over the rights to lands in Denby: for example, TNA: PRO, C1/146/55, C1/535/11–14, C1/579/31, C1/844/39. The family also faced the wrath of their tenants when Laurence and Humphrey enclosed lands at Ashbourne: Blanchard (ed.) *Duchy of Lancaster estates*, pp. 27–29, 53–55. For the sale of Coldeaton, see Jeayes (ed.) *Derbyshire charters*, no. 1121.

[57] McFarlane, *The nobility*, p. 10. For success stories see Carpenter, *Locality and polity*, pp. 116–19 and, of course, the Pastons. 'The Pastons were made by marriages': Richmond, *The Paston family in the fifteenth century*, ch. 4 (p. 117).

[58] Payling, *Political society*, pp. 66, 80; Carpenter, *Locality and polity*, p. 98. It was those families recently elevated in the ranks of the gentry who were 'most determined in the search for heiresses': Payling, 'The economics of marriage', p. 427; Ives, *The common lawyers*, pp. 370–3.

the Newtons held land from the Milton inheritance. This may suggest that, while his father remained alive and resident at Newton, Humphrey and Ellen established a new household in this area.[59]

We do not know how this marriage was brokered or the nature of Humphrey's feelings (though he clearly came to it as an adult), but an alliance between the Newtons and Fittons was a formal recognition of a working and neighbourly association that can be traced back many decades.[60] In common with other marriages below the county elite, it was a union of local families – in this case living less than three miles apart – whose interests were confined to the county.[61] It was a very good match for Humphrey because it allied the Newtons with a family of better lineage, greater landed wealth and wider social connections. The Fittons were descendants of the lords of Bollin who had been the largest landholders in the parish of Wilmslow in the thirteenth and fourteenth centuries. The fifteenth-century Fittons had firm connections to some of Cheshire's knightly elite. Ellen's great-grandfather was Sir Lawrence Fitton of Gawsworth (d. 1456–7), while her father took as his second wife, Elizabeth, daughter of Sir William Booth of Dunham Massey (knighted 1498). Both families were significant powers in the North West, and would prove useful allies to Humphrey in subsequent years.[62]

The Pownall Fittons hardly matched the wealth of their Gawsworth cousins, yet they could boast a number of important and substantial holdings. As Chapter 4 reveals, Humphrey secured an impressive estate: the main possession was Pownall hall, eight tenancies and several hundred acres of land in the townships of Pownall and Bollin; additional lands and tenements were held in several areas in the Northwich hundred of Cheshire. The Fittons had a greater county profile because the family undertook a wide range of military, judicial and administrative duties. Humphrey's father-in-law, Thomas Fitton, appeared on grand and county juries, and also an important commission of array in 1497.[63] It reflects well on the Newtons that they were able to secure an alliance with a family which was clearly notable in terms of lineage, land and county connections. During the sixteenth century the Newtons reaped the full rewards of the manor of Pownall and the increase in social standing it bestowed.

---

[59] Heal and Holmes, *The gentry*, p. 69, for household residences following marriage.

[60] For example, in 1463 Humphrey's father was among those bound to John Fitton of Pownall for £200 of silver during the latter's attempted reconciliation with the Davenport family. CRO, ZCR 63/1/43, p. 135.

[61] Payling, *Political society*, pp. 71, 82–3; Carpenter, *Locality and polity*, p. 99; Acheson, *A gentry community*, p. 158. Two-thirds of Cheshire gentry married Cheshire women: Thornton, *Cheshire*, p. 32.

[62] Humphrey noted the Fitton of Gawsworth pedigree in his commonplace book: fo. 57r. For the help he secured from the Fitton and Booth families, see pp. 102, 208 below. For their wealth see Thornton, *Cheshire*, p. 30.

[63] TNA: PRO, CHES 25/18, m. 35; 37th *DKR*, App.II, p. 280. An exemption from those duties on account of old age is found in TNA: PRO, CHES 29/206, m. 28.

Such rewards did not come cheaply. Although little is known of the marriage settlement, it appears that the Newton family made a substantial cash settlement. A rough estimate can be extracted from a series of notes in Humphrey's commonplace book, where he refers to 'my dowzer payment to my fader in lawe'. According to these accounts, Thomas Fitton had already received £20 and five marks (66s 8d) by 1499/1500.[64] Further payments or 'obligations' of five marks each were to be made bi-annually in February and August. Humphrey's yearly payout was therefore £6 13s 4d. How many more payments Humphrey had to make in 1500 is not easy to tell. In one page of his accounts he jotted down the contributions to be paid from the fifteenth to the nineteenth year of Henry VII (that is c.1499–c.1504), which in itself indicates that Humphrey was continuing to pay for his marriage over ten years after the nuptials. In another account dating to the harvest of 1501, Humphrey noted a debt to Thomas Fitton of seven obligations, plus a further seven 'in sute'. The 'suit' may well refer to the plea of debt Fitton brought against Humphrey at the Chester Exchequer (1506). If so, he was yet another gentleman seemingly overburdened with heavy marriage portions.[65] If these fourteen obligations alone (seventy marks in total) are added to the £20 and five marks already paid, Humphrey's marriage payment would appear to be £70, a very impressive sum, and recognition of the gains to be made from the Pownall estate.[66]

There is sufficient evidence to show that Ellen Fitton was an attractive partner in terms of her land and connections, but what of the person? As with much of the available evidence for medieval women, Ellen makes her appearance in fragments and marginalia; she can only be hazily drawn. Her year of birth is unknown, but it is possible that she had just entered adolescence when she married in 1490. Her first child was not born until five years after the wedding, hinting at a deliberate delay in consumption. While there are well-known examples of young aristocratic wives giving birth close to the age of consent (twelve), society at large did not push for early pregnancies. On medical and moral grounds, England's parents and wider kin voiced a desire to delay conception for at least a few years after puberty.[67]

Ellen is partly met through her clothes. Accounts reveal Humphrey's purchases of kirtles, hats, shoes and 'pynys'. The most colourful comes in an account for Lent 1500, when Ellen had a new scarlet kirtle costing 8s 4d.[68] Most of the clothes have a more practical ring about them. Being a gentleman's wife was not a life of leisure. Conduct literature from the period did not expect her to spend the day sitting, quietly reading. The fifteenth-century writer Christine de Pizan advised in her *Treasure of the City of Ladies* that 'wives should be wise and sound administrators and manage their affairs well'; they should

---

[64] Bodl, MS Lat. Misc.c.66 fo. 30r.
[65] TNA: PRO, CHES 24/71. Cf. Kirby (ed.) *The Plumpton letters and papers.*
[66] Bodl, MS Lat. Misc.c.66, fos 45v, 47v.
[67] A good discussion can be found in Phillips, *Medieval maidens*, pp. 36–42.
[68] For example, Bodl, MS Lat. Misc.c.66, fos 29r, 30v, 34cr, 41ar.

have knowledge of income and revenue and be able to discuss finances with their husbands. Studies of medieval gentlewomen have shown the active and important part the wife would play in the economic and familial organisation of the gentry household. In late medieval East Anglia Thomasin Hopton, Margaret Paston, and Eleanor Townshend were all trusted and highly competent managers of their families' estates.[69] Such a wife was Ellen Newton, whose brief appearances in the commonplace book are sufficient to show her supervisory powers and management skill. Phrases in Humphrey's accounts show that Ellen was treated as a decision-maker: he wrote that the servant Katherine Skenham had agreed to accept any payment that would 'plese my wife and me'. Ellen crops up in these accounts either witnessing wages handed to the servants, or paying them herself. She also dealt with tradesmen, as when she paid the dyer for cloth for her sister-in-law's wedding. Humphrey valued his wife's good opinion. When he paid Ralph Rider his outstanding wages he stated that it was in order 'to have his goode report afor my wife', a hint perhaps at a strong power in the Newton household.[70]

Despite the business element of aristocratic marriages, it is evident that the feelings of the couple, before and especially after marriage, were considered important to the success of the alliance. While unbridled passion was frowned upon, there was a recognised need for affection, kindness and faithfulness. Sir Peter Idley, for instance, exhorted his son 'Thy wyffe þou loue in perfit wyse, in thought and dede, as hertely as þou can', even if the reason was to make her a good wife.[71] Humphrey valued his wife's role at Newton, and he never forgot that she was an heiress who gave him Pownall. Her name appears in land deeds and in court cases, she has her own inquisition *post mortem*, and it is her ancestry that is celebrated in Wilmslow parish church. All of this is conventional, but it does underline that Ellen, like other medieval heiresses, retained a dual identity following her marriage: both a wife and an heiress with her own lineage. On a more personal note, there are the love lyrics in Humphrey's manuscript. Admittedly, they are within a 'literary miscellany', and there is much that is formulaic to the verse, as was common to the genre. Nonetheless, Humphrey specifically chose to compose two lyrics using the acrostic 'Elyn', and it is possible that the emotions expressed were close to Humphrey's true feelings; he was at least capable of using the vocabulary:

> Ever lastynge lof to me I have tane
> Leyn me youre hert & be ye stidfast

---

[69] Christine de Pisan, *The treasure of the city of ladies*, p. 130. Shahar, *The fourth estate*, pp. 149–52; Harris, *English aristocratic women*, ch. 4; Richmond, *John Hopton*, p. 127; Britnell, 'The Pastons', p. 136; and Moreton, *The Townshends*, p. 144.
[70] For example, Bodl, MS Lat. Misc.c.66, fos 25r–v, 27ar, 33v, 39av.
[71] D'Evelyn (ed.) *Peter Idley's instructions to his son*, lines 1226–7, p. 101. Richmond, *John Hopton*, pp. 117–20.

> Ye have my hert me ravesshed & tame
> Never to forsake you while my lif wil last[72]

And he never did forsake her. The marriage lasted a considerable time in a period when life expectancy was low and the chances of widowhood high.[73] Humphrey and Ellen were together for forty-six years; they died within six weeks of each other in 1536. A romantic might read this as an indication of their close union. Perhaps we may also infer from the tombs of Ellen and Humphrey at Wilmslow, where they lie if not side to side then top to toe, that there was an intention that not even death would part them.

Both Humphrey and Ellen would have known that the main purpose of their union was to have children. Pressure would have come from family, friends and society at large, and England was awash with recipes and devices to aid fertility. The Newtons did not take any chances and Humphrey transcribed recipes 'for to make a woman to conseyve child'. These were among other recipes, prayers and charms aimed at helping Ellen through pregnancy and childbirth.[74] The patriarchal nature of early Tudor England, especially in relation to the laws of inheritance, meant that the gentry were culturally conditioned to wish for sons. While Humphrey had no recipe to influence the outcome, he did copy a well-known experiment for discovering the sex of the child. The mother's milk was placed in water. If the milk floated the baby was male; if it sank, it was female.[75] Overall, Humphrey must have felt himself well blessed. Five years after their marriage Humphrey's first son was born. He eventually fathered eleven children over a period of sixteen years. Ellen produced a baby in 1495, 1496, 1497, 1499, 1501, 1502, 1504, 1507, 1509 and 1511; the birthdate of his son Francis is unknown, but his position in the genealogy places it between 1504 and 1507.[76] Ellen would have spent much of her young adulthood pregnant, but this was far from unusual for a woman of her social status. Among the aristocracy of England in the period 1450–1550, forty per cent of women had five or more children.[77] The regularity of the Newton births suggests that a wet nurse was employed; breast feeding is known to have some contraceptive effect. Ellen would have required some help with so many young children around, and gentlewomen were accustomed to handing menial chores to servants. At least three women – Elizabeth Patrick, Agnes Walton and one simply called Katherine – were employed as

---

[72] Bodl, MS Lat. Misc.c.66, fo. 92v. For discussion of the poetry, see pp. 191–3 below.
[73] Harris, *English aristocratic women*, p. 128; Rosenthal, *Patriarchy*, p. 183.
[74] Bodl, MS Lat. Misc.c.66, fo. 89v. For others, see pp. 113–14 below.
[75] Bodl, MS Lat. Misc.c.66, fo. 129r. The opposite was said to result in 'The secrets of women' (published 1480): Thorndike, *History of Magic*, II, p. 739; Ogden (ed.) *The Liber de diversis medicinis*, p. 56.
[76] Bodl, MS Lat. Misc.c.66, fo. 1v. Humphrey wrote both the king's year and the calendar year, but the two do not always correspond. I have used his calendar years.
[77] Harris, *English aristocratic women*, p. 30.

nurses at Newton, and worked within the household.[78] Their milk and care helped most of the Newton children to grow into adults, but four (or thirty-six per cent) died in infancy. Demographic studies show that this was about normal for the period because around a third of children born in non-plague years were likely to die in pre-modern England.[79] For Humphrey, at least, the survival of four boys (along with three girls) into adulthood ensured that he would never suffer the possibility of dying without an heir.

Humphrey carefully copied both the time and date of birth for each of his children into his commonplace book. During the fifteenth century, the practice of recording births had become increasingly common among the literate of Western Europe. Florentine merchants' families listed the births and baptism of their children in family memoirs (*ricordanze*), while, in France, birthdates were recorded in *livres de raison*. In England, comparison can be found in the early sixteenth-century commonplace book of the London merchant, Richard Hill, who listed the hours and dates of birth of his seven children as well as their godparents and baptismal gifts.[80] Such books were ostensibly private records, but they would have proved useful if any question had arisen over an age of majority. Although he may have appeared meticulous, Humphrey was not always accurate. He appears to have misremembered or miscopied the birthdates of his first three sons. For example, the birthdate of his second son, Humphrey, was recorded as Thursday, 10 January 1496; but 10 January fell on a Monday in that year. One might assume that this son was named after his father, though unfortunately nothing is known of the children's godparents, from whom names frequently came. It is possible that the image-conscious Humphrey named his eldest son, William, after the founding ancestor of the Newton family. At the same time, no other son was given a traditional Newton family name like Richard or Thomas, which were also two of the most popular names in England at the time. Instead, 'new' names such as Hugh, Ranulph and Francis were introduced. The earls of Chester may have influenced the choice of Hugh and Ranulph, as both remained popular in the county because of this association.[81] At the same time Humphrey and Ellen gave more traditional Newton (and Fitton) family names to their daughters – Anna, Margaret, Matilda and Sybil – although none were named after Humphrey's mother.

---

[78] Bodl, MS Lat. Misc.c.66, fos 25r, 41av, 43v. Katherine, for example, was hired for a year at 7s. Humphrey gave her 16d 'to pay for her childe', revealing her own recent birth. She stayed in service for two years. Orme, *Medieval children*, pp. 58–60; Ward, *English noblewomen*, p. 95; Fleming, *Family*, p. 63.

[79] Hollingsworth, 'A demographic study', pp. 4–26, shows that among English ducal families, 1330–1479, thirty-six per cent of boys and twenty-nine per cent of girls died before the age of five. See too Shahar, *Childhood*, p. 35; Hanawalt, *Growing up*, p. 55.

[80] Dyboski (ed.) *Songs, carols*, pp. xiii–xiv; Youngs, *The life cycle*, pp. 13–14.

[81] In late medieval England over eighty per cent of males shared the top five names: John, Thomas, Robert, Richard and William: Bennett, 'Forms of intellectual life', p. 123. See Thornton, *Cheshire*, pp. 49–50, for the popularity of Ranulph among Cheshire gentry.

Humphrey's affection towards his children as they were growing up is difficult to measure. The children make only rare appearances in his writings, usually in the provision of food and clothes.[82] One, albeit ambiguous, comment on Humphrey's parental attitudes relates to the children who did not live to adulthood. Historians no longer hold the view that medieval parents were indifferent to their children's deaths, but modern sensibilities may still feel uneasy at Humphrey's written reaction to their demise.[83] The names of Robert, Ranulph, Matilda and Petronella were struck out with long wavy lines and the words 'mortus est' written alongside. A cynical reading would be that they no longer formed part of the Newton lineage and – like the paid accounts that were deleted – were thus a closed matter. A comparable case can be found in Richard Hill's book, where lines cross out his deceased children.[84] There is simply no evidence to gauge the feelings lying behind those pen strokes.

What can be said is that, for those who reached an age of understanding, Humphrey did his duty in terms of their upbringing. While unfortunately nothing is known of any formal tutoring, whether at school or in the household, Humphrey was more than capable of providing early instruction.[85] A number of entries in his commonplace book are likely to have been copied with his children in mind. One was the well-known Middle English alliterative list of proverbs, the *ABC of Aristotle*, which Humphrey hung on a wall in his hall. Taking the form of an *abece*, commonly used to instruct children, its messages preach moderation in all things, alongside a desire for ordered and Christian behaviour.[86] Another item, this time in Latin, was an Aesop's fable. While not specifically directed at children, the fables did appear in classroom texts in schools across Europe.[87] Humphrey, therefore, had works of moral teaching to hand; other didactic texts in his manuscript, discussed in Chapter 6, may also have been collected for his children. The survival of the Newton cartulary demonstrates that his heir, William, was proficient at writing in both Latin and English. But education and training for the medieval gentry was equally concerned with experience and Humphrey followed the conventions of his day by involving his children in a variety of household tasks. In particular, his heir

---

[82] For example, coats were bought for William, Humphrey and Hugh: Bodl, MS Lat. Misc. c.66, fo. 27av.
[83] Shahar, *Childhood*, p. 7 and ch. 6.
[84] Bodl, MS Lat. Misc.c.66, fo. 1v; Dyboski (ed.) *Songs, carols*, pp. xiii–xiv.
[85] The only reference to schooling in Humphrey's commonplace book comes in an account where he notes a debt in a book of a schoolmaster at the Peele (fo. 45v). This probably refers to Northenden school because Peele manor lay in Northenden. It was a jointure house of the Tattons of Wythenshawe and the first reference to Northenden school concerns Robert Tatton of Wythenshawe (d. 1579) who had attended in 1514. Intriguingly, during those schooldays, Robert had lodged with James Barlow, Humphrey's brother-in-law: Furnivall (ed.) *Child marriages*, p. 139.
[86] Rust, 'The "ABC of Aristotle"', pp. 63–78. See p. 151 below.
[87] Bodl, MS Lat. Misc.c.66, fo. 92v. Orme, *English schools*, pp. 103–4; Orme, *Medieval children*, p. 184; Wheatley, *Mastering Aesop*, ch. 3.

needed to know the ways of estate management. At the age of seven William was sent to pay labourers for their work at Newton, while as an eleven-year-old he, as Humphrey's heir, was named alongside his father as feoffee in the lands of Thomas Davenport of Fulshaw.[88] Humphrey was ensuring that his son learnt all facets of managing a landed estate.

Marriage: Humphrey's sisters

When Humphrey fully inherited Newton at the age of thirty-one, he already had three children to consider and another was on the way. The focus of his household, as was commonly the case among English gentry, was on the nuclear family.[89] By 1498, Humphrey had no mother or grandmother to support, but his sisters were still living at home: at least four were in residence at the time of his inheritance. Humphrey had no intention of supporting them for long. Like many new inheritors, he lost no time in seeing siblings safely married off.[90] In just under a year (1498–9) three of his sisters were married to local men. Their cases provide useful indications of Humphrey's status in his early years at Newton.

The marriages followed in quick succession. On 24 June 1498 one sister, possibly Elizabeth, married Robert Vawdray.[91] Less than four months later, on Monday 1 October 1498, a second sister married James Barlow of Northenden (d. before 1530).[92] Early in the following year, a third sister, Anne or Agnes, married John Birtles. It also appears that a few years after these three marriages, a second marriage was arranged between a Newton sister and the Vawdray family, this time Thomas Vawdray (d. 1546).[93] Little is known of the nuptials, but the sisters enjoyed the proper festivities. A glimpse of the ceremony for the third alliance is recorded in a short account of outstanding debts, which Humphrey entitled 'Anes weddyng'. Entertainment was laid on in the form of a minstrel, to whom Humphrey paid 7*d*, and extra meat was ordered for guests. Clothing was a major concern and new garments were bought for

---

[88] Bodl, MS Lat. Misc.c.66, fo. 39ar. CRO, ZCR 63/1/43, p. 157. Compare Shahar, *Childhood*, ch. 10; Orme, *Medieval children*, pp. 242–46; 307, 313–17.
[89] Heal and Holmes, *The gentry*, p. 56; James, *Family*, p. 21.
[90] Bennett, *Women in the medieval countryside*, p. 90; Mertes, *Household*, pp. 54–5.
[91] No name is mentioned in the commonplace book. Elizabeth is suggested because in a sixteenth-century deed involving the widow, Elizabeth Vawdray, it mentions that she was once Elizabeth Newton: TNA: PRO, C1/1073/8–9. In addition, following Robert's death several years later, Humphrey noted a debt to his executors. Underneath he wrote 'ij nobles to Elizabeth': Bodl, MS Lat. Misc.c.66, fo. 59av.
[92] Bodl, MS Lat. Misc.c.66. fos 29v, 30r.
[93] Genealogies for the Vawdray family commonly state that Thomas had married Anne, the daughter of Richard Newton. Those collected by J.P. Earwaker are CRO, ZCR 63/1/200/1. See n. 112 below.

Humphrey, Ellen and a remaining sister, Joan. For the bride, more than eight yards of cloth were bought to be made into a violet wedding dress.[94]

The husbands were local men. English gentlemen regularly preferred to choose husbands for their sisters and daughters from among thriving local families. Susan Wright has uncovered several examples of Derbyshire gentry marrying off their female relations, often quite cheaply, to those who wanted to 'improve their social connection'.[95] All three grooms of the Newton sisters fall into that category. The Birtles were arguably the oldest family, having held a small, compact estate at Birtles (Prestbury parish) since the time of Edward I.[96] Robert Vawdray came from an established family of freeholders who had entered the lower reaches of the gentry in the fifteenth century.[97] Their landed possessions included holdings, though no coherent estate, in Baguley, Sale and Hasilhurst, on the northern borders of Cheshire.[98] Family members were regulars in the administration of fifteenth-century Cheshire; Thomas Vawdray acted as a grand jury member and worked with local yeomen and gentry in the Northenden area.[99] Hovering on the hazy border between yeomanry and gentry, the Barlows of Northenden were descended from a prominent family residing at Barlow in Chorleton, Lancashire.[100] James Barlow seems to have been considered a useful man: he was probably the James Barlow, yeoman, who was retained in 1489 by John Legh of Bradley, esquire. He acted as an attorney and witness for William Tatton of Tatton, esquire; and he was one of several Barlow family members who were accused of rioting and illegally entering land belonging to James Mascy at the instigation of Sir Edward Fitton of Gawsworth in the early sixteenth century.[101] He was someone who worked for – and indeed did the dirty work for – members of the greater gentry.

The bridegrooms' modest backgrounds are reflected in the dowries that Humphrey provided for his sisters: all three were settled at £10. Such a sum would not have secured a groom of the rank of esquire or above. Looking at the local marriage market, Sir George Calveley of Lea (d. 1536) assumed his daughter would need a dowry of £70 to make an alliance with a family of

---

[94] Bodl, MS Lat. Misc.c.66, fos 27ar, 34cv.
[95] See Wright, *Derbyshire gentry*, pp. 44–5.
[96] Ormerod, *Chester*, III, pp. 709–10.
[97] Genealogies of the medieval family are few and contain a large element of fiction, particularly in their Conquest origins: CRO, ZCR 63/1/200/1.
[98] Ormerod, *Chester*, III, p. 611. Earwaker, *East Cheshire*, II, p. 269.
[99] TNA: PRO, CHES 24/80; TNA: PRO, CHES 5/2, mm. 1–3; Earwaker, *East Cheshire*, II, p. 158; Clayton, *The administration of the county palatine*, p. 233.
[100] The Barlow interest in Northenden dated from at least the fourteenth century, when John Barlow was granted a licence to make a mill attachment and weir on the Northenden side of the Mersey river: JRUL, Tatton MSS 39 and 40. Farrer and Brownbill, *VCH, Lancashire*, IV, p. 298.
[101] TNA: PRO, CHES 25/18 m. 13r; JRUL, Ryland Charter 826; JRUL, Tatton MSS 409, 446 and 854; TNA: PRO, STAC 2/28/66.

comparable status to his own; and William Davenport of Bramhall, esquire (d. 1541) bequeathed his daughters £80 each. Even the less wealthy esquire Richard Winnington gave £20 each to his sisters for their dowries. However, as Humphrey's case shows, £10 was adequate to secure an alliance among socially aspiring families.[102] Providing a total of £30 in around a year was still a substantial payment. His father's will may have provided for them, and his mother's death in 1498 would have released some income. Nevertheless, Humphrey did not have to pay the three dowries in one lump sum and he made arrangements with each brother-in-law for the money to be paid in instalments. Robert Vawdray was to receive yearly sums of 20*s* each Martinmas – either in cash or kind – and they were paid on time; by 1502 Vawdray had received £5.[103] Similarly, 20*s* was the yearly amount given to John Birtles: one instalment was made before the marriage, with a second and third given in July and November of 1500.[104] With James Barlow the yearly payments were higher, at 40*s* each Martinmas, with several made in kind: in 1500 Humphrey gave James twenty lambs *in lieu* of 20*s*, and two coverlets and two blankets instead of 11*s* 4*d*. Thereafter, Barlow was given land in Mottram St Andrew, collecting the revenues to the value of 40*s*.[105]

The speed with which Humphrey had paired off his sisters was not so hasty as to blur his judgement in selecting his brother-in-laws. Both Thomas Vawdray and James Barlow increased their landed wealth and status subsequent to the marriages with the Newton sisters. During the early years of his marriage, Thomas Vawdray made grants and purchases to obtain lands in Timperley, Altrincham and Chester, and finally brought the family a compact settlement in Riddings and Bowdon. In the subsidy assessment of 1546 he was assessed on land worth 20*s*.[106] The marriage produced eight children, of whom the eldest son, Robert (d. 1576), achieved several prominent positions: vice-chamberlain of Chester in 1533 and sergeant-at-law for the palatine in 1545.[107] Similarly, the Barlow family, headed by James Barlow and his Newton wife, increased their lands in the early sixteenth century, acquiring messuages, lands and rents in the areas of Ashton, Timperley, Baguley, Northenden and Kenworthy.[108] Both son-in-laws are likely have owed some of their success to their Newton marriages. Certainly, Humphrey put land Barlow's way: to the

---

[102] CRO, ZCR 63/1/94/1 p. 3; Piccope (ed.) *Lancashire and Cheshire Wills*, I, pp. 79–81; JRUL, Arley 27/47. Further examples can be found in Irvine (ed.) *A collection of Lancashire and Cheshire wills*, pp. 21–3, and Driver, *Cheshire*, p. 124.
[103] Kind included a grey horse, calves and sheep. Bodl, MS Lat. Misc.c.66, fo. 29v. For paying in instalments see Wright, *Derbyshire gentry*, p. 45; Ward, *English noblewomen*, p. 25.
[104] Bodl, MS Lat. Misc.c.66, fo. 27av, fo. 34cv. Humphrey also noted a debt to Birtles of 'vi li et di', fo. 47v.
[105] Ibid., fo. 36r.
[106] CRO, ZCR 63/1/200/1; TNA: PRO, E179/85/26, m. 1.
[107] Piccope (ed.) *Lancashire and Cheshire wills*, I, p. 87.
[108] Irvine (ed.) *A collection of Lancashire and Cheshire wills*, p. 61; JRUL, Tatton MSS 96, 98, 1185.

property in Mottram St Andrew was added Huxley House (Broxton hundred) and land in Minshull Vernon (part of the Pownall inheritance).[109] In Barlow we see again a case where kinship had turned to friendship. Humphrey chose Barlow as one of his feoffees in a small land transaction in 1520 because, he stated, he was a 'trusty' friend. On that occasion, Barlow was working alongside Humphrey's second son; a year later he acted as a feoffee for a local man, John Bradley, alongside Humphrey's eldest son, William.[110] Such actions support the view that kinship formed the basis for 'collusive action' in late medieval gentry society.[111]

Humphrey also took back family members. The brevity of many early Tudor marriages because of high death rates is witnessed in Anne's short alliance. John Birtles was dead by November 1501, forcing Anne to return to Newton as a boarder. Humphrey became his sister's guardian once more, but not her provider: Anne had to pay 26s 8d as her board. The sum was apparently paid in four instalments, as Humphrey noted that she had 'found' him 6s 8d.[112] No one, it seems, was allowed to be a drain on the Newton resources.

These sibling marriages were useful in terms of establishing ties with local, socially mobile gentry, but they were never ones that would bring in land or raise the status of the Newtons. Such aims were better attempted with one's children.

Marriage: Humphrey's sons

It was a father's duty to set his children up for life, and for the gentry this also meant ensuring the future of the lineage. When it came to arranging the marriages of his children, Humphrey looked to broaden the family's connections and improve its wealth and status. The most important alliance was that of the heir, William, and examining his marriage will help shed light on the social position attained by Humphrey and the Newtons by the 1520s. It was one that sought to make connections rather than increase acreage: an alliance was made with the Mainwarings of Peover, one of the most important and influential rising gentry families of late medieval Cheshire. During the fifteenth century the Mainwarings had established their local power and connections by advantageous marriages, military prowess and land accumulation. Extensive holdings were held in mid-Cheshire, with the administrative

---

[109] Bodl, MS Lat. Misc.c.66, fo. 60v; CRO, DVE 1/MX/10. See also p. 91 below.
[110] TNA: PRO, WALE 29/427; CHES 29/223, m. 3.
[111] Carpenter, 'The Stonor circle', p. 183.
[112] Bodl, MS Lat. Misc.c.66, fo. 38v. It is likely that Anne took Thomas Vawdray as her second husband. In his commonplace book, Humphrey noted a £4 debt he owed 'Thomas Vaudray wife', and commented that 'I must have a loan for her borde' (fos 45v, 47v). Could he be referring to his sister and boarder, Anne, by her new name?

centre at Peover. At the turn of the sixteenth century the head of the household, Sir John Mainwaring (d. 1515), played a prominent role in local administration. His responsibilities included those of sheriff of Flintshire (1506 and 1509), constable of Heighly, Staffordshire (1512), and steward of Nantwich; and he was one of several prominent Cheshire men who granted the subsidy of 1,000 marks to the king in 1497.[113] At the same time he continued to deploy the family's traditional military skills: in the 1513 campaign in France he took with him 100 men in the division known as the King's Ward, and he was subsequently knighted at Tournai.[114]

It was Sir John Mainwaring's younger daughter, Katherine, who became the wife of William Newton. The wedding took place on 12 May 1522, when William was at the relatively late age of twenty-seven. Unfortunately, the marriage articles have not survived and the actual dowry Katherine brought with her is unknown. However, the potential can be established from the surviving will of Sir John Mainwaring, which shows a man of significant wealth.[115] Mainwaring bequeathed to his two unmarried daughters dowry funds that were commensurate with his status: 300 marks to the elder, Margaret, and 200 marks to the younger, Katherine.[116] These considerable sums were available on condition that the sisters married according to the wishes of their mother, brother and friends. The Newtons may have benefited from Katherine's mother being the sister of William Handforth (d. 1513), with whom Humphrey had a close working and personal relationship.[117]

William Newton's suitability as a groom would have been measured by the jointure the Newtons offered. A feoffment made by Humphrey concerning the marriage jointure in March 1522 reveals that an estate worth £10 was made available for the use of Katherine Mainwaring during her lifetime. Humphrey's inquisition *post mortem* provides a detailed breakdown of these lands and their relative annual value, a large proportion of which came from

---

[113] JRUL, Mainwaring 323, 324; 37th *DKR*, App.II, pp. 501–2; 39th *DKR*, App.I, p. 183; Driver, 'The Mainwarings of Over Peover', pp. 35–6. Thornton, *Cheshire*, pp. 21, 30.
[114] *LP* i (2) 2053, 2301.
[115] His will was dated 3 March 1515; JRUL, Mainwaring 328.
[116] Barbara Harris calculated that the median dowry for a knight's daughter in the period 1450–1550 was 200–300 marks: *English aristocratic women*, p. 47.
[117] William and Humphrey worked together as feoffees on at least three known occasions: for Thomas Verdon in 1507, for Sir Thomas Boteler in 1508, and in an undated marriage agreement between the families of Tatton and Chauntrell. At these times, Humphrey would have observed Handforth's competence, which he evidently found to his liking. In 1508, William was one of the feoffees of Humphrey's entire landed possessions in Newton and Pownall. He also witnessed three quitclaims Humphrey had secured from neighbours in Foxtwist. One of the title deeds of Newton was kept at Handforth, and it is possible that it was entrusted to the family's safe keeping: Irvine (ed.) *A collection of Lancashire and Cheshire wills*, pp. 73–4; CRO, ZCR 63/1/43; TNA: PRO, CHES 3/62/14 and CHES 29/211 m. 7; BL, Add MS 42134A, fos 1–2; JRUL, Bromley Davenport, 'Newton by Mottram', no. 9.

the Newton inheritance.[118] A £10 estate is considered by historians of other English counties as typical for gentry marriages. In examining Derbyshire gentry jointures, Susan Wright calculated that between £10 and £20 of a family's patrimony was considered sufficient to secure a good marriage. Christine Carpenter calculated the 'fairly standard' jointures of fifteenth-century Warwickshire gentry as follows: £4–7 for a small estate, £13–27 for a larger estate and rising to £40 for the 'big league'.[119] Comparison with these figures suggests that while Humphrey was able to negotiate with the bigger players of Cheshire in the matter of his son's marriage – far more so than he had with his sisters or indeed his own marriage – it was still at the lower end of the scale. The Newton family was not arranging, and presumably was not expected to make, one of the major partnerships in Cheshire.

Nevertheless, if the Newtons had collected a dowry close to 200 marks then they had struck a good deal. Studies of aristocratic marriages calculate that dowries were somewhere between five and eleven times the annual rental value of the jointure promised the daughters. Harris sees the jointure as commonly worth ten per cent of the dowry.[120] Yet, working with the figure of 200 marks would mean that the Newton family received a dowry thirteen times the jointure. Katherine was not an heiress and did not bring with her any land. Yet she was from an established county family with important social connections; she had the potential to raise the Newton family's profile. With those benefits, the jointure was probably not considered expensive by the Newton family, and it left the manor of Pownall untouched. From the Mainwaring point of view Katherine was to become the next mistress of Pownall hall and had cemented a connection with a socially mobile gentry family. The Newtons were keen to broadcast the alliance and a shield celebrating the marriage, by the traditional method of quartering the families' arms, was placed in a window of Wilmslow church (Plate 1). The marriage and the birth of the first grandchild in July 1524 are the last dated items that Humphrey added to his commonplace book.[121]

One would expect considerable effort to be made for an heir, but a measure of a family's resources is how much could be achieved for younger sons who could potentially lose out to the elder brother.[122] In Humphrey's case, all his surviving sons eventually made useful alliances and established themselves in

---

118 It comprised lands in Golbourne (worth 6s 8d), Huxley (47s 4d), Mottram St Andrew (57s 8d) and – from the Newton estate – four messuages (out of a possible six), thirty acres of land, ten acres of meadow and four acres of pasture (worth £4 8s 4d per annum). JRUL, Mainwaring 332. TNA: PRO, CHES 3/67/4. Deeds concerning the transfer also appear in the Mainwaring family cartulary *Chartularium Mainwaringianum*, nos 15a, 15b
119 Wright, *Derbyshire gentry*, p. 32 and Carpenter, 'The fifteenth-century gentry and their estates', p. 42.
120 Harris, *Aristocratic English women*, p. 50; Fleming, *Family*, p. 37.
121 Bodl, MS Lat. Misc.c.66, fo. 1r. See p. 135 below.
122 Wright, *Derbyshire gentry*, p. 48; Carpenter, *Locality and polity*, p. 221; Friedrichs, 'Marriage strategies', pp. 54–6.

landed society, although it is not known how long they had to wait after the marriage of William, or indeed after Humphrey's death. Humphrey's second son and namesake made an exceptionally good alliance with Ethelreda, the daughter and heiress of two well-connected Lancashire parents. Her father, Laurence Starkey (c.1474–1532), an active and successful official in Lancashire, was mayor of Lancaster in 1495 and 1523 and MP for Lancaster in 1523 and 1529. He had a close working and personal relationship with Sir Edward Stanley, Lord Mounteagle (c.1460–1524), and the connection helped bring Starkey lands and properties in Lancashire, Staffordshire, Cheshire and Yorkshire.[123] Even more impressively, Ethelreda's mother, Anne, was the daughter of Sir Thomas Boteler of Bewsey, Lancashire (d. 1522), one of the richest landowners in the county. Anne had already been married twice before and the dowers she received from both alliances amounted to an annual jointure of £80 for life as well as considerable goods.[124] Ethelreda was therefore a very lucrative heiress. It is not known whether the betrothal was agreed before Starkey's death in 1532; the couple were, however, married by 1536 when they sent a petition to the court of the duchy of Lancaster.[125] Ethelreda appears to have been born around 1520, making her sixteen at the time of the petition and about fourteen years younger than her husband. The inheritance was not easily obtained, with Humphrey and Ethelreda embroiled in dispute with the daughter of Starkey's first marriage throughout the next two decades.[126]

Following William's marriage, Humphrey had few ancestral lands to offer any of his younger sons and the Fitton inheritance was preserved for the heir. Instead, Humphrey chose a common route and set up his second son with lands more recently acquired.[127] In 1530 Thomas Verdon and Humphrey Newton senior farmed out Verdon's lands in Fulshaw (near Pownall) to Humphrey Newton junior. In 1537 the latter secured a release of all these lands, and later obtained more property in the area.[128] In the subsidy records of 1546 he was assessed on land worth £6 in Fulshaw township. Humphrey's two remaining sons secured more modest estates in neighbouring areas. Francis (d. 1581) came to hold Saltersley in Mobberley, while Hugh Newton found a base in

---

[123] He was a descendent of the Starkey of Stretton family: Brownbill (ed.) *Moore Manuscripts*, nos 196, 1032–3; Irvine (ed.) *A collection of Lancashire and Cheshire wills*, p. 20; Bindoff (ed.) *The House of Commons*, III, pp. 376–8; Clay (ed.) *North country wills*, pp. 111–16; Fishwick (ed.) *Pleadings and depositions in the duchy court*, 2, p. 237.
[124] Anon, 'Lancaster jottings V', p. 199.
[125] Ibid., p. 196
[126] Ibid., p. 209. Humphrey Newton junior had some powerful connections of his own. In the 1540s and 50s he was said to be 'servant and doth weare the cote and livery of one Sir Edmond Trafforth knyghte'. Ibid., p. 207.
[127] Wright, *Derbyshire gentry*, p. 46; Payling, *Political society*, pp. 70–1; Carpenter, *Locality and polity*, p. 358 for comparison.
[128] For further details see pp. 103–4 below.

Lostock, near Poynton (worth £4 according to the 1546 subsidy records).[129] Humphrey's sons had therefore become landed gentry of varying degrees of wealth. None appears to have entered the law, nor did any of them enter the Church, which appears to be something generally avoided by all male Newtons. By the mid-sixteenth century eastern Cheshire was home to four houses of the Newton family.

Humphrey would live but a few months shy of his seventieth birthday, a fair old age in early Tudor England when, assuming one had survived childhood, the average life expectancy was around fifty.[130] Perhaps it owed something to his family. His parents had lived into their late fifties, his paternal grandmother to seventy-seven, and none of the fourteenth-century Newtons appears to have died leaving an under-age heir. Perhaps it was born of contentment. The Newton family was thriving and had not succumbed to the infighting or recklessness that bedevilled other gentry families.[131] His sons worked for, not against, him, with the two eldest involved in family land agreements. Humphrey junior seems to have enjoyed a particularly close relationship with his father. He was chosen as a feoffee and singled out, like his uncle James Barlow, as Humphrey's trusty friend. He may even have been the executor of his father's will because it was apparently in his hands, along with other deeds, in the 1540s.[132] The younger sons, Hugh and Francis, were useful in other ways. Francis was accused of being one of a gang under Humphrey's instruction which in 1527–8 cut down a tree and rioted in the neighbouring holding of the Dean. Similarly, Hugh, in 1529, had apparently caused damage in the Dean at the instigation of his father, and had earlier, in 1522–3, been involved in his father's dispute over Norcliffe mill.[133] Humphrey had therefore managed to persuade his kin to uphold the family's interests.[134] On a final note, it is worth pointing out that Humphrey junior, Francis and Hugh each named his eldest son and heir Humphrey. It suggests recognition of a respected patriarch.

The family image

Humphrey's researches had demonstrated that he came from a long line of ancestors who had been lords of Newton for two centuries. It was an achievement to be advertised and Humphrey was conscious of the importance of his

---

[129] TNA: PRO, E179/85/26, mm. 2–3. Now Lostockhall Farm. See Map 2.
[130] Howell, *Land, Family*, pp. 225–6; Thrupp, *The merchant class*, p. 194; Rosenthal, 'Medieval longevity', p. 288; Fleming, *Family*, p. 68.
[131] Acheson draws attention to occasions among the Leicestershire gentry where trust in the family proved misplaced and many showed wariness in relying too much on family members: Acheson, *A gentry community*, pp. 81–2.
[132] TNA: PRO, E315/419, m. 16; Earwaker, *East Cheshire*, II, p. 266.
[133] TNA: PRO, WALE 29/417, WALE 29/456, STAC 2/6/204–205.
[134] Cf. Carpenter, 'The Stonor circle', p. 192.

family's image. During the Middle Ages, the nobility and, increasingly, the gentry celebrated their lineage – and their separateness from the masses – with the adoption and display of coats of arms. The use of heraldry became, in the words of Maurice Keen, 'emblematic of the pride of birth, station and culture of the nobility in its broadest sense'. By the sixteenth century, the heralds were proclaiming that arms were the sign of a person 'beynge of good name and fame and good renowne (with) lands and possessions of free tenure'.[135]

An astute gentry family with ample resources could secure widespread publicity for its arms, as is illustrated by the well-known fourteenth-century armorial dispute between Sir Richard Scrope and Sir Robert Grosvenor (from Cheshire) over the right to bear the arms *azur a bend or*. The witness testimony generated during the enquiry reveals the extent to which the Grosvenor coat of arms was known across Cheshire: it adorned several church windows, appeared on an altarpiece, and even on an old stone cross on a highway. As Michael Bennett has pointed out, there could have been few places in the county where one would not have seen the Grosvenor coat of arms.[136] In early Tudor England virtually all churches exhibited a fine array of shields. Humphrey's own parish church at Wilmslow contained a large number of heraldic windows, far outnumbering those depicting saints and the apostles, a situation repeated elsewhere in Cheshire.[137] Arms were also prominently displayed in the gentry's own houses. At the Legh family's manor of Adlington, less than two miles east of Newton, a gallery of shields ran along the walls of the main hall, ordered in line with the family's social status. Manuscripts and rolls of arms became fashionable among the gentry, and provided evidence for the heralds. Two surviving Cheshire rolls show that more than 200 families claimed the right to bear arms in the county: the so-called Chester Roll contains some 298 coats of arms, and a roll later secured within a book owned by Sir George Calveley of Lea (d. 1585) contains 220 shields dating to the mid-fifteenth century.[138]

Humphrey's claim to bear arms rested on ancestral right. While there are no surviving images of a Newton arms before the early sixteenth century, Humphrey claimed the traditional family arms as *azure* three popinjays with a chevron *or*. He also knew from his collection of Newton deeds that the seal used by his ancestor Thomas Newton, and more recently by his grandfather Oliver Newton, was a popinjay 'looking to the left as if it sate on the right

---

[135] Keen, *Chivalry*, p. 128; Keen, *Origins*, pp. 17–19; Fleming, 'The character and private concerns of the gentry', p. 23; Coss, 'An age of deference', p. 38; Morgan, 'The individual style', p. 17.
[136] Bennett, *Community*, pp. 82–3.
[137] Ridgeway, 'Coloured window glass in Cheshire', p. 68. And see pp. 135–6 below.
[138] BL, Harley MS 2187, fos 1–5 and Harley MS 2116, fos 13–8. Presumably Calveley's work was the same source used by Laurence Bostock in 1572: 'an old book of armes whiche Sir George Calveley knt. shewed me at his manor house of Lee in Com. Chester anno dom. 1572', BL, Harley MS 139, fo. 27.

hand of the man'. Given the modest social position attained by Humphrey's ancestors, it is unlikely that the popinjay achieved a Grosvenor-like exposure or was well-known around the county. This may have been just as well for Humphrey, because he appears ambiguous on the merit of the Newton arms, particularly when the family became the Newtons of Pownall. As his family's status grew, so did the sense that a refashioning was necessary.

Humphrey wanted an emblem that both distinguished his family and had a good visual impact. Quality of birth would be reflected in the patterns or objects used and the colours selected. Humphrey may well have turned to the discussion and depiction of armorial designs contained in the *Blasing of arms*, one of the component parts of the *Boke of St Albans*, printed in 1486. A copy of the manuscript was once bound within Humphrey's commonplace book, and provided an extensive list of England's most famous coats of arms. Humphrey was highly sensitive to the multivalent readings of the images. What he was aiming for above all was an armorial design that gave the most 'aucthoritie':

> howbeit a question is whech is more of aucthoritie to beare azure iij popinioes betwene a cheveron gould aftr the picture or gould a popiniay vert aftr the seale or a tunne siluer in sable aftr the name, because it may bee seene formost off all colors and metals; or iij tunnes because of Neuton Milton and Phitonn to whom I am heire, or azure a tunne of gould because the richest of all metals and colours, or siluer iij cheverons gules as Neuton Longdendale beires.[139]

In weighing up the possibilities, therefore, Humphrey considered the existing arms and seal of Newton, and turned for inspiration to the Newton family of Mottram-in-Longdendale (near Stockport). In the sixteenth century those assuming arms were widely influenced by similarity of name, even where there was no apparent genealogical connection; this resulted in a number of similar arms being adopted by those of shared surname.[140] A third possibility was the creation of an entirely new coat of arms, using a tun or tuns, which played on the surnames of his relations. Such puns – or canting arms, as they were technically known – were highly popular in medieval Europe. Another example from Cheshire would be the calves' heads used on the shield of the Calveley family of Lea. In this way the arms drew attention to the importance of the family name in symbolising what Keen has called 'the unity of the house'.[141] Humphrey finally decided to adopt a new image of a single tun, while he retained the traditional Newton colours of green and gold: *vert* a tun *or*. Humphrey made several sketches of the tun, and it was publicly displayed

---

[139] BL, Add MS 42134A, fo. 19v. Printed versions can be found in Earwaker, *Eastern Cheshire*, II, p. 265, and Noyes, 'Notices of the family of Newton', p. 318. For the *Boke of St Albans*, see pp. 172–3 below.
[140] Fox (ed.) *English historical scholarship*, p. 41.
[141] Keen, *Chivalry*, p. 130.

in two heraldic windows in Wilmslow church financed by the family in the 1520s (Plate 1). In these the Newton of Pownall shield contained six quarterings: the first was the Newton tun, the second represented Milton, while the remaining four (Fitton of Pownall, Eardswick, Wrenbury and Oulton) all came from the Fitton inheritance: the three 'tuns' – Newton, Milton and Fitton – that underpinned the Newtons' wealth and status. In addition, Humphrey altered the Newton seal. He took the gold ring and seal that had once belonged to Oliver Newton, smoothed out the popinjay from it and engraved a tun in its place. It was a simple but striking image.[142]

The tun, however, does not appear to have survived much beyond Humphrey's death, and the Newton arms suffered an identity crisis in the later sixteenth century. At times the popinjays make a reappearance. The shield used by William Newton of Pownall in 1574 was argent a chevron sable below three popinjays collared, beaked and legged *qu*; his seal was three popinjays.[143] At other times, there is the introduction of a lion rampant. The arms awarded in the 1580 Visitation of Cheshire retained six quarterings, five of which remained the same as those appearing in the Wilmslow windows. The tun, however, was replaced by argent, a lion rampant double grieved sable, charged on the shoulder with a cross *formee or*.[144] This was also used to symbolise the Newton family in the gallery of Adlington Hall.[145] It was not until the eighteenth century that the tun was revived in the shield of the Bromley Davenports, as descendants of the Newtons of Pownall. And it was not until the nineteenth century, in the major new building of Pownall Hall, that the tun became so prominently displayed again in stone and glass. By then antiquarians could list seven alternatives for the shield of the Newtons of Pownall. Evidently Humphrey's choice of arms for his family had not made a significant impression or attained a continued 'aucthoritie'. No arms were ever recorded for the Newtons in the College of Arms.[146] It is perhaps a reflection

---

[142] Very few of Humphrey's seals survive, and most have no impression. One that does has a letter 'H' on it: CRO, ZCR 63/1/43, p. 69. A worn seal which might have been a tun is attached to JRUL, Egerton 1/2/1/16.
[143] Bodl, MS Top Chesh. e.5. fo. 129. Some of the rolls and books of arms available for Cheshire also show the popinjay. In BL, Harley MS 1535 (fo. 34v) the Newton of Pownall arms is similar to that borne by Oliver Newton; there is a slight change in colours, with the Harley arms showing *vert iii popinjays, a chevron sable*.
[144] BL, Harley MS 1424, fo. 114v; Harley MS 1505, fo. 118v. This also appeared in the 1633 Visitation for Sussex as the arms for the Newtons of Mascall in Linfield (descendants of one of Humphrey's grandsons). The note appended to the entry states that 'a certificate under the hand of Sir George Calveley knt.' testified that the coat was from Cheshire: Bannerman (ed.) *The visitation of the county of Sussex*, p. 180. To add to the confusion, the Cheshire visitation of 1566 attributed those arms to the Newtons of Coole and in the 1663 visitation they were given to Thomas Pownall of Barneton: Rylands, 'Impressions', p. 73.
[145] As described in the Adlington manuscript, Chetham Library, Manchester, E. 8. 22, fo. 32v.
[146] Rylands, 'Impressions', p. 73.

of the family's ultimate inability to establish itself as the great landholding lineage that Humphrey had envisioned.

Conclusion

Humphrey was descended from a long line of Newtons who had held land freely in Newton since the late twelfth century or, in Humphrey's words, 'from tyme out of mynde'. His direct line lacked lustre, but it offered him a narrative of continuity and the basis of his gentility. In compiling his genealogy, Humphrey made no overt attempt to disguise his obscure origins, or the odd case of illegitimacy; nor, unlike a number of late medieval families, did he try to fabricate a glorious military past.[147] Humphrey, whose coat of arms was completely devoid of martial imagery, is a good example of someone during the demilitarised sixteenth century for whom heraldry and chivalry had become completely separated, while other aspects of gentility became more important. Later chapters will show that his tomb and his literary interests bear out the view that military capacity never became a facet of Humphrey's identity.

Humphrey was not interested in battle glory; nor did he compile his family trees for sentimental reasons. It was for the prosaic yet vital concern of landholding. All the genealogies in his book, including those of neighbouring families, were about the descent of pieces of land, whole manors or specific rights. His accounts illustrate the clear conjunction of blood and tenure that formed the lineage. The focus was squarely on inheritance. The Newton males may not have led spectacular lives, but they knew whom to marry. It was marriage that had secured Humphrey's inheritance, and alliances with significant families of the North West that had furthered the family's impact in regional society. Marriage had also brought some sheen to the family tree: the link with the earls of Chester was symbolically important to an image-conscious gentleman. Humphrey's own marriage had been a major turning-point for the family in its rise up the social scale. With the Mainwaring marriage, the Newtons had nudged – though clearly not joined – Cheshire's elite.

When Humphrey died in 1536, he was the head of an established gentry household, with the future of the Newton name apparently safe. Ultimately, Humphrey's achievement was that which every landed family strove to accomplish: the ability to pass on an entire estate to a mature heir who could continue the lineage and consolidate the recent social and territorial gains.[148] For that he had his wife Ellen to thank. She not only provided a healthy heir, but conveniently died six weeks after her husband; the Pownall estates passed

---

[147] Moreton, *The Townshends*, p. 5; Morgan, *War and Society*, pp. 3–4. But compare with examples in Denton, 'Image, identity', p. 8.
[148] Mertes, 'Aristocracy', p. 47; Heal and Holmes, *The gentry*, p. 51.

in full to William. Longevity in a line enhanced a family's authority; it was a sign of success. In 1621 William Webb wrote that the township of Pownall was in 'the possession of the best race of Newton, and none I take it of them yet in minority'. Ironically it was the year in which the Newton family finally failed in the male line.[149]

---

[149] Smith and Webb, *The Vale-Royal of England*, p. 89. It was in 1621 that the last male heir, William Newton, died and the estate passed to his daughters.

3

Humphrey and the Law

In 1475 William Worcester may have lamented the numbers who had chosen 'to lerne the practique of law or custom of lande' to the neglect and ultimate detriment of arms,[1] but this was an increasingly old-fashioned view by the fifteenth century as the middling and upper echelons of society came to see law as an advantageous career path for the socially ambitious. The growing laicisation of government, important new developments in the law (such as the making of enfeoffments to use) and the growth of the commercial land market had all furthered opportunities for and increased the prominence of lawyers.[2] Financial and social gains were both possible and quickly achieved, earning lawyers society's suspicions, even opprobrium. Studies have made familiar the success stories of Thomas Kebell (1439–1500) and Sir Roger Townshend (c.1435–93); the latter's career – culminating in his creation as a judge of common pleas – helped to raise his family from the ranks of yeoman-farmers to join the leading gentry families in Norfolk. Such prosperity has led Professor Ives to talk of the law allowing 'the small landowner to make the transition to the substantial squirearchy in one bound'.[3]

Thumbing through Humphrey Newton's commonplace book, with its legal definitions, deeds and fees, gives the impression that he too had chosen law as a route to social advancement. However, defining the lawyer of fifteenth- and early sixteenth-century England is no easy task, especially as the law was not yet fully professionalised. Those engaged in legal work were a heterogeneous group who undertook a wide range of activities. Beyond the courts of Westminster, in the towns and villages around England, worked hundreds of those whom Ives has termed the 'proletariat of local legal officials', who offered services to a broad section of society.[4] They included county court attorneys, minor legal officials such as town clerks, and stewards who presided over the plethora of manorial courts that covered the country. Late medieval England was highly litigious and an obsession with law and its procedures resulted in

---

[1] Worcester, *The boke of noblesse*, p. 77.
[2] Ramsey, 'What was the legal profession?', p. 65.
[3] Ives, *The common lawyers*, p. 32; Moreton, *The Townshends*. For a fifteenth-century view, see Sir Peter Idley's advice to his son: 'To grete worshippe hath the lawe/Brought forth many a pouere man'. D'Evelyn (ed.) *Peter Idley's instruction*, p. 83 (lines 141–2).
[4] Ives, *The common lawyers*, p. 20; Ives, 'Common lawyers', particularly pp. 149–51; Musson, *Medieval law in context*, ch. 2.

knowledgeable amateurs at most levels of society. For the gentleman landowner, a working understanding of family and land law was imperative, the local courts familiar.[5] In addition, in Cheshire, like other counties, the gentry assisted in the administration of justice by participating on juries and making peace bonds.[6]

The range of legal work being undertaken in these and other contexts has led some historians to suggest that there was no single profession; others claim that only the Inns of Court and Chancery supplied a unifying element.[7] For a number of legal historians, the professional lawyer would comply with two conditions. First, he would possess a specialised knowledge and expertise that distinguished him from the layman. Second, he would spend the majority of his time in this activity, deriving much of his income from the law.[8] By these criteria it is difficult to classify Humphrey Newton as a professional lawyer. His commonplace book and his actions show him to have had legal knowledge, to have been employed for his legal skills, and to have administered local justice. But the law was not his career or a substantial source of income. He was never styled a 'man of law'. Instead he appears to be a gentleman-bureaucrat of a type already familiar to Cheshire (and elsewhere) by the late fourteenth century. Michael Bennett has identified a number of men whose legal and administrative expertise made them 'indispensable' to 'the affairs of their more distracted peers'. Among his examples is John Leicester of Tabley, who supplemented his income by acting for his neighbours in legal matters and was rewarded for his counsel.[9] With few scholarly discussions of these men, an analysis of Humphrey's work sheds light on a hazy and poorly understood, but significant, group on the fringes of the legal profession.

Influences

Humphrey's introduction to the workings of the law would have begun at home.[10] As Chapter 2 has indicated, his relatives were well equipped to offer advice and to demonstrate the benefits of legal knowledge. During

---

[5] Maddern, *Violence*, p. 68; Musson, *Medieval law in context*, ch. 3.
[6] Clayton, *The administration of the county palatine*, pp. 214–16, 242–3.
[7] Ramsey, 'What was the legal profession?', p. 62; and Baker, 'The English legal profession', pp. 16–17, 24; Musson, *Public order*, p. 147.
[8] For example, Palmer, *The county courts*, p. 89, n. 1; Brand, *Origins of the English legal profession*, p. vii; Musson and Ormrod, *The evolution of English Justice*, pp. 62–3.
[9] Bennett, *Community*, p. 197. Examples of similar men in the hazy area between professional and amateur can be found in Brand, 'Stewards, bailiffs', particularly p. 145, and Musson, *Public order*, p. 147.
[10] Griffiths, 'Public and private bureaucracies', pp. 120, 132; Ramsey, 'What was the legal profession?', p. 63; Ives, *The common lawyers*, p. 53; Musson, *Medieval law in context*, p. 85.

Humphrey's childhood, his step-grandfather, Laurence Lowe, was at the height of his legal career, and his uncle, Ottiwell Lowe, was completing his education at an Inn of Court.[11] The environs of Newton had also produced several eminent lawyers who advertised the power and connections achievable through the law. A celebrated local hero who drew Humphrey's attention was John Davenport (d. 1390) from the Davenport family of Wheltrough (near Macclesfield). In his commonplace book, Humphrey recounted how John's performance in school had encouraged his father to send him to London to learn the law. He later returned to Cheshire and used his knowledge to the benefit of his county and for his own personal advancement. His most notable act, according to Humphrey, was when he successfully 'contraried or countered a greate man ... send by the king to sytt at the justice of Eyr at Macclesfild'.[12] Two further lawyers from neighbouring families also found their way into Humphrey's book. The earlier was John Pigot of Butley, whose string of titles included justice of Chester in 1388 and sergeant-at-law in the counties of Chester and Flint in 1400. Humphrey carefully transcribed a letter of advice that Pigot had received concerning the rights of inheritance.[13] A more recent neighbour was Thomas Duncalf of Foxtwist, whose long career in the law, lasting over fifty years, included the position of sergeant-at-law of Cheshire in 1436 and 1442–3, and deputy justice for the Cheshire County Court in 1480–1. Humphrey copied Duncalf's written advice on how to set land to feoffees.[14] In the Newton family's immediate locale, therefore, examples of past and present successful lawyers – and local role models – were available when a decision was made regarding Humphrey's education.

Contact with eminent lawyers continued throughout Humphrey's life as he came to work alongside or employ several of the Cheshire men who had joined the growing numbers attending the Inns of Court and Chancery.[15] They include a close-knit group bound by common work and personal ties who can be connected to the Inner Temple. Sir Richard Sutton (d. 1524), from Sutton near Macclesfield, was governor of the Inner Temple seven times in the period 1508–22 and chief governor in 1519–20. A wealthy and successful man, he was also deeply pious and committed to education; he would later be one of the founders of Brasenose College, Oxford. It is likely that it was through Sutton that John Port (c.1472–1540), the son of a Chester mercer, first entered the Inner Temple in the early 1490s. He became treasurer and governor of the Inn and was eventually sergeant at law in 1521. A successful

---

11 See pp. 19–20 above.
12 Bodl, MS Lat. Misc.c.66, fo. 14r.
13 Ibid., fos 10r, 19v.
14 Ibid., fo. 16r. Humphrey prefaced the advice with 'The copie of thadvyse of a lerned man for settyng of lond to feefe'. For information on Duncalf: TNA: PRO, C1/778/5; Clayton, *The administration of the county palatine*, p. 160; Renaud, 'The family of Foxwist', pp. 43–55.
15 Between 1450 and 1550 an estimated 6,000–10,000 men went through the Inns. Baker, 'The English legal profession', p. 32; Jurkowski, 'Lawyers and Lollardy', p. 167.

judge, he subsequently moved to Derbyshire, focusing his career in the North West: he held a number of administrative posts, including that of attorney general of the county palatine of Chester in 1509–21. He was succeeded in that post by another Inner Temple alumnus, Richard Sneyd (reader at the Inn in 1511), who later became recorder of Chester and deputy justice of the county in 1523, 1528–9 and 1531. Their contemporary, John Salter, was an active member of the bench (1505–31/2) who became a reader and governor of the Inn before similarly turning westward, becoming a notable official in the Marches of Wales.[16] As this and later chapters will show, Humphrey had several opportunities to see these men in action and to learn from their experience.

Humphrey's own legal knowledge was not gained through an Inn, and it is much more likely that he adopted a practical approach to learning the law. For many, a course of regular attendance at the local and county courts was the best education available for learning their procedures.[17] Offering a more theoretical grounding was the growing industry of written guides, aided in the later fifteenth century by new commercial printers who considered legal works potential bestsellers. There was a rich selection: registers of writs were owned by both secular and religious landowners; yearbooks of transcribed court cases continued in circulation; while more user-friendly summaries of those cases and of statute and common law were available in abridgements. Added to that was a large corpus of literature that provided instruction on the laying out of documentation and directions for estate officials.[18] Of equal importance were the notebooks which lawyers compiled in an attempt to bring order to the mass of available legal material; data were commonly sorted alphabetically under a series of heads.[19] Some were skilfully organised volumes, such as Sir John Port's notebook, which contains extracts from statutes, yearbooks, abridgements and his observations from the Inner Temple.[20] As in this case, notebooks generally reflected the environment in which the lawyer operated. When, in the early sixteenth century, a member of the Brereton family of Malpas, Cheshire, compiled a register of writs, he included deeds and information relevant to Cheshire, among them a list of contemporary coroners of the county.[21] A proportion of these manu-

---

[16] Contacts between the men are several. For example, John Port co-operated with Sutton in endowing the new foundation of Brasenose College, Oxford, in the early 1500s, and Port's daughter married Richard Sneyd's son, William. Earwaker, *East Cheshire*, II, pp. 445–6; Inderwick (ed.) *A Calendar of the Inner Temple*, pp. 1, 7, 10, 22, 100; Baker (ed.) *The notebook of Sir John Port*; Thornton, *Cheshire*, pp. 92, 147, 149.
[17] Harrison, 'The social and economic history of Cannock and Rugeley', p. 120; Musson, *Medieval law in context*, pp. 68, 122.
[18] Baker, *The common law tradition*, ch. 10; Baker, 'Common lawyers and the inns of court', pp. 448–9; Musson, *Medieval law in context*, pp. 39–41, 69, 122–8.
[19] Simpson, 'The legal treatise', p. 14.
[20] Baker (ed.) *The notebook of Sir John Port*.
[21] *Registrum Brevium*: TNA: PRO, CHES 38/13. The obit of Randolph Brereton (d. 1530)

scripts took the form of commonplace books, which during the sixteenth and seventeenth centuries became complex volumes packed with indispensable knowledge drawn from formulary deeds, lists of legal definitions, legal treatises and records of new legislation or landmark decisions by judges.[22] Early Tudor legal commonplace books took a more amorphous form, but had a comparable value. Sir William Stanford (1509–1558), Justice of the Common Pleas, compiled a miscellany containing a twelve-folio dissertation on the statutes of Westminster, lecture notes from Gray's Inn and accounts showing his financial gains from the law.[23]

Humphrey made a similar attempt at compiling a legal miscellany, although what survives lacks the breadth and sophistication of the better-known notebooks. It comprises fifteen folios, with the material organised under a series of heads, usually document types. It has the feel of a working document; a few entries have been heavily corrected.[24] The entries are akin to those selected for other legal miscellanies, but the compilation is Humphrey's own and reveals the kind of work with which he was involved: it overwhelmingly relates to land law and issues of inheritance. Items were drawn from a variety of sources. First, there were those copied from professional or semi-professional documents, among them a parchment bifolium discussing different forms of land tenure,[25] a formulary booklet, what appears to be an extract from a yearbook,[26] and articles on holding court. We may also note here the Biblical texts (from the books of Deuteronomy, Numbers and 1 Kings) which Humphrey cited in relation to inheritance and landholding. Second, there are copies of advice or opinions made by other lawyers, such as those by Thomas Duncalf mentioned above. Third, there are the items which Humphrey came across in the course of his legal work and as a landholder. These included his copy and discussion of 'a writ of right' concerning 'my lord Fitzwarren', for whom Humphrey acted as steward in Staffordshire.[27] As in this case, a number of the deeds date to the 1490s, and hence were contemporary decisions on legal disputes. It was both natural and useful for his collection to be dominated by regional material, and within the commonplace book can be found a brief list of the customs of Macclesfield.[28] Yet there are docu-

---

appears on the Sarum calendar under 10 June, fo. 17r.
[22] Brooks, *Pettifoggers and Vipers*, pp. 176–8, provides seventeenth-century examples of legal commonplace books.
[23] BL, Royal MS.17 B XLVII, fos 4–140.
[24] Bodl, MS Lat. Misc.c.66, fos 2–17.
[25] Ibid., fos 31b–c. It is written in law French. Humphrey transcribed part of the booklet onto fo. 10v.
[26] The extract, written in law French, concerns a writ of formedon. It opens with the date: Michaelmas term 13 Edward IV.
[27] Ibid., fo. 3r. The deed is dated 1495/6 and documented the sale of a manor by Fitzwarren to Sir John Legh of Stockwell, another notable lawyer. For Humphrey's stewardships see, pp. 56–7 below.
[28] Beginning: 'All these goodez upon olde tyme aftr the custom of Macclesfied ben

ments relating to the Westminster courts too – a writ of right and a *dedimus potestatem*, for instance – reflecting the increasing use made of these external courts by Cheshire people during the early Tudor period.²⁹

The scribe

Humphrey's legal work covered a diversity of tasks which made him useful to his neighbourhood. There was a focus on advocacy, involving the skills of draughtsmanship, offering advice and acting in arbitration cases. One of his more routine duties was the drafting of documents, traces of which may be seen in his purchases of paper and parchment, his recipes for ink and the number of formulary documents included.³⁰ Scribal work was not usually high-powered, and was generally undertaken by the lower ranks of the legal profession or even its fringe members; only in matters of great significance were legal men of stature involved. None of Humphrey's known work would place him among the latter, hinting at his modest status when it came to the law.³¹ It was clearly not always lucrative work; on one occasion Humphrey received merely 12*d* for three pieces of writing.³² Other commissions paid better, underlining the view that there was no such thing as cheap litigation.³³ Two of his clients were regional businessmen who required a scribe with some degree of expertise. One was Ryle of Etchells, a cloth merchant, for whom Humphrey wrote four indentures at 6*s* 8*d*, some indentures that cost 4*s* and a copy worth 6*d*.³⁴ The second was his cousin William Rode, burgess and the mayor of Congleton in 1503–4. Rode thought well of Humphrey, whom he called his 'trustie cosen': he visited Newton on at least two consecutive Christmases and, in 1499, invited Humphrey to his son's wedding to the sister of James Spencer (later Lord Mayor of London, 1527). In his commonplace book Humphrey referred to the 'many times' he had written for Rode; these included several conveyancing deeds and probably Rode's will and testament.³⁵ He, however, seemed less impressed with his cousin, who did not always pay for this work: Humphrey complained that he 'neider had reward' from Rode, and was owed 2*s* 6*d* for a writ, 8*s*

---

conseyved'. Bodl, MS Lat. Misc.c.66, fo. 69r.
²⁹ Ibid., fos 3r, 6r and 8r. Thornton shows that Cheshire cases trickled towards Chancery and Star Chamber before 1515, with the flow increasing significantly during Wolsey's years as chancellor. He writes of Chancery becoming 'suddenly busy' with Cheshire cases in 1515–18: *Cheshire*, pp. 5, 107.
³⁰ Bodl, MS Lat. Misc.c.66, fos 29v and 32v for paper and parchment purchases.
³¹ Baker, 'The English legal profession', p. 27; Ives, *The common lawyers*, p. 143.
³² Bodl, MS Lat. Misc.c.66, fo. 35r.
³³ Ives, *The common lawyers*, p. 318, for comparisons.
³⁴ Bodl, MS Lat. Misc.c.66, fos 45v, 47v. Humphrey records the payments as possible deductions or 'allowances' for previous debts he owed Ryle.
³⁵ BL, Harley 2077, fo. 43v; Bodl, MS Lat. Misc.c.66, fos 30v, 34cr, 47v.

for 'the sheriff', 2s for a copy of a return, and travelling expenses incurred on a trip to London. Humphrey's legal work, therefore, had the potential to take him beyond Cheshire and, presumably in this last case, to the courts at Westminster.[36]

The diverse range of documents that he was called upon to write can be gauged from the formulary items Humphrey collected and copied. These provided templates for the correct phraseology and layout of numerous deeds. They are easy to identify because letters – usually 'a', 'b' and 'c' – have been substituted for proper names, and witness lists contain seemingly fictitious names. One heavily corrected deed in Humphrey's book, headed 'pro manero', used letters for the grantor and includes the surprising witnesses Lambio Sternebergh and Ludkyno Grambek.[37] Other documents may well have been transcribed more for their form than for their specific information: an indenture, an inspeximus and a statute merchant are all headed by their function and most personal names have been reduced to initials. This may also explain why Humphrey copied an interesting fifteenth-century petition to Edward IV in which Hugh Wiot, yeoman, asked to become bailiff of Cleeton and Farlow, Shropshire.[38]

It is reasonable to suppose that Humphrey transcribed these documents because they informed on aspects of legal procedure and were deeds he had written or could expect to be called upon to write. One that he evidently had penned was a declaration of chastity to be stated and signed by a widow, or a male relative on her behalf, who wished to announce the decision in public. Such a deed would have been important to landholding families in ensuring that no further potential claimants to an estate were produced, and important for the widow in protecting herself against pressures to remarry. Note the substitution of 'a', 'b' and 'c' for the proper names:

The othe of a lady of the mantyll and ryng
In the name of the fader the son and the holy gost, I A B sum tyme wife to C & nowe wedowe nat weddet nor ensiret to no man, make avowe unto God, Our Lady & Seynt Paule, & to alle the seynts in heyven, in the presens of yeu, Reverend fader in God, R Bisshop of Panadens, to liffe chast of my body the days of my lif under the rule of Seynt Paule. In nomine patre et filii etc.[39]

An accompanying note reveals that Humphrey had written an oath of chastity for Humphrey David, who had paid, on behalf of his sister, £4 'to alle affaers'. The costs of the decree did not come cheaply, as Humphrey wrote underneath the oath: 'the decrees therof the chauncelor will desir a 100s for

---

[36] Bodl, MS Lat. Misc.c.66, fos 45v, 47v.
[37] Ibid., fo. 5v.
[38] Ibid., fos 5r, 104. For a thorough analysis of the letter's contents see Bennett, 'Memoir of a yeoman', pp. 259–64.
[39] Bodl, MS Lat. Misc.c.66, fo. 6r. Punctuation and capitalisation added. Compare the examples used in Swanson, *Catholic England*, pp. 173–4.

the bishop, the registr 13s 4d, the chaunceler 20s, the issher 7s and 53d the suffryan'. As in other cases, it was often the procedural work of the court and clerical expenses that inflated the cost. Officials at ecclesiastical courts would need extra monetary inducements to undertake this work because their salaries alone would not be adequate.[40]

In writing these deeds, Humphrey needed to be proficient in a variety of scripts. Different documents demanded distinct writing styles and, by the end of the fifteenth century, numerous books had been produced containing model letters and deeds that provided useful illustrations for the aspiring scribe.[41] The works survive in various shapes and forms, with some elaborate scrapbooks made from the cuttings of other deeds and manuscripts.[42] At other times, short booklets of capital and lower-case letters, usually locally produced, provided the basics. An example is a six-page parchment booklet traced to Herefordshire, which contains lists of letters and petitions for local offices.[43] This has particular relevance because it closely compares with the ten-page parchment booklet of letter-forms that Humphrey owned and illustrates a standard design.[44] Humphrey's also has capital and lower-case letters, followed by folios of model petitions to the king. Its scribe was a professional, although the booklet itself is incomplete. It was once in the hands of John Bird, whose name appears (very elaborately) on the cover and in a deed within the booklet, strongly suggesting that he was the scribe.[45] What is revealing in Humphrey's case is that he decided to practise these letter-forms, and copied his efforts on several pages of his commonplace book.[46] Humphrey had a careful eye and he tried to copy out the forms precisely, but he lacked the skill of the original scribe. His painstakingly drawn letters contrast with the fluidity and roundedness of the professional's hand.

---

[40] I owe this point to Maureen Jurkowski.

[41] Clanchy, *From memory*, pp. 127–8; Louis, *The commonplace book of Robert Reynes*, p. 7.

[42] One extraordinary example in the British Library is a sixteenth-century manuscript filled with letters cut from manuscripts and printed material: BL, MS Add. 27869. While beautiful to look at, the scrapbook has obviously left a number of manuscripts without their illuminated initials.

[43] The Herefordshire booklet dates to the late fifteenth century and is attached to the beginning of Bodl, Ashmole MS 789. Another shorter example can be found in the commonplace book BL, Sloane MS 1584, fos 23, 27r–33v.

[44] Bodl, MS Lat. Misc.c.66, fos 112–21. In the seventeenth century Humphrey's booklet appears to have been borrowed by William Brereton of Handforth, whose name and initials are found on the last two leaves.

[45] Unfortunately the name is too common to identify a specific individual, but it is worth noting that the Birds of Locko (Derbyshire) were neighbours of Humphrey's relatives, the Lowes.

[46] The first folio number denotes the letter book; the second is the folio on to which Humphrey transcribed the letters: 112v/96v, 113r/97v, 114r/98r, 115r/100r, 115v/100v, (116r–117v not copied by Humphrey), 118r/99r, 119r/105r, (120–121 not copied by Humphrey).

Humphrey also chose to depart from the booklet in several noteworthy ways. Thus he could not resist adding his signature to the copied deeds, proud perhaps of his efforts. He also chose to add a couple of his own, which reflect the northern context within which he was operating. One, and possibly both, involve the Hawarden family of Chester, which provided several sheriffs and mayors to Chester in the fourteenth and fifteenth centuries.[47] It is not clear why the two deeds particularly attracted Humphrey's attention, but again the form rather than the people are likely to have been the significant point. Elsewhere in his commonplace book, his letter practising involved standard legal phrases which he must have written numerous times: 'to the honourable & most ymportent lord', 'Noverint universi per presentes', and 'be it knowen to all'.[48]

A third difference was the addition of capitals A–H in the elaborate and particularly demanding letterform known as strapwork. It was a design favoured in northern counties in the early sixteenth century.[49] It appeared both in manuscripts and, in a more pedestrian form, in land deeds and family documents. In the will of Richard Hockenhall of Cheshire (dated 1525), for example, the initial 'I' contains the same strapwork design found in Humphrey's letter booklet.[50] It was also becoming increasingly popular with book artists and printers of the early Tudor period, and perhaps Humphrey was seeking to keep his letter practices up to date.[51] Given the repetitive nature of deed writing, learning how to add the odd flourish would be a welcome and individual show of creativity.

Humphrey did not simply copy deeds: for his own sake, and in his work for others, he needed to record information that would help in the interpretation of documents. This motive is reflected in his list of kings of England, which was a regular item in legal miscellanea, probably because documents were generally dated by regnal year. In his list, Humphrey noted famous statutes in the history of the common law: the date of Limitation (1189) and the Statutes of Westminster, numbers II (*de donis conditionalibus*) and

---

[47] Only a few lines are noted from each. The first is a deed of John Stathum, son of Thomas Stathum of Morley in Derbyshire, concerning the actions of Thomas Hawarden, and dates to around 1486. The deed appears to be that transcribed in TNA: PRO, CHES 2/158, m. 7d (calendared in 37th *DKR*, p. 688). A second contains merely the opening lines of a deed written by Brother John Kendale of the knights of St John of Jerusalem. A Lancashire deed, dating c.1480, has the same opening lines and is a licence to choose a confessor for John Hawarden, who is described as a crusader in Rhodes defending it against the Turks. The original can now be found in Lancashire RO, RCHY 3/6. For the Hawarden family, see Lewis and Thacker (eds), *A history*, pp. 308–11.

[48] Bodl, MS Lat. Misc.c.66, fo. 92r.

[49] Bodl, MS Lat. Misc.c.66, fos 99v, 101av. Meale, 'The social and literary contents of a late medieval manuscript', pp. 309–10.

[50] CRO, DLE/15 and Bodl, MS Lat. Misc.c.66, fo. 101av. See also Chetham Library, Manchester, MUN A.6.31.

[51] Meale, 'The politics of book ownership', p. 119. For further discussion, see pp. 187–8 below

III. Most dates are correct, but a poor mistake was made with the third Westminster statute, the famous *Quia Emptores*, which was placed in the reign of Edward III rather than in its rightful position in the reign of Edward I, hinting perhaps at a rather amateur grasp of the law.[52] Another helpful guide, and which circulated widely in late medieval Cheshire, was a list of definitions by which to interpret more complicated and obscure legal jargon.[53] Humphrey's search for definitions may have been prompted by a particular deed. He had transcribed the ancient and, to the uninitiated, baffling privileges claimed for the Aldford fee (in 1364–5). These were enjoyed in the late fifteenth century by John Stanley, who employed Humphrey as steward of Etchells manor, which lay within the fee. Among the terms defined were *ingfanthief, homesoken, blodewite, frithsoken* and *mynde breche*.[54] Yet understanding individual words could not alone aid interpretation, and Humphrey copied opinions or advice that drew out the significance of deeds or acts. This can be seen in short notes such as those following 'a relees with warantie speciall' that involved the Berkshire lands of Thomas Wode, sergeant at law (d. 1502); Humphrey made two points on the extent of the binding of the warranty. Brief discursive notes were also made on 'a case wherby a writ of right was avoided', 'setting a land to feoffe' and on a *dedimus potestatem*.[55] In all cases it was information that Humphrey required for his own purposes and for those of his prospective employers.

Giving counsel

The nobility and major religious houses had long appointed advisers on a regular basis to assist them in their household and political affairs. During the fifteenth century, the value of retaining legal expertise was recognised by a wider landed and commercial society. In giving advice, a lawyer could benefit in a number of ways because it placed him in a strong position in the competition for land and privileges. The Norfolk lawyer Roger Townshend, for example, had his legal work for the Paston family in the 1470s rewarded with the manor of East Beckham.[56] Humphrey's own counsel was

---

[52] Bodl, MS Lat. Misc.c.66, fo. 2r. It was not simply Humphrey's mistake because he was copying a list originally written in the reign of Henry VI: on a few occasions, the number of years between a famous event and Henry VI's reign has been calculated.

[53] These lists proved popular with seventeenth-century Cheshire antiquarians such as John Booth (CRO, ZCR 63/2/30 fo. 1) and William Vernon (BL, Harley MS 2079, fos 66r–68v).

[54] Bodl, MS Lat.Misc.c.66, fos 11v–13v.

[55] Ibid., fos 3r, 7r, 8r, 16–17. *Dedimus potestatem*, meaning literally 'we have given the power', was a commission authorising persons to perform an official duty such as taking the answer of a defendant or conducting examinations outside London.

[56] Moreton, 'A "best bestrustyd frende"'. See also the remarks made by Ives, *The common lawyers*, p. 103; Musson, *Medieval law in context*, p. 48.

sought and he had the opportunity to benefit from imparting legal knowledge, as two examples illustrate. One comes from a dispute that had arisen between Reginald Legh of Adlington (along with the vicar of Prestbury) and his elder brother Thomas, lord of Adlington (d. 1519). Reginald had sought Humphrey's advice and it had led to a successful outcome. Humphrey lost little time in securing his reward, as he himself wrote:

> Memorandum, for asmoche as ther was dyvers variaunces betwene Thomas Legh of Adlyngton, Reynold his broþer and þe vicar of Prestbury and oþer, which Reynold come to me & desired me to be of his counseill to help hym out of trowble: and so I was of his counseill. Wherefore he seid if he cold do me a pleasur he seid he wold, & so I desired hym to get his moder to seall me a relesse of Neuton heith & oþer land as it appears by the dede, & he seid he wold & so I wrote a relessh & gaf it hym & he brogt it to me from her wt specill tokyns sealed.[57]

In 1500, therefore, Reginald Legh persuaded his mother, Ellen, to sign a release that Humphrey had written, thereby quitclaiming to him all her claim to lands and tenements which she held in the area known as Newton Heath. It was a contentious gift which did nothing to heal the rift in the Legh household. Some years later Reginald Legh felt it necessary to endorse his mother's release in front of witnesses.[58] On a second occasion, in 1502, Joyce Crowther of Foxtwist quitclaimed to Humphrey and his heirs all her rights and possessions in the vill of Newton 'pro bono concilio suo'.[59] The advice is not known, but it may again have been the result of troublesome offspring because it was Joyce's son, Gilbert, who 'caused her to seale it'. Humphrey did not instigate a quarrel and it may be assumed that his advice was needed and gratefully received. Yet, as Chapter 4 explains, the quitclaims were important to Humphrey's landed position in the area.[60] Humphrey knew when to take advantage of those who sought his help, particularly when Fortune appeared in the guise of pliant widows.[61]

Humphrey's presence and opinion were further sought among the gentry of the North West. A man of good legal knowledge was a useful choice as a feoffee in land and family settlements, and several local gentry chose Humphrey as trustee for their lands. These included John Tatton of Witheshaw, esquire, and Nicholas Jodrell of Yeardsley, gentleman (d. 1528).[62] One of his most important engagements occurred in 1507 when Humphrey was among twenty men enfeoffed in lands worth £20 as part of a settlement to

---

[57] JRUL, Bromley Davenport 'Newton by Mottram', no. 5; BL, Add MS 42134A fo. 1r.
[58] See p. 98 below
[59] BL, Add MS 42134A fo. 2r.
[60] That is, in his dispute with Butley township: see pp. 97–8 below
[61] Compare with Joan Mariot's vulnerable position discussed in Richmond, *The Paston family in the fifteenth century*, pp. 87–8.
[62] TNA: PRO, CHES 3/62/14; JRUL, Jodrell 38a–b.

end a long, bitter dispute between Sir Thomas Boteler of Bewsey, Lancashire (d. 1522) and Sir Piers Legh of Lyme (d. 1527), two substantial knights and landowners. The twenty, comprising knights, esquires, clergymen and gentlemen of the North West, were listed in terms of their rank and authority. Order mattered to the gentry. In declaring their gentle ancestry, the Paston family 'showed a great multitude of old deeds ... wherein their ancestors were alwaies sett first in witness and before all other gentlemen'.[63] On this basis, Humphrey's position as last on the above list suggests that he was not recruited for his social weight, but for his abilities: he was an 'active' feoffee.[64]

Authority could also be gained from acting as an arbitrator. Well before the early Tudor period, the process of arbitration had become an established way of dealing with disputes among the gentry. It offered a speedier, less expensive and less adversarial alternative to litigation, and was undertaken with a view to restoring long-term harmony.[65] The negotiations might be led by anyone with sufficient authority to ensure that the disputing parties observed the arrangement. In some areas it was a means by which the nobility exercised control over the gentry; however, in Cheshire arbitration was firmly in the hands of the gentry.[66] While it was not necessary to involve lawyers, research on the subject emphasises the presence and importance of men with sound legal knowledge.[67] Humphrey did not act regularly as an arbitrator, and the two examples which have come to light suggest again that his competence mattered more than his social influence. One involved a long-running dispute in the period 1503–6 over a rent on lands in Godley (north-eastern Cheshire) between Thomas Assheton of Ashton, knight (d. 1516), and Robert Legh of Blakebroke, Derbyshire. The case brought Humphrey into contact with Roger Legh of the Ridge (d. 1506), a fellow arbitrator, and a graduate of the Inner Temple with wide legal connections.[68] Humphrey's gentle status, connections and standing in the community could hardly match those of

---

[63] Davis (ed.) *Paston letters and papers*, vol. 2, 897 (p. 551)
[64] JRUL, Legh of Lyme Box R.A.10; Irvine (ed.) *A collection of Lancashire and Cheshire wills*, pp. 73–4. For the dispute see Beamont, *Annals of Warrington*, vol. II, pp. 351–2, 371–5. Humphrey might fit the profile of the type of person whom Carpenter described as 'bringing up the rear among the property transactions of others': Carpenter, 'The Stonor circle', p. 181.
[65] For example, Powell, 'Arbitration and the law' and see n. 67 below.
[66] Thornton, *Cheshire*, p. 29. This study shows that between 1480 and 1560 the gentry acted as arbitrators to the exclusion of the aristocracy.
[67] Rawcliffe, 'Parliament and the settlement of disputes', p. 321; Ives, *The common lawyers*, pp. 126–30; Rowney, 'Arbitration', p. 373; and Moreton, *The Townshends*, p. 16
[68] For the dispute, see *Manchester Guardian*, 13 January 1849, p. 11, and Earwaker, *East Cheshire*, vol. I, pp. 159–60. Legh had close associations with Sir Richard Sutton (they were both trustees of Macclesfield grammar school), as well as two other Cheshire men made wealthy by the law: Sir Humfrey Starkey (d. 1486), Justice of the Common Pleas, and Sir John Legh of Stockwell (d. 1523), knight of Bath.

Roger Legh, nor indeed of Assheton or Robert Legh. It is far more likely that ability and local knowledge had earned him his selection.

The same may be said of Humphrey's second arbitration case, which involved adjudicating between William Davenport of Bramhall, esquire (d. 1528), and Robert Hyde of Norbury, esquire (d. c.1528), over the boundary between Bramhall and Norbury.[69] Neither would have been swayed by Humphrey's social presence: Davenport was a substantial landowner from one of Cheshire's elite families and very well connected.[70] What is significant about this case is that it was not the only example of Humphrey acting for William Davenport. On another occasion, dated to 1512–13, Humphrey had witnessed an arbitration deed between Davenport and John Warren of Poynton.[71] In this instance, Humphrey may have been there at Warren's behest because the latter had employed Humphrey as steward at Stockport manor. However, a more tempting possibility is that Humphrey was being retained by William Davenport and was perhaps of his counsel. Davenport was involved in a number of disputes in Cheshire, was accused of protecting wrongdoers, and had fallen foul of Henry VII's laws against retaining.[72] He was someone needing sound advice. During 1519–21, at least, Humphrey was receiving a regular fee from Davenport. A note in his commonplace book refers to a sum of 5s a year that he owed Humphrey each Martinmas.[73] It connected Humphrey to an important man in the area, and one who supported him when troubles arose. The paying of the fee would have acknowledged Davenport's superiority while recognising Humphrey's worth.[74]

---

[69] BL, Harley MS 2074, fo. 29r. Taken from a later antiquarian's summary of the original deed, which no longer survives. The copy is undated.

[70] His family is among Thornton's list of thirty-nine elite families: *Cheshire*, p. 30, table 1. Davenport himself had a high profile. He was rewarded in 1486–7 for his services to Henry VII with an annuity of twenty marks. In Cheshire, he appeared on the most significant commissions: in 1481, he was placed on a commission to arrest outlaws in Macclesfield hundred; in 1484 he was appointed on a commission of affray for the same hundred; he was collector of subsidy for Macclesfield in 1489 and 1502; was a final concord panellist in 1519; and served at the county court until he secured exemption in 1512. Campbell (ed.) *Materials for a history of the reign of Henry VII*, II, p. 30; TNA: PRO, CHES 24/72, CHES 31/38; 37th *DKR*, App.II, p. 488.

[71] CRO, DDA/1533/1.

[72] TNA: PRO, C1/456/17; CHES 25/18, m. 26; JRUL, Mainwaring 303; Stewart-Brown (ed.) *Lancashire and Cheshire cases in the Court of Star Chamber*, pp. 47–8.

[73] The note reads 'and so he [Davenport] ozes me Vs for my fee for Martynmas anno X⁰ & oþer Vs for Missom anno XI⁰ & for XII⁰ and XIII⁰ howebeit I suppose I rec' Xs of þos þer': Bodl, MS Lat. Misc.c.66, fo. 60v.

[74] Horrox, 'Local and national politics', p. 394. For Davenport's support in Humphrey's land disputes, see p. 102 below.

The steward

The position that gave Humphrey a high profile in several manors in Cheshire and north Staffordshire was that of steward. The size and complexity of many landed estates, along with the potential absence of their lord, demanded some form of organisation, and the steward was a key official.[75] As head of the administration, he (and it was always 'he') had powers to oversee other manorial officers, even to recommend their dismissal, and he could become a valuable adviser to the lord.[76] The highest position was that of the chief steward, found on the most extensive estates, and with responsibility for an entire receivership.[77] Below him were the manorial stewards, who were attached to a single manor or small group of them. Their work could encompass the entire estate administration, including agrarian exploitation, drawing up leases and arranging repairs; some stewards were very probably chosen for their managerial skills. However, the most important function of the steward (both chief and manorial) was the holding of the customary and seignorial courts. From the time of Edward I it became increasingly necessary for the steward to have a good legal knowledge, and lawyers became preferred appointees.[78] The popular estate manual known as the *Seneschaucy* declared that 'he ought to know the law of the country so that he can defend actions outside the lord's estate, can give confidence to the bailiffs who are under him, and can instruct them'.[79] On some estates the steward was employed only to hold the courts (the *seneschallus curie*, or the steward of the courts) and did not fulfil any other administrative duties.[80] His work was part-time and took place largely when the court sat. By the fifteenth century, the position of steward was widely seen as an important opportunity for the nobility to offer patronage to the gentry, and the posts became sinecures. Consequently there emerged a group of deputy or sub-stewards who undertook the work of those holding honorary positions.[81]

---

[75] No full-length discussion of the role of the medieval steward exists, although brief discussions are available: Bennett, *Life on the English Manor*, pp. 156–60; Denholm-Young, *Seignorial administration*, pp. 66–85; Rawcliffe, *The Staffords*, pp. 49–50; Saul, *Knights and esquires*, pp. 85–8; Saul, *Scenes*, pp. 99, 102; and most recently Brand, 'Stewards, bailiffs', pp. 146–51 and Musson, *Public order*, pp. 155–8. For their use in the patronage system, see Kelly, 'The noble steward', pp. 133–48.
[76] Oschinsky, *Walter of Henley*, p. 269.
[77] For example, there were two chief stewards in the duchy of Lancaster administration, one covering the northern regions and one the south: Somerville, *History of the Duchy of Lancaster*, p. 111.
[78] Ives, *The common lawyers*, p. 11; Brooks, *Pettifoggers and vipers*, p. 45.
[79] Oschinsky, *Walter of Henley*, p. 265.
[80] Examples can be found on the manors of the duke of Clarence: Hilton (ed.) *Ministers' accounts of the Warwickshire Estates of the Duke of Clarence*, p. xxvi; Hainsworth, *Stewards*, p. 11.
[81] For example, at Battle Abbey: Searle, *Lordship and community*, p. 422. McFarlane, *The nobility*, pp. 107, 216; Wright, *Derbyshire gentry*, p. 62.

Humphrey never held the prestigious position of chief steward, which was usually bestowed on gentry of knightly status or higher, and there is little to indicate that he played a daily managerial role on any of the manors to which he was assigned. Rather, he was a court-holder who mainly visited a manor when the court sat. Among those who attended the manorial courts, the steward enjoyed a recognised position of authority as the spokesperson of the lord. At the customary court (the civil court for the 'unfree' of a village), the steward acted as the interpreter of customary law and dealt with pleas of debt, trespass and damage.[82] At the court baron (the civil court of the freeholder) the steward was further required to manage a jury, which he had ordered to be summoned and would decide when to adjourn. In both these courts, Humphrey would have upheld the interests of the lord, perhaps adjudicated between lord and tenant, and regulated the lives of the villagers. The most imposing court was that known as the 'leet', where the steward administered private criminal jurisdiction and the common law. In many cases the leet was combined with a 'view of frankpledge', a franchise of the crown which covered public criminal law.[83] In these cases, therefore, Humphrey would have presided as a quasi-royal justice, having the additional responsibility of seeing the king's law done.[84]

The range of issues that he would have considered can be partially gauged from Humphrey's collection of formulary lists of articles that were to be asked at the manorial courts. These lists were very popular in early Tudor England and survive in large numbers in both manuscript and printed form; the manual *Modus tenendi curiam baronis cum visu franci plegii*, for example, was printed in eighteen separate editions between 1510 and 1550.[85] Humphrey transcribed into his commonplace book those articles pertaining to the court baron (nineteen articles), the view of frankpledge (twenty-three), the halmote or manor court (twenty-eight), and the swanimote court, which was the court administering forest law (twenty-eight).[86] His lists contain the average number of articles, although others might include as many as ninety. From the Newton lists it is clear that the information available to the steward was limited and it would have been difficult to run a court from these articles alone. They tell us, for example, that issues dealt with at the court of frank-

---

[82] For a discussion of the court customary (or small court) see Morris, 'The small court', pp. 1–21.
[83] For a discussion of the system of frankpledge as it operated in Cheshire (which was different to most of the rest of England) see Stewart-Brown, *The sergeants of the peace*, p. 99.
[84] Pollock and Maitland, *The history of the English law*, 1, p. 592.
[85] Maitland and Baildon (eds), *The court baron*; Hearnshaw, *Leet jurisdiction in England*, pp. 29–30, 43, 64, 373–7. Both include transcriptions of articles which may be compared with the Newton lists. See also Plucknett, *The medieval bailiff*, pp. 9–10.
[86] They are written in Law French, Bodl, MS Lat. Misc.c.66, fo. 4. For examples of other commonplace books containing articles see Louis, *The commonplace book of Robert Reynes*, pp. 144–5, and Smith, *A commonplace book*, pp. 151–66.

pledge included keeping of the peace, overseeing the assizes of bread and ale, and cases of theft; but they do not divulge how these matters were raised and considered. For Humphrey and other stewards, these articles probably served as checklists of duties.[87]

Humphrey's presence in the court was enhanced by its procedure. On an appointed day those owing suit to the court would gather at a designated place; this might be the lord's manor house, the grander setting of a moot hall, or even at the base of a tree. The steward would then take his position as president of the court, with his clerk on hand to make the enrolment. All complaints and charges were addressed to the steward and any offenders were brought to him by the bailiff. Although it would be the jury who convicted the accused, and other officials who decided the fine, the voice of the steward held authority over those awaiting trial.[88]

Knowledge of Humphrey's stewardships relies mainly on a short series of accounts in his commonplace book dating to 1498–1503 and 1505. These are headed *pro seneschallo* and list the manor, the name of the lord and the fee agreed. Humphrey recorded the information alongside the half-yearly rentals he had made of his Newton tenancies at the festivals of Martinmas and St John the Baptist.[89] These records reveal that between at least 1498 and 1505 Humphrey was retained by eight landlords of varying degrees of wealth and status. He appears to have held the posts for a few years, adopting the common strategy of seeing each position as short-term, rather than a lifetime choice.[90]

Who thought Humphrey worthy of employment? His four main employers were considerable landlords whose holdings and administrations spanned several counties. The largest and most impressive was the duchy of Lancaster, whose base in Cheshire was centred on the barony of Halton.[91] Humphrey followed in the footsteps of a long line of Cheshire gentry when he was appointed steward for the manor of Congleton in *c.*1498–1500. A second employer was the bishop of Coventry and Lichfield, whose lands extended across Warwickshire and Staffordshire into Cheshire. Humphrey was steward of the bishopric's substantial Cheshire estate, which covered the manors of Wybunbury, Tarvin, Farndon and Burton in the Wirral. In 1496 the estimated worth of these manors was £66 17s 2½d.[92] A third employer was nominally the Touchets, Lords Audley, great landholders in Staffordshire and one of the

---

[87] Harrison, 'The social and economic history of Cannock and Rugeley', p. 112.
[88] See Maitland and Baildon (eds), *The court baron*, p. 62; Clanchy, *From memory*, p. 277. For Maddern, courts were 'arenas for the display of authority': *Violence*, p. 66.
[89] Bodl, MS Lat. Misc.c.66, fos 28v, 32r, 35r, 37v, 38v, 41ar, 42v, 43r, and 47r (a single payment for the manor of Tattenhall in 1505). See Map 1.
[90] Denholm-Young, *Seignorial administration*, p. 70.
[91] Somerville, *The history of the duchy of Lancaster, passim*.
[92] 37th *DKR*, App.II, p. 463. In 1535 the lands were collectively valued at £78 6s: *Valor Ecclesiasticus*, 3, p. 128.

few noble families to hold property in Cheshire.[93] Humphrey was steward for the manor of Tattenhall, Cheshire (which was worth around £30), and for the wealthier Touchet manors in Staffordshire at Audley, Horton, Norton and Betley.[94] For most of his stewardships his employers were not specifically the Touchets themselves because, in 1497, James Touchet, seventh Lord Audley, was imprisoned and subsequently beheaded for his part in the insurrection of the Cornishmen. In Humphrey's accounts the Tattenhall fee was accredited first to the king and then to William Smith, possibly the ambitious Staffordshire gentleman who was a page or groom of the wardrobe under Henry VII. The Staffordshire lands went to Lord Fitzwarren (James Touchet's father-in-law).[95] The fourth major landlord was the Trussell family, whose estates encompassed lands in Leicestershire, Essex, Northamptonshire, Norfolk and Berkshire.[96] Their possessions in Cheshire extended to several manors, of which Warmingham – the manor appearing in Humphrey's accounts – was the largest.[97] Again, they were not always the direct employers of Humphrey. In the late fifteenth century the Trussells suffered a succession of minorities, and in 1500 the custody of the Cheshire manors was granted to George Grey, second earl of Kent (d. 1503), who appears in Humphrey's accounts.[98]

There is much to impress here, particularly because Cheshire was not awash with noble families and wealthy ecclesiastical estates offering opportunities for the ambitious gentleman. Humphrey was employed within important bureaucracies where the stewardships were significant sources of patronage. He was part of potentially influential networks of officials, which allowed him to extend his contacts and horizons. Presiding over the courts would also have given him a position of authority over the people covered by each jurisdiction. The leet court of Tarvin was by no means a small affair and covered nearby Kelsall and Hockenhull, while the leet of Tattenhall extended over the entire Tattenhall parish, encompassing tenants from the manors of Burwardsley, Cholmondeley and Huxley. Power could also stretch beyond the manor: the steward of Congleton was expected to administer the oath of office to the newly elected mayor of the town.[99] Humphrey's role in these administrations is glimpsed briefly in an extract copied from a view of frankpledge court roll concerning dower lands in Norton in 1502. Humphrey, who

---

[93] Rowney, 'The Staffordshire political community', p. 9.
[94] Figure derived from ministers' accounts in TNA: PRO, SC 6 HENVII/1559 and SC 6 HENVIII/368.
[95] Ibid. Touchet's lands at his death were worth approximately £1,200: Arthurson, 'Tuchet, James, seventh Baron Audley (c.1463–1497)'. Much of the confiscated lands were returned to the Touchet family in the following decade. For William Smith see Thornton, *Cheshire*, p. 182.
[96] *CPR, 1494–1509*, pp. 203, 234–42, 267–8.
[97] Ormerod, *Chester*, III, p. 228.
[98] *CPR, 1494–1509*, p. 234; 37th *DKR* App. II, p. 423.
[99] Ormerod, *Chester*, II, pp. 306–8, 717. Stephens and Fuidge, 'Tudor and Stuart Congleton', p. 65.

was named as the steward (*seniscallus*), oversaw the writing of the roll and the copy, illustrating his supervision of the clerk who drew up the documentation.[100]

On the other hand, there are reasons to be less impressed by these appointments. In all cases, the Cheshire manors were peripheral to the much larger main estates of these landlords. The stewardship of Congleton was one of the lesser positions in the entire duchy administration. The manor itself had suffered severe decline in the fifteenth century. Surviving accounts put yearly profits at a little over £30, with arrears and decayed rents steadily mounting from the mid-fifteenth century, while profits from the court dropped. By the early sixteenth century the duchy and manor were receding into the background as the market town grew in importance through its woollen and leather trades.[101] Likewise, the lands of the bishopric of Coventry and Lichfield in Cheshire were secondary to the main episcopal estates in Staffordshire and Warwickshire, and somewhat marginal to the bishop's concerns. A similar situation can be claimed for the Trussell estate at Warmingham and Audley's Tattenhall, especially in the years following the attainder.

This information says much regarding Humphrey's importance as a steward. After examining the officials on the estates of the Stafford family, Peter Fleming argued that the status of the officials correlated with the manors' individual importance to the family. Those officials employed on the important properties of the 'central circuit' – the south-west, East Anglia and the midlands – tended to be of a prominent social standing; those on the lesser and distant Kent estates were members of the lesser gentry.[102] The same interpretation can be offered in the case of Humphrey and the estates to which he was feed. The manors themselves were generally holdings of middling size, counting their profits only in terms of tens of pounds. Nor did working in a large administration necessarily imply much power. As steward of Congleton, Humphrey was subject to the control of the chief steward of the Halton fee. It is the latter who is recorded presiding over the view of frankpledge for the entire Halton fee, including Congleton, which might suggest that Humphrey only had authority over the court baron, or acted as the deputy steward.[103] This was certainly his position in Tattenhall because a minister's account of 1508 cites Humphrey as the recent *subseneschallus* – that is, deputy steward – of Tattenhall manor.[104]

---

[100] KUL, S. 401.
[101] Figures taken from duchy accounts in the TNA: PRO, DL 29/9/126, DL 29/10/130, DL 29/10/131. Blake, 'Medieval Congleton', pp. 30, 36, 39.
[102] Fleming, 'The character and private concerns of the gentry', p. 94.
[103] Deputy stewards were recorded for Congleton during the later fifteenth century. Somerville, *History of the duchy of Lancaster*, p. 511.
[104] TNA: PRO, SC 6 HENVIII/368. Deputy stewards regularly operated at Audley too: Boyd, 'Star Chamber proceedings', p. 55.

The four remaining manors on which Humphrey was employed belonged to Cheshire gentry with less substantial estates, but with a comparable pattern of appointment. For at least four years Humphrey was employed on the manor of Stockport, then under the lordship of the Warrens of Poynton, barons of Stockport. Humphrey's employer was Sir John Warren (d. 1518).[105] However, the family's main estate and residence was at Poynton. To give some indication of the relative worth of the two manors, the inquisition *post mortem* of Laurence Warren (1530) valued Stockport at £20 and Poynton at £53 6s 8d.[106] Stockport generally received less attention from the Warren lords, and by the time of Leland's *Itinerary*, the manor had fallen into decay.[107] Similarly, Humphrey's appointment by John Stanley, esquire (d. 1508), was for the manor of Etchells and not Stanley's main Cheshire holdings at the manors of Aldford and Alderley.[108] Only at the remaining two manors, Nether Knutsford and Over Knutsford, did Humphrey work on the lord's primary estates. This was because while the lords Thomas Hulse of Norbury and Sir Philip Legh of Booth were county gentry of some standing, they had few major land bases.[109]

Nevertheless, these smaller manors may have imposed on Humphrey greater responsibility and authority than did his place in the larger bureaucracies. The 1499 *quo warranto* proceedings in Cheshire indicate that the manors at Etchells, Stockport and those at Knutsford were licensed to hold views of frankpledge. At Knutsford a view was held every year and a manor court every three weeks before a steward. The lord of Stockport was entitled to a view held by the steward with a jury of twelve men. He was also granted *infangthief* and *outfangthief*, waif and stray, and tumbrell, meaning that the steward had the power to order pillory, cucking stool and hanging. The lords Warren, Legh and Hulse all had licences to hold fairs and markets at the towns of Stockport and Knutsford.[110] It was the steward of the manor who presided at the leet of Stockport town, to which all adult town residents were summoned, and he represented the lord at the portmote court (a borough court). It may have been for this reason that Humphrey included documents relating to the statute merchant in his commonplace book.[111]

There are two conclusions to emerge from this analysis. The first is that Humphrey was able to secure useful appointments, giving him important

---

[105] That Warren was also called 'of London, and of Westminster' suggests he spent little time on his estates: *CPR, 1494–1509*, p. 24.
[106] 39th *DKR*, p. 285.
[107] Smith (ed.) *The Itinerary of John Leland*, part IX, p. 24.
[108] In a 1492–3 deed concerning the succession of the three manors, their stated collective worth was 200 marks. JRUL, Tatton MS 445.
[109] Over Knutsford was also held of the Duchy of Lancaster. Ormerod, *Chester*, III, p. 464.
[110] TNA: PRO, CHES 34/3 (3, 4, 12, 14), CHES 34/4 (4,14,30), CHES 17/11, CHES 38/26/9.
[111] Bodl, MS Lat. Misc.c.66, fo. 7v. Driver, *Cheshire*, pp. 42–3.

positions of authority, but he did not have the calibre to win the top posts. The second is that these were no sinecures: he worked in his role as steward and was employed for his abilities. What, then, were the qualities Humphrey had to offer? Of considerable significance would be a sound knowledge of the law and, in particular, a familiarity with what the thirteenth-century manual, the *Fleta*, described as 'the laws and customs of his province'.[112] Manorial practice and custom were regional, and it was particularly so in Cheshire, which had its own palatine courts and franchises. Administrations therefore chose men familiar with the local custom, history and traditions of the manor and its environs.[113] Humphrey's stewardships lay near to his own landholdings in Newton (the Knutsford manors, Stockport, Etchells and Congleton), the Broxton hundred (leet of Tattenhall) and the Pownall inheritance (Warmingham); see Map 1. At the same time, his gentle status was significant, even though it was possible by the late fifteenth century for yeomen to become court keepers.[114] Lords chose someone with an influence already established in the area, men with significant local contacts who were capable of utilising them if needed.[115] Humphrey's appointment at Congleton, for instance, could have been influenced by his relatives, the Lowes (who were originally from the area), or William Rode, burgess and mayor of the town.[116] In other appointments, indirect contact and word of mouth are likely to have secured his positions, especially as neither the Fitzwarrens nor the earl of Kent were resident in or familiar with Cheshire. Humphrey was either in position and doing good work, or recommended by others as a local man capable of running the courts successfully. He continued as a steward at Warmingham when the lands passed into the wardship of the earl of Kent in 1500; and he remained at Tattenhall when the king granted the manor to William Smith. In their turn, these employers would prove valuable assistance to Humphrey. As will be shown in Chapter 4, both Philip Legh of Booths and John Stanley of Etchells supported Humphrey's right to the Pownall inheritance in a deed dating to 1508.[117]

Humphrey's suitability would have increased as the number of his fees grew. C.W. Brooks believed that the practice of stewards hired by several lords was a feature of a later age, replacing ties of personal loyalty with a more professional client relationship.[118] However, as many studies have shown, officials feed to a number of lords were a regular feature of medieval lordship. Sir Humphrey Stafford of Grafton took fees worth £71 per annum

---

[112] As quoted in Bennett, *Manor*, p. 158.
[113] Brooks, *Pettifoggers and vipers*, p. 178.
[114] Ives, 'Common lawyers', p. 148.
[115] Wright, *Derbyshire gentry*, p. 62; Kelly, 'The noble steward', pp. 133–48.
[116] Wright, *Derbyshire gentry*, pp. 87–8.
[117] TNA: PRO, CHES 38/26/8. See p. 102 below.
[118] Brooks, *Pettifoggers and vipers*, p. 198.

from eight different lords, including Humphrey, duke of Buckingham.[119] Humphrey was far from being the lawyer with the most fees in Cheshire. In 1515 the Inner Temple alumnus, Richard Sneyd, recorded fees from fifty-three individuals ranging from the earl of Derby to local Cheshire gentry.[120] Multiple employment, rather than being a problem for lords, was welcomed as a chance to find out what other landlords were doing. A servant with numerous commitments was a man clearly conversant with the local power structure.[121]

Fees

A characteristic complaint against lawyers concerned their greedy, grasping nature, whereby nothing was done without a fee. As noted above, examples of men who grew wealthy through the law, including Humphrey's step-grandfather, are not hard to find. The question is whether Humphrey himself drew wealth from his legal work. As a steward, his most important remuneration was the retaining fee, which was dependent upon several factors: the size and wealth of the estate, the number of officials employed, and the exact position held (whether as chief steward, a steward of the courts, or deputy steward).[122] An indication of the range of fees paid to estate officials in the fifteenth and sixteenth centuries has to be extracted from fragmentary sources such as ministers' accounts, account rolls, and the *Valor Ecclesiasticus* (1535), whose detailed accounts of monastic properties include the yearly payments received by each manorial official.[123] For example, officials on the large estates of the Lancashire monasteries were paid well. The fees of thirty-eight officials range from 13s 4d to £6 6s 8d, with around a half paid between £3 and £6 6s 8d; among the middle-range officials, £2 was the common fee.[124] The few accounts surviving for less wealthy estates reveal a more restricted range of fees, with a concentration at the lower end of the scale. Here, fees of 6s 8d and 13s 4d were more common.[125] Within an estate, the difference in fee between individual manors also correlated with size. On the Grey of Ruthin estates, for instance, the steward of the Leicester manor of Burbage

---

[119] McFarlane, *The nobility*, pp. 108–9.
[120] BL, Harley MS 2079 fo. 178r. I owe this reference to Dr Tim Thornton.
[121] Walker, *The Lancastrian affinity*, p. 103; Griffiths, 'Public and private bureaucracies', p. 128; Hicks, *English political culture*, p. 146; Ramsey, 'Retained legal counsel', pp. 104–6; Horrox, *Richard III*, pp. 18–19; Saul, *Knights and esquires*, p. 87.
[122] Denholm-Young, *Seignorial administration*, p. 71.
[123] *Valor Ecclesiasticus*. Professor Ives has a useful table of fees per year received by lawyers attached to large seignorial households: Ives, *The common lawyers*, p. 290.
[124] *Valor Ecclesiasticus*, 5, pp. 219–34.
[125] Ives, 'Common lawyers', p. 288 and *Valor Ecclesiasticus*, 5, pp. 212–13.

Table 1. Humphrey's stewardships: manors and fees.

MANOR	11/11 1498/9	24/6 1499	Lent 1500	11/11 1501	24/6 1501	11/11 1502	24/6 1502	11/11 1503
Audley etc.	–	–	10s	13s 4d	–	–	12s	–
Congleton	6s 8d	6s	6s 8d	–	–	–	–	–
Etchells	–	–	–	10s	10s	10s	10s	10s
Nether Knutsford	–	–	6s 8d	–	–	6s 8d	6s 8d	6s 8d
Over Knutsford	–	–	–	–	13s 4d	–	–	–
Stockport	6s 8d	6s	6s 8d	40s*	40s*	–	–	–
Tattenhall	6s 8d	6s 8d	6s 8d	6s 8d	6s 8d	–	–	6s 8d
Tarvin etc.	6s 8d	6s 8d	6s 8d	6s 8d	13s 4d	–	–	–
Warmingham	13s 4d	13s 4d	13s 4d	13s 4d	13s 4d	–	–	–

* Includes court expenses

received a yearly payment of 40s, whereas the steward of the smaller estate of Braxstead received only 13s 4d.[126]

The fee also related to the status of the official appointed.[127] A man had a definite idea of his worth and might be insulted if the fee were too low. The attorney, Robert Blackwell, took umbrage at Sir Robert Plumpton (d. 1507) for paying him a mere 6s 8d per year. Similarly, Sir John Fortescue refused the fee of 13s 4d in 1437–8 because he considered it too low, although he had accepted it the year before.[128] Nevertheless, some variations according to estate size and the number of officials employed were acceptable and the same man could receive a variety of payments. Richard Sneyd's fifty-three fees from his clients in Cheshire and Lancashire ranged from 6s 8d to £6 13s 4d, roughly corresponding to the status of his employer. His most common fees were 13s 4d (eighteen times) and 20s (eighteen times).[129] While it can never be known for certain why a particular official received a particular fee, there does seem to be a broad correlation between service, status and fee.

Table 1 lists what Humphrey expected to receive from each stewardship during 1498–1503. It can be seen that he was paid by the half-year, an arrangement used elsewhere in England, such as by the Suffolk gentleman John Hopton in paying Sir Roger Townshend.[130] Each column represents a single account of stewards' fees. Humphrey did not receive a fee from every

---

126 Jack (ed.) *The Grey of Ruthin valor*, pp. 64, 128. Similar comparisons can be made on the estates of Richard, duke of York: Rosenthal, 'The estates and finances of Richard, Duke of York', p. 167.
127 Rawcliffe and Flower, 'English noblemen and their advisers', p. 166.
128 Ives, *The common lawyers*, p. 289. Ramsey, 'Retained legal counsel', pp. 105–6.
129 BL, Harley MS 2709, fo. 178r.
130 Richmond, *John Hopton*, pp. 126–7.

manor every half-year, which may suggest that a court did not sit during each period, or else that Humphrey's services were not required.

Overall, Humphrey's single payments ranged from 6s to 13s 4d. The persistence of the 6s 8d figure for either the half-year or the calendar year suggests that this was Humphrey's common retaining fee per court session. This discussion of fee payments has shown that the sum was paid either to the lower-level officials on large estates or to officials on smaller holdings. The former would apply to Congleton; the latter to the manor of Stockport. Slightly higher fees of between 10s and 13s 4d were recorded for the remaining manors. Warmingham provided Humphrey with one of his highest fees, at 13s 4d per year in 1498–1500 and 26s 8d in 1501. This was perhaps the result of the combination of a large estate and an under-age lord in the ward of an absentee earl, both giving Humphrey greater responsibility.[131] From Audley Humphrey received payments of 10s and 13s 4d per year[132] and from Etchells the higher 20s per year. These fees were received by a wider variety of officials and it was a more common fee for the steward of the courts. It was still by no means substantial. The majority of fees which Humphrey commanded, therefore, were at the lower end of the scale. They did vary with the value of the manor, but the range remained appropriate to a small-time official. That Humphrey was not awarded greater fees can be seen by his total fee income. In an average year, it provided a useful but modest return. In 1500, for example, the total figure was 56s 8d, which some administrators could achieve from one lucrative office alone. John Matthews received 53s 4d per annum as bailiff of Boughton for the abbey of St Werburgh (Chester), while Thomas Foulshurst obtained the same sum in 1508–9 as steward of Nantwich.[133] Humphrey appears to have had little prospect of making his fortune through stewardships. Yet he was receiving a fairly regular income, a little and often.

It was not, however, the only remuneration that Humphrey received from his stewardships. Stewards were compensated for a low retaining fee with a number of additional payments, including those of court fees, document searches, the drawing up of documents, and monies from their clientele.[134] Legal cases were expensive and the potential to make money was considerable. Humphrey's own record makes this point when he noted the costs for pursuing the recovery of a writ of entry at the courts of Westminster: the original (2s 6d), the return (12d), three men learned in the law (5s), the crier (4d), the entry of the plea (6s), the copy of the process (2s), the *habere facias*

---

[131] Randolph Birkenhead received the same fee for the stewardship of Warmingham in 1503–4. JRUL, Latin MS 383.

[132] In 1492–3 the fee for the steward of the court was 13s 3d; Boyd, 'Star Chamber proceedings', pp. 256–7.

[133] *Valor Ecclesiasticus*, 5, pp. 205–6; TNA: PRO, SC 6 HENVIII/374.

[134] See the gains made at the honor of Clitheroe, Lancashire: Farrer (ed.), *The court rolls of the Honor of Clitheroe*, III, p. 481.

seisinam (a writ to give possession) 2*s* 6*d*, the return of the same (6*s* 8*d*), and the answer (2*s*) – a total of 28*s*.[135] Gains made from Humphrey's court-holding were varied. One example is the occasion when his fee for Stockport jumped from 6*s* 8*d* to 40*s* because of the 'perquisites' of the court.[136] A further glimpse is offered by an account dating to *c*.1500 which Humphrey headed 'avantages'.[137] The entries are brief and reasons are not always supplied for the sums. Humphrey received payment for essoins (the suitors excused attendance at court) at Tattenhall (21*d*); essoins and pleas at Congleton (13*d*); for the making of two copies at Congleton (7*d*); for entering pleas at Knutsford (2*d*); and for levies and entries at Stockport (3*d*). But he did not record why he received 12*d* from the courts of Warmingham, Wybunbury, Burton and Tarvin, and a further 2*s* 7*d* at the court of Congleton. Two entries mention monies in relation to John Stanley (amounting to 5*s*), presumably in relation to Stanley's manor of Etchells. The sums he received for keeping of 'my lords court at Chester', and 'at Chester a bill for the prince' suggest that Humphrey, as other stewards, was defending his lords' interests at the county court.[138] While it is impossible to calculate how much he gained from these payments, they appear to have been received quite regularly. Humphrey suggests this in a typically obscure note where he writes that his 'vauntages' on three occasions from Horton, Norton, Audeley and Beteley 'beside the fee' were worth 4*s* each time.[139] Finally, benefits came from rents. When Humphrey was steward at Tattenhall he farmed the 'tolbroke' mill on the manor for 15*s*. The farming of mills by stewards may have been common practice. Richard Sneyd, for example, was farmer of the mill pool at Audley in 1492 while acting as steward of the manor and counsellor to Lord Audley.[140] Humphrey's yearly revenue from the law, therefore, was drawn from several sources.

Administration

While Humphrey worked for individual landholders and businessmen of Cheshire, the question remains as to whether he put his skills to use for the county as a whole. The position of manorial steward would have helped to

---

[135] Bodl, MS Lat. Misc.c.66, fo. 27av. For a brief discussion of a writ of entry see Holdsworth, *A history of English law*, vol. 3, p. 12.
[136] Bodl, MS Lat. Misc.c.66, fos 37v, 38v.
[137] Ibid., fo. 29v.
[138] Musson, *Public order*, p. 158; Brand, 'Stewards, bailiffs', pp. 147–8. The bill for the prince may refer to the *quo warranto* proceedings held before Prince Arthur in 1499, see p. 65 below. Humphrey valued the Chester Exchequer for the information it could yield. On one visit, *c*.1511, he quizzed the deputy escheator, Richard Leftwich, over the inheritance of lands in Hanley, Broxton hundred: Bodl, MS Lat. Misc.c.66, fo. 63r.
[139] Bodl, MS Lat. Misc.c.66, fo. 32v: 'the vauntages of horton norton audeley & beteley beside the fee was at the first tyme iiijs the second tyme iiijs the third tyme iiijs'.
[140] TNA: PRO, SC 6 1559, SC 6 HENVIII/368. Wedgewood, 'The "Lists and indexes" of records', p. 257.

increase his stature and make it more likely that other posts and responsibilities would come his way. It was often an important stepping-stone to a career in county administration.[141] However, Humphrey does not appear to have played any substantial, or even a minor, regular role in county administration. This is partly explained by his securing, in 1497, an exemption from working as a juror on assizes and inquisitions, as a tax collector, assessor of subsidies, constable, coroner, bailiff and mayor. It was a repetition of an exemption his father had received three years earlier, and he may have inherited it on his father's death that year. The grant was confirmed two years later in *quo warranto* proceedings, which were held in Chester.[142] All those who claimed any liberties by charter of the earl of Chester were to appear before the justices in eyre, Thomas Kebell and John Mordaunt, to declare and defend their privileges. It was an occasion for expenses and persuasion, as a short entry in Humphrey's book indicates. His payments at Chester were: 12*d* 'at the counsel', 2*s* 6*d* for the writ of *quo warranto* placed at the Cheshire assize, 20*d* for making the claim 'to my lerned man gratia', 12*d* for making the plea to 'philosophers of the same', 4*d* for the return of the *quo warranto* to the sheriff, and small payments to the clerk of the justices in eyre, the crier and the marshalls. For a little gentle persuasion, there was also 'wyne to þe jugez Mr. Keble and Madaunt malmeslee', which appears to have had the desired effect.[143]

Humphrey had therefore opted out of some of the county's routine and mundane administrative and judicial duties. He was not alone, for several members of the gentry and some among the yeomanry of Macclesfield hundred had obtained exemptions from jury service. They allowed people to avoid unwelcome, costly journeys across the county to Chester, especially when old age approached; jury service in general was undertaken by only a minority of those eligible.[144] Humphrey had one of the most wide-reaching dispensations. John Pownall of Pownall, for example, was only exempted from jury duty and not from holding the positions of coroner or constable. Perhaps the Newtons had secured privileges beyond the usual permit for

---

[141] Astill, 'Social advancement', p. 21; Musson, *Public order*, pp. 155–6.
[142] The exemption is transcribed in the plea roll TNA: PRO, CHES 29/198 m. 37. For the *quo warranto* see TNA: PRO, CHES 17/10, CHES 34/3 (6), CHES 38/26/9 (32). Details of the *quo warranto* proceedings can be found in Stewart-Brown, 'The Cheshire Writs of Quo Warranto in 1499', p. 143. Humphrey's heir, William, later claimed the same privileges. On a slip of paper, later inserted into the commonplace book, William emended the exemption awarded Richard Newton, crossing out Richard's name and adding his own: Bodl, MS Lat. Misc.c.66, fo. 27b.
[143] Bodl, MS Lat. Misc.c.66, fo. 30v.
[144] Clayton, *The administration of the county palatine*, p. 238. The age limit was seventy: for example, in the case of Hugh Calveley, TNA: PRO, CHES 29/194 m. 8. It should be noted that Macclesfield hundred had some judicial immunity from the county court at Chester. Instead the hundred was visited annually by the justices/commissioners to hold the 'eyre of Macclesfield': Harris (ed.) *VCH Cheshire*, vol. 2, p. 31.

Macclesfield men in order to escape a trip west. At the same time the heads of knightly families like the Fittons of Gawsworth did not have the list of exemptions that appear on Humphrey's certificate. This is understandable, since men of their standing would not be expected to undertake the duties of coroner, constable or tax collector in the first place. For Humphrey (and the Newtons) to have received those specific exemptions indicates that such work was expected of him (and them). As studies of the English gentry have shown, that type of work was invariably the domain of the lesser gentry.[145] The reluctance of Cheshire gentry to attend their county and local hundred courts is clear to see. In 1523–4, the listed judicators for the Macclesfield hundred court included the most prominent gentry of the hundred: Sir George Legh of Adlington, Sir George Calveley, Sir John Savage, William Davenport of Bramhall, Randulph Ardern and William Swettenham. Yet only William Swettenham turned up in 'propria persona sua'; everyone else was deputised by the lesser landholders of the area.[146] Humphrey and his fellow Cheshire gentry were not unusual in avoiding local government. Across England, the gentry were reluctant to attend the county courts, unless they had private business there, and it has been suggested that only about a third of the English gentry ever became involved in county or regional institutions.[147]

Humphrey himself shows little sense of administrative loyalty to the county, as his absence from the palatinate's records illustrates.[148] Nor, for most of his life, did Humphrey appear on any county commissions. It would be difficult, from this perspective, to say that the county formed a framework for his working life. Even John Hopton of Suffolk, who, according to Colin Richmond, was 'never at any time in his life a very active man in the wider world of county affairs', appears more energetic, being sheriff twice in 1436–7, 1444–5 and on commissions of the peace in 1444–1458 and 1461–68.[149] Again, perhaps Humphrey was good at avoiding such duties, yet he was probably not of sufficient standing to be placed on commissions such as those of array, gaol delivery and collections of the mise. He is only known to have appeared on one commission. In 1531, at the age of sixty-

---

[145] For John Pownall and Thomas Fitton TNA: PRO, CHES 29/194, m. 5. For a discussion of the division of administrative tasks among the Cheshire gentry see Clayton, *The administration of the county palatine*, ch. 5. The positions of coroner, bailiff and tax collector were taken by the lesser gentry in most areas: Saul, *Knights and esquires*, p. 259; Acheson, *A gentry community*, p. 113; Given-Wilson, *The English nobility*, p. 73.
[146] TNA: PRO, SC2/258/7, m. 1r.
[147] Moreton, *The Townshends*, pp. 3, 203–5; Kirby, 'A northern knightly family', p. 90; Carpenter, 'Gentry and community', pp. 346–7; Ormrod, *Political life*, pp. 49–50.
[148] The palatinate records reveal only one reference to a Humphrey Newton in an administrative role. He was one of the men listed on an indictment roll as a potential member of a grand jury for 1501–2: TNA: PRO, CHES 25/18, m. 35. He was not called to jury. Unfortunately, there is no evidence to indicate whether this was Humphrey Newton of Pownall.
[149] Richmond, *John Hopton*, p. 117.

four, Humphrey sat on a commission of inquisition *post mortem* alongside Sir William Stanley, William Venables, John Leicester and the ubiquitous Richard Sneyd to make inquisitions on the lands of several local Cheshire men.[150] Given the standing of his fellow commissioners, it suggests that in later life Humphrey had gained some recognition at county level for his legal and local authority. But he could never be described as one of the workhorses of county administration.

Conclusion

Humphrey was never styled a 'man of law', nor would he have labelled himself as such. Becoming a lawyer was not his route to gentility, or his career, and he never achieved greatness through it. Payments gained cannot compare to the success stories of Ives's *Common lawyers* or even Humphrey's own relations, the Lowes of Denby. He was primarily a gentleman-bureaucrat who supported his family and his business plans with a modest but regular income from his role in the administration of justice in Cheshire and its environs. Was this acquaintance with the law significant enough to influence the way society viewed Humphrey and how he lived his life?

Humphrey was versatile, and the work demanded of him wide-ranging: clerk, interpreter of legal documents, counsellor and arbitrator. He was not as indispensable to the Cheshire gentry as Richard Sneyd appears to have been, with his fifty-three fees – evidently a man of the moment. Yet a wide range of people respected his skills and connections sufficiently to retain his services. Humphrey engaged in a mixed practice, being in the employ of powerful gentry and at least one ecclesiastical lord, as well as gaining *ad hoc* work from neighbouring families, friends and acquaintances. Clients came overwhelmingly from Cheshire, following the links of social and business networks. Humphrey worked in all his roles. He was never employed solely or mainly for his status; indeed, he was more likely to be the person employed to do the work of a sinecure. It was clearly no bad thing to be employed because of competence, and evidently Humphrey was someone who commanded respect. But he appears to have been someone whom other people would describe as useful and dependable rather than powerful. Whether that mattered to him is unknowable.

The provincial nature of Humphrey's working life is unquestionable and unsurprising.[151] Nevertheless, legal work served to broaden the horizons of the gentry, even if individuals subsequently chose to return to their home shire. Work as a steward, feoffee, witness and arbitrator took Humphrey to Staffordshire, Lancashire and Derbyshire, with at least one case prompting a

---

[150] *LP*, v, 166 (51), 364 (17).
[151] Moreton, *The Townshends*, p. 22.

ride to London, a route already well trodden by Cheshire businessmen and lawyers.[152] The notable increase in the use of the courts of Chancery and Star Chamber in early Tudor England served to increase the traffic. Legal work therefore took Humphrey out of the parochial confines of Cheshire and gave him a more urbane and broader cultural experience.

The work and travel helped to shape Humphrey's outlook on life, endowing him with a literate, yet legalistic, view of the world. Chapter 2 has already revealed the extent of the legal mind at work in document collecting and genealogical searches. There is something of the William Worcester (d.c. 1482) about him, a man whose experience with the law sharpened, in the words of P.S. Lewis, 'his aptitude for collecting facts and gave him a knowledge and ability which made him more useful to his employer'.[153] Subsequent chapters will also show the importance that Humphrey placed on written prayers and charms, and how his construction of love poetry seems to owe more to a literate dexterity than to a talent for verse. Knowledge of his work as a scrivener and of his concern with letterform and presentation helps to explain the semi-professional styles featuring on pages of his manuscript. His need to know Latin and some law French gave him access to a broader range of literature than was common among the late medieval laity. It is well-known that several common lawyers were patrons, writers and owners of books, and they have been credited with making 'a sizeable contribution to the intellectual and cultural life of the day'.[154] Humphrey was hardly in the league of men like Sir John Fortescue and Sir Thomas More, but he may have been attracted to literature by similar means.

On a more practical level, the law provided Humphrey with some of the monetary resources and networks to assist in the development of land and family ties. In the same way that Edmund Paston was advised in an oft-quoted letter 'to lerne the lawe', Humphrey's legal skills were beneficial in accumulating and defending his land holdings.[155] The following chapter considers some of Humphrey's own legal cases against neighbours and landlords. Did his legal skills make a significant difference in his own landed pursuits and disputes?

---

[152] Griffiths, 'Public and private bureaucracies', p. 114.
[153] Lewis, 'Sir John Fastolf's lawsuit', p. 2.
[154] Ives, 'The common lawyers', pp. 181–207. Moreton, 'The "library"', pp. 338–46; Jurkowski, 'Lawyers and Lollardy', p. 169.
[155] Davis (ed.) *Paston letters and papers*, I, no. 14. See also Lewis, 'Sir John Fastolf's lawsuit', pp. 1–2, 9–11, for the need for legal knowledge in land disputes and the problems arising through ignorance.

4

Land and Lordship

It is difficult to overestimate the importance of land to England's elite. It was the basis of wealth and the tangible symbol of social and political dominance. Late medieval nobles held vast estates that stretched over several counties, yet it was the gentry, collectively, who held the larger percentage of property. In the North Riding of Yorkshire, the gentry owned forty-five per cent of the manors, while in Humphrey's county of Cheshire the proportion was especially high: over three-quarters of manors were in gentry hands, and the smaller estate far outnumbered the larger.[1]

It was land that formed the basis of Humphrey's gentility, provided his major source of income and played a pivotal role in his upward social mobility. Like many gentlemen, his total landholdings were confined to the county and were geographically concentrated. While he held a few scattered lands and rents in south and west Cheshire, the main *foci* were the estates of Newton and Pownall in Macclesfield hundred, lying in the north-east of the county (Map 2). Newton was the ancestral home and the early focus of Humphrey's energies to improve his family's income and status. It remained his main project for eight years until it was superseded by the larger estate of Pownall, which was acquired through marriage and quickly made the permanent family residence. In common with other gentry landlords, Humphrey invested considerable time and effort in the estates both personally and *via* a team of paid officials. The competitive nature of the gentry meant that it was an accepted part of a gentleman's life to have concerns over inheritance, boundary disputes and grazing rights. Even if Humphrey had chosen to lead a quiet life, it is unlikely that he could have avoided quarrels over land.[2] His area of Cheshire was not struggling with the demands of newcomers, but fomenting with old rivalries of families that had lived next to each other for over a century.[3] In July 1494, for instance, a long-term dispute between

---

[1] Pollard, *North-Eastern England*, pp. 62, 81; Payling, *Political society*, p. 3; Carpenter, *Locality and polity*, p. 36; Cornwall, 'The early Tudor gentry', p. 461; Bennett, *Community*, pp. 68–9.
[2] 'Land was worth fighting over': Saul, *Scenes*, p. 198.
[3] Cheshire has a reputation for the longevity of its gentry families. Thornton's research has shown that during Humphrey's lifetime, thirty-nine of the forty-three major families of Cheshire had origins in the county dating back before the fifteenth century: Thornton, *Cheshire*, p. 32.

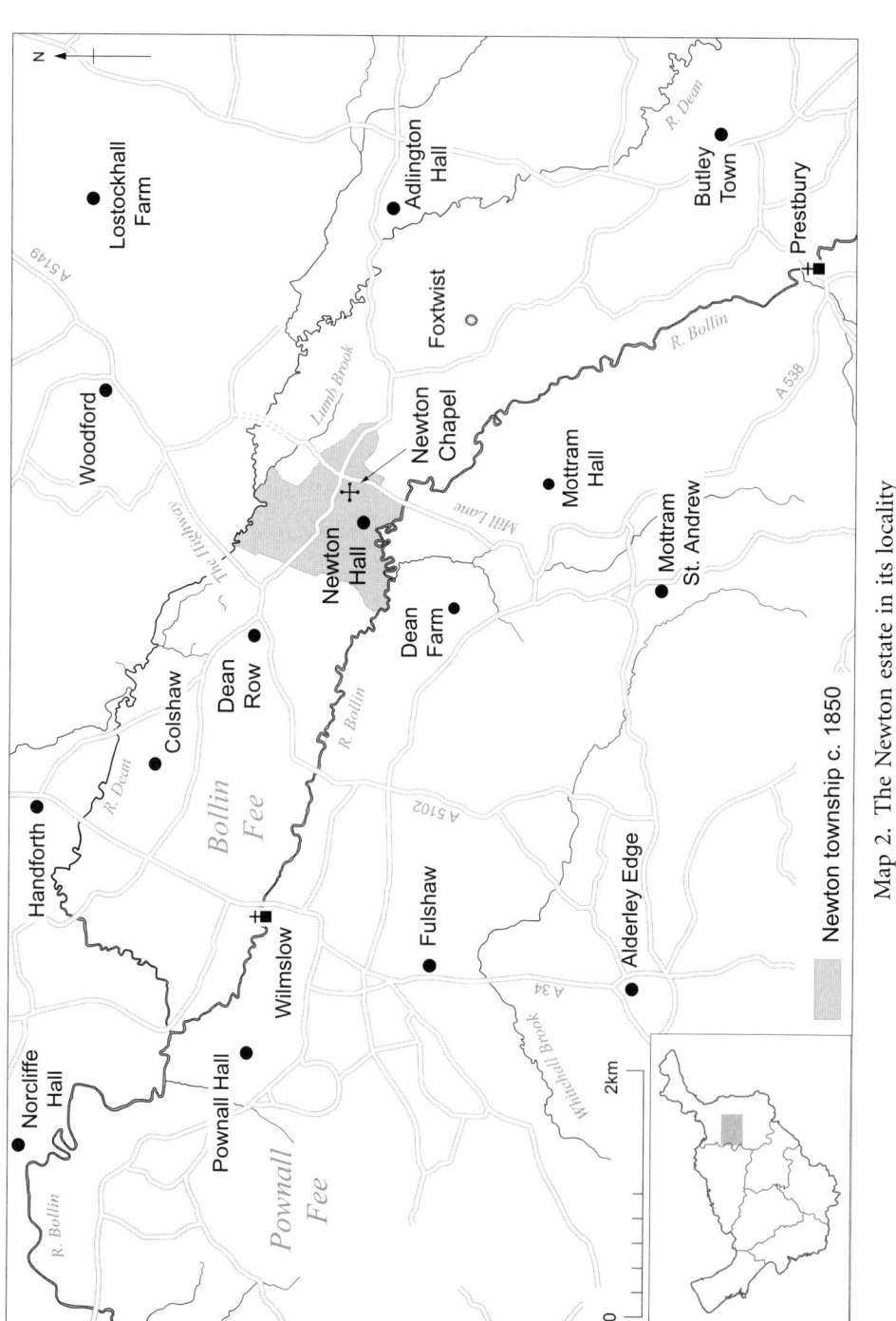

Map 2. The Newton estate in its locality
Map by Anne Leaver

Humphrey's neighbours, the Leghs of Adlington and Davenports of Woodford, erupted in a two-day riot on the streets of Wilmslow involving over 800 locals.[4] Both families would challenge Humphrey over the boundaries of Newton. This chapter discusses how he attempted to prove himself their match and raise his family's status. It discusses the improvements he made at Newton and looks at the acquisition and securing of Pownall. Humphrey adopted a range of strategies to further these aims and in so doing reveals himself a man of ambition and determination.

The inheritance

When his parents died within fifteen months of each other in 1497–98, Humphrey inherited an estate which had been with the Newton family for nearly 200 years. The inheritance centred on Newton, a settlement on the northern banks of the river Bollin. Members of the Newton family had held land there from the twelfth century, but it was in the first years of the fourteenth century that they had secured the chief messuage of Newton and made Newton Hall their sole residence. By Humphrey's day, the settlement of Newton was virtually coterminous with the estate. It would not have taken Humphrey long to walk around its bounds. At less than 500 acres, it was small and compact.[5] It is difficult to gain an accurate assessment of its extent, but Humphrey's inquisition *post mortem* of 1536 presents a figure of 252 Cheshire acres comprising 100 acres of land, twenty acres of meadow, forty acres of pasture, twenty-six acres of wood and sixty-six acres of water, moor, turbary and waste.[6] The land was valued at £6 7s 8d, an underestimation characteristic of inquisitions *post mortem*; the figure probably derived from an assessment made in the 1450s.[7] A more accurate view is gained from a rental drawn up in 1498, which valued Newton at around £11. It was therefore worth over the £10 minimum that governing and heraldic officials considered sufficient to support a gentleman.[8]

---

4   TNA: PRO, CHES 24/65; CHES 25/16, rots. 9–10; Thornton, *Cheshire*, pp. 170–1.
5   Compare Dyer, 'A small landowner', pp. 1–14; Wright, *Derbyshire gentry*, pp. 12–13; Britnell, 'Minor landlords', pp. 3–22.
6   TNA: PRO, CHES 3/67/4. A Cheshire acre was much larger than the standard acre, generally calculated to be 10,240 square yards, or 2.1 times the statute acre: Sylvester, 'The open fields', pp. 27–8. Using this multiple would mean Newton was 529 acres. This poses a problem because the nineteenth-century tithe map and apportionment estimates Newton at 386 statute acres: CRO, EDT 293/1 (see Map 2). Comparing the boundaries claimed in Humphrey's IPM to the tithe map does not indicate much land loss in the intervening 400 years. It may be that Humphrey's IPM contained land the Newtons believed was theirs (below, pp. 89–90), although this does not explain entirely the difference in estate size.
7   A rental dating to Laurence Lowe's management of the estate, *c*.1450–60, has just this total of £6 7s 8d: Bodl, MS Lat. Misc.c.66, fo. 24v. See Saul, *Knights and esquires*, pp. 206–7 for the problems of IPMs.
8   Bodl, MS Lat. Misc.c.66, fo. 24r. Humphrey totals this list as £11 2s 2d, although my

In its economy and management, Newton conforms very closely to the characteristics of other small estates in England.[9] Most of the land was held in demesne and directly managed by the Newtons to provide for the household; only a small percentage of its value derived from rents. Cheshire, in general, was an area where the typical manor comprised a small home farm with a few rent-paying tenant holdings.[10] In 1498 Newton assize rents amounted simply to a single messuage, a group of lands held by two local brothers, and a mill rent. There is no doubt that Humphrey, unlike larger landholders such as the Suffolk gentleman John Hopton, knew exactly who owed him rent.[11] Humphrey would alter and add to his tenancies in subsequent years (as discussed below), but their contribution remained modest: £3 12s 5d in 1498–9, falling to £2 9s per annum in 1502–04.[12] Labour services and dues in Newton, as in other freehold lands of early Tudor England, were negligible.[13] They involved harvesting, the odd day labouring at the mill, and one or two hens, but they were often commuted to cash payments. A greater potential for rent came from a group of holdings in the Broxton hundred of western Cheshire, which had been acquired through the marriage of Humphrey's grandfather, Oliver Newton, to Anne Milton in 1428–9.[14] They had never constituted a coherent estate; messuages, land and rents were scattered across south-western Cheshire. Fragmentation, together with their distance from Newton, meant that they were always rented or leased and seen purely in terms of a steady cash income: Humphrey's rentals indicate a potential £6 18s per annum in 1498, rising to £8 13s 4d in 1504.[15] In drawing up his accounts, Humphrey added the Newton and Broxton rents together: in 1499, for example, the figure totalled £9 11s 7d. Humphrey's need for cash and a desire to consolidate his estates meant, however, that the majority of the Broxton rents were eventually mortgaged, sold or used for dower. The desire, like that of the gentry of Derbyshire and Warwickshire, was for a more manageable unit.[16]

---

reckoning is £10 16s 4d. For the correlation between £10 and a gentleman: Keen, *Origins*, p. 109; Given-Wilson, *The English nobility*, p. 69. Payling's study of the income tax returns of 1436 calculates an income range for a gentleman of £10–£19: Payling, *Political society*, pp. 2–3.

[9] For the criteria of the small estate see: Kosminsky, *Studies in the Agrarian History of England*; Britnell, 'Production for the market', pp. 380–8 and 'Minor landlords', pp. 3–22; Dyer, 'A small landowner', pp. 1–14. This discussion of Newton is based on Humphrey's accounts, for which see pp. 76–8 below. For problems in analysing the small estate see Youngs, 'Estate management'.

[10] Bennett, *Community*, ch. 5.

[11] Richmond, *John Hopton*, p. 165: 'we can be sure that John was not aware of all those who owed him rent'.

[12] Bodl, MS Lat. Misc.c. 66, fos 29r, 32r, 35, 37v, 38v, 41ar, 42v, 43r and 47r.

[13] Acheson, *A gentry community*, p. 55. Richmond, *John Hopton*, p. 167.

[14] See above p. 17.

[15] Bodl, MS Lat. Misc.c.66, fos 28r, 32r, 35–v, 37v, 38v, 41ar, 42v, 43r and 47r.

[16] For Broxton transactions see JRUL, Tatton 130, 131, 408; Bodl, MS Lat. Misc.c.66,

The estate shared the mixed economy of Cheshire, with a combination of arable lands and animal husbandry.[17] The proportion of land that could be cultivated at Newton was limited, but not unusual for an estate of its size.[18] Whereas fifty-two workers supplemented the servants harvesting the 300 acres at Porter's Hall in Stebbing, Essex, only eighteen to twenty-two people were needed to harvest the crops at Newton.[19] In this part of Cheshire, Humphrey would have struggled to achieve very good harvests because the damp, cool climate and the poor-quality soils limited crop growth.[20] This battle with the landscape – which was also evident in nearby Pownall – meant that oats rather than wheat was the dominant crop, and the barley produced was an inferior kind known as 'beire'; it also resulted in the poor-quality 'smale' or small ale being brewed.[21] Rye, wheat and a small quantity of peas were also grown. The neighbouring farm of Dean, which the Newtons had leased for several decades, provided an additional rye crop.[22] But it is evident that the Newton lands were unable to yield sufficient produce to meet the family's needs. Purchases were made from a range of neighbouring estates. In 1500, Humphrey bought over forty bushels of oats, barley and rye from sources including his own tenants, Prestbury parsonage, and the gentry estates of the Davenports of Bramhall (near Stockport) and the Leghs of Adlington.[23] Purchases of wheat were not recorded; it was perhaps too scarce to sell.

During the fifteenth century, following an extended period of falling population and low grain prices, England's landowners increasingly turned their attention to livestock. Pastoral farming was attractive because of its low labour costs and easy maintenance, and rising standards of living had stimulated demand for animal products.[24] In Cheshire this meant cattle farming, and great cattle studs were located in Macclesfield forest. Testa-

---

fo. 60v, and pp. 16–17 above. For comparison: Wright, *Derbyshire gentry*, pp. 26–8; Carpenter, *Locality and polity*, pp. 184–6.

[17] Owen, 'Wales and the Marches', p. 239; Driver, *Cheshire*, p. 92; Compare with Dyer, *Warwickshire farming*, pp. 18–21.

[18] Dyer, 'Small landowner', p. 6; Watkins, 'Landowners', p. 23. It is difficult to calculate the exact acreage of ground sown with cereals. One indication is Humphrey's comment in 1499 that he had sown 31 bushels of seed. Mates has calculated that on average four bushels were sown per acre. If that were the case at Newton it would have meant an area of only 7.75 acres were sown: Mate, 'Medieval agrarian practices', pp. 25–7.

[19] Bodl, MS Lat. Misc.c.66, fos 31av, 34cv, 38r, 43r, 45v, and 48v; Poos, *A rural society*, p. 214.

[20] Sylvester, *The rural landscape*, p. 259; Bennett, *Community*, p. 8; Driver, *Cheshire*, p. 92; Tonkinson, *Macclesfield*, p. 1.

[21] Bodl, MS Lat. Misc.c.66, fo. 46v. For the prominence of oats in Cheshire see Morgan, *War and society*, pp. 82–3. Pownall's dependence on oats is seen in a sixteenth-century inventory where the oat crop was valued at £3 6s 8d, the rye at 50s and the barley at 34s 4d; there was no mention of wheat: BL, Add Roll 37328.

[22] See pp. 91–2 below.

[23] Bodl, MS Lat. Misc.c.66, fo. 36r.

[24] For two recent summations of this development see Dyer, *An age of transition?*, pp. 66, 108; Britnell, *Britain and Ireland*, ch. 20.

mentary evidence shows the dominance of cattle farming among Cheshire gentry families: in 1477 John Davenport of Bramhall boasted a herd of 122.[25] While the total number of Humphrey's herd is unknown, his sales to local fairs and butchers indicate it was a highly lucrative venture. One sale of a bull, two cows and four hides alone brought him more than he obtained from his Newton rents in 1504 (56s). The relative value of cattle and cereals is seen in Humphrey's acceptance of grain as payment for his cattle. The price of one bull, for example, was eight bushels of barley, and he sold one hide for a bushel of rye.[26]

Elsewhere in England, landlords were reaping the benefits of sheep farming, a consequence of the dynamic growth of the woollen industry. Some gentry farmers came to measure their flocks in thousands. In Norfolk, the Townshend family expanded its flock from 7,000 in 1475 to 12,000 by 1490.[27] Most of Cheshire's landscape never offered the opportunity for such large-scale enterprises, but in the upland regions of Macclesfield the prospects for profit were slightly better. The commission of enquiry sent by Cardinal Wolsey in the early sixteenth century found around half of Macclesfield forest occupied by settlers and sheepfolds, with the hill farms mainly sheep runs.[28] Gentry living in the region possessed medium-sized flocks; William Davenport of Bramhall (d. 1541) kept a flock of over 600 sheep on the Peak foothills.[29] Evidence regarding less wealthy sheep owners comes from the Macclesfield hundred court rolls, which list those who had illegally grazed their sheep on surrounding hills. In 1498, for example, over two dozen trespassers were recorded in the areas of Pott Shrigley, Bollington and Sutton. All had more than ten sheep, with a few grazing a flock of forty.[30] Living on the edges of the forest, Humphrey took advantage of these favourable conditions and grazed sheep on surrounding moor and moss, although the information available suggests that his flock was closer in number to those of the small trespassers than the larger landholders. It comprised around fifty ewes, two dozen lambs, and between one and four rams each year. A large percentage was sold annually to local butchers and fairs, and the return was much lower than that on cattle. In 1501 Humphrey sold fourteen old ewes and some male 'swine' for 10s 6d, virtually the same price as one bull. Sheep were, however, useful currency in business transactions; on one occasion Humphrey gave twenty sheep to his brother-in-law to cover a 20s debt.[31] They were a limited, but not negligible, commodity.

---

[25] Hewitt, *Cheshire under the three Edwards*, p. 35; Booth, *The financial administration*, p. 86; Owen, 'Wales and the Marches', p. 239; CRO, DDA/1533/31.
[26] Bodl, MS Lat. Misc.c.66, fos 34cr, 42r.
[27] Moreton, *The Townshends*, ch. 5; Britnell, 'The Pastons', p. 134; Carpenter, *Locality and polity*, pp. 182–9.
[28] Davies, *A history of Macclesfield*, pp. 40–1.
[29] Driver, *Cheshire*, p. 94. Piccope (ed.) *Lancashire and Cheshire Wills*, I, pp. 79–81.
[30] TNA: PRO, SC 2/316/3.
[31] Bodl, MS Lat. Misc.c.66, fos 25v, 29v, 30r, 34cv, 36v, 38r–v and 42v.

These were not the only products in the mixed economy of Humphrey's estate. His accounts reveal that Newton would have reverberated with the sounds of pigs, hens, horses and geese; it produced large quantities of turf; grew hemp and flax; contained a rabbit warren; manufactured cheese and ale; benefited from an orchard; and was the home to swans, which Humphrey marked on one foot with a small hole.[32] The overall impression is that the estate's produce, like that of John Brome's at Baddesley Clinton (Warwickshire), was mainly for direct consumption rather than commercial gain.[33] Nevertheless, as animal sales have shown, the estate did engage in trade, a necessity to raise cash to finance other ventures. Timber sales, for instance, provided a regular income, particularly the selling of ash and birch trees. The majority of Humphrey's transactions, as was the case with those of other landowners, were local.[34] He traded with neighbouring gentry, small yeomen farmers, his tenants and a number of local businessmen. A neat illustration of the informal markets that could be established around gentry estates is seen in Humphrey's account with his tenant Laurence Bennett, probably a butcher. Humphrey sold Bennett cattle, hides and sheep, and in return bought veal, beef, lamb and mutton. It is also one of several cases where 'sales' amounted to mutual exchanges of goods; cash value was only mentioned to ensure equal payment. Newton appears to have experienced the liquidity problems witnessed for other gentry landlords, such as the Plumptons and Stonors, where 'counters' (such as the transaction with Bennett) and complex systems of credit and debt were necessary to ensure the running of the estate.[35]

Country fairs and markets were important to the economy of the estate. Outside the port of Chester, Cheshire had few flourishing commercial centres and most of its towns were small, but five of its thirteen towns lay in eastern Cheshire: Stockport, Macclesfield, Knutsford, Congleton and Altrincham. All lay within a twelve-mile radius of Newton and feature at least once in Humphrey's accounts as a place where he or his servants travelled on business. Leather was purchased at Stockport fair, a horse was fetched from Congleton, and Knutsford was the location of a well-used dyer.[36] Larger towns outside Cheshire are rarely mentioned, but note should be made of the occasions when servants travelled to Doncaster and Manchester (although the reasons are unknown) and, more notably, the market of Chapel-en-le-Frith, Derbyshire, where Humphrey sold sheep, bullocks and oxen.[37]

There is little unusual here: Newton was an estate that drew on various

---

[32] Ibid., fos 24r, 26ar, 27ar, 28r, 29v, 30v and 38v.
[33] Dyer, 'Small landowner', p. 11; Acheson, *A gentry community*, p. 59.
[34] Farmer, 'Marketing the produce', p. 329
[35] Youngs, 'Estate management', pp. 131, 139–40; Dyer, 'The consumer and the market', p. 322; Kirby, 'A fifteenth-century family', pp. 107–8; Carpenter, *Kingsford's Stonor letters and papers*, p. 20; id., 'The Stonor circle'.
[36] Bodl, MS Lat. Misc.c.66, fos 25r, 33v, 39av, 41ar, 43r and 45v.
[37] Ibid., fos 25v, 34cr. Chapel-en-le-Frith lies only ten miles from Newton (Map 1).

sources of income to survive and was firmly embedded in the local economy. The family were proud of its produce. The fourteenth-century poem of Richard Newton proclaimed how

> Hee hadd oxen and kye and corne for the maistrie
> Fatt boars in theyr stye while that they might stand
> Good steedes in his stall well I astande.[38]

However, this was an estate without major franchises. Land alone did not bestow gentility; what mattered was land with rights of lordship. At Newton, there was no parkland and, more significantly, there was no manor court. Humphrey and his tenants were answerable to the court attached to the neighbouring manor and township of Butley. This circumscribed the quality of lordship Humphrey could exercise and would prove a particular point of contention (see below). To some extent the Newton estate would have hardly distinguished Humphrey from the greater yeomen of Cheshire.

Running the estate

The small, compact nature of Newton, together with Humphrey's residence there until at least 1506, meant that no extensive estate apparatus was required. There is no mention of a reeve, bailiff or steward or any other officials commonly found on the large estates of the nobility. Rather, it was Humphrey who oversaw and managed the land, arranged and supervised building projects and dealt directly with local traders. This was not uncommon; research into gentry estate management has regularly stressed the degree of personal decision-making and the lightness of bureaucracy. Yet it is worth emphasising the degree of his involvement. A busy sergeant-at-law like Thomas Kebell spent long stretches away from his Leicestershire estates, whereas Humphrey had fewer reasons to absent himself. He thus knew not only which fields were being sown and with what crops, but who was reaping them, for how long and from whom they had collected their wages.[39]

The intimate knowledge Humphrey acquired of his estate is clearly evident in a series of accounts he compiled in the period *c*.1498–*c*.1506. Originally planned as a distinct booklet, they now form twenty-five folios of his commonplace book.[40] They provide rich information on the Newton and Broxton possessions in the period between Humphrey's inheritance of Newton (1498) and the acquisition of Pownall (1506), when he was most

---

[38] For a full transcription of the poem see p. 196 below.
[39] Britnell, 'Minor landlords', pp. 7–8; Saul, *Knights and esquires*, p. 203; Saul, *Scenes*, pp. 98, 163; Acheson, *A gentry community*, p. 58; Dyer, *An age of transition?*, pp. 106–7; Ives, *The common lawyers*, p. 345; Stone, *Decision-making*, pp. 12–3, 226.
[40] Bodl, MS Lat. Misc.c.66, fos 24–48. Further discussion is provided in Youngs, 'Estate management', pp. 126–7.

fully focused on the Newton estate. They are all written from his perspective, punctuated with sentences such as 'I began to sher the wenysday aftr thassumpcion of our lady in þe Brighouse anno xv'; and 'I hav bozt ij bale of flax at Hugh Dale pric iijs viijd to be paid within xiiij days'.[41] Such personal writings are exceptionally scarce and make for an absorbing, yet at times perplexing, read. These are not the neat formulaic documents of noble or ecclesiastical estates. Instead they reflect the increasingly informal accounting produced in the fifteenth and sixteenth centuries, which can also be seen elsewhere in the account books of Roger Townshend I (d. 1493).[42] They are not daily reckonings, nor yearly totals of profit and loss, and will frustrate any attempt to provide an overall assessment of estate finances. They are best described as a series of annual summaries of key incomings and outgoings, and residual debts, over a six-year period (see Plate 2).

In drawing up these accounts, Humphrey juxtaposed a great mix of items relating to both consumption and production, to income and expenditure: there are rentals, servants' accounts, harvest accounts, tithe payments, Lenten purchases, building works and the sales and purchases of cloth, animals and food.[43] A variety of expenses are often brought together in a single line. In one entry Humphrey recorded a 16*d* payment for 'alez & a hat & a play': were they united by a single event, or just the day on which the debt was paid?[44] Humphrey's informal handwriting, short-hand and squashed marginal notes can suggest a rough readiness to accounting. His sums do not always appear to add up, which might be the consequence of mental adjustments he omitted to record, or the result of memory lapse. Not all of Humphrey's contemporaries agreed with his calculations either, and there were quarrels with servants and local traders. He thought Thomas Pymlot owed him 12*d* 'bot he denies & seys ijd'.[45]

However, the odd memory slip does not betoken incompetence and Humphrey's informal style was not uncommon at a time when some landowners still relied on verbal reckonings.[46] Rather, his accounts reveal the complicated nature of the transactions that often lie behind the polished final accounts drawn up by officials for their lords. Humphrey's tally with his tenant Christopher Lees, for example, offset Christopher's debt for cloth, rent, the tax known as the mise, and the loaning of a plough and a cart, against Humphrey's outstanding payments for wages and the purchase of pigs and barley.[47] In grappling with such minutiae, Humphrey took a professional approach to his accounts, no doubt employing some of the

---

41 Bodl, MS Lat. Misc.c.66, fos 32v, 34cv.
42 Moreton, *The Townshends*, pp. 130, 143; Woolgar, *Household accounts*, I, pp. 59–60.
43 For comparison see Dyer, *An age of transition?*, pp. 98–9.
44 Bodl, MS Lat. Misc.c.66, fo. 29v.
45 Ibid., fo. 29r.
46 Dyer, *An age of transition?*, p. 99; Saul, *Scenes*, pp. 99, 161.
47 Bodl, MS Lat. Misc.c.66, fo. 27av.

skills he had learned as a steward. There is a consistent attempt to organise the material: cross-references were employed, rentals were drawn up every half-year, outstanding debts were re-recorded, and he noted where his debts were recorded in other people's books. Overall, they show that Humphrey embarked on a detailed survey of his estate in 1498, and carefully monitored it thereafter. A stray set of accounts dating to 1519/20 implies that he still kept a close eye on Newton after moving to Pownall.[48]

He was not without help, however. A 'counsel' assisted in the drawing up of the Newton rental, and was on hand to oversee the transfer of property between tenants.[49] Who formed the counsel is unknown, but it may well have comprised family servants, an arrangement which can be observed in the Norfolk household of the Pastons and elsewhere.[50] While Humphrey and his wife, Ellen, kept firm control over the daily management of Newton, they inevitably relied on a range of wage labour to work and maintain the land.[51] There was a constant need for short-term contractors paid by the day. Skilled men, such as the smith, found regular work mending the plough and other equipment, while craftsmen were hired for large building projects. A more regular group of day labourers were agricultural workers, who were employed for three overlapping purposes: to support craftsmen in transporting materials; to undertake regular maintenance of the estate through tasks like trimming hedges and clearing gutters; and to assist in seasonal tasks, primarily to gather the harvest.[52]

The harvest workers were the largest single group and numbered between sixteen and twenty-two at any one harvest. They were paid 2*d* a day, which appears to have been the going rate in midland and northern England.[53] Interestingly, and in contrast to other estates such as those in the East Riding of Yorkshire, the rate was the same for both men and women: Christopher Lees was paid 2*s* 2*d* for thirteen days and Elizabeth Fandon 13*d* for six and a half days.[54] This presumably reflected the low-skilled, low-status nature of the reaping process and it is noteworthy that the majority of this work at Newton was undertaken by women (both married and single), with some children

---

[48] Ibid., fos 59–61.
[49] Ibid., fos 24r, 60v.
[50] Britnell, 'Pastons', p. 135; Saul, *Scenes*, p. 85; Richmond, *John Hopton*, pp. 151–5.
[51] Acheson, *A gentry community*, p. 55. For Ellen, see pp. 23–4 above.
[52] Youngs, 'Servants and labourers', p. 156.
[53] Winchester, 'The castle household', pp. 90–1 and TNA: PRO, SC 6/988/12, m. 1d (for Stafford Castle estate, Stafford).
[54] Disagreement continues over women's wages. Those who believe that women could receive similar wages as men for doing the same work include Hilton, *The English peasantry*, pp. 101–3; Penn, 'Female wage earners', pp. 8–9; and Hanawalt, *The ties that bound*, pp. 150–1. By contrast Poos, *A rural society*, pp. 212–9 and more recently Bardsley, 'Women's work reconsidered', pp. 3–29, argue for wage differentiation at all levels. However, the debate has overwhelmingly focused on fourteenth-century material and provides only limited context for the early Tudor period, a very different economic climate, especially for women.

assisting.⁵⁵ Unlike harvesters in later periods, they were neither migrant nor simply employed for the cereal harvest. A significant proportion – around a half to two-thirds – returned each year, seeing Newton as a regular source of wages. The majority lived within a short distance of the estate and were already connected to it as tenants, servants or agricultural labourers, or as relatives of these individuals. The reapers Richard, Margery and Kate Wyatt, for instance, were more than likely related to John Wyatt, the miller. This was only one of a significant number of family units working at Newton, an employment arrangement found in other parts of England where groups offered themselves to an employer, often for a collective fee.⁵⁶ The impression given is of a long-term connection between Newton and agricultural workers that often passed down the generations. Humphrey – who listed their names, where and for how long they worked – appears to have known all of his harvesters, if only at times by their relationship to others: he noted payments to Wyatt's daughter, Gee's wife and to Williamson's son.⁵⁷

The bulk of the daily work was undertaken by full-time employees whom Humphrey labelled 'servauntes'. He used this term to describe those employed on a contract, for a fixed wage and a stated time period, usually a year, a type of servant commonly found across England.⁵⁸ Whereas some late medieval servants were hired at annual fairs, Newton's workers were more informally employed. Like his harvesters, they were recruited at various points throughout the year from the neighbourhood (including his tenants) and through kinship ties. There are examples of lengthy associations. John Hough of Wilmslow, who worked for Humphrey's father in the 1480s, was followed consecutively by his sons William, James and John during Humphrey's lordship.⁵⁹ The absence of a single hiring date and the use of tenants make it difficult to calculate the number of servants employed each year. The best estimate is that, at any one time, there were approximately five servants working at Newton, which would be commensurate with the estate's size. The manor of Elvethall (Durham), which totalled 240 acres, employed seven full time agricultural workers, while the larger estate of Porter's Hall (Essex), with 300 acres of arable, hired eleven servants.⁶⁰

---

55 In 1500, seventy-five per cent of reapers were women: Youngs, 'Servants and labourers', p. 157. Bardsley, 'Women's work reconsidered', p. 10.
56 Bardsley, 'Women's work reconsidered', pp. 5, 16.
57 Bodl, MS Lat. Misc.c.66, fo. 34cv.
58 It is rare to have such detailed accounts of servants working on a gentleman's estate. Humphrey's accounts bear close similarity to those drawn up by Nicholas Wendover (1468–72) for his employers, the Stonor family: Carpenter, *Kingsford's Stonor letters*, p. 99. For a thorough discussion of the servant see Goldberg, 'What was a servant?', pp. 1–22. For the post-1500 period see Kussmaul, *Servants in husbandry*, pp. 6–7.
59 TNA: PRO, STAC 2/30/86; Bodl, MS Lat. Misc.c.66, fo. 41av. The pattern follows what Goldberg has called 'a succession of youngsters': Goldberg, 'What was a servant?', pp. 13–14; Whittle, *The development of agrarian capitalism*, p. 272.
60 Lomas, 'Elvethall', p. 36; Poos, *A rural society*, p. 213.

Newton did not have the lands, rooms or administrative structure to warrant a large staff with finely demarcated duties.[61] None of the male servants specialised in one particular task, nor were they divided between domestic servants and agricultural workers, as would have been the case on larger estates. Rather, responsibilities were shared and their work overlapped. Their tasks were connected to the soil (digging, ditching, marling and cutting turf), crop management, looking after livestock and its produce, and maintaining buildings such as the mills and fishery. These were combined with various non-manual tasks, such as travelling to local towns and fairs on Humphrey's behalf. James Hough, for example, went to Macclesfield to pay a dyer the 6s 8d debt that Humphrey owed. A select few took on more managerial roles. They were delegated the tasks of overseeing or paying other estate workers, duties traditionally associated with a bailiff. William Hough's key position in the household is seen on the occasions when he acted alongside Humphrey's wife in the payment of servants' wages. He was also trusted, alongside Thomas Astill and Philip Grene, with receiving dowry payments, collecting Humphrey's stewardship fees, and witnessing local land deeds.[62]

The special position of this Newton elite is reflected in their relatively high wages – between 11s and 14s 4d – compared with the 7–8s received by most servants. These wages were fairly typical for northern estates, and comparison can be made with the contemporary estate of Millom in Cumberland in the period 1513–14, where wages ranged from 8s to 13s 4d.[63] In addition, Humphrey's servants benefited from food, drink and clothing, with many receiving the gift of a bountieth or 'tip' as part of their contract. Nicholas Lees, for instance, was hired for half a year for a wage of 5s 4d and a pair of shoes.[64] All of the above were men, and Humphrey followed prevailing views on the sexual division of labour by excluding women from managerial roles. Female servants were generally paid lower wages (never above 8s) and were placed on shorter-term contracts. Where their work is specified, it is the typically domestic tasks traditionally associated with women: brewing, cheese-making and spinning.[65] With their marital status not noted, it is impossible to know whether they were looking to supplement household wages or accumulate a dowry. But, like women workers elsewhere, they were transient labourers, being part-time and short-term.

---

[61] For comparison with other gentry estates see Britnell, 'The Pastons', p. 144; Saul, *Scenes*, p. 161.
[62] Bodl, MS Lat. Misc.c.66, fos 29v, 33v; JRUL, Bromley Davenport, 'Newton by Mottram', no. 7. Cf. Fleming, 'Household servants', p. 30.
[63] Winchester, 'The castle household', pp. 89–95.
[64] Bodl, MS Lat. Misc.c.66, fo. 33v. These tips can be compared to those discussed in Saul, *Scenes*, pp. 121–2; Carpenter, *Kingsford's Stonor letters*, p. 99; Hatcher, 'England in the aftermath', p. 29.
[65] Youngs, 'Servants and labourers', p. 153; Bennett, *Women in the medieval countryside*, pp. 130–8; Graham, '"A woman's work"', pp. 126–48; Whittle, *The development of agrarian capitalism*, p. 261.

Humphrey was never a distant employer, not even after the move to Pownall. He or his wife often dealt with the servants directly, and Humphrey's use of the first person ('I have giffen him', 'I paid hym', 'he has delivered me') underlines the personal contact. He knew when his servants had failed to turn up for work, or had bungled their tasks. He was adamant that Ellen Porter had feigned her sickness and had marred the ale, and he docked the wages of Ralph Rider for losing a fork shoe, sickle and a pick fork.[66] Servants would not get the better of him. Any absences for any reason, including genuine illness and funerals, were financially penalised. They also experienced irregular wages, a reflection of the estate's cash-flow problems, and would often receive payment in kind rather than in cash, which was the more favoured remuneration of fifteenth-century servants.[67]

Yet while Humphrey exercised full authority and discipline, there is no indication that he acted 'as a lyon wylde, or as a tiraint to hem that they servauntis be' (as Peter Idley counselled his son not to be).[68] Admittedly, these accounts are written from Humphrey's perspective, but they do suggest that his servants were not afraid to complain about wage arrears and expose errors, and a level of negotiation was involved in hiring and wage settlements. Two female workers were hired on the proviso that they 'shall be lose opon a quarter warnyng'. Either Humphrey was acknowledging that he could not sack a servant without notice, or, which seems more likely, these female servants were insisting on the flexibility of short-term contracts.[69] At the same time, Humphrey became involved in his employees' lives and there are indications of close ties. He attended the wedding of William Hough, and he dated one of his accounts in relation to the marriage of his servant and tenant, Thomas Lees, suggesting that it was the most memorable event that came to mind. Perhaps, like other English landlords, he even assisted his servants in their marriage plans.[70] David Stone has argued that the success of an estate often lay with the relationship between the lord and his workforce; good managerial skills could markedly improve an estate's performance.[71] The close relationship between Humphrey and his key servants, the trust he placed in them and the 'good lordship' they felt, may well explain why several men chose to stay, electing not to move on when their yearly contract ended. John Aleyn, for example, worked at Newton for at least six years.[72] This would have brought a degree of stability and expertise to the estate.

---

[66] Bodl, MS Lat. Misc.c.66, fos 25r, 33v.
[67] Hanawalt, *The ties that bound*, p. 165; Lomas, 'Elvethall', p. 46.
[68] D'Evelyn (ed.) *Peter Idley's instructions*, p. 102.
[69] Bodl, MS Lat. Misc.c.66, fos 33v, 39av. For examples of women negotiating similar flexible contracts see Poos, *A rural society*, p. 203 and McIntosh, *Working women*, p. 53.
[70] Bodl, MS Lat. Misc.c.66, fos 27ar, 33 and 35v. Goldberg, 'What was a servant?', pp. 17–18; Goldberg, *Medieval England*, p. 21.
[71] Stone, *Decision-making*, pp. 227–8.
[72] Youngs, 'Servants and labourers', p. 149.

Investment and enterprise

Humphrey was fortunate that he inherited his estate during a favourable time for England's landholders. The sluggish economy and low rents that had blighted landlords in the early fifteenth century were replaced from the 1470s by much improved conditions. Many lords saw their revenues increase during the period 1470–1520. In Derbyshire, for example, rents rose on several gentry properties and new rentals were drawn.[73] Yet success was not achieved without effort. Property needed to be maintained and profits maximised in order to stem or ward off decline. Landlords acted in different ways, but the gentry have gained a reputation as an enterprising group, far more so than the more conservative nobility. Christine Carpenter considered the fifteenth-century Warwickshire gentry 'enthusiastic exploiters of profitable ventures', while Eric Acheson argued that Leicestershire gentry were flexible opportunists, with their financial interests marked by 'opportunism and diversity'. Christopher Dyer's analysis of a wide range of evidence concluded that the gentry were 'careful and adaptable managers' who were 'responsive to change'.[74] Praise indeed, yet the impression has sometimes been given that the gentry were pragmatic adapters, merely reacting to the economic climate, rather than forward planners. This can be seen on the issue of investment, where the gentry are shown to focus overwhelmingly on repairs and the replacement of stock. Only gradually have the gentry been credited with taking more active measures.[75]

Humphrey Newton was both an enterprising opportunist and a man with a long-term investment plan. He was not satisfied simply to keep the estate ticking over, although he clearly did replenish stocks and maintain pathways, fences, hedges and gateways.[76] Rather, his view on improving Newton rested on a thoughtful assessment of what could be achieved. This careful planning is evident in the opening items of the account booklet, which bespeak of a man familiarising himself with his new estate. The first folio contains a rental, dated 1498, which lists all possessions and their yearly rentable value. The drawing up of a rental was an expensive business, usually only undertaken for special reasons, such as inheritance, and Humphrey had made it a priority on entering his estate. A second rental drawn up 1504/5 may well have been a

---

[73] Dyer, *Making a living*, p. 338; Wright, *Derbyshire gentry*; Carpenter, *Locality and polity*, pp. 155, 177. That recovery could be patchy, however, see Britnell, *The closing of the Middle Ages?*, p. 241.

[74] Carpenter, 'The fifteenth-century gentry', pp. 36–60; Acheson, *A gentry community*, p. 75; Dyer, *An age of transition?*, p. 97; Dyer, *Making a living*, p. 340; Watkins, 'Landowners', pp. 31–3; Stone, *Decision-making*, p. 11.

[75] Hilton, 'Rent and capital formation', p. 213; Britnell, 'Minor landlords', pp. 15, 18; Watkins, 'Landowners', p. 27. Compare with the more positive assessment in Dyer, *An age of transition?*, p. 108.

[76] For example, Bodl, MS Lat. Misc.c.66, fo. 26ar.

means of assessing the first years of change.[77] Other observations were made in 1498. Tithes were annual outgoings and Humphrey listed those due to the vicar of Prestbury, alongside the formula for calculating those amounts.[78] The most regular expenditure was the daily feeding of the Newton household. With this in mind, Humphrey recorded the amount of seed sown in 1498, followed by the yield or 'increse' in the harvest.[79] At the same time, he estimated the demand from the Newton household by making a tally of the bushels of corn used in the household between 1 August (the first full month of his inheritance) and 30 November 1498. It came to a total of twenty-six. With this figure Humphrey estimated that a household numbering thirteen to fourteen persons 'with strangers' would require around seventy-seven bushels of corn for bread and ale per annum. The figures are a little low for a gentry household, but the accounts offer little by way of explanation.[80] What matters here is that they show a man methodically investigating the productivity of his new estate and the demands upon its resources.

Armed with this information, Humphrey instigated a series of improvements to develop Newton's economy. The range and extent of investment undertaken in the period 1498–1502 is remarkable. Some landlords improved their income by specialising – sheep farming being a common example[81] – but Humphrey's plan continued to reflect the mixed economy of his estate. In those first four years, he oversaw the completion of four major projects: the intensive marling of his arable fields, the rebuilding of a corn mill, and the building of a fishery and a fulling mill. Lying behind the programme were the twin desires of augmenting his income and better providing for the household.

Given the demands placed on the estate, food was a priority. To improve the quantity and quality of the harvest meant deploying fertiliser and one of the most commonly used was marl. It was particularly widespread in Cheshire; the sixteenth-century traveller John Leland attributed the numerous pits that pock-marked the county to the 'digginge of marle for fettynge the baren ground there to beare good corne'.[82] During the period 1499–1502 Humphrey marled the fields used most regularly for growing cereal, and reclaimed three acres of wasteland. The marl pit was dug at Newton itself

---

[77] Bodl, MS Lat. Misc.c.66, fo. 24r; BL, Add MS 42134A, fo. 9r. Dyer, *Warwickshire farming*, p. 164; Carpenter, *Locality and polity*, p. 163.

[78] That he wrote 'I am agreed with þe vicar as my fader was' suggests a recent meeting to confirm terms. Bodl, MS Lat. Misc.c.66, fo. 26ar.

[79] It is difficult to comment on these figures because whereas the seed was measured in bushels, Humphrey measured the output in terms of thraves (an indeterminable measurement commonly used in the north): Bodl, MS Lat. Misc.c.66, fo. 28ar.

[80] Compare with the amount of corn expected to be eaten in a knight's household: Myers (ed.) *The Household of Edward IV*, pp. 108–9. Dyer, *Standards of living*, pp. 152–3.

[81] Ives, *The common lawyers*, pp. 348–51.

[82] Hewitt, *Medieval Cheshire*, p. 21. For Leland's observations: Smith (ed.) *The Itinerary of John Leland*, part VII, p. 5, part IX, p. 6.

and measured around four roods in length and fifty-eight yards in width.[83] We know this because Humphrey carefully recorded the dimensions, and the whole project was carried out under his close personal attention. His instructions to the marlers were specific: the marl had to be set 'verrey thick', and only good-quality or 'able marl' was to be dug; neither 'stepmoder nor fey nor any other stuff' was permitted on the Newton fields.[84] The biggest project in the Highfield (1502) took eight carters and seven 'spreaders' ten weeks to complete, generating a wage bill that approached £6, twice the value of the Newton rents.[85] Such costs would have been anticipated because marling was an expensive, though ultimately worthwhile, investment. As the sixteenth-century gentry writer John Fitzherbert of Norbury (Derbyshire) wrote: 'though it [marl] be exceeding chargeable, yet through good neighbourhood it quieth the cost'.[86] Humphrey certainly appears to have reaped the benefits within a few years. Comparing the Newton rentals of 1498 and 1504/5 indicates that three of the four fields marled had improved in value. The 'Bridgehouse' had increased from 10s to 13s 4d, 'Chokechurle' from 13s 4d to 20s and the Highfield had doubled from 10s to 20s.[87]

While increasing the potential for more bread and ale, Humphrey simultaneously sought to improve the fish stocks of his estate. Fish were an important resource and were already kept in Newton's millpond and water-filled marl pits. These did not satisfy Humphrey's needs and in March 1501 he organised the damming of a tributary of the river Bollin to create a new fishery in Newton. The building costs and labour services amounted to a manageable 20s besides meat and drink; stocking the pool and maintenance required additional expenditure. Humphrey transferred a number of fish from his existing pools, while others were bought from nearby estates such as Bramhall and Foxtwist halls. Perch, tench, bream, fenders and eels were the main stock and were placed in the pool in 'couples'.[88] Humphrey realised that the return from this investment would be delayed for several years until the fishpond became fully stocked. He valued the pool's return at 13s 4d per annum: 10s was the yearly rent, but the additional 3s 4d goes unexplained. The value of the dam is modest when placed against the profits made by larger landowners, yet it remained a significant source of revenue for the small landowner.[89] Fish was a necessary component of the gentry's diet, with large quantities of both preserved and freshwater fish required at Lent and other fast days. The importance of variety is illustrated in Newton's Lenten

---

[83] A rood appears to vary in measurement, lying somewhere between 6 and 8 yards.
[84] Bodl, MS Lat. Misc.c.66, fos 32v, 39ar. Stepmoder – stepmother – was the name given to cold, blue clay. As marl was a blue, clayey soil it was fairly easy to mix the two. Fey refers to the unwanted dirt and grime that clung to the marl.
[85] Ibid, fo. 40r.
[86] Fitzherbert, *Booke of Husbandrie*, p. 29.
[87] BL, Add. MS 42134, fo. 9r.
[88] Bodl, MS Lat. Misc.c.66, fos 37r, 60v.
[89] Aston (ed.) *Medieval fish, fisheries and fishponds*.

COUNTY of CHESHIRE

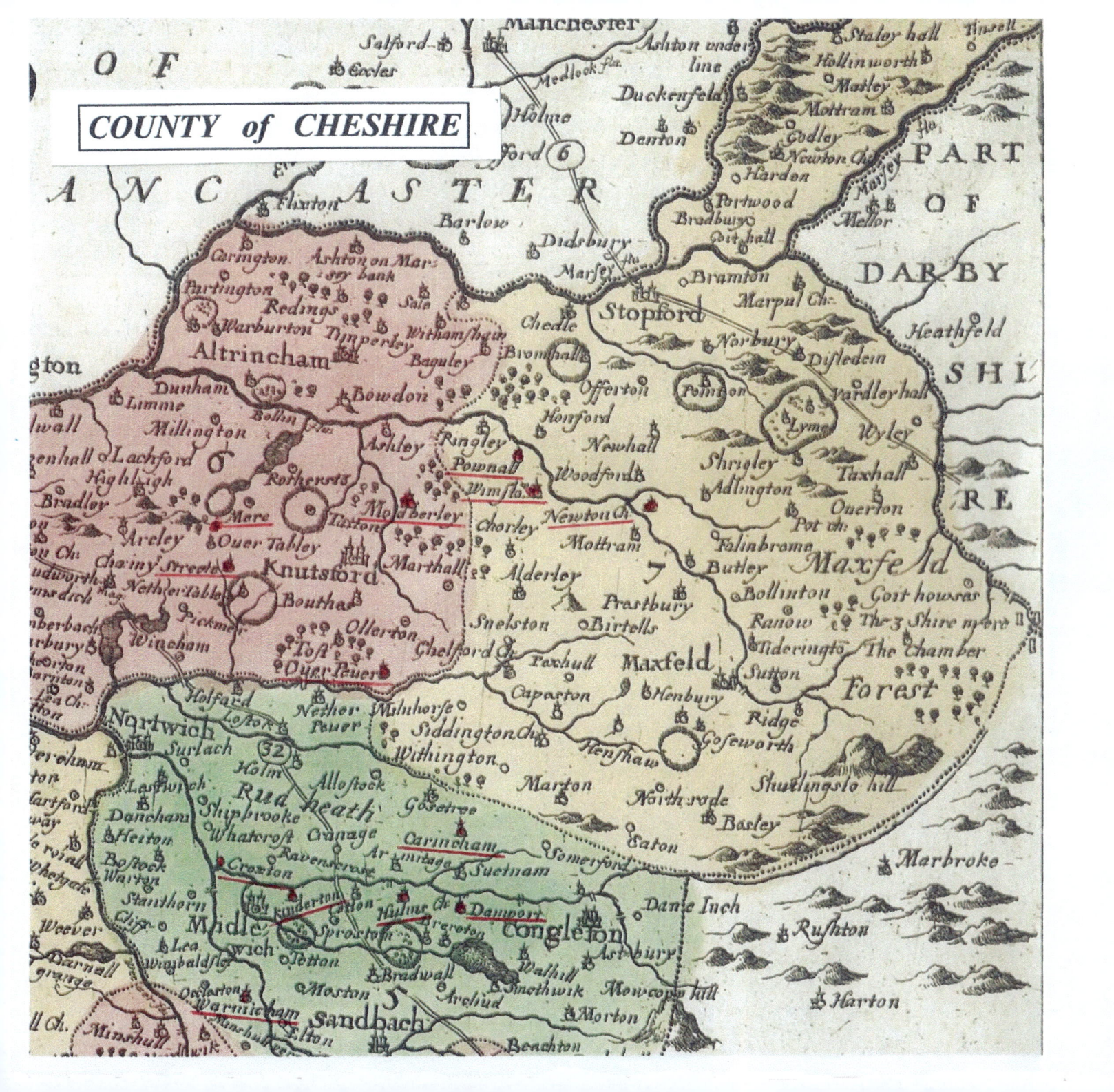

MAP KEY

Cheshire noble families, in direct line of ancestry to Beck and Warden and their Estates

Newton, Pownall (Wilmslow):
  Newton and Fitton

Mobberley, Mere, Strettell:
  Strettell

Over Peover:
  Mainwaring

Carnicham:
  Mainwaring

Davenport:
  Davenport

Hulme:
  Hulme

Kinderton:
  Venables

Croxton:
  Croxton, Mainwaring

Warmichan:
  Mainwaring

purchases of 1499–1501, which included salmon, oysters, mussels, sparling, mulwell (cod), herring and ray. The absence of tench, perch or bream suggests that these were provided from the home farm.[90] The fishery itself symbolised lordship, with fishing rights an important franchise. Practical considerations like costs of construction and ongoing maintenance of ponds (regulation of the flood waters and the ditching of gutters) further ensured that fisheries remained the preserve of the wealthy.[91]

The two larger projects at Newton involved mill-building. Rebuilding the Newton corn mill was one of Humphrey's earliest tasks on the estate, mainly because it had recently 'brok out' and rent was in arrears. The person he employed for the build, Thomas Cross of Norton, received a wage of £3 13s 4d, which indicates the extent of the damage.[92] While this represents significant outlay, Humphrey knew he would benefit greatly from the repair, and not simply financially. The mill's prominent position on the estate helped to establish Humphrey's seigniorial authority while acting as a vital amenity for the local population. Times were more conducive at the end of the fifteenth century for such a project. The 'milling crisis' that had struck England in the first half of the century, with low rents and low mill prices, had given way to the prospect of profit. Mills were rebuilt and many were rented, such as those on the large estates of the bishop of Worcester.[93] Mills in general rated highly in overall manorial values, with significant milling exploitation witnessed in the North West.[94]

Humphrey followed suit and in 1499 he leased the corn mill to its sitting tenant, John Wyatt, for ten years at the common rent of 20s 4d (later rising to 22s 4d) and half the fish in the mill pool.[95] Like other landlords in England, Humphrey made a maintenance agreement that established a division of labour between the miller and lord.[96] Whereas Humphrey oversaw the timber and ironwork and supplied the millstones, Wyatt was responsible for the wheel and stocking the pool with fish (that is, those areas likely to acquire attention on a regular basis). This type of shared agreement was common in the late fifteenth century, although Humphrey had not secured one of the more favourable contracts which arranged for the lessee to pay all maintenance costs. Millstones in particular were expensive.[97] Nevertheless, there were clear advantages to rebuilding and renting the mill. Humphrey himself valued the mill at 40s in his rental of 1498, a figure which meant he would

---

[90] Bodl, MS Lat. Misc.c.66, fos 26av, 34cr, 37v. See also p. 150 below.
[91] Dyer, 'The consumption of fresh-water fish', p. 27.
[92] Bodl, MS Lat. Misc.c.66, fos 27av, 31av. Youngs, 'Estate management', pp. 133–4.
[93] Holt, *The mills*, p. 164; Dyer, *Lords and peasants*, p. 173.
[94] Langdon, *Mills*, pp. 281–2.
[95] Ten years was the most common term in the last quarter of the fifteenth century: Langdon, *Mills*, p. 192, table 5.3. Mills in fifteenth-century Warwickshire were, similarly, bringing in rents of 20s or more per annum: Carpenter, *Locality and polity*, p. 164.
[96] Holt, *The mills*, p. 97; Langdon, 'Water-mills', pp. 437, 439.
[97] Langdon, *Mills*, p. 192, table 5.3.

recoup Cross's building wage in two years. That he was satisfied by his investment is visible in the phrases he used when calculating his profit: the mill would bring 'vantage and pleasur' and 'pleasur and ease'.[98]

Gentry landlords are known to have diversified their interests in a bid to improve their income. In Derbyshire this involved the exploitation of mineral wealth, with many landholders having some kind of smelting enterprise.[99] In Cheshire, Humphrey turned his attention to the cloth industry and built a fulling mill. It was in his mind in 1498 when he appended a sum to his rental for 'a walke milne I may have'. A short while later, Thomas Cross (the corn mill builder) and his team were re-employed for fifteen weeks to build the mill on the river Bollin.[100] Humphrey was not merely an investor: the mill account offers another example of his extraordinarily close involvement in his estate's development. This is most evident in his decision to find timber from his own woods. Humphrey made a careful list of the specialised parts of the mill building and the number of trees and length of wood required to produce them. The key item was the 'walkstock' which was to be twelve feet long and a yard broad. In December 1499, Humphrey walked with Thomas Cross through Newton selecting the most suitable trees for the mill and noting where they were located on the estate. They identified ten of a needed thirteen such as 'a tree nez the wey to the milne for þe tail sill'.[101]

Nevertheless, as with the corn mill, and, again, as on other English estates, the cost and time required for constructing the mill buildings were shared with the first mill tenant.[102] At Martinmas 1499 Humphrey set the proposed mill to John Casker. He provided Casker with thatch and wood to build a two-bay cottage and gave him a reduction in his rent, but the actual construction of the mill house and any additional buildings came out of Casker's pocket. He also entered into a contract for shared upkeep: Humphrey was to maintain the weir, timber and iron work, whereas the tithe and daily maintenance were Casker's responsibility.[103] The role played by Casker probably accounts for the rent of 26s, Humphrey's highest rent at Newton, but not particularly high compared to sums collected elsewhere in England.[104] These actions – using Newton's wood, a trusted builder, and the ambitions of a miller-tenant – must have minimised costs and disruption. Yet, mill building and maintenance was an expensive business, and returns from fulling mills could be low and in no sense a safe investment.[105] Langdon has drawn attention to the 'relative lack of interest' among lords in building

---

[98] Bodl, MS Lat. Misc.c.66, fo. 31av.
[99] Wright, *Derbyshire gentry*, p. 21; Dyer, *An age of transition?*, p. 104.
[100] Bodl, MS Lat. Misc.c.66, fo. 30r.
[101] Ibid., fo 31a.
[102] Acheson, *A gentry community*, p. 62.
[103] Bodl, MS Lat. Misc.c.66, fo. 30r.
[104] Langdon, *Mills*, p. 197.
[105] Holt, *The mills*, pp. 158, 169; Langdon, 'Water-mills', p. 436.

mills for non-agricultural purposes, a reluctance noticeably prominent in the North West. In late medieval England it was more likely to be the tenants, rather than the lords, who were the mill-building entrepreneurs, with fulling mills multiplying through the actions of clothiers or wealthy artisans.[106] Why did a Cheshire gentry landlord decide to build a fulling mill?

Humphrey's reasons may have been with thoughts of rent or suit of mill, with tenants having to bring their raw cloth to be shrunk; actions which would acknowledge Humphrey's seigniorial power.[107] He clearly saw mills as a good investment for, in addition to the two at Newton, he was a lessee of a mill on the Audley estate where he worked as a steward, and appears to have some rights in Norcliffe mill, near his Pownall estate.[108] At Newton there was an opportunity to benefit from local clothiers and neighbours who brought their cloth to the mill. In the later Middle Ages the expanding cloth industry became the largest and most important of England's industries, with cloth-making a useful by-employment in rural areas.[109] Cheshire was not one of the major counties for cloth, but it was surrounded by the nascent cloth centres of north Wales, south Lancashire (especially active from the 1490s) and Yorkshire. There were the fast-flowing rivers and sheep-filled Pennine slopes of Derbyshire to the east, and the growing port of Chester in the west.[110] East Cheshire towns all had expanding cloth industries with their own fulling mills, tailors, weavers and fullers, and Humphrey himself indicates the number of cloth merchants operating in his area.[111] He made several payments to one 'Kelsall', a name connected with prosperous clothiers of Reading and Southampton, and to 'Ryle of Etchells', very likely the clothier found trading in London and Antwerp at that time.[112] Nevertheless, Cheshire's industry was assisted by few of the rural fulling mills that traditional cloth-making areas such as Wiltshire could boast. Only two rural fulling mills have so far come to light in eastern Cheshire: one on the estate of the Worths of Titherington near Macclesfield, and the other on the land of the Leghs of Adlington, Humphrey's most powerful near neighbours.[113]

---

[106] Langdon, 'Lordship and peasant consumerism', pp. 13–15; Dyer, *An age of transition?*, pp. 163, 166.
[107] Bridbury, *Medieval English cloth making*, p. 21; Langdon, *Mills*, p. 232.
[108] TNA: PRO, WALE 29/456; SC 6 HENVIII/368.
[109] Bridbury, *Economic growth*, p. 46; Bridbury, *Medieval English cloth making*; Britnell, *The closing of the Middle Ages?* p. 234.
[110] Coates, 'The origins and distribution of markets and fairs', pp. 92–111; Lowe, *The Lancashire textile industry*; Wilson, 'The port of Chester', pp. 1–15 and Kermode, 'The trade of late medieval Cheshire', pp. 286–307. Cheshire's cloth industry has received little attention from historians. See, for example, Miller (ed.) *The agrarian history of England and Wales, 3*, where Cheshire is only briefly discussed.
[111] Cunliffe-Shaw, 'Two fifteenth-century kinsmen', p. 16; Bennett, 'Sources and problems', pp. 81–2; Beck, *Tudor Cheshire*, p. 53.
[112] Bodl, MS Lat. Misc.c.66, fos 30r, 45v, 47v, 59av and 61r. Bennett, 'Sources and problems', pp. 81–2. For Ryle see TNA: PRO, C1/609/42, C1/321/16.
[113] TNA: PRO, CHES 3/62/4, Earwaker, *East Cheshire*, II, p. 335.

Humphrey appears to have been seizing an opportunity to benefit in rent and tolls from a growing cloth industry in an area poorly served by fulling mills, and making a speculative investment.

Humphrey could simply have been a rent collector on this project, but there are hints that he had further stakes in the fulling process. He made purchases from a webster who had woven cloth (the process before fulling) and to shearmen who cut the cloth (the process after fulling) and it may be that Humphrey was avoiding middlemen and employing craftsmen directly, a much cheaper option.[114] The cloth produced on the estate may then have been passed to servants – which is what occurred on the estates of Roger Townshend (d. 1551) in Norfolk – or sold to tenants.[115] There is also an intriguing set of accounts between Humphrey and Pole the shearman that refer to the selling of cloth. They include 'Item for anoþer pece of vij yards to by & sel xd ob. Item iiij yards to by & sel vid.'[116] Without knowing exactly who was doing the buying and selling, it cannot shed clear light on Humphrey's negotiations. It does, however, suggest an investment in trade, which can be supported with other entries from the commonplace book. His manuscript once contained 'the marchand signe of the said Humfrey' and he was interested in Morgan Milton, a great-great uncle who lived at the close of the fourteenth century. Morgan not only held lands, messuages and burgages in the town of Southampton, but also had a license to trade in the town in gunpowder and saltpetre. Humphrey claimed to be Milton's heir to the land and trading rights. While there is no evidence that he ever became involved in Southampton trade, he may have been on the lookout for business possibilities.[117]

In 1504/5 Humphrey would walk around a much improved inheritance. It had more buildings and more diverse activity, and the rentable income had risen from £11 to £14.[118] Humphrey was prepared to invest in upgrading his estate, recognising that returns might take time. There was an element of risk, notably associated with the fulling mill, but the ventures were traditional ones and all were based on a careful consideration of the estate's potential. His small enterprises were to some extent borne of necessity, but they were not the result of any prevailing adverse economic conditions. The estate was not in dangerous decline; it just needed to be better. Humphrey would have left the daily running of the estate in the hands of trusted employees and he looked to his counsel and family for assistance, but their actions and

---

[114] Bodl, MS Lat. Misc.c.66, fos 27av, 30r. Compare with the examples in Dyer, 'The consumer', p. 323.

[115] Moreton, *The Townshends*, p. 145. At Newton, the tenant, Cisely Lees, bought 40s worth of cloth from Ellen Newton, Bodl, MS Lat. Misc.c.66, fo. 27ar.

[116] Bodl, MS Lat. Misc.c.66, fo. 45r. 'ob' refers to ½d. The cloth was the course, common threads of kersey, ware cloth and russet: Youngs, 'Estate management', p. 138.

[117] Bodl, MS Lat. Misc.c.66, fos 63v, 64ar; BL, Add MS 42134A, fo. 3.

[118] Bodl, MS Lat. Misc.c.66, fo. 24r; BL, Add MS 42134A, fo. 9r.

his projects were undertaken under Humphrey's watchful eye. As a result he would have realised that there was a limit to what a small estate could achieve. The only sure way to increase landed income was to accumulate more land. That is what Humphrey set out to do.

Expansion

Medieval England was full of competitive lords seeking new lands while protecting their own. During the fifteenth century, the trend was towards developing the core of the inheritance. Richard Clervaux of Croft, for example, spent large sums of money consolidating his estate at Croft for no other reason, says Pollard, than to satisfy his pride and honour.[119] Humphrey's early ambitions centred on Newton and he attempted to expand the borders on all sides. It was possible, of course, for expansion to be achieved simply and straightforwardly by purchase or exchange. In April 1519 Humphrey exchanged his lands in Cleyley – one of the Broxton rents – for an area in Mottram St Andrew held by Sir George Calveley (d. 1536). For both men, it meant rationalising their landholdings. In Humphrey's case it added an area of fifty-six Cheshire acres to the south-east corner of Newton.[120] Humphrey did not have this option on other sides of his estate, however, and he was forced to employ a range of strategies in the hope that one or more would work.

Like many landholders, Humphrey's active attempts at expansion were couched in terms of a policy of reclamation. He never saw himself as an aggressor, but as a campaigner attempting to regain Newton's supposedly lost land and rights. Humphrey's searches through legal documents and family papers had left him in no doubt that Newton had once been a larger, thriving township; it was now time to turn back the clock. His starting point was a collection of thirteenth-century deeds, dating to the time of Henry III (1216–72), which showed the existence of several tenements located across a township.[121] Unfortunately, so the story went, the area was hit severely by the fourteenth-century plague. Humphrey described how 'ther fell þe pestilence & was a deth of people & then these tennementez deccessed which was called þe greate deth: aftr whos decessez the londez of Neuton wer in

---

[119] Wright, *Derbyshire gentry*, p. 46; Saul, *Knights and esquires*, pp. 227–81; Pollard, *North eastern England*, p. 82; Heal and Holmes, *The gentry*, p. 104.
[120] A mix of arable, meadow, pasture, wood and moor. JRUL, Bromley Davenport 'Newton by Mottram', no. 6.
[121] Bodl, MS Lat. Misc.c.66, fo. 20r. They were the chief mansion of Newton, and tenements in the 'Bridgehouse', the Cockshead, the Highfield, *Sleyburniscroft*, the Stone field and 'Harperscroft' in the New Garden. The document Humphrey mentions does not now exist. For the gentry establishing viable foundation stories for their estates see Morgan, 'Making the English gentry', p. 24.

decay'.[122] It was a plausible claim because neighbouring localities suffered significantly during the Black Death: the death rate in Macclesfield manor has been estimated at fifty per cent.[123] Some of the Newton lands were leased out, but Humphrey alleged that the wealthy lords of Bollin, holders of neighbouring Dean Row, grabbed the opportunity to snatch land located on the western edge of Newton. In the fifteenth century, Sir Robert Booth of Dunham Massey, Lord of Bollin (d. 1460), took advantage of the minority of Humphrey's father and enclosed the lands, subsuming them into Dean Row. It was unfortunate that Richard Newton's minority coincided with the 'great slump' of the mid-fifteenth century; Booth may well have annexed vacant or dilapidated holdings to increase his own profits through enclosure.[124]

Humphrey, lamenting the continual lack of redress, launched his bid with several courses of action involving both written and oral testimony. Because the western border of Newton ran along the parish boundary of Prestbury and Wilmslow, Humphrey sought the testimony of Richard Clerk of Prestbury who, as a youth in the early fifteenth century, had gathered the tithe corn for Prestbury church. In a sworn testimony in August 1498, Clerk (now said to be eighty-five) outlined the circuit of his tithe collecting and in so doing confirmed Humphrey's border claims.[125] That this action was carried out within a month of Humphrey's full inheritance, and witnessed by several prominent people, including the mayor of Macclesfield, demonstrates the seriousness with which Humphrey was pursuing his case, and his determination to make an impact as soon as he became lord of Newton. A second argument addressed the question of what constituted a boundary line. Humphrey drew attention to the 'Highway' – described variously as the 'old way', the 'King's way' and a 'saltway' – which ran alongside the western edge of the Newton estate. To Humphrey it was obvious that this should be the major dividing line between the holdings of Dean Row and Newton. It is possible to hear the frustration in his voice as he argued that a boundary would be 'by liklyhod sum thing that hath ben or may be long knowen certeyn & redy, which is a heghway'. However, the late fifteenth-century boundary between Newton and Dean Row did not follow the highway, but bisected fields that, Humphrey declared, had once been one; old plough marks showed the continuity 'as a man may see'.[126] Unfortunately, what was lacking was written proof. Humphrey could make a claim based on 'a manys sizt', but he acknowledged that he had no documentation that could prove his case. An even bigger issue was the lack of political opportunity. The land still belonged to the powerful Booth family, which was headed by healthy,

---

[122] Bodl, MS Lat. Misc.c.66, fo. 20r.
[123] Booth, *The financial administration*, p. 2.
[124] Hatcher, 'The great slump'. The losses were listed as the highway and the fields of Jack Jill, 'Ebot's Croft' and 'Prestknave House'.
[125] BL, Add MS 42134A, fo. 12r.
[126] Ibid, fo. 20r. See Map 2 for the Highway.

successful adults. Only inheritance by a minor or weak lord would be promising. In the hope that this might arise, Humphrey decided to align himself with William Fitton of Fernleigh (d. 1523), a rival claimant to Dean Row and one who was sympathetic to the Newtons' cause. Should William succeed in taking the Bollin lordship from the Booth family, he promised Humphrey 'a release with warranty' of the lands in dispute. Humphrey took the case very seriously and – this time with deeds to hand – he laid out Fitton's claims to the lordship in great detail in the commonplace book. Nothing, however, appears to have come of it and it remained a paper exercise.

With his western boundary, therefore, Humphrey was prepared, but also realistic: the Booths were too powerful for active measures. However, this was not the case with Humphrey's lesser neighbours on his southern border with Mottram St Andrew. Lying on the southern bank of the river Bollin was an area known as the Dean. It was a holding of around forty acres of lands, meadows and pastures worth around four marks.[127] The Newtons had been lessees of the Dean farmhouse and lands since at least the 1440s, when a family dispute was put to arbitration and the farm settled on Humphrey's great-grandmother for life.[128] In the later fifteenth century, the land was held by the Brown family of the Marsh, Derbyshire, distant cousins of Humphrey's and his tenants at Milton Hall (Broxton hundred).[129] Initially Humphrey benefited directly from its crops and pasture land, but eventually he sub-let a large part of the Dean to his son-in-law James Barlow.[130]

Significantly, the arrangement with Barlow was made during a minority in the Brown line. Over a decade later when the heir, Nicholas Brown, achieved his majority, he claimed that Humphrey had no right to the house, and, in a petition to Chancery, complained that 'one Humfrey Neuton toke or caused to be takyn away of the seid lands and tenements the seid meyse or building thereof'.[131] Brown cancelled the tenancy of the Newtons and relations between the families deteriorated. Disputes occurred over the rights to land and to the Bollin river which separated Newton and the Dean. The ongoing problems are glimpsed in Humphrey's commonplace book where, around 1519, he wrote that Nicholas Brown had 'toke the deyn fro me ayenst his promes'.[132] There was no quick resolution and, in 1527–9, Brown brought two cases against Humphrey to Star Chamber.[133] Brown accused Humphrey of sending over twenty armed men into Dean wood in order to cut down trees to build

---

[127] TNA: PRO, C1/458/22 and STAC 2/6/204.
[128] BL, Add MS 42134, fo. 23. She held it for life because Humphrey recorded her death 'apud Deynes house' in the first folio of his commonplace book.
[129] Brown had acquired the Dean in an exchange with the Legh family of Adlington. It was not a smooth transaction and disputes rumbled on into the sixteenth century as Chancery petitions show: TNA: PRO, C1/458/21–26 and C1/654/38.
[130] Bodl, MS Lat. Misc.c.66. fos 30, 33r, 36r, 39ar.
[131] TNA: PRO, C1/458/21.
[132] Bodl, MS Lat. Misc.c.66. fo. 60r.
[133] TNA: PRO, STAC 2/6/204–208.

a weir that redirected the river Bollin. In response, Humphrey accused Brown and his men of destroying the Newton fulling mill and turning the river away from it; he had already seen the men indicted at the hundred court at Macclesfield.[134] There are no surviving letters to view 'behind the scenes' of this dispute as one can for the Paston family; nothing to tell us whether insults were traded or who was legally in the right. What can be said is that local order had clearly broken down, and Brown had felt that his complaint would only be properly heard in a court outside Cheshire.[135]

It was, however, disputed land on the eastern edge of Newton that drew most of Humphrey's attention. Adjacent to Newton lay a large heath (usually called Foxtwist Heath) which had been the subject of dispute since the thirteenth century.[136] Clashes between virtually all the families in the area appear to have arisen over boundary confusion between the settlements of Newton, Foxtwist and Butley, and because the heath was in an area with few opportunities for expansion. During Humphrey's lifetime his neighbours the Davenports of Woodford and Leghs of Adlington made claims to the heath and Humphrey was forced to respond. In the case of the Davenport claim, it included commissioning a land survey to delineate the border between Newton and Woodford.[137] More threateningly, the Leghs made great effort to prevent lands they held, or had interest, in Foxtwist falling into the hands of their neighbours. When in May 1503 Thomas Legh granted the estate of Foxtwist to Griffith Willot and his heirs, he made it conditional on Willot never alienating the lands to a specified list of men and their heirs who had a landed interest in the neighbourhood; among the names were the Davenports and Humphrey Newton.[138] In November that same year, Humphrey, along with Willot himself, let a house on the heath to their neighbour William Smale on terms that he 'take nor make not his lande to us such persons bot as be lovers to us'.[139] Landholders circling the heath were very watchful: if they could not get their hands on more land, then they were going to make sure that no one else could either.

Humphrey himself made a bid to a sizeable part of Foxtwist Heath. His claims focused on an area extending from the east of Newton hall to a lane called the Shaw Lane on the western side of Foxtwist Heath, and to a ditch joining the lane to the Lumb brook. Humphrey declared the area to be

---

[134] Mills were often a focus of discontent. In 1523 Humphrey was involved in another dispute over the mill at Norcliffe near Wilmslow: TNA: PRO, WALE 29/456.

[135] For the resort to law as a sign of local breakdown, see Carpenter, 'Gentry and community', p. 355.

[136] The area of Foxtwist is now lost, but its location can be seen on the nineteenth-century tithe map (CRO, EDT 293/1, 293/2). Its coordinates for the 1-inch OS map are SJ8967797, see Map 2. For earlier disputes see Stewart-Brown (ed.) *Chester county court roll*, p. 15; Bodl, MS Lat. Misc.c.66, fo. 19v.

[137] BL, Add MS 42134A, fos 17v–18r.

[138] Legh of Adlington deeds, DLA 71/28/2a+b.

[139] Bodl, MS Lat. Misc.c.66, fo. 25v.

'Newton Heath' and asserted that it belonged to the township of Newton alone. Adopting this position meant he faced the opposition of the lords of Butley and other locals who believed that the heath was part of the adjacent township of Butley, and was under the jurisdiction of Butley's manor court. At one level it was simply an issue of whether the heath belonged to Newton or to Butley, but what elevates this case above a common boundary dispute is that the claim became entangled with Newton's legal status. This was because the lords of Butley (the Pigot family) argued that Newton was not an independent township, but that it, like the heath, fell under the authority of the manor and township of Butley. To understand the implications of that claim a closer look at the township is required.

Township (re)creation

Throughout his lordship, Humphrey persistently declared that Newton was a distinct township. In the late 1530s and 40s, his son, William, furthered that claim in a more aggressive manner, provoking the lord of Butley, Thomas Pigot, to take the case to Star Chamber in 1546. The first question posed to the witnesses gathered on behalf of Newton was 'whether Newton near Butley be a township of itself and no part of the said towne of Butley and so known and taken'.[140]

What was a township and what were the Newtons asserting? A township (*villata*) was a settlement with a recognised, often defined, boundary. In Cheshire, like other northern regions, this was an important administrative, fiscal and law-enforcing unit, as well as a focus of loyalty. During the thirteenth century a series of laws, which culminated in the 1285 Statute of Westminster, laid down the duties of a township. Every township had to make representation at the county and hundred court; it had to have one or two constables; it was bound to arrest malefactors; arms had to be provided at the expense of the township; and watch had to be kept throughout the night.[141]

The Newtons were therefore claiming a considerable degree of power and responsibility for themselves. According to Humphrey, Newton had long been an independent township, at least before the Black Death; all he was doing was stating the obvious and retrieving lost rights. William Newton's witnesses in the sixteenth-century Star Chamber case declared that Newton had always

---

[140] TNA: PRO, STAC 2/30/86. The case against William and his servants highlighted their refusal to pay dues to Butley township, the digging up of turf on the heath, and an assault on a Butley tenant.

[141] Pollock and Maitland, *The history of the English law*, 1, pp. 563–5; Cam, 'The community of the vill', pp. 71–84; Jewell, *English local administration*, pp. 60–1; Winchester, 'Parish, township and tithing', pp. 4–7, and figure 1, which clearly shows Cheshire as part of the 'township country'.

been 'named, reported and taken as a towne of itself'. His opponents, the Pigots of Butley, had a very different view. According to their witnesses, there were several clear and fundamental reasons why Newton was only a principal messuage and 'a parcell' of Butley township. The Newton family and their tenants had kept, and were expected to keep, watch and ward for the township of Butley. Several tenants of Newton had been elected constables for Butley township at Macclesfield hundred court. Any affrays or assaults occurring on the disputed heath were dealt with by the constables of Butley. Newton was subject to Butley manor court, which regulated the township, and residents of Newton paid dues and services to the lordship of Butley. Thomas Duncalf of Foxtwist, the steward of the Butley estate, confirmed that he collected an annual rent from the Newton household for such services. Moreover, when Humphrey wanted to build his fishery and a chapel on the heath he appeared several times before the Butley court to plead his case. It seems that, by their actions, the residents of Newton were participating in the community of the township of Butley.[142]

As in all legal disputes, the 'truth' is relative, but records show that the early Tudor lords of Butley had a strong case.[143] On the one hand, it is possible to see a degree of self-regulation within Newton. It was Humphrey's responsibility to equip his tenants with arms, and he collected the tax known as the mise from them, noting any arrears in his accounts.[144] On the other, there is simply no proof that Newton was a township in the late Middle Ages. Forceful evidence is to be found in the lists of townships made for the assessment of the Cheshire mise: Newton does not appear on the earliest surviving list, dating to 1406.[145] Nor is Newton listed as a township in the puture rolls. Puture was a service or payment exacted by the sergeants of the peace of Macclesfield from particular lands within the hundred. Lands in Newton were included because a thirteenth-century deed detailing the transfer of the Newton estate between the Davenport family mentions the reserve of puture to the sergeantry.[146] However, no fourteenth-century puture roll records a township called Newton and where a member of the Newton family is mentioned paying the due – as was the case in 1355–6 and 1356–8 – his name appears under the township of Butley.[147]

As all the evidence available post-dates the Black Death, it cannot show whether Newton, as Humphrey claimed, was a township in earlier years.

---

[142] TNA: PRO, STAC 2/30/86.
[143] Unfortunately, the local action on the Star Chamber case was lost during disruption caused by Anglo-Scottish wars in the 1540s: Thornton, *Cheshire*, p. 230.
[144] Bodl, MS Lat. Misc.c.66, fos 27ar, 29r, 42v and 43r. As regard the arms, Humphrey wrote on a slip of paper: 'Thomas a bill, a gasterne, a salet, a paire of splenters, Harry Bramely a ball and a gasterne, John Facon a bill and a gasterne, Piers Upton a bowe, Jamys Pymlat a bowe, It. the walker a bowe'. Ibid., fo. 64b.
[145] JRUL, Tatton MS 345.
[146] BL, Add MS 42134A, fos 13v, 16r.
[147] Highet, *The Early History of the Davenports*, pp. 69, 72, 77.

Between the eleventh and thirteenth centuries there had been a considerable growth in old settlements and the establishment of many new ones in Cheshire. It is likely that Newton (the 'new settlement') was cut from the outlying woods of the manor of Butley just prior to the Norman Conquest.[148] In some thirteenth- and fourteenth-century documents Newton is referred to as a *villa*.[149] Yet whether it was ever a township in a legal sense is unknown, and the creation of townships during this period remains poorly understood. What is important is that Humphrey, and later his son, fought to get Newton recognised as a township, and they did so with dogged conviction rather than legal support.

This is a remarkable attempt and a significant historical case because town 'creators' or 're-creators' are uncommon finds in pre-Reformation England. Comparison, however, can be made with those who tried to create a manor, the more common vehicle for lordship in central and southern England. In all cases, the goals pursued were the powers of lordship and the apparatus of authority. In theory, no new manors could be created after the thirteenth century because a manor operated by tradition, but the importance of manorial jurisdiction led a number of families to establish a manor illegally. The most well-known example is that of William Paston, who obtained bond tenants and a manor court in Paston in the 1430s and 40s. Naturally it was not paraded as new, and with 'divers old deeds' the family proclaimed that the manor had existed 'sithen the time that no mind is to the contrary'.[150] Such manor creations continued into the late sixteenth century. Richard Weston, for example, created the manor of Hagley (Staffordshire) by introducing a manor court in the 1570s, thereby increasing his local status.[151]

Humphrey shared this desire to improve rights and status by elevating his family holding. There was, however, a major stumbling block to claims of independence and it came in the form of a rent that the Newtons were required to pay to the Pigot family. Witnesses in the Star Chamber case highlighted the rent – either stated as 4s or 6s – as proof of Newton's dependency on Butley, and they recounted the times the money had been paid. It is likely

---

148 The early history of Newton is obscure, but the use of 'tun' to mean an enclosed settlement suggests a pre-conquest origin. Macclesfield hundred was the most wooded shire in Cheshire and several place-names derive from clearings, such as Butley, or Butta's clearing: Higham, *The Origins of Cheshire*, p. 171. Although Newton is not referenced by name in the Domesday Book, two entries do survive for the manor of Butley. They are so similar that duplication has been suspected but the few differences they exhibit suggest they are distinct areas: Tait (ed.) *The Domesday Survey of Cheshire*, pp. 131, 213; Morgan (ed.) *Domesday Book*, nos 2, 30; 26, 8. One plausible explanation for the two entries is a recent and even division of the area where one part eventually became Newton: Harris and Thacker, *VCH Cheshire*, I, p. 351.
149 As in JRUL, Bromley Davenport, 'Newton by Mottram', nos 1 and 2.
150 Richmond, *The Paston family in the fifteenth century*, pp. 4–6.
151 Harrison, 'The social and economic history of Cannock and Rugeley', p. 111. See also Kerridge, *Agrarian problems*, pp. 17–28.

that the payment is the sum first mentioned in an early thirteenth-century title deed whereby Robert Hyde of Norbury granted Newton to Robert Davenport of Davenport as a reward for good service. Davenport was to present annually a pair of white gloves to Hyde and his heirs, and a rent of 4s to William Pigot of Butley for all services, exaction and demands except foreign service.[152] In fifteenth-century inquisitions *post mortem* of the Pigot family, notice is made of this rent issuing out of Newton and Foxtwist.[153] Whatever the origins of this payment, in the late fifteenth century it symbolised Newton's dependence on Butley.

Humphrey constructed his case for the ownership of the heath using the kind of legal skills that made him an attractive employee to his fellow gentry. Behind the evidence appears a man obsessed with abolishing the payment and, like the Paston family, he used 'divers old deeds' to do so. These were later transcribed into the Newton cartulary by William Newton, quite possibly as a result of the Star Chamber case.[154] Trying to follow these arguments several centuries later is no easy task, especially as they often turn on the interpretation of an archaic legal term, or the position of a topographical feature. With painstaking detail, Humphrey attacked the rent from various angles, questioning its validity, the power it rendered, and the land and the individuals bound by it. Not only did it demand a thorough knowledge of the technicalities of land law, but all the written evidence had to be carefully recorded. Humphrey had at least three early deeds inspected to support his case,[155] while the Newtons carefully concealed others: under one deed was noted 'this deed may not be shown to pigot in anywise nor noother'[156]

Nevertheless, the attempts to win Newton through the law were repeatedly thwarted. Before Humphrey's time, an agreement had been reached between Richard Newton (Humphrey's father) and the Pigot family, when Lawrence Lowe convened a special meeting to help his step-son. While no specific mention was made of the township issue, it was agreed that John Pigot (d. 1513), head of the family, would release to Richard all 'colourable claims of iiijs [four shillings] and of things'. It came to no avail, however, and Pigot refused the release. Humphrey had a similar problem with John's son Robert Pigot (d. 1536). Humphrey noted his many requests to Pigot to demonstrate his claim to the lands and put the matter to arbitration: 'I the said Humfrey have oftymes required it and shewed my evidence before Robert Pigot and his counsel and praied him to show his and whether it were right or wrong

---

[152] JRUL, Bromley Davenport 'Newton by Mottram', no. 4; BL, Add MS 42134A, fo. 14v. Throughout the court case the Newtons claimed that the payment of white gloves was their one and only rent.
[153] For example, John Pigot (d. 1428) TNA: PRO, CHES 3/34/6.
[154] BL, Add MS 42134A, mainly fos 12–18.
[155] CRO, CR 63/1/45/6; Bodl, MS Lat. Misc.c.66, fo. 23b; BL, Add MS 42134A, fos 12v–13r.
[156] BL, Add MS 42134A, fo. 15r.

I would agree with him'.[157] Nothing happened. Humphrey was facing the power of custom, which proved more forceful than written documents and legal knowledge. Before and during the dispute, Humphrey and his tenants were seen paying the dues and participating in the township management of Butley. Regardless of whether the rent was appropriate or not, by making the payment the Newtons were continually validating the custom in the eyes of their neighbours. This is not to say that Humphrey ever gave up on the law and the value of arbitration. On another occasion, a meeting was arranged between Robert Pigot and Humphrey at Newport, Shropshire. The place was selected because it was the home of the sergeant-at-law John Salter, a Cheshire man with some experience of arbitrating local gentry disputes.[158] Humphrey, well advanced in years, had ridden down to Newport, but *en route* fell ill and was forced to turn back. A sick and desperate Humphrey sent word to Pigot that he would give him £6 13*s* 4*d* 'in hand' to have the release of the heath.[159]

Nevertheless, Humphrey had long realised that legal negotiation was not the only answer and more direct action was needed. In the opening years of the sixteenth century Humphrey approached the freeholders who held rights on the heath. This may have been in their capacity as freeholders of the manor of Butley, but possibly implies that Foxtwist Heath was a 'community' field whereby consent of all freeholders was required before the land could be converted to other uses.[160] It is a measure of Humphrey's powers of persuasion in the area that he succeeded in obtaining the necessary releases. Quitclaims were secured from William Willot (August 1500), Ellen Legh of Adlington (September 1500), Griffith Willot following the death of his father (June 1502), Joyce Crowther (October 1502) and Thomas Duncalf, the steward of Butley (1510) on various titles, messuages, lands, tenements, waters, paths and bridges they held in the area of Newton, Foxtwist and the heath. Securing the quitclaims was not without some opposition and Humphrey had to keep in mind the resistance of Thomas Legh, lord of Adlington who, as noted above, attempted to prevent neighbours increasing their control over the heath. The care with which Humphrey registered his dealings is worth detailing, and he provides interesting examples of what needed to be done at a time without an efficient and inexpensive system of land registration. The Willot release, for example, was sealed in the presence of witnesses and then delivered to Humphrey in a 'hole which is a mere

---

157 BL, Add MS 42134A fo. 16r.
158 TNA: PRO, STAC 2/30/86, m. 10r. For Salter, see p. 44 above. Among Salter's arbitration cases was the dispute between Sir Thomas Assheton and the Mainwarings of Peover, William Newton's in-laws (JRUL, Mainwaring 325). He was also a feoffee of Philip Legh of Booth who employed Humphrey as steward of Over Knutsford (KUL, Legh of Booths Charters L.94): see p. 59 above.
159 TNA: PRO, STAC 2/30/86.
160 Sylvester, 'The open fields of Cheshire', p. 32.

dych' in one of the Newton fields. Two witnesses confessed in front of two gentlemen that they had knowledge of this public event, and one later wrote a statement to 'beir true record' of the event in case 'varyance may hap to fall for want of wittenes'.[161] Such actions were doubly necessary when it came to Ellen Legh, Thomas's widowed mother. Obtaining her signature behind Thomas's back was a coup, and in need of security. Thomas's brother, Reginald, who had persuaded his mother to sign, was worried at the potential fallout. Thus he oversaw and signed his mother's quitclaim, he confessed the event in front of George Calveley, knight (who signed a deed to that effect), and confessed again in the presence of John Bradley so that if 'Reginald went furth the cuntry' John would bear record of what Reginald had seen.[162] All of the events, including Humphrey's attainment of the deed, took place outdoors in well-observed places. He was taking no chances.

A more obvious encroachment onto the heath was through the creation of a number of tenements, cottages and gardens. The importance of tenants lay in their ability to demonstrate the existence of seignorial rights. William Paston had attempted to realise this when he obtained the unfree and copyhold tenants for his new manors in Paston and Edingthorpe.[163] Similarly, too few residents would render a township too small to operate as an administrative unit.[164] When Humphrey inherited Newton in 1498 there was one messuage and a group of lands rented out at Newton, nothing like the six messuages Humphrey had read about in earlier deeds. According to the witnesses in the Star Chamber case, Humphrey set about creating another five or six tenements with cottages, and had dug out two or three places of ground for gardens on the heath. There are inconsistencies in the evidence, but the move to expand is clear, and can be corroborated by the gradual increase in tenants in the Newton rentals. By the time of Humphrey's inquisition *post mortem*, 1536, six messuages were recorded.[165] Placing tenants on the heath was a more effective way of declaring ownership than the construction of the odd fence or ditch. They would also bring in a steady source of income.[166] Yet, at the same time, tenants created problems: they had to answer to the court of Butley, and they were officials for the township. Pigot's witnesses drew attention to the occasions when the bailiff of Butley was observed demanding rents from Newton's tenants. From this point of view, a less ambiguous and more enduring mark had to be made.

---

[161] JRUL, Bromley Davenport, 'Newton by Mottram', no. 7.
[162] The original deeds of Legh and Griffith Willot are JRUL, Bromley Davenport, 'Newton by Mottram', nos 5 and 8. Copies of all four deeds can be found in BL, Add MS 42134A fos 1–2, 13r. For details of Ellen Legh's quitclaim given as a response to Humphrey's good legal advice, see p. 51 above.
[163] Richmond, *The Paston family in the fifteenth century*, p. 4.
[164] Winchester, 'The medieval vill', p. 61.
[165] Bodl, MS Lat. Misc.c.66, fos 24r, 25v. TNA: PRO, CHES 3/67/4.
[166] Dyer, *Making a living*, p. 331.

This was accomplished by the building of a chapel at Newton. Humphrey had no free right to build on the heath and he required the permission of all the freeholders of the area. He acted legally in this and consulted each relevant person in turn. In the Star Chamber case Thomas Duncalf, Thomas Willot and John Kelsall all testified that they, or their fathers, had given Humphrey permission to build on the heath. Humphrey also appeared several times before the manor court of Butley to press his claim. The main obstacle again was Robert Pigot. Thomas Duncalf, as steward of Butley, recalled that he was asked by Humphrey on numerous occasions to persuade Pigot to permit the chapel building. The strength of that wish can be gauged from Humphrey's willingness to pay the impressive amount of £6 8s (or two swans) yearly to Pigot and his heirs 'for ever'. In the end his resolve was rewarded and the chapel was built. That the chapel was later used for the manor court of Butley suggests that some deal had been struck.[167]

The chapel was a successful investment. Undoubtedly it brought spiritual benefit and this will be discussed in Chapter 5. In the context of Humphrey's landed interest, it had significant strategic value. One tempting possibility is that the chapel was intended to establish a chapelry, which would have helped create a semi-autonomous area.[168] Even if this was not Humphrey's intention, the chapel did successfully ensure that the heath became widely known in the area as 'Newton Heath'. It is striking that even Pigot's witnesses in the court case, who asserted it should be called Nether Foxtwist Heath, admitted that 'sythens the building of the same chapel' it was called 'after the name of Newtons hethe'.[169] Placing any prominent building in a landscape affects the name by which the land is known: a chapel was perhaps the quickest and most lasting way in which this name change could be effected. Again, how one interpreted documents appeared to be less important than, in this instance, what the land was called.

The issue of the heath was not settled by the time of the deaths of Humphrey Newton and Robert Pigot. To have any claim to the heath the sons, William Newton and Thomas Pigot, had to prove that their fathers had died seised of that land. The document that declared this information was the inquisition *post mortem*. The Pigot and Newton sons manipulated the inquisitions to declare the state of play at their fathers' deaths: the dispute was to continue.[170] Both Humphrey and Robert died in 1536. Robert Pigot's inquisition in April of that year claimed he had died seised of the manor of Butley and of five messuages, 200 acres of wood and 400 acres of heath and marsh in Old Foxtwist, Nether Foxtwist and Newton and Lyehall within the fee of Butley.[171] Humphrey's death in March produced an inquisition

---

167 TNA: PRO, STAC 2/30/86, m. 10r.
168 Winchester, 'Parish, township and tithing', p. 7.
169 For example, TNA: PRO, STAC 2/30/86, m. 7d.
170 Cf. Carpenter, 'The Stonor circle', p. 176; id., *Locality and polity*, pp. 285–6.
171 39th *DKR*, App.I, pp. 214–15; TNA: PRO, CHES 3/27/4.

(in September) that declared that Humphrey had died seised in his demesne as of fee in the *villa et manero de Neuto*n and in one chapel called Newton Chapel and sixty-six acres of water, heath, moor, turbury and wasteland *vocat Neuton Heth in Neuton*.[172] The eastern boundary described in the document repeated that recorded in thirteenth-century deeds. At the end of 1536, therefore, both sides had struck the opening blows that ended in the Star Chamber case a decade later.

Throughout his lordship, Humphrey attempted to recreate or elevate Newton into a township, significantly improving the status of a holding that was far less distinguished than its gentry neighbours. It was a project that paralleled the improvements in produce and industry at Newton. Acquiring Newton heath was a lifelong campaign, which was not concluded by his death. Humphrey never gained an independent Newton, although it should be remembered that independence was not an end in itself but a means to expand the boundaries of Newton and develop the estate. On that point he achieved some success by placing more tenants, gardens, the fishery and the chapel on the heath. Humphrey would have realised, however, that his prospects at Newton were limited. He lived in a crowded landscape, surrounded by families of extensive property who had held their lands for centuries. The holdings in that part of east Cheshire did not quite 'jostle' on the scale of the better-known Norfolk parishes, but the intensity to get out of the 'ruck' was almost as great.[173] For that he had to look beyond Newton.

Acquisition

As Chapter 2 explored, a common strategy and indeed the easiest way to obtain land among rising gentry families was securing a good marriage. Humphrey's marriage to Ellen Fitton, and the death of her father, Thomas, in 1506, brought the Newtons a substantial estate. The Fitton inheritance was located over a wide area of eastern Cheshire, yet the main holding and residence at Pownall was less than three miles from Newton. This quickly became the *caput* of the Newton family, and would be their main estate for the rest of the family's history. According to the inquisition *post mortem* of Ellen Newton (d. 1536) the estate included Pownall Hall, eight messuages, 100 Cheshire acres of land, forty acres of meadow, 100 acres of pasture,

---

[172] TNA: PRO, CHES 3/67/4, my emphases. Antiquarians still associated Newton with Butley into the nineteenth century. In 1810 it was as 'Butley cum Newton' that the area appeared in Lyons, *Magna Britannia*, II, part II, pp. 731, 340. In the first census of 1801, the population of Newton was included within the figure for Butley. However, in the mid-nineteenth century Newton was made a civil parish; in 1858 poor law guardians considered Newton a township, and it was stated as such in the nineteenth-century tithe assessments: Harris, *VCH Cheshire*, II, p. 227; Renaud, *Contributions*, p. 1.
[173] Richmond, *The Paston family in the fifteenth century*, pp. 1–3.

twenty acres of wood and 200 acres of moor, turf and waste in Pownall and Bollin. The stated financial worth was £6. In addition, the Fittons held lands in the Northwich hundred and Ellen's share, according to her inquisition, comprised holdings in Church Minshull, Minshull Vernon, Wrenbury and Oulton to the value of £14 14s 2d.[174] Even allowing for the likely undervaluing of the inquisition, the Fitton estate was worth in excess of £20 and had more than doubled the land and the wealth of Humphrey and his family. Pownall also carried a superior form of lordship, being the chief messuage of the Pownall fee (one of the four fees that comprised the parish of Wilmslow), and Humphrey benefited from the non-residence of the three wealthiest and knightly landholders in the parish: the Traffords of Trafford (Lancashire), the Booths of Dunham Massey and the Fittons of Gawsworth. His closest resident neighbours in the area were gentleman like himself, or below.

However, securing the inheritance was not without problems, and Humphrey would again face another long dispute, this one lasting over twenty years. Ellen Fitton had a much younger sister, Margaret (d. 1557), who was twice married: first to James Mainwaring of Croxton esquire and, secondly, to William Minshull of Minshull (d. 1557).[175] From an agreement dating to 1496, it would appear that Margaret's original portion from the inheritance was the manor of Eardswick and lands in Wrenbury and Minshull Vernon (the majority of Fitton holdings in the Northwich hundred). She would have gained a substantial area: the manor of Eardswick, thirty messuages, 360 acres of land, moieties of 400 acres of pasture and wood, and a third part of 240 acres of land, heath and turf in Wrenbury and Minshull Vernon. The value was approximately £22 a year.[176] The division of inheritances among co-heiresess, however, was prone to dispute, and so it proved with the Fitton estates.[177] The settlement was not accepted by either of the daughters and their respective husbands. Each tried in the name of his wife to procure the larger portion of the estate.

The case had all the ingredients of a protracted dispute. It involved a change of heart. The initial arrangement had conferred a large share of the Fitton estate on Margaret, but shortly afterwards Thomas Fitton publicly cancelled the agreement: Sir Edward Fitton of Gawsworth (d. 1510) recalled burning the relevant deeds in front of witnesses.[178] There were concerned parties guarding inheritance rights. In 1498 Humphrey secured from Charles

---

[174] See Map 1. The estate was held in socage tenure from the lords of Bollin, the Booths of Dunham Massey and the Traffords of Trafford, for the rent of 3s 10d per annum: TNA: PRO, CHES 3/67/5 and SC 6/HEN VIII/297, m. 6; Earwaker, *East Cheshire*, I, p. 119. In the subsidy of 1546 William Newton was assessed on lands worth £22 (TNA: PRO, E179/85/26, m. 2). In 1598 the estate was valued at £77 12s 4d (BL, Add Roll 37328). Unfortunately no estate accounts have survived for Pownall.
[175] Earwaker, *East Cheshire*, I, pp. 120–1.
[176] TNA: PRO, CHES 1/2/72, m. 4.
[177] Cf. Carpenter, *The Armburgh papers*.
[178] TNA: PRO, CHES 38/26/8. In this document Margaret is described as 'under age'.

Mainwaring, Margaret's potential father-in-law, an indenture confirming Ellen's right to half the lands and tenements in the towns of Wrenbury, Minshull Vernon, Church Minshull, Worleston and Oulton. That the Fitton–Mainwaring marriage had not yet occurred is evident from the deed's reference to the espousals of Margaret and James, or any other son of Charles Mainwaring who married Margaret.[179] There were forgeries to contend with too. In 1507 James Mainwaring reportedly falsified a deed to state that lands in Pownall and Bollin would pass to Margaret Fitton and her husband. The forgery was revealed in 1509 during an inquiry conducted by the mayor and several burgesses of Macclesfield.[180]

Mainwaring had perhaps attempted this route because Humphrey had an important advantage: he had weighty support. The feoffees of the Fitton estate included his uncle Humphrey Lowe and the overlords of Pownall, Edmund Trafford and William Booth, knights, who consistently backed the Newtons.[181] With the Pownall lands Humphrey also had the geographic advantage of living near, and then in, the Pownall estate; he was well known in the neighbourhood. In 1508 eight neighbouring landlords supported the case of Ellen Newton and declared that it was never Thomas Fitton's wish for any lands or rights in Pownall or Bollin to descend to Margaret Fitton. The witnesses included prominent county gentry such as Sir Edward Fitton of Gawsworth, Sir John Legh of Baguley and three men who had employed Humphrey for his legal and administrative skills: Sir Philip Legh of Booth, John Stanley of Etchells and William Davenport of Bramhall.[182] With their collaboration Humphrey and Ellen safely secured Pownall manor without recourse to the courts or violence, and would make further gains. In January 1508 Humphrey and Ellen acquired the lands and rights that comprised the dower of Elizabeth, widow of Thomas Fitton, in return for an annual sum of £20.[183] In August, they managed to obtain the bigger prize of Eardswick in exchange for lands in Minshull Vernon, Wrenbury, Church Minshull, Worleston and Oulton.[184]

Nevertheless, even with powerful friends, it was never a good idea to become complacent. The more distant manor of Eardswick became a growing problem, especially when Ellen's sister married William Minshull, a native of those parts. In this case Humphrey chose the increasingly common route of the central courts. In 1519–20 he and Ellen petitioned Chancery, asking for a

---

[179] 37th *DKR*, App.II, p. 501.
[180] TNA: PRO, CHES 38/26/8. Bodl, MS Lat. Misc.c.66, fo. 44r.
[181] On the advantage of powerful friends: Carpenter, *The Armburgh papers*, pp. 40, 68; Wright, *Derbyshire gentry*, ch. 5.
[182] TNA: PRO, CHES 38/26/8 and pp. 53, 59–60 above.
[183] It amounted to seven messuages, three tofts, eight gardens, 310 acres of land, meadow, pasture, wood, heath and moor in Pownall and Bollin, along with an annual rent of 28s. TNA: PRO, WALE 29/485; CHES 29/211 m. 4; WALE 30/25. Humphrey placed these lands on long lease and used them for rent: TNA: PRO, WALE 29/417.
[184] CRO, DVE 1 MX/10; CRO, ZCR 72/13/1.

dedimus potestatem to be directed to certain men acquainted with the wishes of Thomas Fitton concerning Eardswick. Humphrey wanted the answers of the chosen men to be taken to the court of Chancery and remain there as a 'recorde for the ferther knolege herafter to be had if case shall requyre'.[185] No provocation is mentioned in the deed, but it certainly produced a reaction. Not long afterwards Humphrey was again petitioning Chancery, this time accusing Minshull of using deeds to convey to himself and family an estate out of the Fitton inheritance in the Northwich hundred centring on Eardswick. In this, Margaret's status is ignored; she is merely Minshull's wife, and Ellen Newton is named as 'sole heir' to the Fitton estate.[186] In the end Humphrey and Ellen might have relented because, according to her inquisition *post mortem* of 1557, Margaret was seised in the manor of Eardswick (worth 54s 6d).[187]

The desire to expand the estate continued through the last decade of Humphrey's life. In his late sixties, Humphrey managed to extend the Newton interest in the parish of Wilmslow by initiating the gradual acquisition of Fulshaw, a manor once at the centre of the Bollin fee and lying less than a mile from Pownall. The manor was divided into two main parts: the first was held by the ubiquitous Legh of Adlington family, and the second sub-divided between the families of Verdon of Fulshaw and Davenport of Fulshaw. In the sixteenth century the Newtons gradually took hold of the share held by Verdon and Davenport. The Verdon family had close relations with the Newtons, which can be traced through land deeds to the late fourteenth century; by the early sixteenth century kinship further connected the families. Humphrey himself had acted as one of the feoffees of the Verdon estate and was an executor for the Wilmslow lands of John Verdon (d. 1522).[188] He must, therefore, have had early knowledge of the Verdon's decision to move their landed and social interests to Yorkshire. In 1530 Humphrey, alongside Thomas Verdon, then head of the family, farmed out to Humphrey's second son and namesake a number of messuages, lands and rents in the area for seven years at four marks in rent. At the end of that term in 1537 Thomas Verdon granted to the younger Humphrey Newton the farm of all his lands in Fulshaw. That the deed consistently called Humphrey 'the younger' despite the fact his father was dead, suggests that the deal had been brokered a year or two before. Eventually Humphrey junior purchased the Verdon share in

---

[185] TNA: PRO, C1/548/77. For the use of Chancery among the middling ranks of English society as 'pre-emptive action', see Haskett, 'Conscience, justice and authority', pp. 161–2.
[186] TNA: PRO, C1/548/81.
[187] TNA: PRO CHES 3/72/7. Eardswick was not included in Ellen's IPM: TNA: PRO, SC 6/HEN VIII 297.
[188] *Cheshire Sheaf*, ser. III, vol. XVII, pp. 65–6 (PCC, 25 Maynwaring).

1567, adding it to the Davenport's Fulshaw holding he had bought in 1562.[189] While the final stages of the acquisitions occurred after Humphrey's death, he had paved the way for this extension of Newton influence.

Conclusion

In 1509 Humphrey and Ellen placed all their lands in the hands of feoffees, which provides a useful survey of the Newton acquisitions by that year. It was clearly a substantial estate: it amounted to the *villae* and *maneria* of Newton, Pownall and Eardswick, twenty-six messuages, ten cottages, twelve tofts, one water mill, one fulling mill, 500 acres of land, 150 acres of meadow, 300 acres of pasture, 120 acres of wood, 180 acres of heath and 100 acres of moor and turf in Newton, Eardswick, Pownall, Bollin, Wrenbury, Minshull Vernon, Church Minshull, Wrenbury, Oulton, Milton, Handley, Huxley and Golbourne Bellow.[190] This was a considerable improvement on the Newton estate (worth £11) that Humphrey inherited in 1497–8. He could measure his land in terms of hundreds rather than tens of acres. These holdings would have lifted Humphrey above the ranks of many of his Cheshire neighbours, and indeed much of English society too. In Leicestershire and Warwickshire the majority of the gentry are shown to hold only a single manor, and a significant number held none at all.[191] In terms of land and wealth, there was no mistaking Humphrey's gentility and membership of England's elite.

Marriage evidently played a key role in forming this new estate, but Humphrey's personal drive and ambition cannot be understated. He appears a man of conviction, with a reluctance to accept failure. His enterprise and desire for change can be seen in the notes penned in his commonplace book, the letters sent to Chancery and the numbers of witnesses he dragged out into fields and in front of local gentry to support his case. In particular, his ride down to Shropshire, while at an advanced age and ill, suggests a man who would make every effort to win. It is noteworthy that, although Newton's projects have been considered separately, they were organised simultaneously. The date 1498 has figured on several occasions and in the 1520s, when the Newtons were still trying to secure the Fitton inheritance, Humphrey was keeping up the pressure to gain 'Newton Heath' and assert township rights.

Overall, Humphrey's strategy represented the steady accumulation of lands in a limited area of eastern Cheshire. There are no records of Humphrey actively seeking lands elsewhere. Indeed, the holdings in the Broxton

---

[189] Transcriptions of the Fulshaw deeds by the nineteenth-century antiquarian J.P. Earwaker can be found in CRO, ZCR 63/1/43 pp. 49, 51, 59, 69, 157; Earwaker, *East Cheshire*, I, pp. 151–2.
[190] TNA: PRO, CHES 29/211 m. 7.
[191] Acheson, *A gentry community*, p. 49; Carpenter, *Locality and polity*, p. 89; see also Saul, *Knights and esquires*, p. 225.

hundred, too few to render Newton any potential weight in the area, were mortgaged or leased out in order to finance the eastern expansion. Reducing and rationalising the possessions was a strategy that overcame the friction of distance, the problems of travel costs and added bureaucracy. It is possible that Humphrey wanted to further his influence in the area by connecting his estates of Pownall and Newton, seen in the gradual purchase of Fulshaw and attempted encroachments into Dean Row. No records voice that claim or suggest he thought it feasible in his lifetime, but Humphrey may have seen it as an aim of his descendants.

It was not an estate built on violence. Humphrey was not a man prone to personal feuding or political power struggles and he was accused of few hostile acts, although it has to be admitted that when one act did occur (against Brown) it was against his weakest neighbour. Rather than adopting the aggressive strategies of families such as the Pastons or the Armburghs, Humphrey compares more closely to the families of Plumpton and Townshend: he put considerable faith in the legal process and the power of the written record.[192] The concerted effort Humphrey made to collect relevant material and the meticulous detail with which he analysed the records show his legalistic mind at work. On the whole Humphrey appears to have stayed within the letter of the law. He put matters to arbitration and he went through the proper channels of securing quitclaims from resident townspeople. Whatever devious interpretation of deeds occurred, no obvious criminal activity was involved.

But what had been demonstrated to Humphrey time and again was that documents could not work by themselves. It depended on the witnesses, on the acceptance and enforcement of arbitration, and on local power structures. Proximity to the desired land was of some importance: Humphrey had the advantage in both Newton and Pownall in being a resident landlord, and he appears to have had a good relationship with the freeholders in the neighbourhood. More importantly, power lay with who you knew. Humphrey secured Pownall because he persuaded the most powerful men of that area to support his claim. In the environs of Newton, lesser neighbours were willing to risk the wrath of the Leghs or Pigots and allow (or perhaps could not stop) Humphrey's encroachment on the heath. Humphrey's influence would not have spread much outside of the Pownall–Newton axis, but in this part of Cheshire, he was someone to watch.

---

[192] Richmond, *The Paston family in the fifteenth century*; Carpenter, *The Armburgh papers*, p. 51 and *passim*; Moreton, *The Townshends*, p. 194; Kirby, 'A fifteenth-century family', p. 109.

5

Beliefs

We know much about the gentry's personal responses to land disputes, prominent as they are in court records and family letters of the fifteenth and sixteenth centuries. Uncovering personal religious beliefs, however, proves more of a challenge.[1] Too often the evidence that survives is associated with the end of life, such as a will or a monument. These inevitably carry the heavy presence of death and can only obliquely reveal what might have been a person's religion during his or her lifetime. Fortunately, while the most conspicuous relic of Humphrey Newton's piety is his tomb, the survival of his commonplace book permits a rare glimpse of his 'living' religion. It may not offer a window into his soul, but it does shine a spotlight on several aspects of his spirituality and the influence the Church had upon his everyday actions. We can see what he knew of Christianity, what he was particularly devoted to; we can consider his contemplative and active piety, and assess the relationship between his personal devotion and communal practices. Through this discussion the nature of Humphrey's piety will be compared to pre-Reformation society at large, and specifically to the gentry. The spiritual outlook of England's landed society and its commitment to parish worship has divided scholarly opinion, and Humphrey offers a fascinating case study through which to review the debate.[2]

The written word

Humphrey's beliefs would have been formed during his childhood and informed by the teachings and example of his parents, godparents, relatives, neighbours and friends. Most of this early instruction would have been passed on verbally and would have focused on basic prayers and moral behaviour. The household, and communal occasions such as meal-times, provided a focus for instruction. Humphrey's list of prayers to be said before and after dinner exemplifies the systematic saying of grace that had become a feature of many aristocratic households since the fourteenth century.[3] As Humphrey

---

[1] Swanson, *Catholic England*, p. 1; Aston, *Faith and fire*, p. 1.
[2] The debate will be outlined on pp. 124–5 below.
[3] Bodl, MS Lat. Misc.c.66, fo. 34b. Pantin, 'Instructions', p. 339; Mertes, *The English noble household*, pp. 140–8; Orme, *Medieval children*, pp. 204–5.

grew older, the written word became a significant source of his spiritual knowledge. During the fifteenth century the devotional works in circulation, particularly in the vernacular, grew in number. By the early Tudor period, a gentleman could be familiar with collections of sermons, confession manuals, or a vernacular bible, as well as a number of 'how to' books that recounted the correct way to live and die well. The dissemination of spiritual writings was promoted by the Church, which wanted the laity better instructed in leading a Christian life in order to assess their own lives and aim for improvement. These writings found their way into the personal manuscripts of fifteenth-century gentlemen. The collections of Robert Thornton, lord of East Newton, Yorkshire, reveal that he looked for guidance in texts such as the *Lay Folk's catechism*, Hilton's *Epistle of Mixed Life*, and *The Abbey of the Holy Ghost*.[4] Humphrey's own selection indicates access to a wide range of religious material, and shows his familiarity with both Middle English and Latin texts. Extracts from the *Old Testament* books of Numbers and Deuteronomy, St Augustine, Mirk's *Festial* (a collection of English sermons arranged for the ecclesiastical year), William Lynwood's *Provinciale* (a Latin codification of canon law) and a treatise on the seven deadly sins were transcribed alongside several copies of Marian and Christocentric prayers.

In surveying Humphrey's choices three conclusions can be drawn. The first is the strong practical nature of the selection. What they all offered was a basic knowledge, instructing on how to live well, rather than detailed theological exposition. In this regard Humphrey's choice compares closely to the religious entries found in two near-contemporary East Anglian commonplace books: that of the church reeve Robert Reynes of Acle and the so-called 'Book of Brome'. In his analysis of these works Eamon Duffy pointed to the lack of 'deep religious introspection', and the focus on moralistic writings and the need for self-discipline.[5] Their belief that an individual could avoid God's wrath simply by not swearing is echoed in Humphrey's extract from a book on the seven deadly sins. This comprised around fifty lines from Chaucer's *Parson's Tale*, although Humphrey knew it as a penitential treatise entitled a 'Boke of Schrift'. This is the diatribe that begins 'What sey we of hem þat delites þaym in swerynge and holden it a gentrye or manly dede to swere gret oþes'.[6] A similar 'lightweight' feel can be sensed in Humphrey's sermon extract from Mirk's *Festial* and his two short Latin pieces from St Augustine, which centred on the last days. They provided easy, moralistic information that was not intellectually challenging.[7] The Latin excerpts from the book of

---

[4] Erler, 'Devotional literature', p. 495; Brown, *Popular piety*, pp. 205–6; Swanson, *Church and society*, p. 276; Arnold, *Belief and unbelief*, pp. 58–65; Nicholls, *Seeable signs*, pp. 150–7; Hughes, *Pastors and visionaries*, p. 295.
[5] Duffy, *The stripping of the altars*, pp. 71–5.
[6] Bodl, MS Lat. Misc.c.66, fo. 128r. *The Canterbury Tales: The Parson's Tale*, lines I 600–21, 626–8.
[7] Bodl, MS Lat. Misc.c.66, fos 62r, 65v. Swanson, *Catholic England*, pp. 51–2. That the

Numbers and Deuteronomy demanded more thought, but their application to a legal argument on the wrongfulness of disinheritance points to ruminations of a more secular kind.[8]

Humphrey's sources were not as populist and entertaining as those preferred by Robert Reynes and the writers of Brome. Humphrey favoured more sober and serious works to the rhymed saints' lives and religious plays found in the East Anglian collections. Yet, at the same time, there are no traces of the sophisticated spiritual writings found in other miscellanies. Humphrey's book is far less doctrinal than Robert Thornton's works or the contemporary commonplace book of London merchant Richard Hill, which contains longer, detailed works on the laws of the church, the sacraments, the merits of the mass, a Latin tract on the Ten Commandments and a Latin guide to confession.[9]

A second conclusion is that Humphrey appears highly sensitive to current trends of worship. Late medieval religion was not a static set of practices, but was continually developing, with new cults emerging. During the fifteenth century the new observances were overwhelmingly Marian and Christocentric devotions, and these were central to Humphrey's faith. His worship of the Virgin Mary, shared by his fellow parishioners at Wilmslow, can be seen throughout Humphrey's book, and he purposely sought out prayers and places associated with the Virgin.[10] On a visit to a church in Newark (presumably Nottinghamshire) he copied out lines from a chained book entitled 'Miraclez of Our Lady with oþer marveils'. Such miracle collections circulated widely in medieval England, and often appear in miscellanies such as that compiled by Robert Reynes. Interestingly, Humphrey did not transcribe any miracles – at least not into his commonplace book – but, rather, selected a short devotional prayer to *Virgo fecunda piissima*.[11] Perhaps it was the book that drew him to the church; it at least indicates that Humphrey was in the habit of visiting non-local churches. On another occasion he went on a pilgrimage to a place called Radcliff. It was evidently worthwhile because he gave his sister money to travel there too. Again the exact place is unknown, but the nearest geographically would be Radcliff in Lancashire, where the

---

Festial as a whole was an accessible text intended for the 'common people' rather than an intellectual elite is argued in Ford, *John Mirk's Festial*, pp. 11–13.

[8] Bodl, MS Lat. Misc.c.66, fo. 9r.

[9] Duffy, *The stripping of the altars*, pp. 75–6.

[10] Wilmslow church was dedicated to Mary, and gentry of the parish supported an image and a Marian service. See the wills of John Verdon (d. 1522) and Thomas Davenport (d. 1523). *Cheshire Sheaf*, 3rd ser. XVII (1920), p. 65; Piccope, *Lancashire and Cheshire wills*, I, p. 40.

[11] Bodl, MS Lat. Misc.c.66, fo.18r. Louis, *The commonplace book of Robert Reynes*, p. 228. For manuscripts of Marian miracles see Meale, 'The Miracles of Our Lady'. For the importance of Mary to the landowning elite see Hughes, *The religious life of Richard III*, pp. 18–23; Gibson, *The theater of devotion*, ch. 6.

parish church was dedicated to the Virgin.[12] Alongside the Marian devotion, Humphrey shared the growing fascination with Christ, his humanity and his bodily sufferings. He transcribed a copy of *Richard de Caistre's Hymn*, a highly popular fifteenth-century lyric, which survives in at least seventeen manuscripts. It is a simple Middle English prayer that praises Jesus as 'heyven kynge' and 'almyghty god in trinitie' while asking for his compassion: 'Brynge the saules into blisse'.[13] Humphrey's interest in the physicality of Christ and the details of the passion is reflected in his copy of the measurement of an imprint of Christ's foot, and in his drawings of Veronica and the vernicle, the Sacred Heart and the five wounds of Christ.[14]

There is nothing unexpected here, but it is noteworthy that Humphrey's devotion focused wholly on the universal cults promoted by the Church. There is little local about his observations; no regional saints are mentioned and there is nothing comparable to the verse life of St Anne found in Robert Reynes's book or the verse life of St Margaret in the Book of Brome.[15] The only significant reference to a saint comes in Humphrey's Purgatory treatise (of which, more below), where a spirit leading the protagonist through the otherworld is identified as St George. His name was a later interpolation, and it is difficult to judge whether its being an afterthought should lessen or increase its importance. What is striking is that this again is an international (and a national) saint, rather than a local figure of note. The huge popularity of St George was spreading through Cheshire in the 1490s, as witnessed in the fraternity of St George at St Peter's Chester and in an impressive wall painting at Astbury parish church.[16] Was Humphrey persuaded by his power, or by the fashion? Given the emphasis often placed on local saints and their relics in pre-Reformation worship, their absence in Humphrey's manuscript is perhaps surprising, although it is a situation shared with contemporary Cheshire testators.[17]

The spread of religious literature in the fifteenth century assisted the move towards private devotion as individuals aimed for a more personal relationship with God. The third conclusion to be drawn from Humphrey's writings is the meditative nature of parts of the book, linked to the Church's

---

[12] Bodl, MS Lat. Misc.c.66, fo. 29v.
[13] Bodl, MS Lat. Misc.c.66, fo. 106r. *NIMEV*, no. 1727; Brown (ed.) *Religious lyrics of the fifteenth century*, no. 64, pp. 98–100, 313–14. Humphrey's version does not have the first three verses and begins on the third line of the fourth verse (line 15 in Brown).
[14] Bodl, MS Lat. Misc.c.66, fo. 9v. For footprint and Veronica see p. 168 and p. 188 respectively.
[15] Louis (ed.) *The commonplace book*; Smith (ed.) *A commonplace book*, pp. 107–18.
[16] Youngs, '*A vision in a trance*', p. 217 and ns 25–7; Richmond, 'Religion and the fifteenth-century English gentleman', p. 197; Gill, 'Now help St George', pp. 91–102.
[17] For example, Whiting, *Blind devotion*, ch. 4; Brown, *Church and society*, ch. 3; Duffy, *The stripping of the altars*, ch. 5. For Chester: Jones, *The church in Chester*, p. 115.

drive to encourage people to contemplate the Passion.[18] On the final folio of his commonplace book Humphrey drew a large red heart to represent the Sacred Heart of Christ. As can be seen in Plate 3, the crown of thorns hovers above and the names of Jesus, John and Mary are prominently written; the wounds to Christ's hands and feet are marked with four black circles, while a lozenge shape cut represents the side wound. It is the picture of Christ's crucifixion, seen on so many rood lofts, reduced to its bare essentials to emphasise Christ's sufferings.[19] Both the Heart and Wounds were widespread observances in fifteenth-century Europe and depictions can be found on many devotional objects of late medieval England, including woodcuts, carvings and jewellery, particularly rings.[20] At the same time they gained new symbolic presence in masses, prayers, candles and mourners at many funeral services, particularly among the gentry. In 1527 Humphrey witnessed the will of Nicholas Jodrell of Yeardsley, gentleman, who requested 'five massez of the blessed woundez' to be said for his soul.[21]

The placing of a Sacred Heart image in a personal manuscript was encouraged as a focus for contemplation. Humphrey's eye-catching drawing would have found favour with writers such as Lanspergius (d. 1539), a Carthusian of Cologne, and an enthusiastic promoter of the Sacred Heart. He urged worshippers to 'have an image of the Divine Heart, or of the Five Wounds … (and) put it in some place by which you often pass, so that it will recall you to your practice and exercise of love towards God'.[22] These images were believed to be an important part of Christian instruction, particularly among the illiterate. Humphrey alludes to this quality in the prayer he wrote underneath the Heart: 'Pray to Owr Lady aves seven / the crede of þe appostelis ffor þe mede of heven / ffor his lofe þat ȝou bozt/ teche þaym þat rede can not'.[23] The most visually striking of the wounds was the side wound, which had come to enjoy a worship of its own by the late fifteenth century.[24] It was perceived as an entry into Christ's heart, a route to grace and a source of redemption. It was a powerful image in the meditations of the mystics and Humphrey may

---

[18] Pantin, 'Instructions'; Carey, 'Devout literate laypeople'; Duffy, *The stripping of the altars*, p. 62 and, id., *Marking the hours*, p. 55. For new forms of personal devotion: Brown, *Popular piety*, pp. 202–8.

[19] For the separation of aspects of Christ's sufferings on images see Kamerick, *Popular piety*, p. 166.

[20] Rhodes, 'Private devotions', p. 434; Beckwith, *Christ's body*, p. 58; Middleton-Stewart, *Inward purity*, pp. 122–7.

[21] JRUL, Jodrell 39; Pfaff, *New liturgical feasts*, p. 89; Pfaff, 'The English devotion', pp. 75–90. For the response of the gentry to these new fashionable cults see Brown, *Popular piety*, pp. 103, 253.

[22] Gougaud, *Devotional and ascetic practices*, p. 101.

[23] This echoes the famous opinion of Gregory the Great (590–604) who defended the use of images by Christians as a means to instruct the illiterate in the faith. Kamerick, *Popular piety*, pp. 1–4; Os, *The art of devotion*, p. 157.

[24] Gougaud, *Devotional and ascetic practices*, p. 90, and Simpson, 'On the measure of the wound', pp. 357–74.

have shared their desire to experience Christ's suffering and find security.[25] During the fifteenth century it was thought that the exact size of the wound (the *mensura vulneris*) was known, which is why Humphrey wrote around the wound 'þis is ye mesure of þe wound of owr lord Ihu criste þat be sufferd on þe rode for owre redemcion'. The worship of the measure had received an impetus with the issuing of a seven-year indulgence by Pope Innocent VIII to all those who meditated on the measure of the wound or who wore or kissed the image.[26] Honouring the wounds was a means to gain protection from a range of horrific illnesses and deaths. It would be gained by uttering a simple prayer, such as the common, short prayer that Humphrey copied beneath the heart: 'Vulnera quinque Dei fuit medicina mei'.[27]

Humphrey had therefore filled the page with several interlinked elements of these new devotional cults. There was much to catch his eye and his conscience. One final example relates to the number of wounds on Christ's body. Although there were five principal wounds, Jesus was often portrayed with multiple incisions. Above the Heart Humphrey included one of the traditional numbers of wounds (5,475) that Christ suffered. As such he was reminding himself not only that humankind had inflicted the wounds on Christ, but that it was in the process of inflicting many more. While a point for rumination, there was also a positive side: the wounds could act as antidotes to particular sins because the blood and water that flowed from the wounds symbolised Christ's cleansing power. Veneration of the side wound drew attention to the maker of the wound: the centurion Longinus with his lance. In making the wound Longinus had opened Christ's heart to humanity and allowed the redeeming blood and water of Jesus to wash over the earth. As a result Longinus appears in numerous charms and short prayers and Humphrey himself transcribed one of the most common prayers, appropriately one on the staunching of blood.[28]

The written text therefore performed an important role in Humphrey's piety, facilitating religious practices that were a mixture of the contemplative and the practical. With them Humphrey praised and worshipped God but, as the last example indicates, he was also expecting something in return.

---

[25] Rhodes, 'Private devotions', pp. 438–42.
[26] Gougaud, *Devotional and ascetic practices*, p. 101.
[27] These are the first two lines of what is known as the prayer of the seraphic mother: Gougaud, *Devotional and ascetic practices*, p. 83. Duffy, *The stripping of the altar*, p. 245; Kamerick, *Popular piety*, pp. 180–3.
[28] Bodl, MS Lat. Misc.c.66, fo. 3r. Gray, 'Some notes on Middle English charms', p. 62; Nichols, *Seeable signs*, pp. 14–15.

Protect me

There were physical and spiritual dangers aplenty in early Tudor society. Plague remained a recurrent event and new diseases emerged, such as the sweating sickness, which ravaged England from the late fifteenth century. In Chester, serious outbreaks of disease occurred in 1506 (sweat) and 1515 (plague).[29] Life expectancy and infant mortality rates were poor, with four of Humphrey's own children dying in childhood. Death could strike at any time, as Sir George Booth of Dunham Massey (d. 1531) observed in his will: 'consideryng yt ye lif of man is mortall and that ye houre of death is uncertone and much dredfull'.[30] Equally unpredictable, but infinitely more perilous, were dangers to the soul. Humans were considered weak and easily tempted into sin by evil spirits that walked abroad. The problem of not knowing when death would arrive, or when sin would tempt, drove what Duffy has called 'the Christian's need for eternal vigilance'.[31]

Help was near, however, in the conquering power of Christ, in the intercessory and protective power of Mary, and in a panoply of saints who covered every conceivable disease and problem. Prayers invoking their names in order to battle evil spirits and diseases can be found in many private devotional collections and miscellanies. In viewing these it is obvious that fifteenth-century worshippers did not simply offer up a prayer and hope for the best. Rather, they believed that by following a particular procedure, they would make the spiritual power work for them; a whole range of words and objects were believed to have talismanic qualities. Humphrey was clearly of this mind. In one example, he listed a series of ten masses, which, if sung on ten consecutive days, were said to deliver the commissioner or singer from whatever tribulation, sickness or adversity he or she was currently suffering. The benefits were assumed to be automatic, as long as the masses were sung correctly.[32]

This was not his only protective aid and Humphrey made sure he had several readily to hand. He carried in his purse the widely known 'letter to Charlemagne' and the accompanying prayer, the 'crux christi'. In carrying and reciting the prayer he believed, as the letter explained, that he was protected against evil, disease and sudden death. The power lay in the regular repetition of the name of Christ and in the drawing of the cross, denoting when a person was required to cross himself or herself on the body or in the air. The protection could be personalised by adding the name of choice in spaces specially provided. The fifteenth-century Yorkshire gentleman Robert Thornton chose to do this in his letter, and Humphrey also made sure that

---

[29] Morris, *Chester*, p. 65; Zieglar, *The Black Death*, p. 189. Lewis and Thacker (eds) *A history*, p. 71; Slack, *The impact of the plague*, p. 268; JRUL, English MS 202, fo. 55.
[30] Piccope, *Lancashire and Cheshire wills*, I, p. 93.
[31] Duffy, *The stripping of the altars*, p. 266.
[32] Bodl, MS Lat. Misc.c.66, fo. 16v. Bossy, 'Prayers'; Brown, *Church and society*, p. 77.

he received all due advantages by adding his name in the allotted spaces.[33] Humphrey's faith in the name of Christ, usually combined with the power of the cross, is visible in other protective charms. His prayer against the 'axes' or attacks of diseases – which can similarly be found in Robert Reynes's manuscript – centred on a dialogue between Christ and Peter. The power of Biblical characters is seen in two other prayers, with one, beginning 'Omnipotens sempiterne Deus', containing a lengthy list: Christ and Mary appear alongside the angels and archangels, John the Baptist, the twelve apostles, the four evangelists, the holy martyrs and confessors, and the holy virgins.[34] Again it is noteworthy that Humphrey's prayers are overwhelmingly Christocentric and Bibliocentric. No recent or local saints are ever called upon.

Humphrey's collection was not solely for his own benefit. As head of a household he needed to safeguard those in his care. Late medieval society was sensitive to the dangers and pain which women experienced in childbirth and Humphrey transcribed two prayers with this in mind.[35] One was a Latin prayer widely used by pregnant women, which asked for strength and protection in the times ahead. Humphrey made sure his wife benefited by inserting 'Ellen' in the spaces left for the recipient's name.[36] The whole prayer was often cited over water, which was then drunk by the woman, presumably before childbirth commenced. A second prayer, entitled 'for þe delyverance of childe' was designed for use during the birth itself. The prayer was written on a slip of paper that was intended to be attached to the sole of the right foot of the mother. It used a common formula that listed key biblical births to be said along with three *paternosters* and three *aves*.[37] The prayer illustrates the strong impulse across Catholic Europe to attach words physically to the woman's body during labour. There are numerous examples of similar prayers written in wax, on paper or parchment and attached to a mother's

---

[33] Bodl, MS Lat. Misc.c.66, fo. 69r. Horstman, *Yorkshire writers*, pp. 376–7; Duffy, *The stripping of the altars*, pp. 274–5 and, id., *Marking the hours*, p. 77; Bossy, 'Prayers', p. 42. For the type of purse Humphrey may have carried see Pantin, 'Instructions', p. 398.

[34] Bodl, MS Lat. Misc.c.66: the prayer on fo. 91r was also copied on fo. 69v. That on 91v contains the name of Agnes, which suggests it was meant for one of Humphrey's sisters (for whom see pp. 18 and 28 above). For Reynes: Louis (ed.) *The commonplace book*, p. 30. For discussion: Simpson, 'On the measure', pp. 370–1, and Duffy, *Marking the hours*, pp. 105–6. Another prayer-charm in Humphrey's book employed four red tiles bearing the names of the evangelists (fo. 39b), which can be compared with examples discussed in Pettigrew, 'Observations', p. 401.

[35] Mirk, *Instructions for parish priests*, p. 3 (lines 77–83); Stoertz, 'Suffering and survival', pp. 102–3; Rawcliffe, *Medicine*, p. 200.

[36] Bodl, MS Lat Misc c 66, fos 73v–74r.

[37] It begins 'Anna peperit Samuelem Elizabeth Johannem Maria Ihesu Saluatorem nostrum': Bodl, MS Lat. Misc.c.66, fo. 40br. A similar prayer can be found among Humphrey's medical recipes (fo. 87r). For comparison see BL, Harley MS 1735, fo. 40r; Gray, 'Some notes on Middle English charms', p. 63; Stoertz, 'Suffering and survival', pp. 107–8.

foot or thigh, bound to the right knee, or placed on the woman's stomach.[38] In more ways than one the woman's body was screaming for help.

Together these practices show that Humphrey believed that an individual could draw upon supernatural power for his or her own ends. The goals discussed so far were serious ones: to protect the person at points of vulnerability, at moments of danger. However, the attempt to summon powers could be undertaken for many other reasons, such as protecting animals or property, or even for the purposes of entertainment. Humphrey clearly enjoyed magic tricks and collected several examples, in some measure tempering his sober image.[39] A few were very simple to perform: the heating of an iron hoop to make it hop around a room. For others to succeed a conjuring element was demanded. One mischievous example is the charm intended 'to make a woman to daunce when she comes in to house'. The words 'Anna cadon casua' were written on a clean sheet of paper and placed under the door stone. A woman entering the house would immediately dance and would only stop when the paper was removed. In addition, Humphrey noted how to make a woman talk in her sleep, how to make those sitting at the table fall asleep, how to understand birdsong, and how to become free from chains and fetters. All entailed using a power derived from written words, many nonsensical, which no doubt added to the 'magic' of the formulae. Letters were chosen for what they looked like and how they sounded. It is the repetitive, alliterative sounds that mesmerise in Humphrey's charm against mad dogs: the words 'Arebus alibus rivet rivat apolluit que, ariat arrivat rivet rivat apolluit' were written on cheese and fed to the dogs.[40]

Humphrey was not unusual in his interests and these recipes are regular finds in medieval manuscripts of both country landowners and city dwellers. In early sixteenth-century London, the merchant Richard Hill copied a similar set of puzzles and pranks into his commonplace book, including how to make a man look as if he had two heads.[41] Both Humphrey and Hill may have taken these tricks from a 'book of secrets'. These were filled with recipes, formulae and experiments taken from astrology, lapidaries and herbals that were accredited to the teachings of famous philosophers; they were billed as containing the secrets of nature. Two of the best known were

---

[38] For example, BL, Sloane MS 3160, fo. 169r. For modern printed versions: Ogden (ed.) *Liber de diversis medicinis*, p. 57; Cockayne (ed.) *Leechdoms, wortcunning and starcraft*, p. 362.
[39] Bodl, MS Lat. Misc.c.66, fo. 129r. Compare with Kieckhefer, *Magic in the Middle Ages*, p. 91.
[40] Bodl, MS Lat. Misc.c.66, fo. 41b. This is a scrap of paper torn from a deed and the hand does not appear to be Humphrey's. Cheese was a popular medium for charms and used by Richard Hill: Dyboski (ed.) *Songs, carols*, p. xli. See too Thomas, *Religion and the decline*, p. 219 and Hewitt, 'Medical recipes', p. 75.
[41] Discussed in Parker, *The commonplace book*, p. 73.

the *Book of Secrets* by Albertus Magnus and the *Secretum Secretorum*, and Humphrey certainly had access to the latter.[42]

In post-Reformation England many of these practices would be condemned as superstitious. Even in the pre-Reformation era, episcopal enquiries, religious writers and confessional manuals criticised the credulous masses who placed their trust in charms.[43] One such view is voiced in Chaucer's *Parson's Tale*, where the Parson attacked the 'þilke horible swerynge of adiuracion and coniuracion' of 'false enchantours or nigramanciens' who curse against Christ and 'holy church'. Scorned are those who try to make divinations from the noises of birds and animals, dreams, the creaking of doors and houses, and the gnawing of rats. Nor is he impressed with charms for wounds and illnesses. If they have any effect, which the Parson doubts, it is probably because God had ordained this to happen. These lines have been summarised because Humphrey himself was sufficiently struck by them to transcribe them into his commonplace book on the folio immediately preceding his list of tricks.[44] It is a curious juxtaposition. Did he not appreciate the message of his extract or does it suggest that Humphrey was sceptical about his tricks and charms? More probably the lines demonstrate that he recognised the difference between an appeal to God and the exploitation of the mysteries of nature. The Church itself promoted the idea that objects and words had spiritual power. The force of evil was an important part of the liturgy; baptism used holy water and the sign of the cross to expel the devil; and the power of names was a reflection of the Church's own emphasis on the power of the Name of Jesus. The clerical author of *Dives and Pauper* condemned the use of written charms to ward off sickness, but not if they were the *paternoster*, creed or holy writ.[45] On these grounds, none of Humphrey's 'protective' charms was in opposition to Church teaching; each either begin or end *in nomine patris*. A few of his tricks – trying to catch thieves and understanding birdsong – would have drawn critical clerical comment. But neither his nor Richard Hill's collection of tricks was meant to be malicious, merely amusing. Ultimately, tapping into a source of power was not questioned as long as it was the right kind of power, and was used for good ends.

---

[42] Bodl, MS Lat. Misc.c.66, fo. 123v, and pp. 159–60 below. For books of secrets see Thorndike, *History of magic*, II, pp. 751–812; Best and Brightman (eds) *The book of secrets*; Eamon, 'The book of secrets', pp. 26–49. Recipes for invisible writing, jumping hoops, sleep talking, escaping from chains and catching thieves all appear; a recipe for a dancing woman has yet to be found.

[43] Duffy, *The stripping of the altars*, p. 73.

[44] Bodl, MS Lat. Misc.c.66, fo. 128r–v. The lines from the *Parson's Tale* are taken from Humphrey's own transcription, a full text of which can be found in Youngs, 'The Parson's Tale', pp. 214–16.

[45] Barnum (ed.) *Dives and Pauper*, vol. 1, pp. 157–8, 162; Kieckhefer, 'The specific rationality of medieval magic', p. 835; Duffy, *The stripping of the altars*, p. 279; Brown, *Church and society*, pp. 3, 7. Daniell, *Death and burial*, p. 26; Arnold, *Belief and unbelief*, p. 97.

As Humphrey's examples show, the hazy line between accepted and condemned charms was not one that divided the elite from the lower levels of society, or indeed town from country.[46] Humphrey was not living in poverty; he had a roof over his head, regular food on the table and a choice of warm clothing to wear. It was not simply basic needs or adverse economic conditions that drove people to seek solace in charms. Humphrey used protective devices for reassurance, to help avoid sudden death, and to ward off disease. Despite his everyday, practical knowledge of writing, it did not stop him believing in the symbolic, magical power of the written word; perhaps he was even the more inclined to value it.

Save me

Humphrey's beliefs and charms provided sources of comfort and support throughout his life. Yet his wealth afforded him sufficient leisure time to ponder the reality that earthly life was short; a much longer-term concern was the fate of his soul after death. Humphrey, like his fellow Christians, never doubted the existence of an afterlife. Heaven and Hell were possible destinations, but by the fifteenth century Purgatory had become engraved on the consciences of western Christians as the place allotted to the majority of souls. First officially defined in 1274, it allowed for those who had yet to fulfil the penance for their earthly sins to make satisfaction in the afterlife. Unlike hell, it was a temporary phase, and the general view held that the dead would remain in this transitional state until cleansed, or until the last Judgement and the Second Coming of Christ.[47]

What many Christians wanted to know was the location, appearance and the experiences to be expected of the afterlife. While neither the Bible nor key theological thinkers offered much in the way of description, a range of popular literature provided detailed accounts of Heaven, Hell, Purgatory and paradise. Visions of the otherworld were among the most useful. These told of apparitions visiting the living with tales of purgatory, or of individuals suffering near-death experiences and seeing the otherworld for themselves. They were highly derivative, and were influenced by key texts like the eighth-century *Vision of Drythelm* and the twelfth-century *Vision of Tundale*. During the fifteenth century these tales became readily available in Middle English. They featured in several gentlemen's miscellanies, and were considered suffi-

---

[46] For the possible division between town and country see Duffy, *The stripping of the altars*, pp. 73–7.
[47] In the English context see Burgess, '"A fond thing vainly invented"', pp. 56–84; Duffy, *The stripping of the altars*, ch. 10; Matsuda, *Death and purgatory*, ch. 1.

ciently popular to be printed. *The Revelation to the Monk of Eynsham*, a translation of a twelfth-century Latin prose account, was printed *c*.1483.[48]

Humphrey not only read this literature, but he contributed to it. On six pages of his commonplace book he recorded the otherworld vision of John Newton, a draper of Congleton, who had a near-death experience in 1492. In so doing he provides only the fourth Middle English otherworld vision known to be composed in the fifteenth century.[49] Humphrey's is the only surviving text of the vision he entitled *A vision in a trance*, and possibly the only account ever made of the incident. It is written as a local event and authenticity is implied in the personal details of John Newton's name and occupation, and the names of his wife and brother. There was a prominent family of Newton in fifteenth-century Congleton, with a John Newton holding the position of mayor in 1469–70.[50] It would not be surprising if Humphrey had heard of the vision on one of his many visits as steward to Congleton manor. Given the shared surname with John, this could have been a family story. We do not know. Ultimately, whether it was true or not is less important than the intention that it be seen as an actual occurrence, and in this case a personal revelation. Conventional though the visions were, it was the individual touches that helped to make them appear 'real'.

Humphrey's creative role in producing the account is difficult to gauge. Was he transcribing a story he had heard first-hand or as hearsay? Did he copy it verbatim or in a loose paraphrase, or did he simply reproduce an existing record? The evidence suggests that he at least influenced the style of some of the passages, and it is not too fanciful to see some elements as the product of a gentle outlook. Paradise, for example, was not described as a temple or a church, but as a grand hall with high walls, a dais and central hearth. The dance of the souls around the hearth seems distinctly courtly as they lined up in a row and went 'sobrely and noþer leep nor hopped'. These were heavenly steps, not the manic dances of the damned – or indeed the uncouth leaping of village dances. Moreover, there is a wonderful understatement whereby the noises of the souls in Purgatory – described as ear-piercing screams in other visions – are likened to 'servauntez at their rising in a gentleman place'.[51] One had to live in a certain context to know and write that.

---

[48] Discussions on the late medieval English visions can be found in Keiser, 'The progress of Purgatory', pp. 72–100; Easting, '"Send thine heart into Purgatory"', pp. 185–203; and Matsuda, *Death and Purgatory*. Otherworld visions in the miscellanies of English gentry households include the *Vision of Tundale* in the Heege manuscript: Hardman (ed.) *The Heege manuscript*, no. 35, fos 98r–157v; and *Owen Miles* in the Brome manuscript: Smith (ed.) *A commonplace book*, pp. 80–106.
[49] Bodl, MS Lat. Misc.c.66, fos 21r–23v. A full analysis and complete text can be found in Youngs, '*A vision in a trance*', pp. 212–34.
[50] Stephens (ed.) *History of Congleton*, appendix B.
[51] Bodl, MS Lat. Misc.c.66, fo. 22r. Youngs '*A vision in a trance*', p. 229. See p. 190 below.

What can firmly be said is that Humphrey owned a highly conventional account of Purgatory and Paradise. He could read of Purgatory's harsh and frightening landscape, and the horrific methods used to purify souls. In gruesome detail a range of punishments, echoing those found in the *Vision of Drythelm*, are meted out to sinners: many are burnt, frozen in ice or violated with sharp objects, snakes and toads. Two fiery wheels, common instruments of torture in several visions, turn souls through a rabble of screaming devils.[52] Physical torture is matched with psychological pain: those in purgatory experience exclusion and loneliness. As in other visions, the punishment matches the sin, emphasising the link between cause and effect. In Newton's version, people who had little pity for the poor are forced to stare at a beautiful crystal wall while being prevented from reaching it. The thrust of the vision is that no one could escape the need for penance and that the punishments in the otherworld are far more tortuous than anything exacted on earth. Repent, says the vision, before it is too late.

There is much here to support Duffy's view that English accounts (in contrast to southern European ones) portrayed Purgatory as 'an out-patient department of Hell, rather than the antechamber of Heaven'.[53] And yet John Newton's vision also offered a more positive message: the passage to earthly and celestial paradise was not closed to those who had confessed their sins. The vision graphically shows the saved walking into paradise and experiencing the presence of God. They could enjoy the community of the blessed and be reunited with family, friends and the Godhead. It was a beautiful image and for that reason one that could engender another type of fear: the fear of missing out. The vision was a tale of spiritual enlightenment and self-knowledge as, in paradise, John Newton is brought face to face with his own sins and his failure to confess and be absolved of them. Interestingly, his sinfulness is symbolised by his appearance in poor, tawny clothing, which contrasts with the pure and well-dressed souls surrounding him. Only after his confession would he 'be clad with clene clothez after his decesse'.[54] Such a line may well have caught Humphrey's attention. While medieval literature commonly used outward appearances to symbolise inward purity, John Newton's public humiliation through his poor dress and loss of status may have had particular resonance for a gentleman reader.

Consumers of vision literature would have been frightened or relieved depending on their state of mind, but the overall message of the narrative was progressive: nothing is fixed; the opportunities were there to reduce time in Purgatory and improve the chances of reaching Paradise. Humphrey's personal reaction to the vision is unknowable; it is likely to have changed with his age and his experiences. His interest might have been piqued by

---

[52] Os, *Religious visions*, p. 68; Zaleski, 'St Patrick's purgatory', p. 475; and Youngs, 'A vision in a trance', p. 218, for further comparisons.
[53] Duffy, *The stripping of the altars*, p. 344.
[54] Bodl, MS Lat. Misc.c. 66, fo. 23r.

the adventure plot of the narrative, or the individual spiritual messages. For a man with protection aids bearing Christ's name, he would doubtless have welcomed the episodes where the power of the name of Jesus frightens away the devils.[55] Yet he clearly believed in Purgatory and there is no evidence to suggest that he was influenced by early sixteenth-century reformers who cast doubt on its existence. Nor does he appear to be like the Paston family, who Colin Richmond has described as having a 'casual' attitude towards purgatory.[56] Humphrey was sufficiently absorbed to write at least six pages of detail about it.

He was also sufficiently troubled by Purgatory to make various attempts to shorten his time there. The medieval Church urged people to undertake a 'spiritual audit', and preached that the individual had the power in their own hands to affect the time they spent in Purgatory. In life, as Newton's vision had effectively broadcast, this meant repenting sins, confessing, and performing penance on a regular basis, as well as undertaking additional acts of good works. One of the simplest ways, and one that promised huge reductions in purgatorial time, was the indulgence or pardon, a remission of the penance imposed on an individual who had confessed, repented and been absolved of sin. The accessibility and popularity of indulgences saw their distribution multiply enormously during the late Middle Ages and by 1500 a person could accumulate numerous years of remission through a wide range of acts, some requiring little effort.[57] Just a few miles away from Newton in Macclesfield church, the brass of Roger Legh, esquire (d. 1506), which depicted the Mass of St Gregory, asked observers to say five *paternosters*, five *aves* and a creed for his soul. In return the person would be rewarded with 26,026 days of pardon.[58] In the minds of English people, this meant a guaranteed reduction of time spent in Purgatory.

Humphrey was an avid collector of pardons and obtained them from various sources. From Dom John Newton (relationship unknown) Humphrey gathered information on the pardon beads from the Charterhouse of St Anne's, Coventry, of Sheen and of Syon, the latter the most famous and widely used beads of the day.[59] He learnt, for instance, that 1,500 days of

---

[55] John was saved by shouting 'Iesu, Iesu, Iesu, that art in Heven, have mercy on me and safe me fro þat company', fo. 21r.
[56] Richmond, 'Religion and the fifteenth-century English gentleman', p. 195.
[57] Lea, *A history of auricular confession and indulgences*, vol. 3; Orme, 'Indulgences', pp. 15–32; Swanson, *Religion and devotion*, pp. 217–25 and, id., 'Indulgences at Norwich cathedral'. Indulgences were popular among the gentry of Kent: Fleming, 'Charity', p. 42.
[58] The brass still remains in the Savage chapel of Macclesfield church, although it is damaged. For a sketch of its original state see Earwaker, *East Cheshire*, II, p. 449.
[59] Bodl, MS Lat. Misc.c.66, fo. 2v. Rhodes, 'Syon Abbey', pp. 12–13; Rhodes, 'The rosary'; and Wilkins, *The rose garden game*. Dom John Newton was from the Diocese of Coventry and Lichfield, but the name is too common to present one definite candidate. The most intriguing possibility is John Newton of Roode (Lancashire) who can be linked with Syon. In Bodl, Laud. MS 416 is the note 'scriptus Rhodo per Johannem Neuton die 25 Octobris 1459'.

pardon would be granted for praying a *paternoster*, three *aves* and a *credo* on the Syon beads. Such supplications to the Virgin were clearly important to Humphrey and they can be found in another example, the so-called 'devotion of the thousand aves', a highly popular prayer that was copied into numerous medieval manuscripts.⁶⁰ More significantly, Humphrey obtained pardons, linked to the Virgin, as a gift. Some time between 1513 and 1517 he received a copy of a letter which Robert Preston, a master's student from New College, Oxford, had sent to his sister and brother-in-law living in the North West. From Humphrey's uniquely surviving copy we learn that Preston had encountered a friar, lately from Rome, who was selling indulgences in Oxford. Preston not only bought for himself, but secured pardons for thirty-nine gentlefolk connected to Wilmslow parish, including Humphrey and his wife. It must have pleased Humphrey that by wearing ten rosary beads at the girdle and by praying an *ave* for each bead, he could expect 10,000 years and 1,010 days of pardon. By merely wearing or looking at the rosary further pardons, in multiples of ten, might also be secured.⁶¹

Performing any one of these prayers or actions regularly would have provided Humphrey with an impressive number of years of remission in the bank. Yet his account was not exhausted by them. On one page of his commonplace book there is a rare and remarkable list of eleven further pardons, drawn from all over England. They were obtained from the guild of St Mary's Coventry, the guild of St John of Jerusalem, the Trinitarian friars of St Robert of Knaresborough, the hospital of Burton Lazars, the hospital of Our Lady of Bethlehem, the hospital of St Anthony of Vienne, the hospital of St Sepulchre at Lincoln, St John's Chester, the hospital of St Thomas of Canterbury at Rome, the Jesus guild at St Paul's Cathedral, and the chapel of Talke (near Audley, Staffordshire).⁶² It is an impressive collection, comprising several of the wealthiest and most significant guilds in the country. Humphrey detailed the benefits received from each institution, and it is clear that the primary aim was to tot up the gains – or 'thresur' as Humphrey called them – thus far attained. There are some substantial individual items. The benefits from St John's Church, Chester, were enumerated as 45,200 years of pardon, with two priests singing daily for the living and the dead, and the prayers of all fellow brothers and sisters at various feasts.

An inscription on the back board mentions Anne Colvylle and Clementia Thasebrough, who were both nuns at Syon in 1518 (I owe this reference to Dr Julia Boffey). Syon Abbey owned lands and churches in Lancashire, including Newton near Lancaster.
⁶⁰ Bodl, MS Lat. Misc.c.66, fo. 69v. Rhodes, 'The rosary', p. 185.
⁶¹ Bodl, MS Lat. Misc.c.66, fo. 62. For the text and analysis: Youngs, 'A spiritual community'. The list of recipients was headed by the Trafford family, and included the Fittons of Gawsworth, both important gentry families in the North West (see p. 22 above and p. 208 below). For comparative examples of popes granting indulgences for praying with a rosary see Winston-Allen, *Stories of the rose*, p. 28.
⁶² Bodl, MS Lat. Misc.c.66, fo. 17v. The Trinitarian friars of Hounslow (Middlesex) are also mentioned in the entry on Robert of Knaresborough.

While not quite on the scale of the famous collection of Frederick the Wise, Elector of Saxony, with his 2 million years of pardons, Humphrey had still managed to accumulate at least half a million years of pardon, and time off purgatory. Like other collectors, Humphrey clearly did not see purgatory as a brief interlude, nor did he know how much would be considered enough.[63]

This was no death-bed collection, but was drawn together over a number of years. Humphrey would have accumulated them in either of two ways. He could have made personal journeys, perhaps pilgrimages, to the sites. Both the chapel of Talke and the church of St John's at Chester lay in areas that Humphrey regularly visited. But, equally, he could have stayed at home. All the remaining institutions in the list were large and wealthy enough to send out agents – quaesters, proctors or pardoners – to collect funds by promising pardons to those who donated to them; they carried letters of confraternity that listed the benefits obtained through a regular subscription. Sometimes this was prompted by a specific fund-raising drive, such as when Bishop Alcock of Ely issued an indulgence in 1491 to finance the repairs of St Robert of Knaresborough.[64] Proctors had evidently convinced Humphrey to buy letters from the Burton Lazars, St John of Jerusalem, Our Mary of Bethlehem and St Robert of Knaresborough, as indeed they had convinced others in sixteenth-century Cheshire.[65] Humphrey had received a similar letter from the Bishop of Coventry and Lichfield as part of the annual attempt to garner contributions to the fraternity of St Chad at Lichfield. Humphrey's précis of this circular listed the benefits of (presumably his) membership of the fraternity.[66]

Proctors travelled all over England and their movements can be partially traced because permission to operate was needed from the bishop in whose diocese they intended to work. Episcopal registers, such as those of the dioceses of Durham, Exeter, Hereford and Lincoln, reveal the most popular pardons – or the most persistent proctors – within a particular period.[67] What they show is that Humphrey's choice of pardons was less a personal selection and more to do with who was selling them in late medieval England. It is striking that six of the nine institutions that received the largest number of

---

63 This is my total from adding up the number of pardon years for each entry. Humphrey's own total reads as if he was expecting over a million, although I have no idea how he reached that figure. For Frederick the Wise see Bainton, *Here I stand*, p. 53.
64 Wordsworth, 'On some pardons', p. 404, n. 6.
65 Bodl, MS Lat. Misc.c.66, fo. 17v, 34cr. For another Cheshire purchaser see the will of Edmund Mascy, priest (d. 1516), who left money to the proctors of Burton Lazars, the Friary of St John and St Paul's: TNA: PRO, PROB 11/19/1.
66 Bodl, MS Lat. Misc.c.66, fo. 18r. See Kettle (ed.) 'A list of families in the archdeaconry of Stafford', p. ix. Humphrey's list of benefits can be compared to the circular issued by the bishop in 1440: Swanson, *Catholic England*, pp. 218–19.
67 Clark-Maxwell, 'Some further letters of confraternity, pp. 179–216; Haines, *Ecclesia Anglicana*, pp. 184–91; Swanson, 'Indulgences for prayers for the dead'.

episcopal grants in the Hereford registers also appear in Humphrey's list.[68] Such cases of seemingly unsystematic collecting can be found elsewhere in England. Multiple memberships of confraternities were encouraged by the sales-pitch of pardoners, the printing of letters in the early sixteenth century, and the affordability of the product.[69] In Lent 1499 Humphrey paid 2*d* apiece to the collectors of Robert of Knaresborough and the Burton Lazars, and 1*d* to the 'procurator' of St John of Jerusalem.[70] These may have been tips or instalments, but they were amounts small enough for most of society, including Humphrey's servants, to afford.[71] From such modest amounts, the institutions themselves benefited tremendously. St Anthony's Hospital received £228 10*s* from a collection made in 1513, with the sum of £5 10*s* gathered in Cheshire.[72]

We do not know whether Humphrey's pardon account was the result of panic buying triggered by a specific event such as a new case of plague, a family death or advancing age. Was it an account that he regarded with a degree of satisfaction, or feelings of inadequacy? What is apparent is that the prospect of Purgatory did not make him hide away or break down; he took control of the situation and sought a practical solution to the uncertainties of death. Indulgences meant one simply had to pay the money and keep an account, very much like managing an estate or any other business matter. Such an attitude drew increasing criticism during the sixteenth century; Robert Preston's letter circulated at a time when both Thomas More and Martin Luther were voicing their disquiet. Humphrey appears the type of person whom Erasmus had in mind when, in his *Praise of Folly*, he scoffs at those who thought they could measure their length of time in Purgatory 'as if from a mathematical table'.[73] In his way, Humphrey had gained a substantial number of pardons in a mechanical fashion, and without much effort or suffering involved. Nevertheless, Humphrey's collection also lends support to revisionist approaches which have highlighted the advantages of indulgences: they encouraged people to do good works, confess their sins

---

[68] The hospital of St Thomas of Rome, the hospital of St Anthony of Vienne, the hospital of the Burton Lazars, the hospital of St Mary of Bethlehem, the hospital of St Sepulchre (Lincoln), and the Jesus guild of St Paul's. See Clark-Maxwell, 'Some further letters', p. 197.
[69] Swanson, *Church and society*, pp. 283, 294. Tanner, *The church in late medieval Norwich*, p. 75. Printed pardons appeared for the Burton Lazars in 1510, the Bethlehem Hospital in 1519 and Robert of Knaresborough.
[70] Bodl, MS Lat. Misc.c.66, fo. 34cr.
[71] Humphrey gave Kathryn the nurse 1*d* for the pardon of the friary of St John: Bodl, MS Lat. Misc.c.66, fo. 25r. For payments see Clark-Maxwell, 'Letters of confraternity', p. 48; Clark-Maxwell 'Some further letters', p. 202; and Swanson, *Catholic England*, p. 202.
[72] Swanson, *Catholic England*, p. 208.
[73] Erasmus, *Praise of Folly*, ch. 20, p. 42. Marshall, *Beliefs and the dead*, p. 32; Marshall, 'Fear, Purgatory and polemic', pp. 289–90; For the practical response: Matsuda, *Death and Purgatory*, pp. 25–6, 33.

and pass on communal benefits.[74] The central thrust of the Preston letter and the Syon beads urged action: *aves* had to be said, prayer and meditation were required. There was an important communal aspect of their giving: when Robert Preston met the pardon seller his thoughts turned to others and he used the pardons both to strengthen living relations and help forge spiritual communities.

It is likely that Humphrey's collection was intended for more than his personal benefit. His pardon account stated that the daily masses purchased would be sung for both the 'wheke & dede'.[75] The cult of Purgatory was one that encouraged communication between this world and the otherworld, creating a bond between the living and the dead as prayers and masses were demanded for departed souls. There are other entries in Humphrey's commonplace book which reflect this relationship. The necessity of post-mortem prayers to help the dead was a message emphasised in the Newton vision, where John is reminded by his dead son 'Fader, wepe nat, bot sey þi pater noster and pray for all cristen souly'.[76] A more colourful example features in Humphrey's extract from a sermon story in Mirk's *Festial*. This told of two souls caught in a horrific cycle of punishment for the adultery they committed together in life. Only sufficient masses and alms-giving from the living would release them, and when the help is forthcoming they are delivered from pain and to 'ever lasting blisse the whech God bring us all'.[77] Such demand for post-mortem prayers and masses grew rapidly during the late Middle Ages, and most gentry wills contain some provision for the dead.[78] In May 1500, several years before his death, Humphrey's father-in-law, Thomas Fitton, placed a tenement known as Colshaw in the hands of feoffees to fund masses at Wilmslow church for himself, his wives, children, parents and ancestors for a period of twenty years.[79] Again we see family and lineage: the gentry's greatest obligations. Humphrey himself took care to ensure that his kin were not languishing forgotten in Purgatory. He referred to the list of the Newton ancestors and children beginning the commonplace book as 'obits of Humffrey Neuton ancestores and byts of his childer', suggesting that it could have functioned as a prayer roll. Prayers in the manuscript and odd notes, such as the ten groups of masses forming St Gregory's Trental,

---

[74] D'Avray, 'Papal authority', pp. 393–408; Haines, *Ecclesia Anglicana*, pp. 183–94; Swanson, 'Indulgences at Norwich cathedral', p. 18.
[75] Swanson has argued that indulgences were largely obtained after death, largely by widows, widowers and executors: Swanson, 'Indulgences for prayers', p. 210.
[76] Bodl, MS Lat. Misc.c.66, fo. 23r.
[77] Ibid., fo. 65v. It is taken from the sermon for the fourth Sunday of Lent: Erbe (ed.) *Mirk's festial*, pp. 105–6.
[78] For example, Fleming, 'Charity', pp. 37, 41; Brown, *Popular piety*, ch. 4 and, id., *Church and society*, p. 130.
[79] TNA: PRO, WALE 29/40. See Map 2.

may have been written with his family's souls in mind.[80] More specifically he made a donation for his father at All Hallows and fulfilled his father's request for the heirs of Newton to finance a silver lamp to hang in the chancel at Prestbury during services.[81] He recorded in his manuscript both the obit of his father-in-law and the epitaph of his grandfather, Laurence Lowe, which may well indicate that he financed prayers for their souls. All three, it will be noted, were male relations; Humphrey never mentions his mother. This may well have been a deliberate omission. Peter Fleming's study of the gentry of Kent has revealed a tendency among testators to restrict the number of prayers to a small group of close family and friends.[82] In other words, Humphrey's obligation was to the patrilineal line and to those male relatives who had helped shape his life.

Communal worship: churches and chapels

Thus far it has been seen that Humphrey invested much in saving his soul and the souls of his lineage. Pre-Reformation spiritual provision meant that he could pray, meditate, collect talismans and buy indulgences, all from his own home. Yet religious writers were wary of those who turned to their books and were in danger of introversion. Robert Thornton's anthologies contained texts that reminded him of his social duties, and communal worship was considered an essential part of medieval spiritual life.[83] Recent research has emphasised the community of the parish and shown it to be a strong religious, social and economic unit. Like any community, it was not necessarily harmonious or constructive at all times, and individuals had varying experiences; but pre-Reformation parish life appears to have been resilient and vibrant, and the focus of religious devotion for many.[84] The extent to which the English gentry participated in corporate parish worship has been an issue of debate, however. One strand of thought argues for very limited involvement, as the aristocracy retreated into private chapels and came to experience a different, and more 'me-centred', religious worship linked to the personal reading of devotional texts. The position has been emphatically expressed in N.J.G. Pounds's claim that 'Everywhere yeomen and gentry were turning

---

[80] Bodl, MS Lat. Misc.c.66, fo. 4v. Duffy, *The stripping of the altars*, pp. 293–4, 370–5; Pfaff, 'The English devotion', pp. 75–90. St Gregory's Trental also appears in the commonplace books of Brome and Richard Hill: Smith (ed.) *A commonplace book*, pp. 121–2; Dyboski (ed.) *Songs, carols*, p. xl, no. 44.
[81] Bodl, MS Lat. Misc.c.66, fos 29v, 74v. For the endowment of perpetual lamps as an option for the less wealthy: Carpenter, 'The religion of the gentry', p. 60.
[82] Bodl, MS Lat. Misc.c.66, fos 17r, 18r. Fleming, 'Charity', p. 38.
[83] Hughes, *Pastors and visionaries*, p. 296.
[84] For example, French, *The people of the parish*, especially ch. 4. Kumin, *The shaping of a community*.

away from communal religion'.⁸⁵ Unease, however, has been voiced over these privatisation claims. Bequests to parish churches, tombs supporting church rituals and the lending of items for the use of the parish, have all been cited in support of the centrality of the parish church in the lives of the gentry.⁸⁶ In recent years a more nuanced view has emerged, one that counsels against seeing the gentry as one monolithic block. Studies have shown that it was those of knightly status who were more likely to pay for a portable altar or private chapel, would leave fewer bequests to their parish church and were almost never involved in gilds apart from those of national or international importance. In contrast, the gentlemen and esquires had, in the words of Katherine French, 'less lofty aspirations' and identified more closely with the parish.⁸⁷ Given Humphrey's sub-knightly status, how did he view the prospect of communal worship?

The answer has to begin at the parish church. We can never know how many times Humphrey turned up to worship at Prestbury or Wilmslow parish churches, but he certainly paid his financial dues as a landholder and parishioner. In addition to his tithes on animals and crops, Humphrey paid the vicar of Prestbury seasonal contributions (Candlemas and Christmas Day offerings), an offering on the day of the saint to whom the church was dedicated (St Peter), and a number of smaller payments (the plough penny, 'amends penny', 'reach half penny').⁸⁸ Parishioners were also expected to contribute to the general upkeep of their church. Often this is apparent in the donations of numerous testators, including the gentry, who chose to express their charity and support for their local churches with payments for the rebuilding of steeples, aisles and windows. In 1436, for instance, Wilmslow church benefited from a £5 bequest from Richard Fitton to maintain the church, churchyard, bells and vestments.⁸⁹ In Humphrey's case, we know some of his life-time contributions to Prestbury church, which included several payments to 'the bell sylvur' and to the 'mason werk' in the early sixteenth century.⁹⁰ Interestingly, he also made a number of donations to Prestbury church ales and to the ales of individual people, such as the 3*d* he

---

⁸⁵ Pounds, *A history of the English parish*, p. 251. Richmond, 'The English gentry and religion', p. 135.

⁸⁶ Carpenter, 'Religion of the gentry'; Carpenter, *Locality and polity*, pp. 238–9; Duffy, *The stripping of the altars*, p. 122. Brown argues for growing privacy and detachment among the gentry, but believes that some private concerns did have public intentions: *Popular piety*, pp. 207–8, 252–6.

⁸⁷ French, *The people of the parish*, p. 92; Fleming, 'Charity', pp. 41–2, 48; Bainbridge, *Gilds*, pp. 135–6; Kumin, *The shaping of a community*, p. 36; Saul, 'The gentry and the parish', especially pp. 253–9.

⁸⁸ And something known as the 'housilling' board, which involved the giving of 1*d* for every man and wife and ½*d* for every single person. Bodl, MS Lat. Misc.c.66, fos 25v, 29v. For the plough penny and the 'amends' penny (which is probably the 'confession' penny) see Moorman, *Church life*, pp. 128, 132.

⁸⁹ *Cheshire Sheaf*, 3rd ser. xviii, p. 24.

⁹⁰ Bodl, MS Lat. Misc.c.66, fos 32v, 45v.

gave to the ale of Ralf Davenport. It is a noteworthy action because the gentry are not considered regular contributors to such collective fund-raising activities.[91] There is nothing to suggest that Humphrey himself attended these ales, though he regularly gave servants money to do so, but he was present at the 'Wilmslow wakes' (c.1499–1500), when he gave 2d to a minstrel. This could be simply an annual festival or holiday, but may well have been the merry-making that occurred during the dedication of a church.[92] Already, there are hints of Humphrey's regular involvement in communal worship.

Where we see him at his most active is his involvement in the running of two local chapels, neither of which, unfortunately, has survived to modern times. The first was the chapel of Mottram St Andrew, whose echoes remain only in place-name evidence: Chapel field and Priest Lane lie near the eighteenth-century Mottram Hall. It was once an important landmark in the environs of Newton. In 1415, Adam Mottram, a native of the area who became precentor of Salisbury, bequeathed to the chapel (*capelle Sancti Andree de Mottrum*) a missal, chalice and a vestment, and 100s to the maintenance of the chaplain.[93] By Humphrey's day, local land transactions were made in its grounds, and tradesmen were paid within its walls.[94]

Significantly, Humphrey was involved in its spiritual provision. In a short note dating July 1504, he wrote that two local men, Edward Mottershead and Robert Barlowe, had hired Thomas Unsworth to say mass at Mottram chapel for a year for 20s. The payments to Unsworth were made by Humphrey himself and the holder of Mottram Hall, George Calveley, knight, who took it in turns to pay the instalments. It is possible that an individual or family had endowed a chantry at the chapel, with Mottershead, Barlow, Calveley and Newton as trustees. In 1415 Adam Mottram had asked that his 100s payment to the chaplain be administered by his relatives living in the area, and Edward Mottershead was a descendent.[95] However, Humphrey also mentions that Unsworth would receive the 'avauntage of his bede roll and stole and geft monay' as well as money from an ale, which would help pay his wages. Any surplus was to be divided between every man according to the 'rate as he giffs his bord'. Such arrangements would seem to suggest that Humphrey was

---

[91] Brown, *Church and society*, p. 134. But again the lesser gentry probably did have a greater part to play in fundraising: Saul, 'The gentry and the parish', p. 258.
[92] Bodl, MS Lat. Misc.c.66, fos 26av, 29v, 30v, 33v, 34cv, 43v. For the definition of wakes: *OED*, qv 'wakes'.
[93] Laughton, 'A note on the place-name Mottram St Andrew', pp. 32–3 (my thanks to Dr Laughton for this information); Jacob (ed.) *The register of Henry Chichele*, vol. 2, pp. 42–3. Apparently a few gravestones survived in the 1840s, although G.Y. Osborne, like other nineteenth-century antiquarians, expressed doubts over the existence of a chapel: *Sketch of the parish of Prestbury*, p. 25.
[94] BL, Add MS 42134A, fo. 1v; Bodl, MS Lat. Misc.c.66, fo. 27ar.
[95] Mottershead also acted as one of four feoffees in land used to fund the perpetual chantry founded by Thomas and Anne Stapleton at Prestbury Church: JRUL, Tatton 603–604. For Mottershead: Earwaker, *East Cheshire*, II, p. 355; and pp. 206–7 below.

actively involved in a local fraternity of some kind. These voluntary associations had grown considerably in number during the fifteenth century. They varied in size, aims and organisation, but their main goal was to provide masses for the living and dead members of the fraternity, and to ensure that members received a proper funeral and burial.[96]

Humphrey's notes make Mottram a lucky find because these associations are difficult to detect, especially as many foundations had no landed endowment.[97] With its regular contributions and the quarterly payments of the priest, this would appear the case for Mottram. It was clearly not a wealthy association, and did not offer its employees a good salary. Another appointed chaplain in 1504 was a man called Piers, who divided his time between Mottram and Newton, presumably at the chapel (discussed below).[98] He was to sing three times a week for the yearly sum of 33s 4d. In that instance Humphrey paid the priest for his time at Newton and Calveley for the time spent at Mottram. Both Thomas and Piers were receiving wages well below the standard rate of seven marks established for chaplains and chantry priests under Henry V, although this was not an unusual situation. Northern regions offered particularly low wages: in Yorkshire there are examples of figures as low as £2 and some Lancashire chantry priests were paid even less.[99] The poor payments of the Mottram priests may reflect the few times a week they were expected to say mass; and their wages were supplemented by the bede roll, gift money and the church ale.[100] It still did not mean that they, any more than Humphrey's servants, were paid on time. Humphrey observed that he owed Unsworth 2s 9d, with the last quarter in arrears by 16d. As this account emphasises, the running of Mottram chapel and the appointment and security of the priest were entirely in lay hands. Unsworth's employment was said to come about by 'the mocian of Edward Mottershed and Robert Barlow'; the priest Piers left after completing only two quarters 'by the hand' of Robert Barlow. Overseeing all the arrangements was Humphrey himself, who perhaps acted as the official record keeper of the fraternity. It was he and Calveley who paid the priest's wages, a reflection of their higher status within the group; Mottershead and Barlow were yeomen. All four were therefore part of the move towards greater lay control and patronage in England's pre-

---

[96] Barron, 'Parish fraternities'; Rosser, 'Communities of the parish', 29–55; Scarisbrick, *The Reformation and the English people*, pp. 19–39; Farnhill, *Guilds*; Swanson, *Church and society*, pp. 280–4.
[97] Orme, 'The other parish churches', pp. 78–9.
[98] Bodl, MS Lat. Misc.c.66, fo. 48r. He was possibly the Sir Piers Mascy to whom Humphrey lent 5s in gold, fo. 47v. Another priest of Mottram, Ralph Astbury, was paid 4d for 'obits': ibid., fo. 36v.
[99] Swanson, *Church and society*, p. 47; Haigh, *Reformation and resistance*, p. 33.
[100] French, *The people of the parish*, p. 103, for the use of bede rolls as part of a clerk's or vicar's salary.

Reformation churches, which can be seen elsewhere in supervising church property and regulating religious affairs.[101]

Humphrey did not confine himself to the organisation of one chapel. In the opening years of the sixteenth century he decided to build a chapel at Newton. This is what he wrote in his commonplace book:

> I wold make a lityll chapell of tymber, and aftr I wold make a chauncell of ston of iiii yards. And þe chapell to be v yards long within þe walls and iiii yards brode, and of heght about vi yards. And þe walplate to be from þe grond iii yards and di or iiii yards. And þe sill of þe wyndowe over the auter to be of heght from þe grond ii yards and a di, and of iij stages, and þey to be of heght a yard and iii quarters. And þen þe rof above to be about a yard and iii quarters. And þe oþer wyndowes on þe sides the syl of þe same heght or lo3er by di a yard, and of ii stages and a yard hegh. Also the auter to be of heght a yard and di quarter or a yard and a handful, and of length ii yards and of brode a yarde. Also the step from þe auter to þe forme a yard and a lytill more. Also the forme to be of length a yard and quarter. Also þe deske most be a yard brode and þen from þe deske to þe chapell end is about a yard and a half within þe walls. And þen þe dur most be on þe end unto þe chauncell were bygged. And so þe church shuld be made ix yards long when þe chauncel is bigged and þe is long end.[102]

Rarely is such a detailed and fascinating description found; there is little with which to compare it. The repetition of 'I wold' suggests that this was Humphrey's personal project: he was not simply throwing money at an idea, or letting others decide the most suitable building plan. The detail reveals a concern with both interior space and overall design. There is a combination of precise and rough measurements – the 'yard and a handful' – characteristic of Humphrey's record keeping in general. The chapel was listed in Humphrey's inquisition *post mortem*, and it appears to have been financed largely from the Newton estate: it was provided with an endowment comprising the corn and fulling mills of Newton, two messuages and 'certain other lands'.[103] When the chapel was actually built is unclear, but it was sometime during the first decade of the sixteenth century: the arrangement to share a priest with Mottram chapel dates to around 1504, which would imply that the new building was at least underway by then.[104] It was a small, simple chapel with a wooden nave and a stone chancel, as is illus-

---

[101] Kumin, *The shaping of a community*, p. 182; McIntosh, *Autonomy and community*, p. 236; Scarisbrick, *The Reformation and the English people*, pp. 19–39; Brown, *Church and society*, ch. 4.
[102] Bodl, MS Lat.Misc.c.66, fo.45v. Punctuation added, contractions expanded. The last few words are extremely faint and this is the best guess at their form.
[103] TNA: PRO, E315/105, mm. 145–6; CHES 3/67/4.
[104] See pp. 97–9 above for Humphrey's attempts at securing rights and land c.1504.

trated in the attempted reconstruction in Figure 2.[105] The main focus was the altar, illuminated from above by a large, three-light window. There was also a desk or board for service books, and a form or bench for worshippers. The chapel was situated near Newton Hall. While the exact position has not been pinpointed, the survival of the name 'Chapel Yard' on the nineteenth-century tithe map suggests that it lay in a corner field bordered by the current Lees Lane and Mill Lane.[106] The chapel continued in use until the late seventeenth century; in 1707, however, it was said to be in a ruinous state.[107]

This, again, was a small, and never particularly rich, establishment. When the chapel was dissolved by the Court of Augmentation in 1546, it was officially valued at £4 per annum, £3 13s 4d of which was the chaplain's wage; better than at Mottram, but still on the low side. Ornaments were returned as one chalice (weighing ten ounces), a paper mass book, a white buckram vestment, a black damask vestment, a blue velvet cope and two bells weighing a total of eighty pounds.[108] In the following year a certificate issued by the Court listed the ornaments as plate and jewels (weighing nine ounces), stocks of cattle, goods and ornaments, lead and bells.[109] Seen in the context of other chapels in Cheshire, it was not particularly well stocked. The chapel of Pott Shrigley, bolstered by its three chantries, had a yearly value of £13 14s 4d, with plate and jewels of eighteen ounces and goods and ornaments worth 28s 11d. But at least Newton was faring better than the Green chapel in Millington (Frodsham parish), which was valued at 60s, with jewels at 6s and no goods or bells; and much better than the neglected chapel at Lyme (Prestbury parish), worth only 17s 4d and with no incumbent or ornaments.[110]

It would be fascinating to know how Humphrey felt and worshipped in the years following the chapel's build. The record is silent on these issues, but there is evidence to suggest that Humphrey took care to provide the right equipment for the chapel. His awareness of the practicalities of worship is seen in the list he made of service books and their respective costs. Most appear in rather cheap versions: a missal (26s 8d), gradual (18s), processional (3s 4d), manual (7s 8d), breviary (£3 6s 8d), psalter, dirige, common

---

[105] My thanks to David Percivall of The Royal Commission on the Ancient and Historical Monuments of Wales for the reconstruction, and to Professor Nicholas Orme for his advice on interpreting the chapel description.
[106] The tithe map can be viewed in CRO, EDT 293/1, /2. See also the early OS maps for 'Buxton and Stockport' (1st revision of 1899 to 3rd revision 1938–46), which place the site of Newton chapel in this area. Earwaker attempted to narrow the location, seeing it as lying between two yew trees near one of the cottages that still stands on the field: CRO, CR 63/1/93/8. A gravestone was apparently found in the garden of the cottage on the north side of the field in the mid-twentieth century (information from the Cheshire County Council Historic Environment Record).
[107] In 1672 a warden was sworn to the chapel. CRO, ZCR 63/3/32; Renaud, *Contributions*, p. 12.
[108] TNA: PRO, E315/419, m. 16; SC 12/6/24.
[109] TNA: PRO, E301/8/18.
[110] Ibid. and TNA: PRO, E301/8/28; SC 12/6/24.

Figure 2. The Newton Chapel

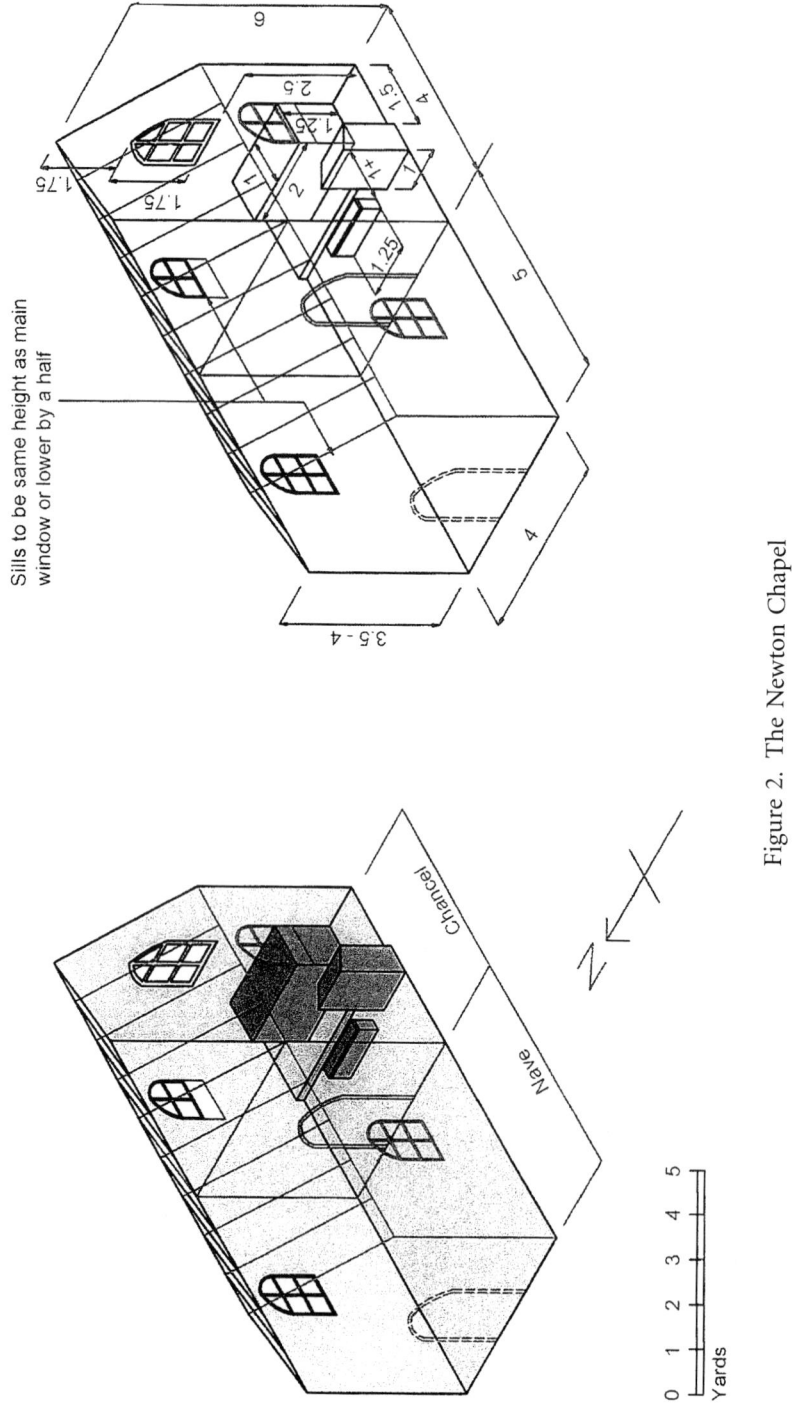

book and a matutinales.¹¹¹ Admittedly there is no indication that they were meant for a particular chapel, but the list is almost identical to the inventory of service books considered a 'complete set' for the medieval parish church.¹¹² Humphrey's purchase of a mass book *c.*1519–20 points to chapel use, and there is also his brief extract from William Lyndwood's *Provinciale*, a fifteenth-century codification of English provincial Canon Law. Humphrey summarised the section on mass and paid specific attention to a passage on the correct metal to be used in making a chalice.¹¹³

A chapel was neither an easy nor a cheap project. What lay behind this level of commitment? It is possible that the chapel was built with the sole intention of increasing the number of prayers and masses said for Humphrey and his family. Given what is known of Humphrey's belief in Purgatory and his pardon collection, this would not be surprising. The chapel appeared suspiciously like a personal foundation for it to be included in the dissolution of the chantries in the 1540s. There were important social advantages too. As Chapter 4 has detailed, the chapel played a crucial role in Humphrey's claim to the neighbouring heath, and his bid to build the chapel can read like a one-man campaign. Gervase Rosser has drawn attention to the way landlords used chapels to 'recruit support' for their predominance in an area.¹¹⁴ At Newton, Humphrey was surrounded by powerful families who boasted better houses and parks. A chapel was a conspicuous means to advertise status and raise his profile.

However, the evidence does not support wholly selfish motives. The chapel was certainly instrumental in securing the heath, but the chapel as much as the land may have been the goal. In the 1540s William Newton argued that the chapel was aimed at the wider community, and the commission established by the Court of Augmentations (to oversee the dissolution of the chantries) agreed. After carefully studying Humphrey's will, the Court chose to believe that he had only a life interest in the chapel. The building, it recorded, 'was and yet is a chappell of ease, and so continually used'.¹¹⁵ In other words, the chapel was specifically created for parishioners who lived at a distance from the parish church at Prestbury. It would enable them to reach the church more quickly and easily, and perhaps more often. The need for a chapel of ease in the large parishes of northern England was a common one, particu-

---

111 Cheap compared with the prices noted in Wordsworth and Littlehales, *The old service books*, pp. 44–5. Churchwardens at St Michael's (Bath) bought a missal at £2 6s 2d in 1349, a processional for 5s 11d in 1426 and a manual for 16s 8d in 1439. Yatton church (Somerset) bought in 1495 a manual for £1 3s 4d and a processional for 9s 4d.
112 Wordsworth and Littlehales, *The old service books*, pp. 68, 256; Owen, *Church and society*, pp. 117–18. Although note that the breviary was not supplied by the parishioners, but by the clergy.
113 Bodl, MS Lat. Misc.c.66, fos 3v, 59av. Ballard and Chalmer Bell (eds) *Lynwood's Provinciale*, Book 3, Titulus 23 ch. iv.
114 Rosser, 'Parochial conformity', pp. 181–2. See pp. 97–9 above.
115 TNA: PRO, E315/105, m. 147.

larly in outlying hamlets. In south Lancashire population increase spurred the foundation of thirty-eight new chapels between 1500 and 1548.[116] In Derbyshire, Humphrey's great-uncle Thomas Lowe had led the township of Alderwasley's bid for a new chapel on the same grounds.[117] Prestbury parish, where Newton chapel lay, extended over a substantial area of thirty-two townships, prompting a number of parochial chapels to be established.

It has to be wondered, too, whether problems within Prestbury church in the early sixteenth century had not influenced Humphrey's decision. A long-running dispute was taking place between Thomas Legh of Adlington, esquire (d. 1519), and John Stanley of Handforth, knight (d. 1527), over the lease of the rectory, parsonage and manor of Prestbury and the tithes of the church. This resulted in the eviction of chaplains and the withholding of tithes. The case went to Chancery and Humphrey was one of the men commissioned to interview the perpetrators.[118] Humphrey had already been involved in Legh's dispute with the vicar of Prestbury, and the men had exchanged angry words over tithe cattle and a mortuary payment. Humphrey had tried to donate a gown to Prestbury church as his mother's mortuary, but Legh had refused the gift. Humphrey wrote of his wish to see the matter resolved 'for drede of þe curse þat he [Legh] made ageynst theym whech held dutiez of þe church'. An alternative chapel may well have been essential for the spiritual health of the community, not merely a convenience.[119]

Newton chapel does appear to have been a communal endeavour. The priest's wages were not only drawn from Humphrey's endowment, but derived from the profits of an ale, and of a stock of cattle and other goods which were in the hands of several local inhabitants. The renting out of stocks of sheep or cattle was a common method of fund-raising in many areas of Cheshire and elsewhere in rural England.[120] There was local support and commitment too. The chapel was situated at a point where four roads crossed, bringing people up from Mottram and down from Woodford. When it first opened, it shared a priest with Mottram chapel, and one of the Mottram fraternity, Edward Mottershead, was present during the chapel's construction. In 1538 it was a neighbouring gentleman, John Davenport of Woodford, who paid the stipend of the priest, and it seems that residents of Woodford in the sixteenth and seventeenth centuries preferred to visit Newton rather than their own

---

[116] Haigh, *Reformation and resistance*, p. 31; Orme, 'The other parish churches', pp. 80, 83; Kitching, 'Church and chapelry', pp. 279–83.
[117] BL, Add MS 6666, fo. 58.
[118] TNA: PRO, C1/411/13–16, C1/511/44; Renaud, *Contributions*, p. 49.
[119] Bodl, MS Lat. Misc.c.66, fo. 60r. Humphrey was so fed up with Thomas's claims for tithe that he was thinking of moving all his cattle to Pownall. See also pp. 51, 92 and 97–8 above.
[120] Richmond, 'The English gentry and religion', pp. 122–3; Addy, *Church and manor*, p. 314; Brown, *Church and society*, p. 91.

township chapel of Poynton cum Woodford.[121] While Humphrey expressed his plans in terms of 'I wold', this does not mean it was an independent enterprise. A local initiative to secure a new chapel usually stood a better chance of succeeding if the project was headed by an influential gentleman.[122] At the same time potential chapel builders recognised that their projects depended on the cooperation of their neighbours. When William Holynshead left £20 for the construction of a new chapel at Holinshead, and when Henry Ryle (d. 1536) wanted to double the size of his chapel in Wilmslow church, both acknowledged in their wills that it would only happen with the support of local people; in neither case does this appear to have materialised.[123] Humphrey's fervour in securing the land for the chapel must have been matched to some degree by local support for his actions.

Altogether, this information shows Humphrey very much involved in the religious affairs of his local community. He contributed to church ales, feast days and the building fabric of Prestbury and Wilmslow; he helped run a small fraternity, and built a chapel of ease on neighbouring heath that served the local community for nearly two centuries. In Newton he did not follow the example of other contemporary gentry – including his neighbours the Leghs of Adlington and the Davenports of Bramhall – and build a private chapel within his manor house.[124] It is likely that a chapel already existed in Pownall Hall, and hence he would have benefited from a private chaplain.[125] But that did not stop Humphrey from fighting to build the chapel at Newton even when it was no longer his chief residence. His actions can be seen as consonant with a lesser gentry status. Unlike wealthier gentry, whose multiple properties often made them 'part-time' parishioners, the geographical proximity of Humphrey's holdings meant that he could be on hand at the chapels of Newton and Mottram, and at Prestbury and Wilmslow parish churches. While we cannot ignore the possibility that his involvement was an exercise in power and domination,[126] he was attempting to improve the spiritual resources of his locality, and he succeeded to a significant extent.

If the evidence gathered thus far cannot prove his intentions, a few accounts in his commonplace book lend further support to the view that Humphrey was heavily involved in public spiritual provision and the matter of people's souls. These are lists labelled 'restitution & detts'. Restitution was a debt a penitent owed his or her victim(s), either in money (usually) or prayers, and calculated by a person's confessor. It was to be paid to the victim in the first

---

[121] TNA: PRO, STAC 2/30/86; CRO, DDS/509; Irvine (ed.) 'List of the eleven deaneries', p. 11.
[122] Kumin, *The shaping of a community*, pp. 170–1.
[123] TNA: PRO, PROB 11/19/19 (Holynshead); *Cheshire Sheaf*, 3rd ser. XVIII (1921), p. 61 (Ryle).
[124] Earwaker, *East Cheshire*, II, p. 237; Piccope (ed.) *Lancashire and Cheshire Wills*, I, p. 76.
[125] BL, Add Roll 37328.
[126] Brown, *Church and society*, p. 109.

instance and, if that was not possible, then to the poor, a broad grouping that included the Church.[127] Most of Humphrey's accounts relate to named individuals, for example, 'to syng for the soule of Stephen Strete or else to deile to por folks iijs iiijd' and 'Item a ryng to maistres Jane Delamer or els to syng for her in massez or in alms'. An exception is the general 'a peny to offer I knowe not wher. Gif it in silver to a por nezbur to pray for theym & all halows Cristyn soules'.[128] To what do these refer? Was Humphrey rendering payments for his own misdemeanours? He clearly wrote as if he owed Stephen Street money: he stated his need 'to get masses for Stephen Strete soul whoz I ogh iijs iiijd'.[129] However, a more likely possibility is that Humphrey was either an executor of these people's wills, or had been delegated tasks by their executors. This would appear to be the case from his entry on James, Lord Audley (d. 1497), for whom Humphrey acted as steward in his Cheshire and Staffordshire manors: 'Also I most agre with the heirs of my Lorde Audelay, or els do for his soule for asmoch as Raufe Huxley & I cold reken no better bot þat I was behynde xxviijs xid; howe be it parte liez in þe tenants handes'.[130] Testators with troubled consciences could request that their executors pay debts of restitution to those whom they had harmed. Sylvia Thrupp found a number of examples in London merchants' wills: the result of selling bad goods or overcharging, or of acts of youthful wrong-doing.[131] We may never know the exact nature of these payments, but they suggest that Humphrey was a man who could be trusted to pay spiritual debts. What is also striking is that Humphrey included these payments among other transactions, such as those for a millstone to a Chester tradesman, and his dower payments. There is no distinction between the sacred and the profane, just as it is impossible to divide spiritual and social intentions when it comes to gentry involvement in religion. It is a point firmly underlined in the next section.

Remember me

If death did not end the soul's existence, it certainly took away the physical being. In time it would erase the memory of the person too. Medieval people hoped that they would be remembered, at least for a while, after death. Sentimental reasons may have played a part but, for most, the desire for remembrance was inextricably linked to the need for prayers that would speed the passage through Purgatory. While people placed trust in family, friends and

---

127 Lea, *Auricular confession*, vol. 2, pp. 43–63 and Tentler, *Sin*, pp. 340–3.
128 Bodl, MS Lat. Misc.c.66, fo. 65r. 'Jane Delamer' was Lady Delamere of Aldermaston, Berkshire.
129 Ibid., fo. 59av.
130 Ibid., fo. 60r, p. 57 above.
131 Thrupp, *Merchant class*, pp. 176–7. For further examples see Duffy, *The stripping of the altars*, p. 356; Gibson, *The theater of devotion*, pp. 27–8.

executors, there were worries about negligence and forgetfulness. A lasting, more tangible, prompt to prayer was required.

By the late Middle Ages attention was increasingly focused on the parish church. Virtually every part could be used to request prayers; its fabric and fittings acted as an obit roll.[132] Donations of chalices, service books or altar cloths were intended to catch the eye, especially that of the priest, during mass. Richard Starkey of Stretton, esquire, for example, wanted a chalice made with the words 'Ex dono Ricardi Starky' imprinted on it to be placed in the chapel of Stretton.[133] Those wealthy enough to organise or contribute substantially to the rebuilding of a church could arrange for their names to be incorporated into its fabric. Anyone walking into the newly remodelled east end of Wilmslow church in the mid-1520s would have had a clear impression of the leading men and families of the parish, who presumably helped finance the restructuring.[134] A few old windows of saints had survived the rebuilding, but antiquarian notes of the later sixteenth century describe its three chapels and the chancel filled with the arms of local gentry and businessmen. That most of these windows date to 1523 suggests that the fenestration marked the end of the rebuilding and, like modern sponsorship, was recognition of financial patronage. The use of portrait windows heightened the effect of the ubiquitous requests for prayers. Those financed by the knightly families of Trafford and Handforth depicted the donor, his wife and children all in prayer. Those of William Booth of Dunham Massey and Henry Ryle showed individuals kneeling in front of an open book on a rest.[135] For the Traffords and the Booths, whose main residences lay in other parishes and who used alternative churches, representations of them in worship were probably the nearest they ever came to a regular presence in the church. They nevertheless presented themselves as part of the community of worshippers.

These collective 'armigerous' requests for prayers at Wilmslow were shared by the Newton family. Two of the windows in the north, or Jesus, chapel were glazed under its instructions. Only one survives today, celebrating the marriage of Humphrey's eldest son, the shield quartering the arms of Newton and Mainwaring (Plate 1). A second window, containing the same shield of Newton, asked for prayers for Humphrey and his wife, this time noting Ellen's ancestry: 'Orate pro Humfrido Neuton de Pownall armigero et Elena uxore eius filia et herede Thome ffyton armigero filii Johannis filii Ricardi

---

[132] Richmond, 'Religion', p. 186; Rogers, 'Hic iacet ...', p. 261.
[133] Piccope (ed.) *Lancashire and Cheshire wills*, I, pp. 19–22.
[134] During 1490–1522 the main body of the church underwent extensive rebuilding. The complete rebuilding of the chancel was overseen by Henry Trafford (rector 1516–37): Earwaker, *East Cheshire*, I, p. 97. On completion in 1522, Trafford had his initials engraved in the chancel ceiling. For comparison: Brown, *Popular piety*, p. 111; Saul, *Scenes*, pp. 151–60; Whiting, *Blind devotion*, pp. 219–20.
[135] As depicted in antiquarian drawings of *c*.1572: BL, Harley MS 2151, fos 61–2. Discussion of similar portraits can be found in Griffith, 'A portrait of the reader'.

filii Thome filii Hugonis ffiton fratris Ricardi ffiton quondam domini de Bolyn qui istam fenestram fieri fecit anno domini Mccccxxiij'.[136] With these windows, therefore, the Newtons declared their links to past greatness (lords of Bollin) and present power (Mainwaring). Nevertheless, in their design the windows betray Humphrey's comparatively lesser status. Both merely contained shields and were relatively plain works in contrast to the portrait windows discussed above.

All of these windows were financed during the donors' lifetime, but the most prominent monuments in England's churches were those commemorating death. For those individuals with the resources a range of memorials was available, including stone slabs, brasses and tombs. It was in this way that the Newtons made their mark in Wilmslow church. Both Humphrey and Ellen Newton were commemorated in tomb effigies, which still survive in the north wall of the Jesus chapel (Plates 4–5). It is not known whether they were commissioned before Humphrey's death, or were planned and arranged by his sons. But, given that he was mindful of preparing for the afterlife, it would be surprising if Humphrey had not made clear his burial plans.

In examining these tombs, a first point of consideration is the location. Canon law gave individuals the right to choose where they wished to be buried, and the surviving testamentary evidence from England and Western Europe suggests that most exercised that right. In Vanessa Harding's sample of Londoners who left wills in the period 1380–1520, around ninety to ninety-eight per cent stated where they wanted to be buried.[137] The choice was influenced by family, association, residence, age and finances. Among England's aristocracy, family was a crucial factor, and was closely linked to what Philip Morgan has called 'place-loyalty'.[138] For the gentry, this usually meant the parish church. The choice could be personal, intending to express family allegiance, as when Margaret Paston chose to be buried with 'myn aunceteres'.[139] It could also be a political statement, as powerful local families colonised their parish churches to the extent of turning them into private mausoleums. A striking example of what Nigel Saul has termed a 'gentry takeover' can be found in Norbury church, Derbyshire, where the chancel is dominated by the monuments of the Fitzherbert family, lords of the nearby manor.[140] Similarly, in late medieval Cheshire, leading gentry families such

---

[136] For Jesus chapel: Earwaker, *East Cheshire*, I, pp. 70–1. For the marriage, see pp. 31–3 above.
[137] Harding, 'Burial choice', p. 122.
[138] Morgan, 'Of worms and war', p. 140.
[139] Davis (ed.) *Paston Letters*, 1, no. 230 (p. 383).
[140] Fleming, 'Charity', p. 51; Rogers, 'Hic iacet …', p. 267; Saul, *Death, art, and memory*, p. 245 and, id., 'The gentry and the parish', pp. 247–52; Brown, *Popular piety*, p. 116; Carpenter, 'Religion', p. 143. Good illustrations of the Fitzherbert tombs can be found in Hadley, *Death*, pp. 149, 154–5, 159.

as Booth and Dutton had long-established ancestral burial places in their parish churches.[141]

While the fourteenth- and fifteenth-century Newton family did not have the status and position to dominate their local church, they did establish a small ancestral burial spot in Prestbury church. Humphrey described how his great-grandfather Richard (d. after 1397) was buried on the north side of Prestbury church 'under the fforme which longeth to Neuton ther, þat is to sey the highmost bott one at þis day'.[142] It is possible that this was at or near the location of the tombstone of Humphrey's father Richard (d. 1497). This no longer survives, but antiquarian notes describe an old and broken gravestone, once in the chancel, that contained Richard's name and date of death.[143] By the late sixteenth century it had been despatched to the churchyard, and probably recycled like many medieval grave slabs. The exact date of death indicates that it was made after Richard's death, presumably under Humphrey's direction. That his mother's name does not appear (she died in 1498) is perhaps a sign that little time was lost in arranging the memorial.

Humphrey did not continue this tradition in Prestbury, nor did he choose to be buried in the chapel at Newton. England's aristocracy usually wished to be buried in the parish of their principal residence. The wealthy Clare family, originally based in East Anglia, had switched their burial place to Tewkesbury Abbey when they inherited Gloucestershire possessions in the fifteenth century.[144] Likewise, when Humphrey moved his family to the new residence at Pownall, he turned his attention to the parish church at Wilmslow. The tombs of Humphrey and Ellen lie immediately below the Newton window in the Jesus chapel. This was a private chapel endowed by the Trafford family and one of the most prestigious burial locations in the church. While in life Humphrey may have facilitated communal worship, his memorial would have marked a clear separation between the Newtons and the ordinary parishioners. Studies have revealed the clear hierarchy that existed in church burial space. The most desirable position was in the chancel, which was dominated by the clergy and a select group of local worthies. The Newtons were never likely to place tombs in this part of Wilmslow church, as it was already occupied with members of the Booth and Trafford families. They therefore went for the next best thing, a site near a specific altar.[145] Both Humphrey and Ellen would benefit from the regular masses and prayers of

---

[141] Irvine, *A collection of Lancashire and Cheshire wills*, pp. 23, 26, 65, 94.
[142] Bodl, MS Lat. Misc.c.66, fo. 1v.
[143] 'Orate pro anima Ricardi Neuton filij Oliveri Neuton qui quidem Ricardus obi di dominica die April anno domini Mcc…' Date is unfinished in the manuscript BL, Harley MS 2151, fo. 28r (42r).
[144] Daniell, *Death and burial*, p. 92.
[145] Ibid., pp. 98–9; Hadley, *Death*, p. 43; Rogers, 'Hic iacet …', pp. 263–4. The chancel floor was already inset with the fine brass of Sir Robert Booth of Bollin and his wife (1453).

the Jesus chapel's priest, Henry Knight, and they were not far away from the masses sung at the main altar.[146]

Effigies were symbols of wealth, intended to attract attention. They were not meant to be anonymous and were designed to convey information about the deceased; in the words of Paul Binski, they 'lent them a voice'. Binski has argued that from the thirteenth century onwards monumental sculpture reflected a growing sense of a person as an individual. This does not mean as a unique individual, but what Binski calls 'a socially and culturally constructed entity'. Through various emblems and motifs, a person was able to convey several messages about the social, familial, religious and political associations that formed their identity.[147] Cheshire gentry who requested memorials, for example, wanted their arms to be present in order to show their lineage. Sir Piers Legh of Lyme (d. 1527) asked for a tombstone of marble with a picture of himself and his wife, their arms and an inscription with their names and the dates of their decease.[148]

The effigies of Humphrey and Ellen are conventional in design. They are shown in a recumbent position in a pose of prayer or contemplation intended to express piety and devotion. They are idealised images. Despite dying at sixty-nine, Humphrey is presented in the prime of life (his mid-thirties), the age that souls were believed to attain at resurrection. He is smooth-skinned and clean-shaven, with the common long bobbed haircut of the early sixteenth century. There is no hint of the actual bodily death that contemporary cadaver tombs or shrouded images conveyed.[149] What is striking, however, is the choice of clothing. He is dressed as a civilian and wears a full-sleeved fur-lined red robe that reaches to his feet; traces of red and black paint can still be seen. Surviving medieval tombs of civilians are unusual; the majority of effigies are those of ecclesiastics or knights in armour. In Cheshire only three out of fifty effigies surviving for the period before 1540 are of male civilians, and such relatively low numbers are common in neighbouring Staffordshire and elsewhere in England.[150] On the one hand, it is not surprising that Humphrey is dressed in this way: no Newton family member had gone near a battlefield for over 100 years.[151] While a number of gentry families continued to choose armour in their effigies, whether they had seen military action or not, the Newtons eschewed

---

[146] Knight was the first and only chantry priest of the Jesus chapel, and was buried beneath the chapel floor: BL, Harley MS 2151, fo. 61r.
[147] Binski, *Medieval death*, pp. 71, 92–111; Saul, *Death, art, and memory*, p. 249.
[148] Irvine (ed.) *A collection of Lancashire and Cheshire wills*, pp. 33–6.
[149] For example, Henry Trafford's tomb chest in Wilmslow once contained an image of a shrouded man: BL, Harley MS 2151, fo. 61r.
[150] For Cheshire: Blair, 'Pre-reformation effigies', part 1, pp. 117–47; part 2, pp. 91–120. Of fifty-four effigies in Staffordshire dating to 1303–1599, only three are civilians, of which only one is pre-Reformation in date: Jeavons, *The monumental effigies of Staffordshire*, part II, pp. 1–35. See also Crossley, *English church monuments*; Gardner, *Alabaster tombs*.
[151] See pp. 16, 18 and 21 above.

this conceit. On the other, those civilian effigies which do survive countrywide generally reflect a higher social status than that of the Newtons. They include a large proportion of wealthy lawyers: the effigies of both Humfrey Starkey (d. 1486) at Shoreditch, Middlesex, and John Port (d. 1540) at Etwall, Derbyshire, demonstrate their careers as sergeants at law with long robes and the characteristic coif and hood of those who reached the top of their profession. In other words, few civilian effigies exist because the lesser gentry and merchants were less likely to commission them.

That this highly visible statement was something almost out of the range of the Newton finances is hinted by the materials and design of the tombs. Unlike the majority of late medieval Midland effigies, they were not carved in alabaster.[152] Instead they were made from red sandstone, typical of the North West of England and easy to acquire. That is not to say that the stone was of poor quality, but it was one of the cheaper materials used for effigy work. Nor, unlike the tomb of Henry Trafford in Wilmslow, could the family afford a full free-standing monument. The tombs were placed under two wall canopies, a device used since the late thirteenth century to give the effect of a standing monument. The recycling of earlier materials also took place. Neither the ogee arches over the effigies nor the sculpture underneath date to the 1530s; they are at least 100 years earlier. It is likely that these pieces belonged to parts of the earlier church and were incorporated into the fabric of the remodelled chancel. Were they made, ready and waiting, for the Newton effigies, or did the family take the opportunity to occupy spaces created for other reasons? Through lack of space or finance, it seems that the Newtons could hardly avoid the use of second-hand materials.[153] It was a downmarket attempt to make a very upmarket gesture.

It is suggestive that, in order to make comparisons with Humphrey's appearance, it is necessary to look at contemporary brasses rather than tombs. These were more common among those of middling rank and a significant number survive across England. They include Robert Casteltown, esquire (d. 1527), who is depicted alongside his wife in Long Dutton church, Surrey. An image closer to home, and which Humphrey is likely to have seen, is the already mentioned brass of Roger Legh in Macclesfield church.[154] Both exam-

---

[152] In Cheshire, eighteen of the twenty-four surviving tombs dating 1400–1540 are made of alabaster: Blair, 'Pre-Reformation effigies', part 1, p. 119.

[153] Victorian work has done much to complicate the dating of the chapel. It is a bit of a mess architecturally and has been neglected academically. Any firm answers to the dating and construction awaits the detailed study currently undertaken by Dr Birgitta Hoffman of Liverpool University. Thus far, there is some nineteenth-century evidence to suggest that the recesses were used as tombs. When the north wall of the chapel was underpinned to support the new vestry building, bones and coffin furniture were found beneath the wall: Fryer, *Wilmslow graves*, p. 61.

[154] Stephenson, *A list of monumental brasses in Surrey*, p. 191. For the Legh brass see p. 119 above; for Legh see p. 52 above. Note that there were also fewer brasses of men in civilian dress than in military garb: Staniland, 'Civil costume', p. 44.

ples show standard features, portraying a similar style of long fur-trimmed gowns with open sleeves, long hair, clean-shaven faces and hands in prayer. No obvious individual traits have been introduced. Humphrey's clothing and hairstyle were standard for the monuments of gentlemen, simply transposed to stone. Nevertheless, the sculptor who carved the effigy was not without skill and chose to make Humphrey's red gown very full, conveying its richness and status. It is much livelier than the rather flat image of Henry Trafford lying nearby.

In contrast, the depiction of Ellen as a widow required a plainer representation. Instead of the elaborate clothing and headdress seen on many Tudor female effigies, there is a simple head cloth that pleats around the face and folds on the shoulders. Her widow's identity is twinned with her status as an heiress: she is shown wearing a purse and her head rests on a wheatsheaf, the symbol of her Fitton family. Her status must explain Ellen's position in the chapel: her tomb lies closer to the east end and hence the altar than does Humphrey's. In a patriarchal society where men would traditionally be placed before women, this is an important recognition of Ellen's personal standing in local society.

Lying behind the effigies were the twin desires of saving souls and promoting family status. The tomb was a strong visual reminder of death and as such should, like the windows above, encourage those entering the Jesus chapel (primarily the priest) to help shorten the time and alleviate the pain of Humphrey's and Ellen's souls in Purgatory. The request for prayers for the dead was made explicit in the words initially engraved on the scroll covering Humphrey's front: 'Orate pro Humfrido Neuton de Pownall armigero et Elena uxore eius filie et herede Thome Fitton et Ceciliae uxoris eius qui obiit anno MCCCC'.[155] The emphasis again on Ellen's parentage is a reminder that the tombs functioned to proclaim a family's past, present and future importance to the local area. In terms of the present, the Newtons were declaring their arrival in the Wilmslow parish as the new lords of Pownall Hall. Death may have been the great leveller, but Humphrey, like others of his class, wanted to assert his wealth and status. He may have felt the need, shared by other recently elevated families, that an impact had to be made. This may have been borne out of pride and confidence, but could also have arisen from feelings of insecurity, perhaps fear.[156] No family wanted to be seen as entirely 'new' arrivals and the Newtons were keen to display their Fitton and Milton connections. Humphrey's head rests on three tuns, recalling his reason for choosing the tun as his insignia – to represent 'Newton, Milton and Fitton to which I am heir'; this symbolism suggests his hand in the tomb's design.[157]

---

[155] BL, Harley MS 2151, fo. 62. Date incomplete in manuscript.
[156] Saul, *Death, art, and memory*, pp. 238, 241; Morgan, 'Of worms and war', p. 139.
[157] BL, Add MS 42134A, fo. 19v.

Finally, the tombs were built for the future, in order that Humphrey and his wife would remain a continual presence in the church; it has so far proved a lasting achievement.

Conclusion

Lest we forget, Humphrey lived through times of considerable religious upheaval. He was an exact contemporary of the reformer Erasmus (1466–1536), but they probably shared little more than dates in common. There is no recognition of new continental forms of piety, no whiff of radicalism in Humphrey's writings; nothing to help historians explain the Reformation, which was gaining momentum in England during Humphrey's twilight years. He was utterly conventional, a conformist by desire, who was fashionable in the cults that he followed and enthusiastic in his support for indulgences.[158] His reading material, rather lightweight and unchallenging, helped to ensure that his views were the common beliefs of the age, and ones shared by both the educated and illiterate: Humphrey's piety retained the folkloric elements that occupied the grey areas of pre-Reformation practices. Nevertheless, he did make choices. While a believer in the miraculous, he neither recorded specific miracles nor appears interested in saints' lives. Christ and Mary were his main succour, with help from a supporting Biblical cast.

Purgatory and the state of the soul preoccupied Humphrey, and like all members of the gentry, he had more money and more options than most of English society to cope with these concerns. He engaged in both private worship and collective activity. It is evident that he did not retreat from the parish, whether because of a personal desire to share in communal worship or because, on a more cynical note, he was too insecure in his locality to turn his back on the parish. The chapel and the tombs could be seen as spiritual equivalents of his township creation and estate improvements. They may even suggest, using Carpenter's view of the parvenu gentry, that he was throwing money 'at things that made an immediate and strong impact'.[159] Perhaps Humphrey himself was unsure about his motivations and felt the need to assuage his spiritual angst with the large accumulation of spiritual credit. Yet while much that he did was conventional, it is worth emphasising that only a minority of the gentry embarked on chapel building, let alone a chapel of ease; only a proportion would be memorialised in effigy, and rarely below the county elite. Cheaper designs and materials in his monument suggest that it was a financial stretch for a gentleman to make. Current scholarship would also suggest that his involvement in parish worship was at a level rarely

---

[158] Cf. Hicks, 'Four studies', p. 3.
[159] Carpenter, 'Religion', p. 141.

considered common for the gentry.[160] While none of Humphrey's actions alone would have appeared unusual to his tenants or fellow landholders, his commitments, taken together, may well have meant that he stood out in his community as a facilitator of worship, and a man to trust with spiritual requests.

---

[160] See Middleton-Stewart, *Inward purity*, pp. 268–74 for tombs; Brown, *Popular piety*, pp. 139–40 for the unusualness of gentry becoming involved in small non-endowed fraternities.

6

Lifestyle

God would judge the soul, but medieval gentle society would judge by outward appearances. Gentility did not merely reside in the solidity of land and wealth, but in the often intangible qualities of presentation and display. Status was reflected in homes and material possessions, in personal appearance and modes of behaviour. While good birth could not be taken away, claims to gentility had to be continually demonstrated and justified: a gentleman was expected to lead a particular way of life.

The dual purpose of a gentle lifestyle was to convey exclusivity and superiority. Peter Coss has argued that one definition of gentility would be the well-developed sense of social difference between the aristocracy and the rest of the population.[1] The formation of a class-conscious group was reflected in the development of distinctive codes of conduct which were predicated on the view that outward behaviour reflected inner virtues. By the fifteenth century, these codes prioritised the qualities of courtesy, generosity, piety, self-discipline, polite conversation, knowledge and wisdom, and were expressed through activities such as service and patronage.[2] Reputation and display were central to the gentle identity. Many of the signs and gestures involved in these actions will not have troubled the historical record. The visual impact of a house or hairstyle, or the reception of a nod or comment, are rarely found. More readily available are the written works that might have informed decisions and set the rules of appropriate behaviour. During the fifteenth century this literature was increasingly available to help the gentry, or those aspiring to be gentle, to form their identity. As Joan Thirsk has argued for the sixteenth century, books in general were 'powerful agents fashioning the gentry, shaping their attitudes, giving them a philosophy of life and directing their actions'.[3] Written material, therefore, had an important role in moulding a group consciousness and shared mentality.

In trying to understand the culture of the gentry, the question of emulation must be considered. Coss, using Georges Duby's theory of cultural patterns, has pointed to the various ways that the gentry imitated their social supe-

---

[1] Coss, 'The formation of the gentry', p. 48. See also Amos, 'For manners make man', p. 26.
[2] Mertes, 'Aristocracy'; Saul, 'Chaucer and gentility', p. 49. Mason, *Gentlefolk in the making*; Mitchell, '"Italian nobilita"', pp. 23–37.
[3] Thirsk, 'The fashioning of the Tudor–Stuart gentry', p. 72.

riors, the nobility, in terms of their literary tastes and possessions. His belief that the 'gentry and higher nobility enjoyed a broad common culture' is supported by a number of studies indicating the gentry's fondness for courtly fashions.[4] The well-known passage in the household book of Edward IV has the esquires 'talkyng of cronycles of kinges and of other polycyes', while great households like that of Richard Beauchamp, earl of Warwick, the De Vere, earls of Oxford, and Cicely Neville, duchess of York, provided milieus conducive for cultural exchange between the nobility and gentry.[5] However, while acknowledging a shared taste, more recent research has sought to emphasise gentry agency in literary culture and argue that they did not simply ape their superiors unthinkingly. Nor were the nobility the only social group with which the gentry shared interests. At times the gentry appear to be at one with the middling sections of society, largely the merchant class, in their choice of reading matter. It is a literary audience A.R. Myers called the 'bourgeois gentilhommes' (and Felicity Riddy the 'bourgeois-gentry').[6]

It is in the context of growing research on gentry culture that Humphrey's lifestyle will be examined, partly through his home life and largely through his reading matter. At the very least, this should demonstrate that his days were not simply filled with the simultaneously mundane and explosive world of land disputes; they contained the finer things in life. More significantly, the discussion will reveal a man conscious of creating a particular impression. His promised and then realised elevation to lord of Pownall may have prompted a need to convince those around him that he was worthy of that position. Humphrey was not simply concerned about personal status and he appears to be another provincial landlord preoccupied with the 'correct' upbringing and social positioning of his family, particularly his heir.[7] For this reason, the present chapter and the next will focus upon the fashioning of a gentle image.

---

[4] Coss, 'Aspects of cultural diffusion', p. 44; Green, *Poets and princepleasers*, pp. 9–10; Doyle, 'English books in and out of court', p. 166; Boffey and Thompson, 'Anthologies and miscellanies', p. 293.
[5] Myers (ed.) *The Household of Edward IV*, p. 129; Armstrong, 'The piety of Cicely, duchess of York, pp. 79–80; Edwards, 'Transmission and audience', p. 166; Hanna and Edwards, 'Rotheley, the De Vere circle'; Lowry, 'John Rous', pp. 331–2; Coleman, *Public reading*, pp. 109; 139; Radulescu, 'Talkyng of cronycles', p. 128; Youngs, 'Cultural networks', pp. 127–8.
[6] Myers (ed.) *The household of Edward IV*, p. 2; Riddy, 'Middle English romance', p. 237; Radulescu, 'Literature', p. 102; Youngs, 'Cultural networks', pp. 128–9; Meale, 'The politics of book ownership', p. 103.
[7] Boffey and Edwards, 'Literary texts', p. 560 for comparisons.

LIFESTYLE

Home

First impressions are important. Humphrey was lord of two estates and visitors to Newton and Pownall would have measured the man by what they saw. The houses of the gentry were not merely practical buildings, but symbols of authority and power. Size was a key indicator of wealth, while decoration could express fashion and taste.[8] Early Tudor Cheshire boasted some fine gentry residences, a number of which have remained *in situ* to the modern day. When the well-travelled antiquarian John Leland made his way around Cheshire in the 1530s, he noted several key families of the county and commented on their residences. The Davenports of Davenport had a 'great old house coverid with leade'; Cholmondely hall was 'a fair house, having a little mere by hit, a fair woode, and a mosse of fyrwod'; and the head of the Needham family was praised for having built 'a faire house. It is motid'.[9] In contrast, neither the Newton family nor their homes were deemed worthy of comment. Newton, which has never caught the eye of any Cheshire visitor, would have been not much more than a farmhouse, although it might have impressed locals with its newly marled fields, well-stocked fishponds and two working mills.[10] It also benefited from a 'fotewey' at 'þe hall dur' and a recently built chimney. The latter was constructed in the opening years of the sixteenth century, when Humphrey employed Master Cheyne of Wybunbury and Richard Breekman of Middlewich to make the necessary bricks. The chimney's position is not known, but with Humphrey's usual level of detail, it is described as being built on red sand and measuring three or four bricks in thickness.[11] Given the reference to sand, it may have been that, like chimneys at the houses of Kent gentry, it was built against a rear wall of the house.[12] Despite these improvements, Humphrey could not have been too sorry to move from Newton and take up residence in the larger Pownall Hall.

Pownall Hall was completely rebuilt in 1830 and all traces of earlier buildings have been erased. There is, however, an inventory of goods made in 1598 for Humphrey's great-grandson, William Newton, and as no major alterations are recorded for the sixteenth century, this may well indicate how the house appeared in Humphrey's day.[13] The design does resemble that of a conventional late medieval gentry house: simplicity combined with a marked

---

[8] Cooper, *Houses of the gentry*, p. 3.
[9] Smith, *The itinerary of John Leland*, part IX, pp. 27–30.
[10] As discussed above, pp. 83–88. The present house is a Grade II listed farmhouse, built in the seventeenth century with later additions. Information courtesy of Cheshire and Chester Archives and Local Studies.
[11] 12,000 bricks were purchased: Bodl, MS Lat. Misc.c.66, fo. 45r. For the footway see fo. 27ar.
[12] Pearson, *The medieval houses of Kent*, pp. 108, 111–12.
[13] BL, Add Roll 37328. The inventory valued the estate at £77 12s 4d.

hierarchical division between service and domestic areas.¹⁴ At the lower range was a room where the servants slept and a maids' chamber consisting of two beds; there was a kitchen and a number of storehouses; and the industry of the estate is represented in the itemised spinning wheel, loom and cheese press. Of the private dwellings, there was a great chamber, a middle chamber, a chapel chamber and William Newton's own chamber. It suggests a suite of rooms, ones that would have been separated from the main hall (here noticeable by its absence in the inventory). The arrangement also implies that, as in the larger country houses, the lord would be able to walk from his own room to the chapel chamber without needing to traverse the more public spaces.¹⁵ In each room the key item was the bed; William's was the most highly valued in the house, at 50s. While essentially private furnishings, beds could make important public statements about a person's wealth and standing. Humphrey himself was sufficiently taken with a bed he saw at Bradley Hall (Lancashire), the home of the Legh of Lyme family, that he made a note of it in his commonplace book. It is no surprise to see that his interest took the form of detailed measurements: he recorded the length and width of the frame, the feather mattress, the bolster, the pillow, the sheets, the blankets and covering.¹⁶

Like all gentry households, Newton and Pownall would be home not simply to the immediate Newton family, but also to a number of resident servants, itinerant guests and wider kin. Household size made as much of a statement about the lord's capacity as the extent of the building itself. At Newton, around 1498, Humphrey estimated that his household would consist of around thirteen to fourteen people along with strangers (the guests). This would make for a small household; it was dwarfed by great establishments, such as that of the Duke of Buckingham in Thornbury, where 157 residents including guests resided in 1507–8. It is also small compared to households of the county gentry. In East Anglia, the Townshend family employed between fifteen and twenty-two servants in the early sixteenth century, and many minor gentry had around twenty household servants.¹⁷ Newton's household appears more like that of the Kentish gentleman William Brent (d. 1490), which consisted of himself, his wife, four children and six servants.¹⁸

The household provided the gentleman with what Felicity Heal has called

---

¹⁴ Girouard, *Life*, pp. 30–1; Grenville, *Medieval housing*, pp. 106, 114.
¹⁵ See Heal, *Hospitality*, p. 44 who describes a similar, but much grander, situation at the duke of Buckingham's residence in Thornbury.
¹⁶ Bodl, MS Lat. Misc.c.66, fo.4v. It is possible that this is the same bed that Lady Newton described in the early twentieth century as 'a very curious old oak bed'. It was said to date to the fifteenth century and was called the king's bed: Newton, *The House of Lyme*, pp. 11–12.
¹⁷ Woolgar, *The great household*, p. 16; Moreton, *The Townshends*, p. 136; Mertes, *The English noble household*, p. 103; Girouard, *Life*, p. 15; Given-Wilson, *The English nobility*, p. 89.
¹⁸ Fleming, 'Household servants', p. 21; see also Saul, *Scenes*, p. 162.

'a stage on which his virtues were displayed', and the key performances came during the important ritual of meal-times.[19] Medieval society placed great emphasis on communal eating. For the elite, the sharing of food was an opportunity to display breeding and hospitality, and therefore good lordship. Kate Mertes has argued that fifteenth-century descriptions of nobility are more inclined to stress a liberal character than a warlike one.[20] Humphrey was no doubt adhering to these principles when he included 'strangers' in his calculations for grain consumption.[21] Upbringing and rank were also demonstrated through the observance of rules, a respect for order and the correct performance of duties and manners. Useful in this regard was the group of 'courtesy' or conduct books, which focused on meal-times. Their production grew significantly in the later Middle Ages and could run to anything from a few lines to a book-length treatise. While attractive to the nobility, they found their main market in the fifteenth and sixteenth centuries among those desiring social advancement, with a number of gentry and merchants commissioning and using conduct books.[22] The London merchant Richard Hill, for instance, owned at least three courtesy tracts, which he transcribed into his commonplace book.[23] Their attraction lay in their anonymity: the rules of etiquette could be learnt without losing face by having to ask.[24] They helped to clarify, in the words of Philippa Maddern, 'the criteria through which the distinctiveness of gentle and non-gentle were reconstructed and reinforced'.[25]

Humphrey had access to two late fifteenth-century courtesy treatises. The first and longer work is entitled *For to serve a lord*, while a second, incomplete, text is devoted to service at a marriage banquet.[26] Both treatises provided him – and indeed his household – with useful information on

---

[19] Heal, *Hospitality*, p. 23.
[20] Mertes, *The English noble household*, p. 187; Mertes, 'Aristocracy', p. 51; Sponsler, 'Eating lessons'; Myers (ed.), *The household of Edward IV*, p. 2.
[21] Bodl, MS Lat. Misc.c.66, fo. 31av.
[22] Nicholls, *The matter of courtesy*, ch. 4; Amos, 'For manners make man', pp. 25, 30; Sponsler, 'Eating lessons', pp. 4–5; Mertes, 'Aristocracy', p. 43; Radulescu, 'Literature', p. 101
[23] Dyboski (ed.) *Songs, carols*, pp. xli, xlii, xliii. See Nicholls, *The matter of courtesy*, pp. 71–2; Riddy, *Sir Thomas Malory*, p. 70.
[24] Nicholls, *The matter of courtesy*, p. 71; Riddy, *Sir Thomas Malory*, p. 72.
[25] Maddern, 'Gentility', p. 26.
[26] Bodl, MS Lat. Misc.c.66, fos 66r–68v. The two treatises were published in Furnivall (ed.) *The babee's book*, pp. 366–77. As this is a reasonably accurate transcription, I have cited Furnivall's version for ease of reference. Discolouration on the outer leaves suggest that the treatises once formed a separate booklet which was later included in the commonplace book. The separate existence is also suggested by the paper where the watermark (lettre P, dating variously 1462 x 1544) differs from the rest of the manuscript, and there are signs that the treatise was once folded along its centre: Briquet, *Les Filigranes* e.g. no. 8597. The discoloration of the final leaf suggests that the latter part of the marriage treatise was lost sometime prior to its inclusion within the commonplace book.

a broad range of issues. As the title suggests, *For to serve a lord* describes the correct procedure for serving a lord, the work requirements of each servant, the exact method to serve and clear away food, the number and correct folding of towels and cloths, the order of the meal and the food suitable for each course. The proper presentation of the meal is important here and imperative for the man anxious to show his guests that outwardly he presided over a well-ordered, dignified gentry household. For the same reasons, the treatise ends with a section on the correct way to carve the meat, an essential skill for the cultivated gentleman to master, as Chaucer famously highlighted in his description of the pilgrim squire who could 'calf biforn his fader at the table'.[27]

Throughout the entire meal, it was necessary to acknowledge hierarchy and to treat guests with the deference their rank demanded. Humphrey's treatise advised that when drinks were served to guests in the chamber 'yf ther be knight or lady or grete gentilwoman, they shall be servid uppon knee with bread and wyne'.[28] The note perhaps gives some indication of the level of society to which the treatise was directed. Whereas John Russell's *Boke of Nurture* was written for a noble household, Humphrey's treatise was fashioned for a humbler estate.[29] Signs of this are the fewer numbers of household staff and the narrower range of dishes served. The section on carving also betrays a vagueness in terms that is not seen in the more detailed treatises aimed at greater households. In the nineteenth century the text's editor, F.J. Furnivall, thought that a well-bred carver would faint at the type of confusions found in the Newton treatise.[30]

At least the Newton personnel would have dressed the part. It was vital that a gentleman's household staff appeared well-groomed in order to reflect positively on the lord's household: an unkempt servant could suggest an impoverished or tight-fisted lord. In the largest households, valets and pages would wear livery to mark their allegiance.[31] Humphrey's accounts reveal regular payments to servants for smocks, kirtles, robes and shoes. As discussed in Chapter 4, some even received part of their wages in clothing, probably spun and woven at Newton itself. One servant obtained a more expensive item when Humphrey passed on a gown that had once belonged to his mother; it was eaten by mites, but still worth around 5s. For William Hough, William Smale and Richard Coke there were also purchases of 'housecloth'. While

---

[27] *The Canterbury Tales: General prologue*: line 100.
[28] Furnivall (ed.) *The babees book*, p. 373.
[29] Ibid., pp. 117–228. Russell was an usher and marshall at the household of Duke Humphrey of Gloucester (d. 1447).
[30] Ibid., p. 366, commenting on the phrase 'unlose, tire or display' in relation to preparing a crane.
[31] For example, Fleming, 'Household servants', p. 24.

Plate 1. Arms of the Newton family quartering the Mainwaring of Peover at Wilmslow parish church

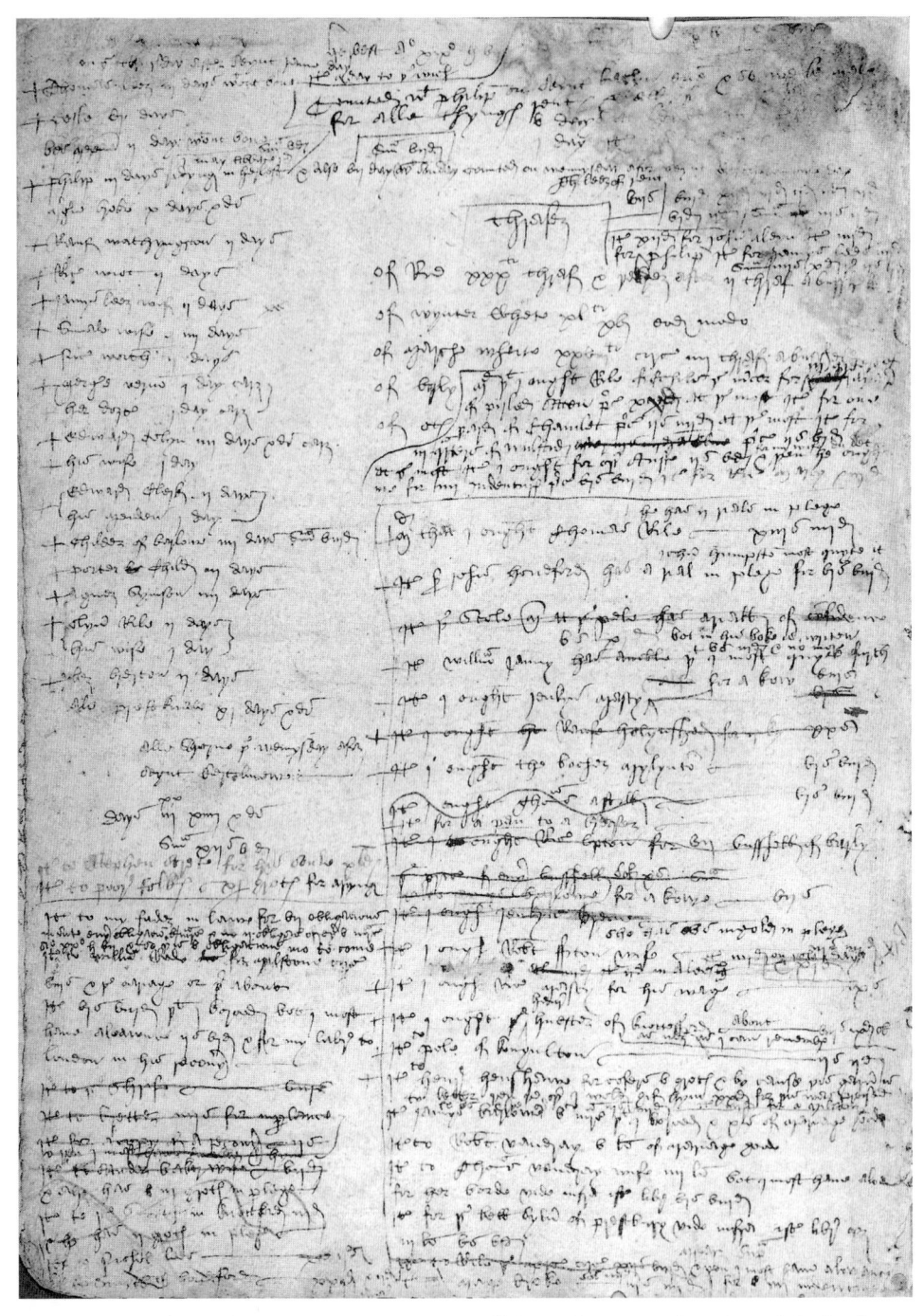

Plate 2. Page from the Newton accounts. Bodleian Library, University of Oxford, MS Latin Misc.c.66, fo. 45v

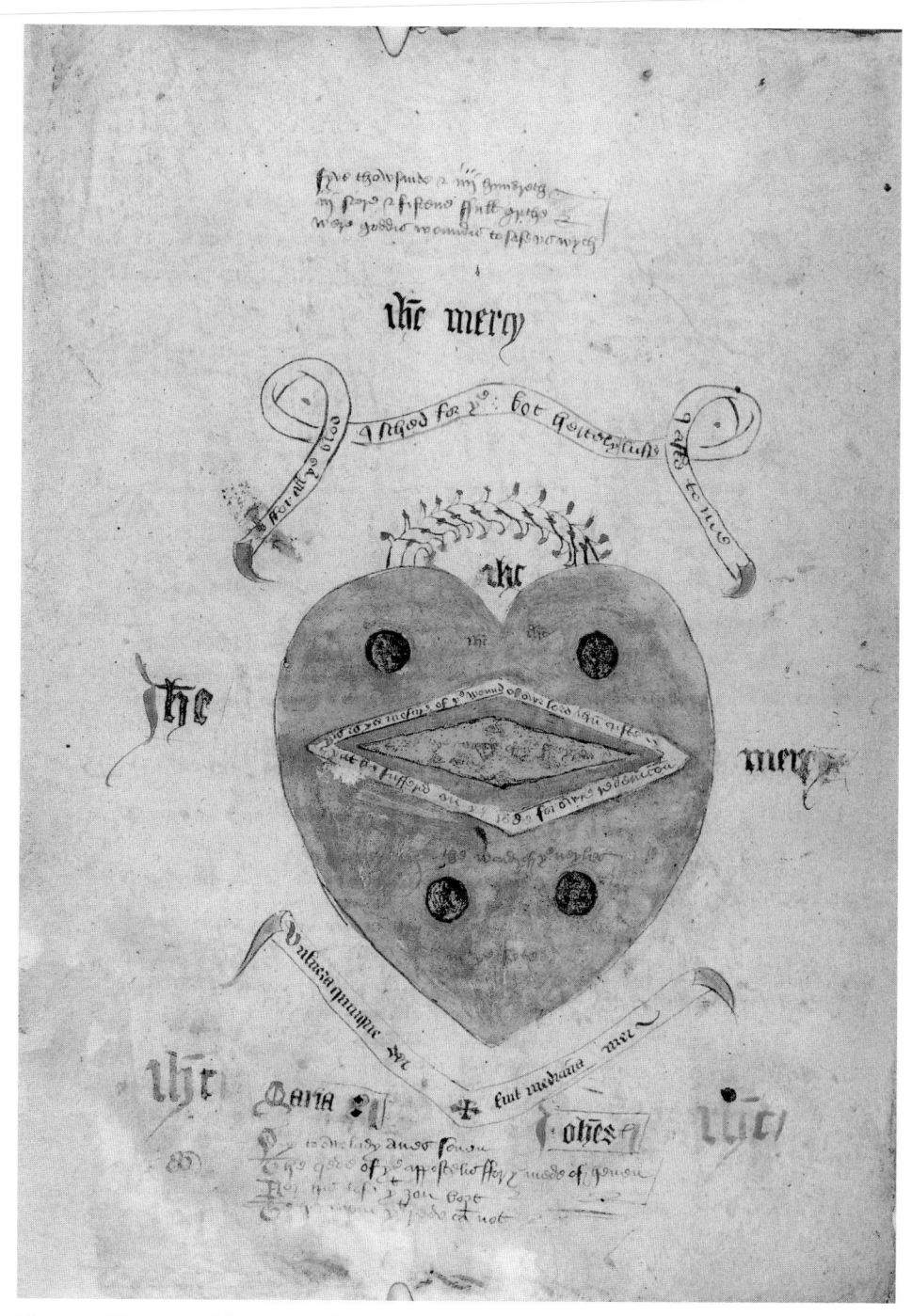

Plate 3. The sacred heart. Bodleian Library, University of Oxford, MS Latin Misc. c. 66, fo. 129v

Plate 4. The tombs of Humphrey and Ellen Newton, Wilmslow parish church. Photo: Conway Library, The Courtauld Institute of Art, London

Plate 5. The tomb of Humphrey Newton, Wilmslow parish church. Photo: Conway Library, The Courtauld Institute of Art, London

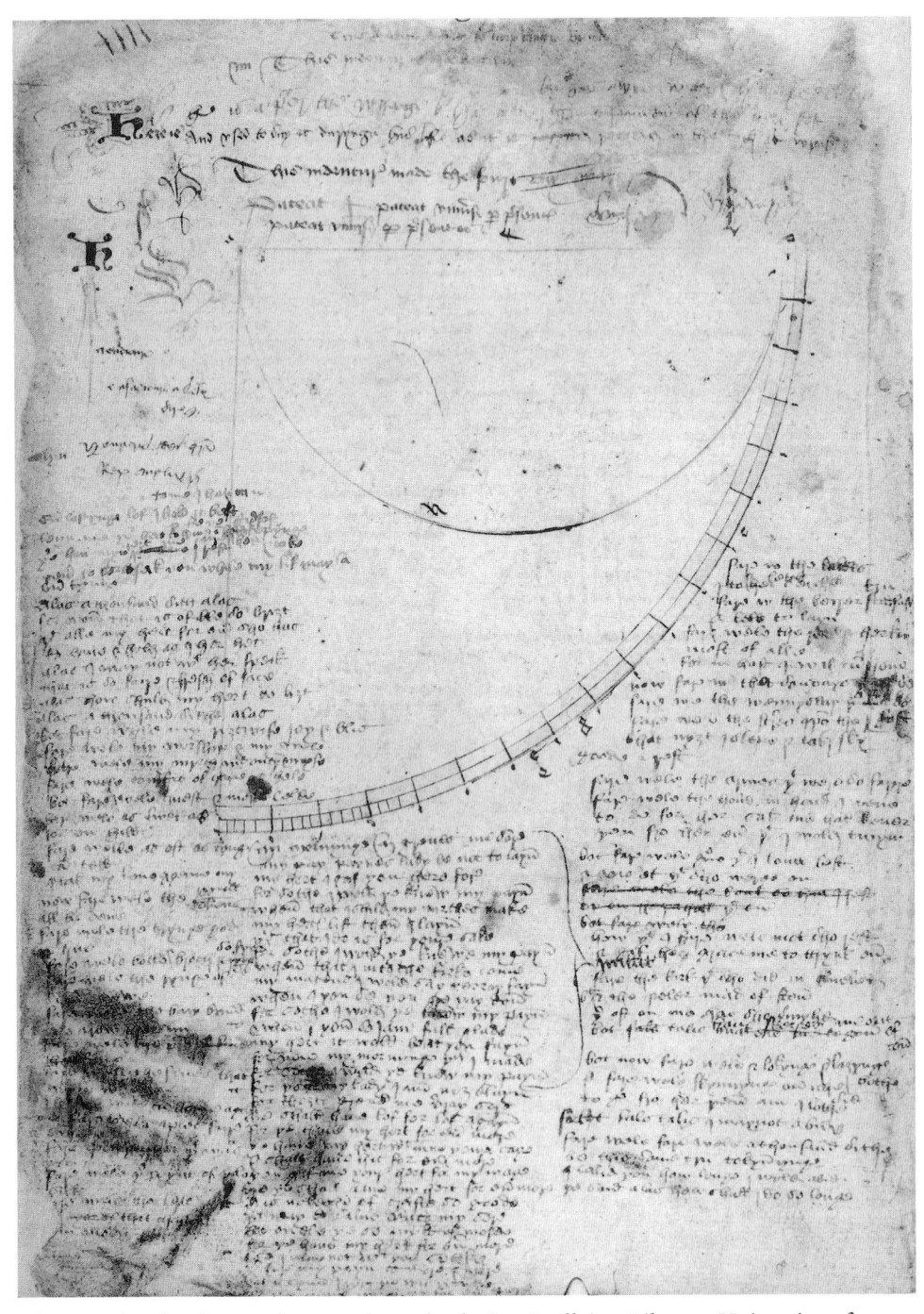

Plate 6. Sketch of a quadrant and secular lyrics. Bodleian Library, University of Oxford, MS Latin. Misc.c.66, fo. 94v

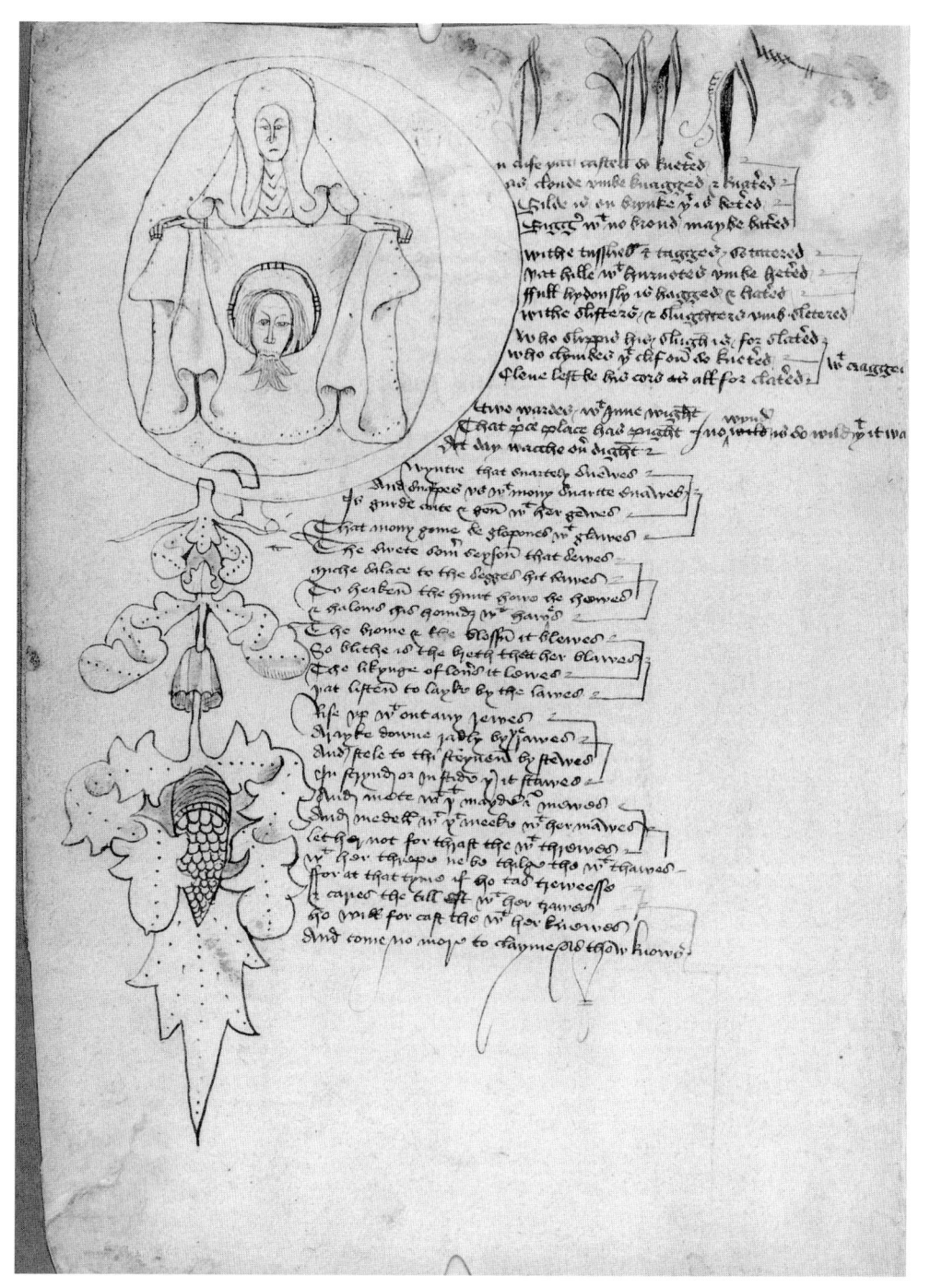

Plate 7. St Veronica and the vernicle. Bodleian Library, University of Oxford, MS Latin Misc.c.66, fo. 106v

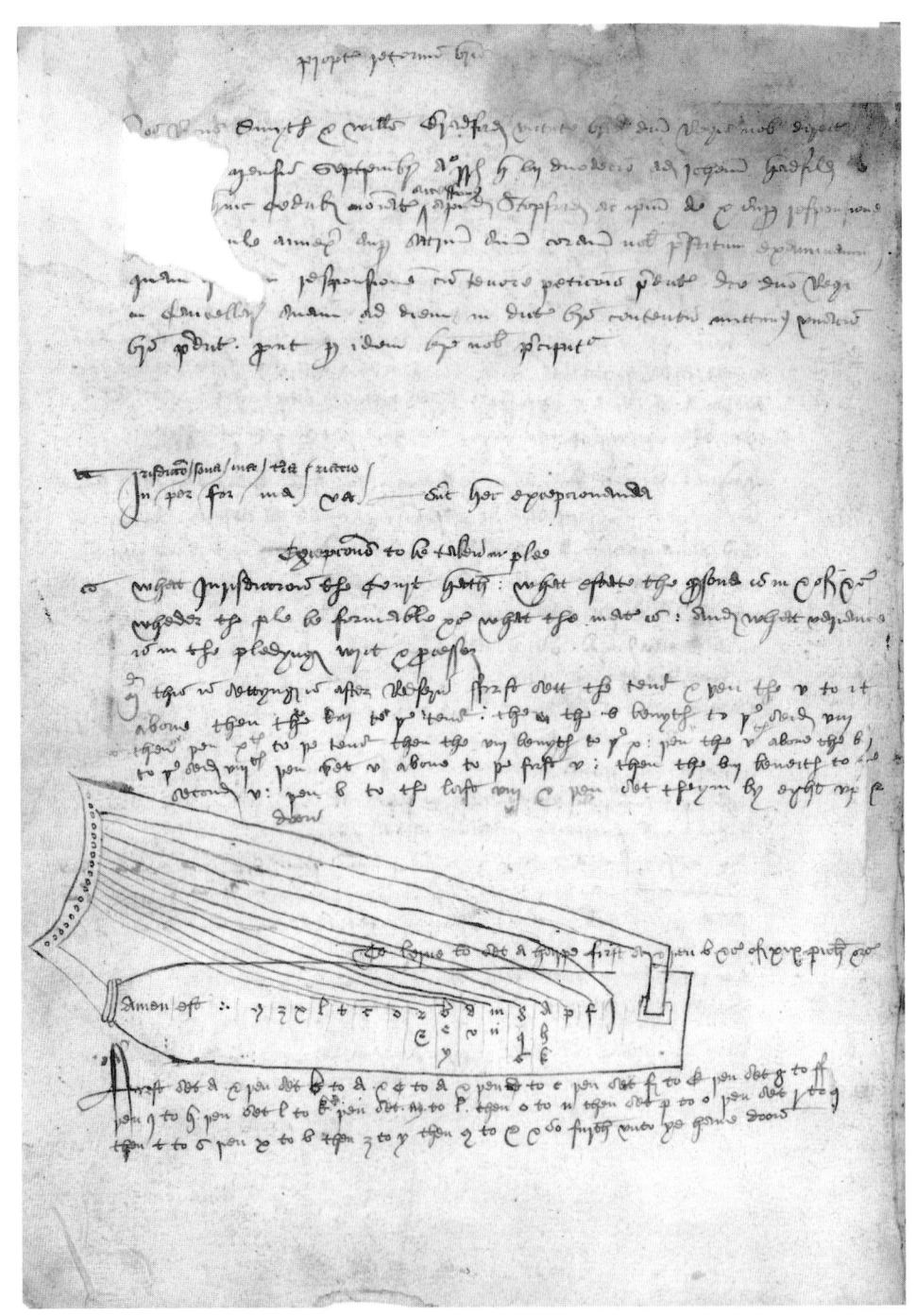

Plate 8. Sketch of a harp. Bodleian Library, University of Oxford, MS Latin Misc. c.66, fo. 8v

there is little to suggest a Newton livery, it is noteworthy that Richard Coke was specifically bought a tawny jacket and white hose.[32]

Naturally, a key part of Humphrey's treatises was the section on food. Aristocratic banquets are renowned for their richness of diet and plentiful courses. Just how many dishes were to be served depended on a person's status and wealth. The issuing of sumptuary legislation during the fifteenth and sixteenth centuries hints at the regular flouting of the rules, but also the continuing relevance of food in social aspiration. According to the regulations of 1517, a cardinal could have nine dishes at table; dukes, earls and bishops were allowed seven; those with land or fees worth between £100 and £200 were permitted four; and those with wealth worth £40–£100 a mere three.[33] Humphrey's treatise did not stipulate the number of dishes, but recognised that the quality and quantity served should be according to 'his degre'.[34] The menu has the standard three courses and presents a rich diet. There was to be beef, goose, rabbit, swan, pheasant, venison and a host of wildfowl, such as woodcock, partridge and plover. Unfortunately, the lack of detailed household accounts for Newton or Pownall means it is not possible to gauge the reality. Odd references do indicate the dominance of meat: there were purchases of beef and veal, while the home farm's pigs, chickens and the more highly valued swans presumably found their way to the table.[35] Rabbit was another prized meat and the warren at Newton (the 'conyes') would have provided a steady supply. Humphrey carefully noted two methods for catching rabbits, one using a scented glove and the other a stuffed female rabbit skin as a decoy. The latter was seen as a sure method to make rabbits 'com aboute ye as tame bestis'.[36] According to *For to serve a lord*, the meat should be washed down with wine 'of the beste that may be had, to the honor and lawde of the principall of the house'.[37] Little is known of Humphrey's wine purchases, but they are likely to have been modest. Transport costs and storage difficulties made wine an expensive drink. While it was consumed daily in noble households and would be purchased in bulk, in gentry residences, such as the Catesby's of Ashby St Ledgers, wine was purchased in small amounts as a rare treat and only served to certain guests.[38]

The household would experience seasonal variations, as diet was dictated

---

[32] Bodl, MS Lat. Misc.c.66, fos 25r, 27ar, 32v, 33r–v, 41av, 43v, 60r. Youngs, 'Servants and labourers', pp. 151, 154. See pp. 80, 88 above.
[33] Hughes and Larkin (eds) *Tudor royal proclamations*, no. 81, pp. 128–9.
[34] Furnivall (ed.) *The babees book*, p. 370.
[35] Bodl, MS Lat. Misc.c.66, fo 26a. Swan was a delicacy enjoyed by gentry families such as the Townshends: Moreton, *The Townshends*, p. 137.
[36] Bodl, MS Lat. Misc.c.66, fo. 128r.
[37] Furnivall (ed.) *The babees book*, p. 373.
[38] The main references to wine in Humphrey's accounts are when (tellingly perhaps) he was sending it to others: the parsonage of Prestbury (fo. 29v) and the justices in eyre (fo. 30v). Woolgar, *The great household*, p. 126; Hammond, *Food and feast*, pp. 72–3; Sim, *Food and feast*, ch. 5.

by weather and religion. At Lent, fish was the principal food, and Humphrey's Lenten purchases consisted of white (pickled) and red (smoked) herring, mulwell (cod), ray, sparling, salmon, oysters and mussels.[39] To these can be added the perch, tench, bream, fenders and eels that had been placed in Humphrey's own pools. It was a mix of the staple and the luxury. The sea fish would satisfy most demand, with the cheaper herring, oysters and mussels the basic provision for the lower orders. Freshwater fish was more highly valued, with the larger pond fish, like bream and pike, considered a delicacy to be served only to the lord and his special guests.[40] Their prestigious status was reflected in their appearance in medieval cookbooks, which were directed at the upper sections of society. Humphrey himself copied a recipe for tench or pike; it was to be fried in parsley, rosemary and onions and served with vinegar.[41] Seasonal variation can also be found in the fruit that was a staple for the final course of the meal. In Humphrey's treatise baked apples and pears were standard winter fare, presumably garnered from his orchards. In larger households these would have been augmented with more exotic fruit, like peaches or apricots, to impress guests.[42] While these may have been beyond Humphrey's budget, he could still enhance what he had: in common with other gentry households, Humphrey purchased spices for taste, colour and interest. Almonds and figs were bought during Lent, and passing references are made to sugar, pepper, mustard and the more expensive saffron.[43]

Special occasions drew a family under closer scrutiny, and none more so than a wedding feast, which was the opportunity to impress new relatives with demonstrations of wealth and hospitality. Whether arranging the marriage feasts of his sisters, or of his sons, Humphrey would have realised that variety was vital. The set menu he owned for the wedding feast was far more lavish than that in *For to serve a lord*, and there is an extra course. No longer was the third serving merely baked fruit: it included almond cream, 'losynge in syruppe', partridge, plover and veal, followed by a fourth course of cheese and cake.[44] The food itself was meant to be entertaining, and hence devices, or subtleties, were placed on the central dishes.[45] The first course had a device proclaiming 'Welcombe you bretheren godely in this hall', and a lamb with a verse denoting meekness; the second had an antelope and a couplet proclaiming gladness and loyalty; while the third course was one that gave thanks for the feast. The final subtlety showed a wife lying in childbed

---

[39] Bodl, MS Lat. Misc.c.66, fos 34cr, 37v.
[40] Dyer, *Standards of living*, p. 62; Woolgar, *The great household*, pp. 121–2.
[41] Bodl, MS Lat. Misc.c.66, fo. 5v.
[42] Sim, *Food and feast*, p. 118.
[43] Bodl, MS Lat. Misc.c.66, fos 34cr, 35v, 36v; Woolgar, *The great household*, p. 130.
[44] It was entitled 'Ffor to make a feste for a bryde', printed in Furnivall (ed.) *The babees book*, pp. 375–7. 'Losynge' refers to a small cake. *OED*: lozen and lozenge.
[45] Similarly used in John Russell's *Boke of Nurture*, see Furnivall (ed.) *The babees book*, pp. 164–70.

with lines promising offspring. All the elements of a successful wedding were therefore present: the meek and loyal wife who would hopefully be very fertile; the richness of the feast for which thanks be to God.

Most of the entertainment came in more animated form, with music, story-telling and juggling – the varied repertoire of the minstrel. This was an essential component of aristocratic feasting at all levels. In the wealthy household of the Suffolk widow Alice de Bryene a harpist was employed twice and minstrels four times during 1412–13.[46] Humphrey is known to have paid a minstrel to perform at his sister's wedding, and Hill the minstrel was present on another occasion at Newton. That they came alone may well suggest that Humphrey did not have the resources to pay for a troop.[47] Feasting, therefore, was designed to be full of colour, and yet it must not be forgotten that mealtimes also formed the focus of worship and contemplation. In *For to serve a lord* grace was to be said just prior to the hand washing.[48] Humphrey's short series of Latin prayers were to be said before and after dinner and supper.[49] They are conventional, praising and thanking God for the food, punctuated by the repetition of *benedicite*. Humphrey may have given these to his sons to recite because children of the gentry were expected to read out Latin prayers in between and sometimes during meals.[50] It is of course possible that *For to serve a lord* was aimed largely at Humphrey's sons; the section on carving might indicate as much.[51] Certainly the behaviour of all present in the household was important. In Chapter 2 it was noted that Humphrey had placed a copy of the *ABC of Aristotle* in a prominent position in the Newton household, 'in þe bordure of þe halle', implying that the hall at Newton remained the focus of communal life.[52] The poem's theme of moderation – 'mesurable mene is best for vs all' – chimed well with the gentry's outlook. The foolery of the minstrel would take place within the confines of a well-ordered Christian household.[53]

Presiding over these festivities, making sure prayers were said and meals were served on time, was the lord, 'the principall soverain'. Taking the spotlight meant his appearance, particularly his apparel, came under intense scrutiny. At a time when clothes were perceived to distinguish 'estates, preeminence, dignities and degrees', Humphrey had to dress as a gentleman to be

---

[46] Swabey, *Medieval gentlewoman*, p. 92. Girouard, *Life*, pp. 24–5. Moreton, *The Townshends*, p. 136.
[47] Bodl, MS Lat. Misc.c.66, fos 26av, 34cv.
[48] Furnivall (ed.) *The babees book*, p. 368.
[49] Bodl, MS Lat. Misc.c.66, fo. 34b.
[50] Orme, *Medieval children*, p. 207.
[51] John Russell's book was specifically aimed at 'alle yonge gentilmen þat lust to lerne or entende': Furnivall (ed.) *The babees book*, p. 198: lines 1236–7.
[52] Bodl, MS Lat. Misc.c.66, fo. 26v. *NIMEV*, nos 471, 3793, 4155. See p. 27 above.
[53] It may also reflect what Riddy has called a 'bourgeois ethos' in the moderating of food: Riddy, 'Mother knows best', p. 84; Sponsler, 'Eating lessons', p. 18; Rust, 'The "ABC of Aristotle"', pp. 63–78.

accepted as one.⁵⁴ He would have seen and digested this message from several sources, including his otherworld vision, where the poor, tawny clothing of John Newton is employed to signify his spiritual and social shortcomings. The only hint at Humphrey's own appearance is found on his tomb, where he is dressed in a long, voluminous gown.⁵⁵ The image is too stylised to be an exact representation of Humphrey, but it does show the fashion in the early sixteenth century, and he may well have sported similar gowns. The clothes he did own were bought from several tradesmen from eastern Cheshire; there are no hints that he made more metropolitan purchases, as the London-savvy Paston family did.⁵⁶ Humphrey's clothes were a standard mix of gowns, doublets, jacket, hose, buskins (shoes), 'pynsons' (thin shoes or slippers), hats, caps and bonnets.⁵⁷ Most of the items have a practical ring about them: the tendency was to buy the thick cotton or woollen cloths of kersey, fustian and worsted. His purchase of a 'pair of shows with double soles' may have been for a servant, but could also reflect his travels on business across the Midland counties and down into London.⁵⁸ Nevertheless, he also purchased garments for more social and leisurely occasions. He bought three quarters of 'piled satin' and a damask doublet along with two yards of large braid to embellish it. Both were richly woven cloth which regularly feature in sumptuary legislation. Indeed, it would appear that Humphrey was technically buying clothing designated for those of knightly rank and above.⁵⁹ These clothes would have been ornamented with a range of jewellery. Again, little is known of Humphrey's preferences – or indeed his wife's – but he did purchase from a goldsmith a turquoise, a ruby, a sapphire and a diamond, which he paid for in instalments.⁶⁰

It has to be acknowledged that these are all mere glimpses of the man, but they are sufficient to confirm his gentry status. Indeed, it is telling that such brief signs can be so obviously read: Humphrey's gentility would have been in question if the clues were obscure or needed to be layered on thickly.

---

⁵⁴ The phrase comes from Sumptuary legislation issued in 1510: Hunt, *Governance of the consuming passions*, p. 310. For discussions on the importance of dress see Crane, *The performance of self*, pp. 10–15 and Scattergood, 'Fashion and morality', particularly p. 255. See also Peter Idley: 'Ffor clothing ofte maketh the man': D'Evelyn (ed.) *Peter Idley's instruction to his son: Liber primus*, line 102, p. 82.
⁵⁵ For both the vision and Humphrey's tomb, see above pp. 118, 138.
⁵⁶ For John Paston III and his desire for fashionable London hats, see Richmond, *The Paston Family*, p. 36.
⁵⁷ Bodl, MS Lat. Misc.c.66, fos 26av, 27ar–v, 29r, 30r, 32v, 41ar and 45v. He also bought lace for his wife: ibid., fo. 41av.
⁵⁸ Bodl, MS Lat. Misc.c.66, fo. 30r.
⁵⁹ In 1463 sumptuary legislation decreed that no one below the rank of knight could wear velvet, satin, counterfeit silk or ermine: Hunt, *Governance of the consuming passions*, p. 307.
⁶⁰ Bodl, MS Lat. Misc.c.66, fo. 65r.

A gentleman's reading

In some quiet corners of Newton and Pownall Hall, Humphrey found the space to read a wide range of material. It will already be clear that the written word performed an important function in Humphrey's life. Treatises, deeds and books informed his legal work, sourced his landed disputes and facilitated his personal worship. Yet Humphrey was no mere 'pragmatic reader', but was what Malcolm Parkes has described as a 'cultivated reader', and he was interested in a variety of literature that would improve his knowledge, satisfy his curiosity and entertain himself and his family.[61]

He was not unusual in this. Levels of readership in the period of Humphrey's lifetime are notoriously difficult to determine, but all the evidence points to a significant growth in lay literacy during the late medieval period.[62] Factors behind this expansion include the demands made by commerce, estate and government administrations; developments in the law; the spread of the vernacular; and the increasing availability of books, especially following the introduction of printing. Among the gentry and mercantile classes education was highly valued as a means of bestowing some social polish and providing the route to social advancement. While the very wealthy could afford to pay for private tuition, wider society benefited from the provision of grammar schools, which grew considerably in number during the fifteenth century. These developments meant that cities like York became home to literate gentlemen, artisans, yeomen and husbandmen.[63] In London in 1533, Thomas More estimated that between fifty and sixty per cent of England was literate. While doubts have been raised about this proportion, J.B. Trapp is of the opinion that it 'might not be wide of the mark'.[64] It is therefore possible that Humphrey was part of a literary world where reading ability was taken for granted. It should be remembered that Humphrey's wedding feast menu assumed that the guests would be able to read the subtleties on the dishes. The pictures of a lamb and a woman in childbed were not left to make statements alone, although both could have done so adequately.

While books figured prominently in the lives of the gentry, just how many volumes an individual might access or own during his or her life is not easy to determine, especially at the lower social levels. Humphrey lived during a period where printing had helped to make books affordable not simply to the wealthy, but also to the financially comfortable. Nonetheless, they retained a

---

[61] Parkes, 'Literacy of the laity', pp. 275, 278.
[62] Ibid., pp. 278, 287; Moran, *The growth of English schooling*, pp. 150–84; DuBoulay, *An age of ambition*, p. 118; Bennett, 'Forms of intellectual life', p. 143; Trapp, 'Literacy, books and readers', p. 34; Meale, 'Patrons, buyers and owners', pp. 201–38.
[63] Moran, *The growth of English schooling*, passim.
[64] Trapp, 'Literacy, books and readers', pp. 39–40.

luxury status and were not owned in large numbers among the laity.[65] The sergeant at law, Roger Townshend, appears exceptional in having forty books at his death, while the bibliophile Sir John Paston (d. 1479) appears to have owned in the region of around twenty volumes.[66] Yet the inventories used as evidence in these cases are rare finds and the dependency on wills for information on book ownership is problematic: religious works dominated as testators considered their souls, while secular and vernacular books were most likely to be overlooked.[67]

Given these notable difficulties, it is fortunate that Humphrey's commonplace book survives to indicate works to which he had access, and that he considered worth quoting. We do not know whether he referenced most of his reading matter or only a small proportion, but altogether Humphrey transcribed part or all of over thirty authored texts, with the impression given of a widely read gentleman interested in the content of the works he came across. More than half appear in the final third of his manuscript, a distinct section or 'literary miscellany'.[68] It is possible that he owned one or several of the texts in book or pamphlet form, but no extant volume bearing marks of his ownership has come to light. There is no evidence that he ever commissioned works, and we know little of his household's collection, although he had married into a family with a history of book owning. In his will of 1438, Richard Fitton of Pownall, Ellen's great-grandfather, bequeathed four breviaries and one missal.[69] Nevertheless, there was no need to buy and possess manuscripts in late medieval England: a healthy market in second-hand books existed, with informal networks of book lending and borrowing operating around the country. Parish libraries provided some reading matter, and not far from Newton lay the chapel of Pott Shrigley, which housed a lending library serving the neighbouring gentry. An inventory of the library dating c.1492 lists nineteen books, mostly of a religious nature, but there were also a *Gesta Romanorum* and – what every gentleman needed – a book of 'goode manners'.[70]

Humphrey's own works were largely in the vernacular, with over two-thirds of the texts in Middle English, which by the late fifteenth century was the reading language of choice for gentry society. He was, nonetheless, comfortable with Latin, transcribing both basic and technical Latin treatises,

---

[65] Ford, 'Private ownership of printed books', pp. 206, 218; Strohm, 'Writing and reading', p. 471; Pearsall, 'The cultural and social setting', p. 32; Fleming, 'The "Hautes"', p. 100; Meale, 'The politics of book ownership', p. 103.
[66] Moreton, *The Townshends*, p. 379; Davis (ed.) *Paston letters and papers*, I, pp. 516–18.
[67] Parkes, 'Literacy of the laity', p. 292; Cavanagh, 'A study of books privately owned in England, pp. 3, 9–14; Vale, *Piety, charity and literacy*, pp. 5, 29; Thrupp, *Merchant class*, p. 161; Goldberg, 'Lay book ownership', pp. 183–9.
[68] For the 'literary miscellany', see p. 184 below.
[69] *Cheshire Sheaf*, 3rd ser. xviii (1921), p. 24.
[70] Dodgson, 'A library at Pott chapel', pp. 47–53. For other libraries see Moran, *The growth of English schooling*, p. 210; Barron, 'The expansion of education', p. 240.

while French was confined to the law French texts described in Chapter 3. He is a reminder, therefore, of the continuing importance of Latin and French in the lives of the early sixteenth-century elite.[71] Most of what Humphrey transcribed has a strong practical edge, which is to be expected of items contained in commonplace books (as discussed in Chapter 7). The following sections explore his choices and what they can reveal about his interests and preoccupations.

Family concerns: medicine and health

With infection and disease a common occurrence in late medieval life, Humphrey was deeply concerned for his family's health. Chapter 5 drew attention to his conventional dependency on spiritual assistance in times of need, and this was complemented by a plethora of more earthly measures. If Humphrey paid for medical attention, he does not refer to it, but it can be assumed that he would never have relied wholly on the services of others. Ineffectiveness and a lack of physicians had necessarily made the period an age where 'medicine began at home'.[72] The early Tudor householder had a range of texts to choose from. In addition to the traditional Latin philosophical works favoured by university-trained scholars, the fifteenth century had witnessed the growth of Middle English treatises aimed at the non-graduate practitioner. They formed part of what Peter Jones has termed an 'information revolution', as the explosion of interest in medical writings fuelled the production of practical material. An eclectic range of items, from recipes scribbled in the margins of estate accounts to the medical knowledge in the intricately woven tales of Gower and Lydgate, makes 'health' material one of the most common survivors of later medieval manuscripts.[73]

The core of Humphrey's medical material is contained in a sixteen-folio pamphlet professionally written in the late fifteenth century.[74] It is not known whether this was prepared specifically for the Newton family or if it was acquired ready-made, but it provided a useful body of work: a Middle English commentary on Giles of Corbeil's Latin poem *De Urinis*; a urinary in English; lines from the English *Trotula* version D; a short section on the *mola matricis* from a Latin *Trotula*; and well over a dozen medical recipes.[75] The

---

[71] See pp. 45 n.25, n.26, and 55 above. Strohm, 'Writing and reading', p. 455.
[72] Jones, 'Popular medical knowledge', p. 421.
[73] Jones, 'Medicine and Science', pp. 433–5. Singer, 'Survey of medical manuscripts', pp. 96–107; Robbins, 'Medical manuscripts', pp. 345–402; Voigts, 'Scientific and medical books', pp. 345–402; Voigts, 'Medical prose', pp. 315–35; Jones, 'Information and science', p. 101.
[74] Bodl, MS Lat. Misc.c.66, fos 75–91. The paper's 'ciseaux' watermark suggests a date c.1470–2. Briquet, *Les Filigranes*, no. 3687 possibly.
[75] *De Urinis* (fos 75–83), *Trotula* Version D (fos 83–86), recipes (fos 87–8), English urinary (fos 88–9), recipes (fos 89–90).

Corbeil was quite a sophisticated treatise aimed at professional practitioners and it offered Humphrey detailed theoretical information on the function of the organs and the passage of blood around the body. Nonetheless, the remaining choices were highly practical, with the texts providing essential guidance on the diagnosis, prognosis and treatment of a wide range of diseases. The urinary was a trusted, painless method of diagnosing illnesses that emphasised the primacy of observation in medical practice. There was a buoyant market in these treatises in both Latin and Middle English. Many versions were written in the expectation that they would be used as part of home diagnosis: the fourteenth-century *Domes of Urine*, for instance, advised the reader to match his own sample with the coloured illustrations of the text.[76] Humphrey's copy contains the prick marks, ruled margins and formal handwriting of a trained scribe, yet its plainness shows it belonged to the cheaper end of the market. While 'jordons' or glass phials are drawn in order to show varying shades of urine, they are not coloured, leaving a person to make decisions based on written description alone.

In treating any ailments found, the most accessible remedies were provided by the medical recipe. Usually these comprised compounds of ingredients taken from plants, animals, minerals and occasionally precious stones. Such recipes are frequent finds in commonplace books – those of Robert Reynes and Richard Hill, for example – and Humphrey collected a wide range. A number were drawn from an unknown authority simply named 'Reynes'. Like many collections, they were intended to serve everyday concerns while preparing for the worst. They included toothache, the cough, sleep talking, migraine, insomnia and nose bleeding, alongside the greater dangers of plague and sweating sickness.[77] Humphrey used his commonplace book to record hopeful cures for whatever might befall his household.

At times it is possible to see Humphrey's attention turn to specific members of that family. His care for his wife's health has been noted in previous chapters, and this extended to collecting various obstetrical and gynaecological texts in circulation. That he owned one of the various treatises attributed to Trotula (English D version) entitled *Secreta mulierum* is not surprising because surviving texts suggest it was aimed at, and uniformly owned by, men.[78] Whether Ellen herself would feel the need to read the opinions on menstruation, conception and cravings in pregnancy cannot be known. But she may have benefited from Humphrey's knowledge of these 'mysteries' and both would have wanted to be aware of particular problems hindering pregnancy. On this subject the short Latin piece attributed to Trotula on the *Mola*

---

[76] Gottfried, *The Black Death*, pp. 119–20; Rawcliffe, *Medicine*, pp. 46–9.
[77] Bodl, MS Lat. Misc.c.66, fos 87v–88r, 89r–90v. Others are referred to or transcribed on folios 27c, 62a and 64ar. Reynes was possibly the Reyneris Osterhusen Daventriensis, Doctor of Medicine who compiled a compendium of medicine. One Latin version can be found at the beginning of BL, MS Sloane 345, fos 1–6.
[78] Green, 'Obstetrical and gynaecological texts', pp. 56–7, 71.

Matricis provided useful information. The *mola* was a large fleshy lump that grew in the womb and exhibited all the appearances of a developing foetus. Evidently it was vital to distinguish a *mola* before embarking on any attempts to dispel the lump from the body. The piece in Humphrey's manuscript lists the various signs and indications that a true pregnancy had occurred.[79] Not for the first time, therefore, Humphrey's notes show a concern with conception and childbirth. These might be dismissed as a gentleman's need for heirs, but Humphrey was not lacking in that area and the care shown for the mother's health may hint at more altruistic reasons.[80]

Astrology

Books also allowed Humphrey to transcend the everyday and stimulate his imagination. He was interested in the way the world worked and what secrets it held. He shared the common view among Europe's educated of a close relationship between heaven and earth and the essential unity of God and nature. A single law was believed to govern the planets, the seasons and the human body, leading to what Jonathan Hughes has called 'a more holistic attitude towards their society and natural environment' than exists in the modern day.[81]

Humphrey's inquisitiveness led him to draw information from the work *Speculum Mundi*, a great compilation of several Latin writers on the structure, size and workings of the Universe. A French version had appeared in 1464 and was subsequently used for an English translation printed by Caxton in 1481 under the title *The Mirrour of the World*. Humphrey had access to a condensed version of the *Mirrour* because, while he references his selected passage as 'Chapter 17', only the first sentence was taken from there; the transcription is an amalgamation of six different chapters.[82] Humphrey was perhaps drawn to the work in the way Caxton hoped his readers would be: the printer promised that they would 'lerne and knowe specially the creacion of this world the gretnes of the firmament and lytilnes of therthe in regard

---

[79] Bodl, MS Lat. Misc.c.66. fo. 87b. An English version has been printed in Rowland, *Medieval women's guide to health*, pp. 140–4.

[80] See pp. 113–14 above. Male physicians also paid particular attention to female gynaecological conditions. The physician Thomas Fayrefold treated forty-two female patients (alongside sixty-three males) and ten per cent of his list of cures concerned cases of suffocation of the womb: Jones, 'Thomas Fayreford', pp. 156–83.

[81] Hughes, *Arthurian myths*, p. 9. Burrow, *Ages of man*, pp. 2, 55; Goodich, *From birth to old age*, pp. 15, 69.

[82] Bodl, MS Lat. Misc.c.66, fo. 34a. Comparing Humphrey's text to the EETS volume of Caxton's *Mirrour*, his referencing should be: Part 1, ch. 17 (the first line); Part 3, chs 19–22 (one or two lines from each chapter) and ch. 23 (the diagram). Prior (ed.) *Caxton's Mirrour of the World*, pp. 51, 171–4, 177–8, 180.

of heven'.[83] Certainly the passages that caught Humphrey's attention tried to express the incredible vastness of the heavens with comprehensible examples: a stone, for instance, would take one hundred years to free-fall from the sphere of the stars down to earth. Beneath the piece Humphrey drew a rough copy of a diagram depicting the concentric spheres that comprised the universe. These spheres were believed to have direct influence over the course of earthly events, and Humphrey was interested in how the planets held answers to the direction the world was heading. He recorded the belief, widespread in medieval philosophical works and usually derived from Ptolomy, that the seven planets corresponded with the seven patriarchs (from Adam to the anti-Christ), who in turn represented the seven ages of the world (each represented by a millennium).[84] While satisfying Humphrey's cosmological curiosity, it also appealed to his apocalyptic beliefs that are visible elsewhere in his writings: the world would end at the seventh stage unless God decided on a new course 'to reyen ageyn'.

It was the planets' impact on individual lives, however, that strengthened the popularity of astrology during the fifteenth century, and saw it gain a broad following among literate citizens, merchants and artisans.[85] They had access to a large spectrum of material, from the complex planetary tables demanding scientific calculations to the very basic lunar calendars, and to the almanacs which became the 'scientific book best-seller' of the fifteenth and sixteenth centuries.[86] For the majority of adherents, astrology's value lay in its everyday usefulness. It could proffer information on the weather or on the whereabouts of stolen goods or an errant spouse, or provide answers to when a pregnancy would take place and the sex of the child. Above all, it was its association with medicine, specifically prognosis, that ensured an enduring appeal. The fifteenth-century notebooks of the provincial physicians John Crophill of Wix (Cambridge), Richard Trewythian of London and Thomas Fayreford of the West Country indicate the value of astrology to medicine. All use the scientific notion that once a person's 'nativity' (the date and preferably hour of birth) was known, calculations could be made to determine whether the patient was curable, the type and duration of the treatment, and the best time for the cure to begin.[87]

Humphrey's own interests were linked to these practical needs. It was perhaps with a view to casting his children's nativity that Humphrey recorded

---

[83] Crotch (ed.) *The prologues and epilogues of William Caxton*, p. 54.
[84] Bodl, MS Lat. Misc.c.66, fo. 70r. A similar scheme is found in the commonplace book of Richard Hill: Dyboski (ed.) *Songs, carols*, p. xxxvii. Discussion of the seven ages can be found in Burrow, *Ages of Man*, pp. 79–80.
[85] Jones, 'Information and science', pp. 97–111; Page, 'Richard Trewythian', pp. 193–228.
[86] Jones, 'Medicine and science', p. 438.
[87] Siraisi, *Medieval and early Renaissance medicine*, pp. 134–6; Rawcliffe, *Medicine*, ch. 4; Green, 'Obstetrical and gynaecological texts', p. 59; Talbert, 'The notebook of a fifteenth-century practising physician', pp. 5–30; Mustain, 'A rural medical practitioner', pp. 469–76; Page, 'Richard Trewythian'; Jones, 'Thomas Fayreford'.

the hour and date of their births. William Newton, for example, was born between the hours of eight and nine in the morning of Tuesday 3 January. Humphrey also listed the three 'perilous Mondays' and scribbled down two circular diagrams of the zodiac. Slightly more demanding were copies of three planetary charts. These provided basic information on the relationship between the planets and the zodiac, and listed the 'unequal' hours of the day and night, essential material for astrological calculations such as the computation of horoscopes.[88] Determining the hours was a common find in almanacs and was, as Carey describes, 'one of the first steps required in astrological investigations'.[89] Humphrey's introductory material may therefore have helped him make his own computations. He was at least aware of the astronomical instruments needed to create them. His partial drawing of a quadrant must have been formed by tracing the pen around an actual instrument; it is no free-hand sketch (Plate 6). The quadrant was employed in angle measurement, in general astronomy and as a variation of the astrolabe; its small size, portability, accessibility and low cost all helped to make its use widespread. Humphrey also made a small sketch of an astronomer holding an armillary sphere, which is very similar to illustrations appearing in surviving fifteenth-century astrological treatises. As well as hinting at Humphrey's awareness of these manuscripts, it suggests a familiarity with the armillary sphere, which showed the paths of the equator, ecliptic, tropics, polar circles and several meridian circles.[90]

Humphrey would not have needed to look solely at the heavens to see what the future held: he could read the messages in and on the body. As is well known, medieval scientists followed ancient philosophy in believing the human body to be composed of four basic elements (fire, water, earth and air) and four bodily fluids or humours (blood, phlegm, yellow bile and black bile), which rendered a particular complexion and personality.[91] Humphrey quoted from the best-known treatise on physiognomy, the exceptionally popular *Secretum secretorum*, traditionally attributed to Aristotle. Its success among the nobility has often been attributed to the work's original intention as a guidebook for rulers. However, its main attraction to wider society was the section on divination and physiognomy, which promised to reveal

---

[88] Bodl, MS Lat. Misc.c.66, fos 1v, 48v, 64r, 122. Smoller, *History, prophecy and the stars*, pp. 14–22. The 'unequal hours' refers to the view that an hour in the summer was longer than in the winter. Compare with the tables found in *A Theater of the planetary hours of all dayes of the year*, pp. 12–14; North, *Chaucer's universe*, p. 78.
[89] Carey, 'Astrological medicine', p. 326.
[90] Bodl, MS Lat. Misc.c. 66, fos 92r (astrologer), 94v (quadrant). Both instruments are discussed in Price, 'Precision instruments to 1500', pp. 599–600, 612–13; Pederson, 'Astronomy', p. 323. See Carey, *Courting disaster*, plate no. 5, where Charles V of France is shown holding an armillary and dressed in a similar fashion to the man in Humphrey's sketch.
[91] For example, Rawcliffe, *Medicine*, p. 33. The scheme is simply tabulated in Burrow, *Ages of man*, p. 12.

Aristotle's secrets of the world and often circulated independently of the *Secretum*. Humphrey's chosen extract concerned 'þe propertyes of vysage' and explained how to interpret facial features. Grey eyes, for instance, were a sign of unstableness, and only ill could be expected of someone with brows that met in the middle.[92] Humphrey seems less interested in the reasoning behind this system than he was in the superficial signs that denoted complexion. Elsewhere in his manuscript a short list provided brief descriptions of the sanguine, choleric, phlegmatic and melancholic personality. As an example, and as we would expect, the sanguine person was of ruddy colour and 'fleschy, riȝt bold, riȝt blessyd'.[93] Hands provided further possibilities for reading personalities, with palmistry or chiromancy a means of predicting future developments. This was sometimes attacked as an illicit occult practice because it appeared to reject the notion of free will. Nevertheless, it had support in the church hierarchy, royal courts and universities, gaining some legitimacy through its accreditation to Aristotle or Albertus Magnus. It was legitimate so long as the lines were read simply as denoting an inclination towards a particular character or event, not that it was fated.[94] Some of the major academic treatises were long and detailed, but Humphrey again chose to copy a text that provided for a quick and easy assessment. A crude sketch of a large right hand is filled with notes inside and adjacent to the palm. All are rudimentary, stating simply what each line and mark signified, rather than offering much in the way of explanation. That Humphrey used a Latin text perhaps reflected the ambiguous nature of chiromancy.

Altogether, Humphrey is a good illustration of the growing audience for astrology and occult material in the late fifteenth and early sixteenth centuries. It would not be surprising if aristocratic fashion played a strong hand. John, duke of Bedford, and Humphrey, duke of Gloucester, were both interested in astrology and commissioned compilations and translations; Sir John Fastolf owned an astrolabe; and Caxton's translation of the *Mirrour* was commissioned by Hugh Bryce, alderman of London, who considered it a suitable volume to present to William, Lord Hastings. Such books and objects operated as marks of culture among both the gentry and nobility.[95] At the same time, Humphrey Newton could be seen as someone with the 'scientific empirical curiosity' which Hughes argues had 'wide currency' in late fifteenth-century England.[96] He was a non-university, non-medical practitioner, interested in the world around him and the practical benefits

---

[92] Bodl, MS Lat. Misc.c.66, fo. 123v. For comparison see Manzalaoui (ed.) *Secretum secretorum*. Carey, *Courting disaster*, p. 35; Eamon, *Science and the secrets of nature*, pp. 45–8.
[93] Bodl, MS Lat. Misc.c.66, fo. 127v.
[94] Thorndike, 'Chiromancy', pp. 674–706; Pack, 'A pseudo-Aristotelian chiromancy', pp. 189–241. For Humphrey's hand: Bodl, MS Lat. Misc.c.66, fo. 95r. Its rough and ready nature is thrown into sharp relief when placed next to the beautifully detailed illuminated hands found in Bodl, MS Ashmole 399, fo. 17r.
[95] Rawcliffe, *Medicine*, p. 9, Hughes, *Arthurian myths*, pp. 107, 256, 310.
[96] Hughes, *Arthurian myths*, p. 309.

of astrology. He was attracted to the belief that nature's secrets could be revealed, and he wanted to be able to read those signs on whatever earthly or heavenly bodies they might appear.

Prophecy

Humphrey's curiosity was further fed by the ancient practice of prophecy. Whereas the predictions of planetary configurations and chiromancy could be detailed with some exactness, prophecy was characteristically vague and, in the words of Sharon Jansen, 'deliberately obscure and wilfully ambiguous'.[97] They were constantly updated with contemporary material – the latest king, a recent battle – in order to strengthen their relevance to a particular period. In this way, prophecies began with a retelling of recent history moulded to conform to the prophetic structure. Having 'predicted the past' successfully, they had the authority to predict the future.

In England, prophecies had been gathering interest since the twelfth century, but they became particularly popular in the early Tudor period, reaching a peak around 1500 and again in the Reformation years under Henry VIII. Attempts to explain their popularity invoke a context of grave political and social disturbance. On the one hand, the prophecies smoothed over changes in history and offered an explanation for events by seeing them as part of God's pre-arranged plan. On the other, they provided a medium through which challenges to the prevailing political order could be voiced.[98] It is this aspect, Lesley Coote argues, which became attractive to the key readership in the fifteenth century, the governing and administrative classes who were 'literate, articulate and politically aware'. They were the men – and Humphrey can be considered an example here – with some local power and status, but with no influence over the political events contained in the prophetic literature. Prophecies therefore provided 'a language of power for the unempowered in later medieval England'.[99] Their popularity was also assisted by a steadily growing circulation in cheap paper manuscripts and the prophecy's similarity to the well-liked 'abuse' literature of the fifteenth century.[100] Both linked moral depravity to social upheavals like famine and plague. Yet, while the prophecies protested against moral and political decadence, they were deeply conservative and not intended to be revolutionary; hence they were highly sought after by both royalty and the nobility,

---

[97] Jansen, *Political protests*, p. 10.
[98] Elton, *Policy and police*, pp. 46–82; Fox, 'Prophecies and politics', pp. 77–94, p. 77. The key study for the period up to 1485 is Coote, *Prophecy*.
[99] Coote, 'A language of power', pp. 25–6.
[100] Hughes, *Arthurian myths*, p. 118; Scattergood, *Politics and poetry*, pp. 299–306.

though often for less social reasons. Noblemen were particularly interested in collecting prophecies relating to their own families.[101]

In a free-flowing hand, Humphrey copied several prophecies into his commonplace book. Although they constitute only two pages of his manuscript, the dozen or so items encompass all the common ingredients of any respectable prophecy collection. There are verses attributed to known 'authorities'. These include an updated version of the sybillic couplet usually ascribed to Thomas Becket,[102] and a six-line prophecy beginning 'when feith faileth in prestes sawes', which was most commonly assigned to Merlin or Chaucer, although Humphrey attributes it to Bede.[103] There is a Latin verse that falls into the category of 'abuse' literature, and assigns society's misfortunes to moral decline. In addition, a six-line verse is in the Merlinic tradition of a battle between a red dragon (Britain) and a white dragon (Saxon), which would result in victory of the former and the end of the name of England.[104] All were well-known prophecies which were passed from book to book; Humphrey may have copied them wholesale from another manuscript. But prophecies, as Tudor authorities were only too aware, travelled more quickly by word of mouth. Humphrey enjoyed the entertainment of minstrels, and one performer, known as Thomas Perkynson, sang something of considerable appeal, enough for Humphrey to attempt a summary:

> Thomas Perkynson sang a song of Thomas Ersholedon and þe quene of ffeiree, rehersyng þe batell of Stoke fild and þe batell of Branston of deth of þe kynges of Scotts. And also rehersyn þat a lion shuld come out of Walys and also a dragon and land in werall þat eny woman shuld stan have rowme to milke her cowe wt many thousands and on a wennysday after to drive don Chester walls. And after to feght in the fforest delamar with a kyng of the southe, which shuld have hundreds of m^l þat shu feght ii or iii days. And þen þer shuld come a ploz of yew with clubbez and clot shone [shoue?] and take parte and wyn alle. And þer þe kyng shuld be kylled with many an oþer to þe nowmber of lxi ml. And never kyng after bot iiii wardens unto domysday[105]

---

[101] Taylor, *Political prophecy*, p. 85; Coote, *Prophecy*, p. 215.

[102] The couplet usually reads: H patre submarcet post R reget J qui relicto/ E post H rex fit E post E., postea mira. See Ward, *Catalogue* I, p. 314, and Taylor, *Political prophecy*, p. 114. Humphrey, however, used the letter G instead of the penultimate E. This use of G is found in two other brief lines (one has the sequence H, J, E, R, H, E, G, E). They reveal a familiarity with the 'Prophecy of G', which first appeared in the 1480s and 90s. G was said to refer to George, duke of Clarence and then Richard, duke of Gloucester: Sutton and Visser-Fuchs, *Richard III's books*, p. 203.

[103] Bodl, MS Lat. Misc.c.66, fo. 104r. Campbell, 'Chaucer's prophecy', pp. 195–6; Robbins (ed.) *Historical poems*, p. 121.

[104] For the *Prophecia Merlini* and British history see Coote, *Prophecy*, particularly pp. 50, 61.

[105] Bodl, MS Lat, Misc.c.66, fo. 104r. See also Thornton, 'Reshaping the local future', pp. 54–5

Thomas of Erceldoune was a popular thirteenth-century Scottish prophesier commonly known as the Rymer. Over time his prophecies were incorporated into a romance called *Thomas of Essholden*, in which the hero is visited by the Queen of Fairies, who recites a lengthy prophecy mainly relating to the Anglo-Scottish wars.[106] By the sixteenth century, this had become synthesised with a series of other prophecies, resulting in the *Prophesies of Rymour, Beid and Marlyng*, one of the most famous examples of prophecy literature of the early Tudor period. Humphrey appears familiar with a written version because – perhaps prompted by Perkynson's song – he recorded forty-eight lines of prophecy beginning 'a fedur in high shall fall in hast'. It shares several lines and themes with the *Prophesies*, although it lacks the personal names and underlying narrative.[107]

In true prophetic form the minstrel Perkynson added other influences to *Thomas of Essholden* and created something specifically tailored to his Cheshire audience. While the prophecy ultimately foretold world destruction, the immediate focus was local; the key battle would take place in west Cheshire. Prophecy had long been adapted by local prophets to regional geography and politics, and Cheshire had a particularly well-known prophesier, Robert Nixon (traditionally living in the time of King Edward IV). Although Perkynson's song does not mirror Nixon's exactly, there are sufficient similarities to suggest that he may have been reiterating a prophecy of the Nixon tradition; in both, for instance, the place of action is the forest of Delamere.[108] There are other adaptations too, which emphasise the regionalism of the verse. In place of the more usual Bosworth Field, Perkynson sang of the battle of Stoke, a more northern battle and one, like the battle of Flodden Field (the prophecy's battle of Branston), where Cheshire men believed they played a decisive role.[109] The battle of Flodden (1513) was also a subject of one of the early sixteenth-century ballads said to have originated within the retinue of the powerful Stanley family, and which celebrated the prowess of Cheshire and Lancashire men. The Perkynson song may well contain fragments of that partisan literature, especially since Delamere Forest

---

[106] Murray, *The romances*.
[107] Two manuscript versions of the *Prophesies* are known and Humphrey's extract shares lines with both: BL, Lansdowne MS 762, as printed in Murray, *The romances*, pp. 54–5; and Bodl, Rawlinson MS c.813, which is printed in Jansen and Jordan (eds) *The Welles anthology*, p. 260.
[108] One surviving manuscript of the Nixon predictions is CRO, DDX 123, which originally came from Vale Royal Abbey, Cheshire. The popularity of the Nixon prophesies continued into the nineteenth century, when they were printed: Axon, *Nixon's Cheshire prophecies*. For further information: Thornton, *Cheshire*, pp. 60–1; Thornton, 'Reshaping the local future', p. 57.
[109] Over 100 Lancashire and Cheshire knights and esquires were retained by Henry VII prior to the battle of Stoke (1487): Bennett, *Lambert Simnel*, pp. 82, 95.

was Stanley territory.[110] In this context it is interesting that Humphrey linked one of his shorter prophecies to Stanley. He bracketed the words 'Stanley' and 'Milfote' next to the couplet 'War bussh burn for þer þe milfote shalbe alto torne/ Nevell blode shall blowe his horne'. What these obscure lines meant to Humphrey is unknown, but he is connecting Milford Haven ('Milfote'), the landing place of Henry Tudor on his way to Bosworth, with the Stanley family ('Neville's blood' through Eleanor Neville).[111] Finally, Perkynson's prophecy suggests some Welsh influence. The lion, after all, is coming out of Wales and destroying Chester's walls. An animosity between the Welsh and Chester was long standing, and there would be several folk memories concerning destruction wrought by the Welsh: the Glyndŵr revolt had devastated the Western half of Cheshire and damaged the trade of Chester.[112] As a Cheshire man born and bred, Humphrey was perhaps amenable to the view that nothing but trouble would come out of Wales.

There were several elements, therefore, that could have drawn Humphrey's attention. There were the authoritative names of Bede and the Rymour, the local elements and the problems of the Welsh. He may have copied them because, like the astrology, they were fashionable, or because he enjoyed a puzzle. At the same time, the revelatory nature of prophecy, showing that God's plan could be interpreted, would have helped him to make sense of the world. There is also the continuation of another theme in Humphrey's manuscript: the moral and apocalyptic associations of prophecy. At some point in time, the immortal, immoral world would destroy itself.

The Past

Humphrey was certainly interested in crisis years generated through sin and disorder. He transcribed two short paragraphs which detailed the destruction wrought in Edward III's reign. The first focused on the 'universall pestylence' of 1349–50 and contained the common clichés that the subsequent chaos had resulted in 'deth without sorowe, weddyng without friendship, wylfull penance and derth without scarsyte and sleyng without sorour'.

---

[110] Flodden was called *Scottish Field*. Lawton, 'Scottish Field', pp. 42–57; Halliwell, *Palatine anthology*, pp. 165–8; Oakden (ed.) 'Scotish Ffeilde'. See p. 198 below.

[111] The spelling of Milford with a 't' is found in the Rawlinson manuscript of the *Prophesies of Rymour*: 'ther shall entre at Milffort Haven / upon a horse off tree / a banneshed buron that is baren / Off Brutes blode shalbe / throughe the helpe of an egle anon / he shall broke bretten to the see': Jansen and Jordan (eds) *Welles Anthology*, no. 60, p. 259. The Stanley badge was an eagle and hence the family might be considered the 'helpers' in this context. Eleanor Neville, sister of Richard, earl of Warwick (d. 1471), married Thomas Stanley, earl of Derby (d. 1504). That their son, James Stanley, bishop of Ely, had 'Neville blood' was mentioned in a version of *Scottish Field*: 'Neere of nature to the Nevills that noble have beene ever': Oakden (ed.) 'Scotish Ffeilde', p. 9, line 284.

[112] Davies, *The revolt*, p. 281.

Only a tenth of the population were left alive and there were too few to 'bury the dede bot kest theym on heipes and holys'. A second extract told of the drought and famine in Edward III's reign that had pushed up wheat prices. Both were taken from a version of the *Brut*, the popular chronicle and standard history of England.[113] Written in Middle English, it survives in around 240 manuscripts in a range of formats, earning it a 'best seller' status and strongly suggesting that it was the most prolific secular text of late medieval England.[114] Its readership appears mainly among the middle strata of society – merchants, and the rural and urban gentry – a group that Felicity Riddy describes as the 'non-specialist, non-academic audience among the governing classes' who were the 'leading opinion formers'.[115] The popularity of the *Brut* and similar historical material among the gentry has been explained in terms of their involvement in local and central government and hence important political events. But perhaps Humphrey had a reason closer to home. Raluca Radulescu has alluded to the attempts made by families to place their own events within broader, national history.[116] It is worth recalling that Humphrey linked the fortunes of his landed estate to the fourteenth-century plague: it was the historic event that had destroyed Newton township.[117]

Humphrey did not record any other passages from the *Brut*, but his historical curiosity can be seen in other small entries. He shared a widespread interest in the genealogy of England's kings that was particularly pronounced in compilers of miscellanies.[118] His king list is far less detailed than the more regularly cited genealogical rolls and verses: it records only the basic information of name, reign length, coronation and burial locations, with some additional events.[119] That this list followed his genealogy of the Newton family suggests that he viewed the world and its history through family relations. If so, it is understandable that the more numerous genealogies in the Newton manuscript are those of the Anglo-Norman earls of Chester, to whom Humphrey could claim a connection. Humphrey recorded three of

---

113 Bodl, MS Lat. Misc.c.66, fos 6v and 7r. Both of Humphrey's extracts were 'fillers', added sometime after the original legal material on those folios. A published version of the Brut can be found in Brie (ed.) *The Brut*. Humphrey's first extract broadly concurs with lines found in Chapter CCXXVIII, a few on p. 301, a few on p. 303. The second extract is a summation of a section in Chapter CCXXIX (p. 304).
114 Radulescu, 'Literature', pp. 54–6; Meale, 'Patrons, buyers and owners', p. 215.
115 Riddy, 'Reading for England', p. 325.
116 Radulescu, *The gentry context*, p. 70; Radulescu, 'Literature', pp. 113–14. See also Hardman, 'Compiling the nation', p. 63: 'the ills of a particular period in the past can readily be reinterpreted to apply to the perceived conditions of the present'.
117 See pp. 89–90 above. Humphrey's recipes for plague also show its continuing medical concern. Bodl, MS Lat. Misc.c.66, fo. 64ar.
118 For a list of chronicles and genealogies see Hartung, *A manual of writings*, 8. For lists of kings appearing in other manuscripts see, for example, James, 'The Anlaby cartulary', pp. 337–47; Gunn, 'Early Tudor dates', pp. 213–16.
119 Bodl, MS Lat. Misc.c.66, fo. 2r and pp. 49–50 above.

these genealogies, ranging from a brief list to one containing a description of the arms of each earl. These descents were part of a common corpus of 'earl literature' which was circulating in Cheshire in the later Middle Ages, showing the continual relevance of the earls to the county's history.[120]

As these genealogies indicate, Humphrey's notes exhibit a sense of place and of regional historical culture. His manuscript compares to other miscellanies around Britain, where the locality of the scribal owner emerges to a greater or lesser degree. The 'London collections' of Richard Hill, John Colyns and Thomas Frowyk reveal their authors' interests in the city's history and topography.[121] Humphrey's commonplace book reflects his Cheshire context in a variety of ways – prophecy, list of Cheshire officials and local laws, and genealogies of neighbouring gentry – while his king-list includes the building of Beeston and Chartley castles (Cheshire) and the abbey of Dieulecres (Staffordshire), all founded by Ranulph III, earl of Chester (d. 1231–2). Yet the mobility of the gentry meant that they were never regionally bound and Humphrey was equally drawn to more national events. His comital lists were dated according to the reigns of English kings; his king list referenced the murder of Thomas Becket and the battle of Shrewsbury; and he transcribed a list of fifteenth-century battles and the numbers of towns, shires, parish churches and knights' fees in England.[122]

More tellingly, an interest in broader British history is evident in a short series of notes Humphrey made on Glastonbury Abbey and its legends.[123] Throughout the Middle Ages, Glastonbury Abbey had been a place of important pilgrimage. It had one of the largest and most impressive relic collections in Britain, with items associated with the Old Testament prophets, New Testament Apostles, Saints, Holy Virgins, Holy Martyrs, the Virgin Mary and Christ. In the mid-fourteenth century the chronicler John of Glastonbury wrote that the 'stone pavement, the sides of the altar and the altar itself are so loaded, above and below with relics packed together that there is no path through the church, cemetery or cemetery chapel which is free from the ashes of the blessed'.[124] Few of these were the focus of Humphrey's notes, however, and it was Arthurian rather than Biblical memorabilia that caught his eye. This is not unexpected given that during the reigns of Edward IV and Henry VII both Glastonbury and the Arthurian legend were experiencing a period of intense interest. Sir Thomas Malory's *Morte Darthur*, printed by Caxton in 1485 and reprinted by de Worde in 1498, had been a notable

---

[120] Ibid, fos 7r, 9v and 63v. See p. 17 above.
[121] Those manuscripts falling under this label are BL, Harley MS 2252 (Colyns), Balliol MS 354 (Hill), BL, Harley MS 541 (Frowyk), BL, Egerton MS 1995, and BL, Lansdowne MS 762. Meale, 'The compiler at work', p. 100; Riddy, *Sir Thomas Malory*, p. 34; Parker, *The commonplace book*.
[122] Bodl, MS Lat. Misc.c.66, fos 62r, 127v.
[123] Ibid., fo. 3v.
[124] Carley (ed.) *The chronicle of John of Glastonbury*, p. 17. In this, as elsewhere, John was expanding on the view of William of Malmsbury: Scott (ed.) *The early history*, p. 67.

success among England's literate society. During Humphrey's adulthood, the fortunes of Glastonbury had improved in the hands of Abbot Richard Beere (abbot 1492–1525), a man fascinated by the Abbey's history and particularly the cult of Joseph of Arimathea (celebrated as a saint and as an ancestor of Arthur). Beere had Joseph's famous hawthorn branch prominently displayed, and built a shrine that, with the help of indulgences, was immediately promoted as the site of numerous miracles.[125]

Humphrey, therefore, shows himself again to be sensitive to contemporary fashions and the prominent topics of conversation. His brief notes are probably scraps of information from several sources which he gathered together as a result of a memory prompt such as a book, visit or conversation.[126] A possible stimulation may have been the recent reading of a chronicle because Humphrey penned a short paragraph on the story of Rainald of Marksbury, which he must have taken either directly from the chronicle of John of Glastonbury or from someone else's summation of the work.[127] It is possible, too, that John of Glastonbury was the source for Humphrey's transcription of the epitaph on the tomb of Arthur, one of the major attractions of the Abbey, and a critical force for keeping the Arthurian legend alive. By the early sixteenth century the tomb had virtually become a national memorial and the epitaph circulated widely.[128] Despite the growing scepticism of the early Tudor period, Humphrey appears to have willingly accepted the reality of Arthur and jotted down other odd 'facts' associated with him: the existence of the isle of Avalon and the lady of the lake, as well as the origin of the name of Glastonbury.[129] Like late medieval English society at large, Humphrey was drawn to the survival of physical remains and the power of relics. In common with the antiquarians Worcester and Leland, he noted the lead cross of Arthur, said to be attached to a stone slab on Arthur's grave and considered the key piece of evidence in validating his resting place.[130] Crosses particularly caught Humphrey's eye and he mentioned a further three, including the crystal cross that legend told had been given to Arthur by the Virgin Mary. It was kept under guard at the abbey as one of its most

---

[125] Carley, *Glastonbury abbey*, pp. 69–70; Carley, 'Arthur in English history'; Thompson, 'Authors and audiences', pp. 371–96; Hughes, *Arthurian myths*, especially ch. 6.
[126] Thompson, 'Authors and audiences', p. 393.
[127] See Carley (ed.) *John of Glastonbury*, p. 41 for Rainald's story. Humphrey's lines roughly summarise this section in a mixture of Latin and English.
[128] Withrington, 'The Arthurian epitaph', pp. 103–44.
[129] Riddy, *Sir Thomas Malory*, pp. 32–3 for the scepticism. William Worcester also believed in his existence, and Caxton, after weighing up the options, similarly agreed: Gransden, *Historical writing*, p. 340; Blake, *Caxton's own prose*, pp. 106–9.
[130] Humphrey's inscription reads 'Hic iacet inclitus Arthurus quondam Rex Britonis'. Numerous versions circulated, although Humphrey's was not the most common; that usually included reference to Arthur's return: 'Hic iacet Arthurus rex quondam rexque futurus'. Alcock, *Arthur's Britain*, pp. 74–80; Withrington, 'The Arthurian epitaph', pp. 113–17.

prized possessions. While all four crosses had high religious importance, Humphrey was clearly alert to the visually spectacular, and this predilection can also be seen in his reference to the blue sapphire: a magnificent altar stone said to have been brought by St David to the monastery.[131] In addition, there is mention of the stirrups of Arthur and the hawthorn of Arimathea. The only saints' relics mentioned relate to two who were concurrently being championed by Abbot Beere: St Benignus, a saint in whose honour Beere built a new church; and St Dunstan, whose relics Beere had promoted in a successful campaign to increase pilgrims. Altogether, Humphrey's list was very much a product of the decade around 1500.

Historical lists of this type were very popular and, as Chapter 7 discusses, they were standard features in miscellanies. The commonplace book of Richard Hill, for example, has lists of places where fairs were kept in England and a list of assizes in Essex. Commenting on this manuscript, Parker highlights Hill's 'impulse to collect' and describes him as more of a 'collector' than a 'doer'.[132] Can the same be said of Humphrey? There is some reason to believe that he was more active and made the pilgrimage to Glastonbury. There is information on size, typical for Humphrey, but which is absent from conventional written descriptions: the crystal cross was a 'span long'; the blue sapphire was also 'a span long'; and Arthur's stirrups were 'bot lytill & thik'. In addition, Humphrey alludes to relics located at 'Edington', which may be the small town lying ten kilometres west of Glastonbury and positioned on the north side of the busy Bridgewater–Glastonbury road. While Edington church was the property of Glastonbury Abbey, it is not mentioned in any surviving text connected with Glastonbury, and does not appear to have been known nationally as a site of interest. It would have been known, however, by those who travelled through it.[133] There is also the possibility that it was at Glastonbury that Humphrey picked up his measure of Christ's foot. In an elongated rectangle at the edge of folio 9v Humphrey wrote 'this mesur within these blake lynes is the true mesur of the fote of Jhu Crist as it is enprynted at seynt Georg'. There is no information on the location of 'St George', but according to legend (later immortalised in Blake's *Jerusalem*), the most obvious place in England to find an imprint of the foot of Jesus would be in Glastonbury. There was (and is) a famous inn at Glastonbury called St George which was a favourite resting place for pilgrims; an appropriate location for a footprint. The case for a first-hand visit is reasonable. But then, right at the bottom of the list, Humphrey notes 'at Warwik' the 'ribbez of þe boor' and 'Sir Guy sword'. These can only refer to the legend of Sir Guy of

---

[131] For chronicle references to these relics: Carley (ed.) *John of Glastonbury*, pp. 24–5, 42–4; Scott (ed.) *The early history*, pp. 78–9, 81, 156–8.
[132] Parker, *The commonplace book*, p. 54.
[133] Dunning (ed.) *VCH Somerset, vol. VIII*, pp. 50–62. Edington was a dependent on Moorlich church, which had been appropriated by Glastonbury Abbey in 1262.

Warwick and his famous relics.[134] Such a tantalising, but laconic, reference means that whether Humphrey toured sites connected to literary heroes or simply gathered information read elsewhere has to remain unknown.

In comparison with the historical information owned by other gentleman, Humphrey's book is a bit of a disappointment for the modern reader. There is no full *Brut* chronicle, no Arthurian romance, nothing of the detail and length found in other miscellanies, such as those owned by John Colyns or Robert Thornton. Humphrey's works are merely odds and ends. Yet they are enough to reveal his familiarity with the latest historical fashions and some of the mainstays of gentry culture. Not for the first time, there appears a little of the William Worcester about him: a bookish nature mixed with the need to see and measure; a historical curiosity that triggered a bout of note taking.

Fashioning the future

A richer range of works is viewed when Humphrey's didactic literature is considered. It has already been noted that Humphrey drew together material, such as the *ABC of Aristotle*, that focused on behaviour. These were included alongside extracts from moralising works containing useful facts or observations that could be introduced into conversation, perhaps during meal-times, in order to demonstrate gentility and portray a particular image. Some of those texts were specifically directed at children, others at the more reflective adult. They appealed to parents unsure of the social skills they needed to teach their offspring, and to middling sorts who strove to isolate the manners and mannerisms of the class to which they were aspiring.[135] Humphrey may well have selected some texts explicitly for his young sons, but his main aim was to familiarise himself with the core tenets of gentry culture.

Instruction in correct behaviour was the central theme of the works collectively known as 'Mirrors of princes', guide books usually made for, or directed to, the young prince or noble with the view to achieving success in government, the household and the estate. They held particular attraction for the gentry on two grounds: they appealed to their pious outlook in urging spiritual reform, and, by advocating obedience as the foundation for stability, they appealed to their concern for the law.[136] Humphrey had access to three key texts of this genre: *De regimine principum*, the *Secretum secretorum* and *The Siege of Thebes*. As a list this is reasonably impressive, but the problem is

---

134 For a detailed discussion of Sir Guy and his relics see Crane, 'The vogue of Guy of Warwick'; pp. 135, n. 25, and 169. The boar was famously killed by Guy in Windsor forest.
135 Riddy, *Sir Thomas Malory*, p. 71.
136 Genet, *Four English political tracts*; Ferster, *Fictions of advice*; Green, *Poets and prince-pleasers*, ch. 5; Coleman, *English literature in history*, p. 43; Radulescu, 'Literature', p. 112.

that it cannot be known for sure why Humphrey was drawn to these works. We know of his *De regimine principum* only because it appears in a contents page (fo. 91). The text itself has not survived and we have to presume that it refers to the famous Latin work written by Giles of Rome in the late thirteenth century for the heir of the king of France. It proved a widely popular text – it survives in more than 350 manuscripts across Europe – with a broad readership, and was translated into Middle English in the late fourteenth century by John Trevisa (c.1342–1402).[137] Frustratingly, there is no knowing which section caught Humphrey's eye. He may have been interested in its main message on the need for dignity, truth, justice, prudence and peace at home, but equally his attention may have been drawn for less grandiose reasons. It has already been noted that Humphrey's interest in the *Secretum secretorum* had more to do with eye colour, a rather simpler aid to judging a person's character than their qualities of leadership. Something similar is observed with the third work, the *Siege of Thebes*, a major poem written by John Lydgate between the years 1421–2. It was popular (there are more than thirty extant manuscripts), and drew the interest of many fifteenth-century gentle readers because its adventurous storyline entertained them while teaching important moral lessons. Alice Chaucer, duchess of Suffolk, owned and perhaps commissioned a version, while Thomas Boyd, the earl of Arran, borrowed a copy from Anne Paston.[138] The *Siege* championed the need for a wise and just rule and exposed the dire consequences of unwise government and the futility of war. Humphrey, however, only included the first verse of that poem in his book, and it goes unattributed, which may suggest that he did not know or was not interested in knowing the fuller context. The introductory lines are on the seasons of the year linked to their astrological constellations, and it is possible, given what is known about his other interests, that Humphrey was simply struck by the natural imagery.[139]

Nevertheless, Humphrey was drawn to the work of Lydgate and its moral messages. Lydgate's writings were fashionable throughout the fifteenth and early sixteenth centuries, and he became a 'name' to quote. Among the gentry this may have been because, in focusing on the problems of governing, Lydgate struck a chord with men who were increasingly involved in local and central government.[140] At the same time there was a moral earnestness to late medieval literature, and to Lydgate's work in particular, which seems to have been

---

[137] Fowler, Briggs and Remley (eds) *The governance of kings and princes*; Sutton and Visser-Fuchs, *Richard III's books*, pp. 15, 123.
[138] Edwards (ed.) *John Lydgate: the siege of Thebes*; Pearsall, *John Lydgate*, pp. 151–6; Thompson, 'Popular reading tastes', p. 89; Davis (ed.) *Paston letters and papers*, I, no. 352.
[139] Bodl, MS Lat. Misc.c.66, fo. 127v. Humphrey's verse came from a corrupt version of the text. Notably, his fourth line replaces 'In virgyne [virgo] taken had his place' with 'In Iubiter [Jupiter] had takyn hym a place'.
[140] Radulescu, 'Literature', p. 112.

especially attractive to the gentry.[141] At one time Humphrey's commonplace book contained a complete copy of *Look in the Mirror*, a moralistic refrain of twenty-seven octavo stanzas. It is not one of Lydgate's best-known works, and survives in only a handful of manuscripts.[142] In its complete form the work exhorts people not to waste time criticising others but to look to themselves and their own sins. The message is transmitted through various birds, such as the peacock, eagle and swan, and Humphrey may well have liked the imagery (or thought it suitable for his children). Elsewhere in his manuscript he enjoyed sketching birds and he even penned a short verse coming from the mouth of a parrot.[143] Nevertheless, it was a strongly religious work that urged readers to think on God's mercy and show compassion. A similar call for spiritual and moral renewal – and again coming from the beaks of birds – can be found in *Philomena*, an allegorical Middle English poem that was once erroneously attributed to Lydgate.[144] Save for the first three verses of the proem, Humphrey copied the entire text and took care to sign the finished result. *Philomena* describes the last song of a dying nightingale as an allegory of the Christian soul. People are urged to ruminate on their life because 'dethe comes in hast he wil not be forborne'. In preparation, the person should turn away from sin, remember the pains Christ suffered for the sake of Christian souls, give praise and make repentance.[145] It is the message Humphrey similarly read in his more overtly religious items, such as his otherworld vision and Mirk's *Festial*, discussed in Chapter 5.

Humphrey's choice of literature is what we have come to expect of the late medieval gentleman: sober, principled and didactic.[146] It is therefore not surprising that in his acquaintance with Chaucer's great compendium, the *Canterbury Tales*, it was the moral rather than the chivalric or bawdy that caught his eye. It has already been noted in Chapter 5 that he copied a section from the *Parson's Tale* that was probably circulating separately as a 'Book of Shrift'. It was hardly the most popular of texts and Chaucer's name is not showcased.[147] A second, and smaller, extract was taken from the *Knight's Tale*. From this adventure tale there is nothing of tournaments or courtly love. What Humphrey copied was several lines from near the end of the work where Theseus is commenting on the death of Arcite at the height of his

---

[141] Pearsall, *John Lydgate*, p. 68; Coleman, *English literature in history*, pp. 43, 71.
[142] A printed text can be found in McCracken (ed.) *The minor poems*, pp. 765–72. For manuscripts see Hartung, *Manual*, 6, pp. 1872, 2130. It was also included in Wynkyn de Worde's printed book *The proverbs of Lydgate* (c.1510). NIMEV, no. 3798.
[143] See pp. 190–1 below.
[144] Glauning (ed.) *Lydgate's minor poems*, pp. 1–15. Among those who have since proven Glauning wrong, see Pearsall, *John Lydgate*, pp. 267–8. Humphrey never attributes this poem to Lydgate, which has been claimed by McCracken (ed.) *The minor poems*, p. xxxiii and Schirmer, *John Lydgate*, p. 181.
[145] Bodl, MS Lat. Misc.c.66, fos 107v–111v (quotation fo. 108v).
[146] James, 'English politics', p. 358; Keiser, 'Practical books', p. 472.
[147] See pp. 107, 115 above. Meale, 'Patrons, buyers and owners', p. 218.

knightly prowess. These express the view that it was best 'as for a worthy fame to die whan a man is best of name'. In other words, reputation was a matter of a 'good death' as well as a 'good life'. What is particularly striking is that Humphrey glossed these lines 'Howe deth is best in medyll age'.[148] When he began his commonplace book, Humphrey had just turned thirty and the bulk of his writings were made during his thirties to fifties, the years which medieval philosophical writings termed 'mid-life'. Humphrey would have gained an understanding of this system of ages from several sources. The *Knight's Tale* is itself a scheme of three ages with Theseus the representative of mid-life, while *De regimine principum* stressed the superiority of middle age.[149] Moreover, in *Philomena*, the nightingale links the ages of Christ's life to the ages of the world and to the ages of man. The most significant stage was that of sext, the hour of Christ's crucifixion, and the 'myddis' of man's life. This was the 'parfite age', the peak of a person's physical and mental abilities, when one needed to use that strength to reform.[150] The sins of youth must be put aside; the sobriety of 'mid-life' brought to the fore.

It was not simply about acting appropriately: it was imperative to know how to speak correctly, both in the sense of controlling the tongue and in knowing the right terms to use. Texts of instruction for the young often urged the regulation of speech. Peter Idley, for example, advised his son to 'restreyne and kepe well thy tongue'.[151] Watching the tongue was also associated with rank: worship could be damaged by slander and in the household book of Edward IV the marshals of the hall were charged with monitoring the speech of those below barons to watch for swearing.[152] This text also reveals how mastering a particular discourse would bring social and cultural profit: the 'mastyr of Henxmen', in charge of the young retainers, was to make sure that they 'haue all curtesy in wordez, dedes and degrees'. In certain cases this demanded the learning of esoteric terms. In Malory's *Morte Darthur* Sir Tristram is honoured because of 'the goodly tarmys that jantylmen have and use and shall do', which means that 'all man of worship may discover a jantylman frome a yoman and a yoman frome a vylayne'.[153]

Humphrey's interest in perfecting this discourse can be seen in the treatise that once lay within the commonplace book, but was removed in the nineteenth century: the 1486 printed book the *Treatise of Hawking, Hunting*

---

[148] *Canterbury Tales: Knight's Tale*, lines 3048–56 (the quoted lines are 3048, 3055–6); Bodl, MS Lat. Misc.c.66, fo. 2r. The gloss comes in the contents page on fo. 64ar.
[149] Burrow, *Ages of man*, pp. 9, 11.
[150] Bodl, MS Lat. Misc.c.66, fo. 111r; Dove, *The perfect age*, pp. 18, 36.
[151] D'Evelyn (ed.) *Peter Idley's instructions to his son, Liber primus*, pp. 82, 84.
[152] Perkins, *Hoccleve's Regiment of Princes*, pp. 14–18; Amos, '"For manners make man"', p. 40; Radulescu, *The gentry context*, p. 23.
[153] Myers (ed.) *The household of Edward IV*, p. 126; Malory, *Works*, p. 232 (lines 18–19); Riddy, *Sir Thomas Malory*, p. 95. See too the comments in Richmond, *The Paston family*, p. 37, n. 106.

and the Blasing of Arms, also known as the *Boke of St Albans*.[154] The book is missing the whole of the hawking section and the final ten pages of the *Blasing of Arms*, and may never have been a complete text: it contains manuscript signatures, and there are numerous uncoloured shields. Rachel Hands suggests that the book was Caxton's personal copy, and he made the several corrections and additions to the text.[155] How the text reached Cheshire is not known, but a connection between Caxton and Newton is not required. The manuscript was only an early and unfinished work which circulated alongside completed printed texts. It probably had little value and could have been picked up cheaply from the workshop or at a fair.

Behind the *Boke of St Albans* lay the desire (echoing *Morte Darthur*) to explain how 'gentilmen shall be knowyn from ungentill men'. Hunting, with its military associations, was naturally the sport of the aristocracy, and hunting rights, privileges of free warren and the keeping of hawks and hounds were highly valued. They were, in the words of Nigel Saul, at 'the very heart of the gentleman's life style'.[156] As well as being enjoyable, hunting also strengthened the body, taught military skills and was considered character building. Among the gentry, possession of parkland grew considerably in the fifteenth century, and Humphrey would only need to walk about a mile from Newton before he stepped on the ancient parklands of the Pigots of Butley or the fine new park of the Leghs of Adlington.[157] Hunting manuals were part of this elite culture, but English works, in contrast to their French counterparts, never became practical teaching aids. Rather the English manuals taught men (young and old) how to talk about hunting.[158] Lengthy glossaries of terms and definitions furnished the reader with the exclusive language of the elite, which can also be seen in the *Blasing of Arms*, which revealed the peculiar vocabulary of armorial bearing. The *Boke of St Albans* reached its intended audience of the landholding classes, but, like the conduct books, works on hunting and hawking were more often owned by the socially aspiring than by nobles themselves. The miscellany BL MS Egerton 1995, for example, was

---

[154] It is uncropped and measures 300mm x 210mm. William Sneyd recollected seeing the *Boke* bound within Humphrey's manuscript in c.1828: Furnivall (ed.) *The babee's book*, p. 366. Sometime before 1874 the work was removed and rebound separately by William Bromley-Davenport at his library in Capesthorne; the separation was noted by A.J. Horwood in the appendix to the second HMC report, *Reports on manuscripts in various collections*. The book was eventually purchased by the British Library, becoming one of the Library's two copies of the 1486 edition. The manuscript currently remains within its nineteenth-century binding. Inside is an *ex libris* of William Davenport; on the book's spine are the words 'Capesthorne Library'. For the Boke of St Albans see Jacob, 'The Boke of St Albans'; Hands, *English hawking and hunting*.
[155] Hands, *English hawking and hunting*, pp. xviii, xx.
[156] Saul, *Scenes*, p. 187.
[157] Pollard, *North-Eastern England*, pp. 198–208. For Adlington: TNA: PRO, CHES 34/14 (15).
[158] Rooney, *Hunting*, pp. 7, 15; Orme, 'Medieval hunting', pp. 133–54; Riddy, *Sir Thomas Malory*, p. 70.

a book of useful information designed for, in the words of Parker, 'the rising London merchant who wants to improve his social position through knowledge of hunting customs and courtesy books'. They offered 'a key to the secret signals which identify members of the aristocracy to each other'.[159] There is no record of how often (if ever) Humphrey went hunting, but like the London merchant, he would have been able to share in this culture.

Another means of learning or teaching appropriate phrases was through collections of proverbs. Humphrey had access to *The dicts and sayings of the philosophers*, a work of proverbs that circulated in the fifteenth century in Latin, French and Spanish. It proved sufficiently popular among the English aristocracy for individuals to translate and promote an English version. It was the translation made by Anthony Woodville, Earl Rivers, which was used by William Caxton for one of his first printed books in 1477. The education of the young occurs again here, as Rivers stated that the translation was for the education of the young Prince Edward (the future Edward V) who was then aged four.[160] Aphorisms were widely used among the fifteenth-century gentry, both in speech and in letters.[161] Because they were short and concise, such sayings were regular entries in miscellanies and commonplace books. The *Dicts* were important in instructing the gentry on worldly wisdom with the intention of enabling man to master his passions and behaviour. Humphrey transcribed a few lines near the end of the treatise, which neatly summarise these characteristically gentle concerns.

> He asked of a wise man what thyng encresed the law and he answered and seid trouth. And what sustened trouth? Reason and witt. And whereby is witt? By keeping of the tong. And howe is the tong kept? With pacience. What causeth pacience? Drede of god. And what causeth drede of god? Often in speke to remember deth and to consider and knowe his frailnes.[162]

In other words: the desire for social order, personal restraint and humility, with recognition of the omnipotence of God. And, of course, the need to watch the tongue.

---

[159] Parker, *The commonplace book*, p. 34; Orme, 'Education and recreation', p. 78; Rooney, *Hunting*, p. 15; Keiser, 'Practical books', pp. 470–2; Putter, 'The ways and words', pp. 354–5.

[160] Bühler (ed.) *The dicts and sayings*; Orme, *From childhood*, pp. 102–3; Orme, *Medieval children*, p. 279.

[161] As seen in the letters of Anthony Woodville, Stephen Scrope and William Worcester: Hughes, 'Stephen Scrope', p. 141. Proverbs appear regularly in manuscripts associated with the gentry: for example, Hardman (ed.) *The Heege manuscript*, nos 14–15 (fo. 61v); Thompson (ed.) *Robert Thornton*, p. 14.

[162] Bodl, MS Lat. Misc.c.66, fo. 74av. Expansions and punctuation added. Humphrey's lines can be found in Bühler (ed.) *The dicts and sayings*, p. 284 (lines 19–24) and p. 318 (lines 33–38).

Conclusion

Humphrey's houses were not noteworthy buildings in early Tudor Cheshire, but they were recognisably gentleman's residences. Guests would have been treated to some fine hospitality as Humphrey (and his household) demonstrated the rules and behaviour of contemporary elite society. His guides on these issues were not only family and peers, but his reading material. His interests were dominated by didactic and improving literature, reasserting the conventional gentry concerns of good governance, good alliances and good manners, and the ideals of loyalty, hierarchy, law and education.[163] There is a worthiness and obviousness to his choice; it is clearly conservative. His preference is the literature of Lydgate and Chaucer, very similar to that contained in the 'London' commonplace books.[164] There is no discernible foreign interest in Humphrey's taste; no sign of the Italian or Flemish culture that was attracting attention in Henry VII's England.[165] The only items mentioned in this chapter that could be considered up-to-date were the prophetical and astrological; while dependent on older traditions, the circulation of these texts owed much to their apparent contemporary resonances.

Nevertheless, in being conventional, Humphrey shows an awareness of the most fashionable texts; indeed the term 'best seller' has been used or implied on several occasions during this chapter: *De regimine principum*, Lydgate's *Siege of Thebes*, *Secretum secretorum*, *The dicts and sayings of the philosophers*, the *Brut* chronicle, the *Prophesies of Rymer* and the almanac-style entries are all cases in point. If a late fifteenth-century gentleman had made a check-list of works that were *de rigueur*, it would look a lot like Humphrey's reading habits.[166] Despite the expansion in the manuscript and particularly the printed book trade, it was still a time where, if a gentleman wanted to appear well-read, it was possible to become familiar with the main authors and texts. This was also a national 'check-list', as Humphrey shared that aspect of gentility which, in the words of Philip Morgan, 'sought to be part of an increasingly national and even island culture'.[167]

In accessing or inculcating this moralising literature and its values, Humphrey's preoccupations dovetailed with wider aristocratic reading interests. There is a sense of trying to ape the nobility: he owned the type of prac-

---

[163] Radulescu, 'Literature', p. 101; Fleming, 'The "Hautes"', p. 85.
[164] Parker, *The commonplace book*, p. 162. Caxton's *Book of Curtesye* (1477–78) recommended the reading of Gower, Chaucer, Lydgate and Hoccleve: pp. 33–41: Amos, 'For manners make man', p. 41.
[165] Meale, 'Patrons, buyers and owners', pp. 204–5; Fleming, 'The "Hautes"', pp. 93, 98, 100.
[166] John Shirley's composite manuscript includes the Brut chronicles, Hoccleve's *Regiment*, Lydgate's *Secrets*, chronicles, genealogies and advice literature. Radulescu, *The gentry context*, p. 46.
[167] Morgan, 'Ranks of society', p. 85.

tical treatises which belonged to 'upwardly aspiring gentry' who wished to achieve what *The Master of the Game* termed 'ryght gentylnesse'. There is an emphasis on manners, on behaviour.[168] This is not surprising given many of the shared interests of the landed elite; the competitive nature of the gentry and nobility witnessed in land disputes also extended to style and conversation, and Humphrey would not have wanted to put a foot wrong.

However, there is an important ingredient missing: romances. It has generally been assumed that these were an essential part of gentry reading matter. Christine Carpenter believed that 'chivalric fictions were the common property of the whole of landed society in this period' because military prowess was 'the spiritual *raison d'être* of the landed class'.[169] Humphrey did not imagine himself as a military man, and while he clearly knew of Arthur and Sir Guy of Warwick he shows no interest in romance literature. There is little to compare with John Paston's *Grete Boke* – or indeed any 'grete boke' – and its heavily chivalric influences. Only in the final folios of Paston's book, which contain the *Secretum secretorum*, the *Secrets of old philosophers* and a book of governance, do his and Humphrey's worlds appear to overlap.[170] At the same time, it can be seen that Humphrey's interests coincided with merchants such as Richard Hill, and others of the so-called 'middling classes': they are moralistic, rather than chivalric. In this he could be said to reveal a lesser gentry status. Gerald Harriss has recently outlined the distinction made between the culture of the knightly elite, who were reading traditional chivalry and manuals on manners, hunting and medicine which did not reflect any developing social trends, and the lesser gentry, who were anti-clerical and anti-chivalric, exercised about moral reform and more likely to focus on the abuses of the age than on courtly love.[171] Humphrey does not fall neatly into either camp, but has a foot in both.

---

[168] Mertes, 'Aristocracy', p. 54; Keiser, 'Practical books', pp. 478–80.
[169] Carpenter, *Locality and polity*, p. 49; Radulescu, 'Literature', p. 104; Orme, 'Education and recreation', p. 70.
[170] Lester, *Sir John Paston's 'Grete Boke'*; Cherewatuk, '"Gentyl audiences"', p. 209.
[171] Harriss, *Shaping the nation*, pp. 159–60.

7

Writer

Humphrey was not only a reader but a writer, and a confident one at that. There can have been few aspects of his life that did not involve making a written record. As previous chapters have revealed, Humphrey placed a great deal of trust in written documents, while recognising the issues of forgery and mistakes. Debt repayments, the selling of sheep, a new medical recipe or a snippet of local history were all reasons to take up the pen and make a note. While this was not a rare action in late medieval society, it was far from common among the general population. Humphrey had grown up at a time when writing was still considered a specialised skill, usually taught separately from reading.[1] Not everyone would have bothered or needed to write on a daily basis. It was hardly necessary to the labourer in the field, and the nobility could pay to have the onerous task executed for them. The use of secretaries was widespread among the landed classes, letters were dictated, and oral testimony still valued.

Nevertheless, a growing need to write can be found among tradespeople, in the expanding bureaucracies of England, and within the houses of the gentry. Alison Truelove's work points to the increasing likelihood of gentlemen writing their own letters in the fifteenth century.[2] How many of the gentry could or chose to write is difficult to gauge, and it is impossible to generalise on the degrees of competence or the regularity with which the skill was used. Occasionally someone will helpfully draw attention to his or her own writing. The will of Robert Reddich of Grappenhall, near Warrington (1508) was 'written wt my simple hand'.[3] Yet such pronouncements are not frequent finds. Without a sufficient cluster of personal writings, such as those found in the well-known letter collections of Paston and Stonor, it will not be easy to establish whether the sender is using his or her own hand or is dictating to a secretary. This is especially true of the North West, where only odd letters from the gentry survive. One limited insight can be achieved by examining the use of signatures. It is questionable whether being able to sign

---

[1] Clanchy, *From memory*, pp. 13, 47 and 126–7, 232.
[2] Truelove, 'Literacy', pp. 85 and 90; Moran, *The growth of English schooling*, p. 178. For the literacy skills of gentlewomen see Boffey, 'Women authors and women's literacy', pp. 159–82.
[3] TNA: PRO, PROB 11/16. Truelove, 'Literacy', p. 89 and Moran, *The growth of English schooling*, pp. 151–2, have further examples.

one's name should be taken as an indication of basic skill, but it is the case that signatures had become important identifiers by the early Tudor period.[4] They acted (like seals) as confirmation marks of witnesses or parties to a legal agreement. The deed recording the arbitration settlement between the Cheshire gentlemen John Sutton and Nicholas Jodrell (1500) was described in related documents with reference to the signatures of Richard Sutton and Humphrey Newton, which appeared at its foot: 'a paper subscribit wt the hands of Richard Sutton & Humfrey Neuton'.[5]

Not all members of the Cheshire gentry did or could sign their names. In a bond of 1519–20 Thomas Hulse of Norbury, esquire (who had been Humphrey's employer as steward at Knutsford), and John Mere of Mere, esquire, simply signed with a cross.[6] While it is possible that they chose a religious symbol as their mark, this does not appear a regular occurrence among the Cheshire gentry. Instead, a range of deeds shows that most leading gentry in north-eastern Cheshire were at least able to sign their names, even if they rarely wrote anything else. Signatures are noted for the heads of the Booth family of Dunham Massey, the Calveleys of Lea, Davenports of Bramhall, Downes of Worth, Fittons of Gawsworth, Leghs of Adlington, Leghs of Booths, Tattons of Withenshaw, Traffords of Trafford and Warrens of Poynton.[7] There is a mix of hands, with some considerably neater than others. John Tatton of Withenshaw (sheriff of Chester in 1503 and baron of the exchequer, 1515) had a more stylish and obviously more practised hand than the wealthier Lancashire knight, Sir Edmund Trafford (d. 1513). In 1504, Sir George Calveley of the Lea was capable of penning 'This was seyd in presens of me Gerage Calveley' when he confirmed a witness's statement for Humphrey. It is perfectly legible, but its very scratchy appearance suggests a man not used to wielding a pen on a daily basis.[8]

On the other hand, a more accomplished level of literacy is seen in surviving manuscript evidence. Several gentlemen across England are known to have written and created their own books. One of the most well known is Robert Thornton, lord of the manor of East Newton, Yorkshire, who compiled two manuscripts of devotional and literary texts between 1425 and 1450. Thornton drew his material from around fifteen to twenty different exemplars that were circulating in his locality.[9] Gentry of the North West also produced their own manuscripts. John Leche of Nantwich, for example,

---

[4] For the potential of signatures see Cressy, *Literacy and the social order*. For a discussion of the limitations of using the signature see Thomas, 'The meaning of literacy', pp. 101–2.
[5] JRUL, Jodrell 36 and 38c
[6] CRO, DDA 1533/30.
[7] See, for example, CRO, DDA 1533/30; JRUL, Mainwaring 332; Legh of Adlington DLA 69/1/4b; 69/10/7; Legh of Adlington 10/11.
[8] JRUL, Bromley Davenport, 'Newton by Mottram', no. 5. See p. 98 above.
[9] Thompson (ed.) *Robert Thornton*; Brewer and Owen (eds) *The Thornton manuscript*; Thompson, 'The compiler in action'.

transcribed a copy of the *Canterbury Tales* in the mid-fifteenth century.[10] In Humphrey's locality, the Booths of Dunham Massey (a 'remembrance book'), the Fittons of Gawsworth, the Warrens of Poynton and the Trafford family (the 'Black book of Trafford') all owned manuscripts of family memoranda, which may have contained autograph writings of the household.[11] There was certainly an assumption in Humphrey's parish of Prestbury that gentlemen wished to make copies of literary and spiritual texts. The library at Pott Shrigley chapel is a tantalising glimpse of what may have existed in several rural churches. According to the will of its founder, Geoffrey Downes (1494), gentlemen could borrow any book in the chapel 'either for to read or to take a copy'.[12] Naturally, a scribe could have been employed to make the copies, but the library's existence allows for the possibility that gentry would write their own. Humphrey lived under four miles from Pott Shrigley and is known to have had contact with members of the Downes family and the chaplain of Pott chapel. Given his transcription of a Marian prayer from a church at Newark, he was evidently familiar with drawing information from church holdings.[13]

This fragmentary evidence suggests that within England's gentle society Humphrey was doing nothing special in being able to write, and he was not the only gentleman in Cheshire and Lancashire to pen his own manuscript. Yet he is the only known person from the North West to have compiled a commonplace book in pre-Reformation England, and one of the few manuscript makers who can be identified. It is an important point that deserves emphasising. In writing regularly and during his leisure time, he was going beyond what many of the gentry, particularly at the higher levels, would choose to do.

The book-maker

During the last decade of the fifteenth century and the first quarter of the sixteenth Humphrey wrote the pages that would eventually form his commonplace book. This type of manuscript, appearing in growing numbers in the fifteenth and sixteenth centuries, is not a frequent survivor from the period, and only around two dozen currently exist. Defining a commonplace book is not without its problems. The term has been used quite loosely, and scholarly attempts to narrow the definition have resulted in disagreements over exactly

---

[10] Manly and Rickert (eds) *The texts of the Canterbury Tales*, vol. 1, pp. 535–44.
[11] Marsh, '"I see by sizt"', pp. 86–7.
[12] Dodgson, 'A library at Pott Chapel', pp. 47–53. See also p. 154 above.
[13] TNA: PRO, CHES 38/26/8; BL, Add MS 42134A, fo 2r. For the Marian prayer see p. 108 above.

which manuscripts should be categorised as commonplace.[14] Recent scholarship lays emphasis on three characteristics. The first, and undisputable, is its miscellaneous and idiosyncratic content. This is summed up in the merchant Richard Hill's description of his book as 'a boke of dyversis tales and balettis and dyversis reconyngs etc'.[15] There is no particular theme, as may be found in poetry anthologies or devotional collections. Second, it is work compiled for personal consumption, reflecting the writer's interests, amusements and practical needs. Guddat-Figge forcefully argues that it was not professionally written for a 'book market' or commissioned by a wealthy patron. Signs of professional craft such as ruled margins and catchwords should therefore be non-existent or negligible.[16] Third, and on a related point, the book would not have been planned from start to finish, but would be an incremental, unsystematic accumulation, drawn together over time and adapting to the compiler's taste. Some books were miscellanies compiled over many years, perhaps involving more than one scribe; others were wads of blank pages that were filled by one writer. All, however, were gradual and piecemeal creations.

What these factors underline is that these books have claim to be some of the more personal items surviving from the late medieval period. A compiler would write only what was necessary for his (and it always is a 'his') life, perhaps not bothering to finish a text, or choosing to elaborate; he may add 'odds and ends' in small blank spaces by scribbling a quick note or a doodle. Inevitably, these manuscripts would only be created by those familiar with the writing process, and for this reason the lay commonplace book is largely the work of a specific stratum of society. Where ownership can be identified, it is the book of small landholders, merchants and professionals; a work, therefore, reflecting the tastes of the aspiring middle classes. Fifteenth- and early sixteenth-century compilers include John Colyns and Richard Hill, who were London merchants; Robert Melton, a steward of the Cornwallis family (Suffolk); Reginald Andrews, an official of William Uvedale of Wickham (Hampshire); John Crophill of Wix (Essex), a bailiff and amateur physician; and Robert Reynes of Acle (Norfolk), church reeve, lawyer, petty officer and alderman of a local guild.[17] A characteristic that all these owners shared with

---

[14] Definitions can be found in Robbins (ed.) *Secular lyrics*, p. xxviii; Rigg, *A Glastonbury miscellany*, p. 24; Louis, *The commonplace book of Robert Reynes*, pp. 100–1; Meale, 'The social and literary contents', part 2; Guddat-Figge, *Catalogue of the manuscripts*, pp. 22–8; Youngs, 'The medieval commonplace book', pp. 58–65; Pearsall, 'The whole book', pp. 23–4. For the differing manuscripts identified as commonplace books compare those found in Robbins and Guddat-Figge to that of Parker, *The commonplace book*, pp. 7, 11–12. Parker does not list Humphrey's book.

[15] Dyboski (ed.) *Songs, carols*, p. xxxiv.

[16] Guddat-Figge, *Catalogue of the manuscripts*, pp. 22–8; Pearsall, 'The whole book', pp. 23–4. While Guddat-Figge excludes professional compilations, Parker believes that they can still be attributed the term commonplace book: *The commonplace book*, p. 10.

[17] Robbins (ed.) *Secular lyrics*; Louis, *The commonplace book of Robert Reynes*, p. 102;

each other and with Humphrey Newton was their regular need to register accounts and record memoranda. In contrast to the nobility, it is highly unlikely that they employed anyone, certainly not on a permanent basis, to compile their records. Indeed, it is apparent that some of these compilers were precisely those employed for their scribal skills. They were also unlikely to be able to afford to buy large numbers of books, and therefore the miscellanies were borne of a need to copy texts – often quite quickly – when they came available.[18] With the spread of paper in the fifteenth century, this new cheaper medium facilitated the construction of personal books.[19] In compiling his manuscript, Humphrey can be said to share the aims of a widening literate group of bureaucrats, professionals and businessmen.

The commonplace book was therefore the work of those who were in the habit of writing, and having near them materials to which they would frequently refer for information. It explains the mix of household, legal accounts, formulary letters and deeds often to be found within commonplace books, as they are in Humphrey's miscellany. The juxtaposition of literary work and household accounts also shows the shifting balance that could occur between practical and recreational writings. The commonplace book belonging to Glastonbury Abbey was originally an account book before it took the form of a literary miscellany. Conversely, the 'Book of Brome' was a literary miscellany that was later used for accounts and other notes.[20]

These manuscripts also reflect the strong impulse throughout the late medieval period to gather information together. It can be seen in the range of collections circulating among the middle and upper strata of society, from sermon exempla to quotations from classical authors (the *florilegia*), and to composite manuscripts of a range of literary items. The development of commercial exemplars or booklets, readily available for copying and collecting, meant that small units could be purchased and brought together in an anthology of a person's own making.[21] Among commonplace book compilers there was a desire to make lists and draw together a range of seemingly disparate information. Parker writes of Richard Hill's collection as the product of his wish 'to put everything under one roof, as it were, to contain all of his smaller lists and arrangements into one comprehensive whole'.[22]

What were Humphrey's reasons for compiling a commonplace book? There was a degree of necessity about the process. This appears most obviously the case in the estate accounts, where rents, wages and outstanding

---

Smith (ed.) *The commonplace book* (Melton); BL, Harley MS 2252 (Colyns); BL, Harley MS 1735 (Crophill); Bodl, Lyell MS 35 (Uvedale).
[18] Gillespie, 'Balliol MS 354', p. 57.
[19] Lyall, 'Materials', pp. 11–30.
[20] Rigg, *A Glastonbury miscellany*, p. 5; Smith, *The commonplace book*.
[21] Boffey and Thompson, 'Anthologies and miscellanies', pp. 279–315; Robinson, 'The booklet'; Hardman (ed.) *The Heege manuscript*, pp. 14–17; Hanna, 'Booklets in medieval manuscripts'; Hanna, 'Miscellaneity and vernacularity', pp. 49–50.
[22] Parker, *The commonplace book*, p. 83.

debts had to be noted. It also applies in his more leisurely and spiritual items, where Humphrey needed to make copies of writings he would not have regularly to hand. The prayers he copied down from the chained book at Newark Church are cases in point. Several items, from his legal material to literary works such as *Philomena*, may have been borrowed and would have needed to be returned.[23] On the other hand, Humphrey did not simply transcribe items that he lacked, but also works that he owned. These include the Crux Christi prayer, which he kept in his purse, and a legal treatise in French, from which he copied a few opening paragraphs.[24] The former may have been copied as a surety against loss; the latter because he was extracting the relevant lines for reference. Both relate to the need to keep writing safe and easily accessible. As is well known, the Middle Ages witnessed a growth in record keeping; it was no longer simply the preserve of monasteries and royal administrations. Lay cartularies, such as that compiled by William Newton, chart the progress of document storage among the landholders of England. Comprising material from personal and sometimes neighbouring archives, their aim was to meet present and future landholding demands.[25] In making his transcriptions, Humphrey was creating something tailored to his immediate needs as landlord and bureaucrat, and to his longer-term interests as a leisure reader and worshipper.

At the same time, Humphrey was influenced by fashion and convention. A significant number of items he copied were ones favoured by other miscellany makers. John Fortescue's *Notes on the purchasing of land*, for instance, appears in several commonplace books besides Humphrey's as well as in other contemporary miscellanies.[26] While direct borrowing is a possibility – as has been suggested for those collections produced in London – the similarity more likely reflects the compilers' backgrounds and common experiences, and a general understanding of material suitable for miscellanies.[27] Pithy poems and extracts were universally appealing. In all likelihood Humphrey came across his two short pieces of St Augustine as extracts rather than as extended pieces; one of the quotations is found in a miscellany compiled by the scribe and translator John Shirley (d. 1456).[28] Some short lists appear so frequently in commonplace books that they became standard entries: lists of kings, or fifteenth-century battles, and the lists of towns and knight's fees in England. London booksellers were sensitive to the market and begun producing the more popular lists in booklets among plenty of blank pages

---

[23] Bodl, MS Lat. Misc.c.66, fos 3v, 18r, 107v–111v.
[24] Ibid., fos 10v, 31, 69r. See p. 112 above.
[25] For example, Foulds, 'Medieval cartularies'; O'Connor (ed.) *A calendar of the cartularies of John Pyel and Adam Franceys*; Marsh, '"I see by sizt"'.
[26] Bodl, MS Lat. Misc.c.66, fo. 101r; *NIMEV*, no. 4148. A printed copy of Humphrey's text can be found in Robbins, 'The poems of Humfrey Newton', p. 275.
[27] Parker, *The commonplace book*; Moss, 'A merchant's tale', p. 158.
[28] Now Bodl, Ashmole MS 59, fo. 73r. Bodl, MS Lat. Misc.c.66, fo. 62r.

for the owner to fill in for his or herself. The commonplace book of the wealthy London merchant Sir Thomas Frowyk (d. 1485) is a good example, as it contains a list of mayors and sheriffs of London to 1437, followed by a number of blank pages for subsequent office holders to be added.[29] The steer from booksellers may have helped to crystallise a standard design for miscellanies. In this sense, Humphrey could well have had a set idea about what his miscellany should contain.

A final consideration is the potential for the book to serve more than Humphrey's personal needs. This relates to what Philippa Hardman has highlighted as the 'home-centred' concerns of miscellanies.[30] It has been noted in earlier chapters that entries within Humphrey's commonplace book could satisfy a range of reading, social and health interests, with some items specifically for the family: medical recipes for his wife; didactic works for his children; and land deeds, estate accounts, genealogies and local histories that would assist future generations. It was this storehouse of family information that attracted later antiquarians to Humphrey's manuscript, and probably secured its survival. In 1656, John Warde, whose mother had been a Newton, retrieved the commonplace book from the antiquarian John Booth of Twemlow, to whom it had been lent. Warde was worried at Booth's treatment of his ancestor's manuscript and he rescued and bound it because the contents 'were of ordinary concernment to my selfe and neare relations of the Wardes my father's kindred'.[31]

Humphrey's commonplace book therefore served multiple purposes, perhaps multiple readers. There was no unifying theme or governing principle to the manuscript, nor had there been from the beginning. It is evident from the structure of the manuscript that Humphrey did not gather a wad of blank leaves together and gradually fill them up; nor did he start with page 1 and work his way through to 129. What has become Humphrey's commonplace book comprises a series of distinct quires, bifolia and odd leaves. Scraps of paper were pasted to others, and four professional texts were tucked inside, three of which provided Humphrey with material for copying. There was a liberal use of 'fillers' as Humphrey added new entries to his work: for instance, a description of a bed, a note on a forged deed, and the masses of St Gregory's Trental were copied onto a page originally containing only arti-

---

[29] BL, Harley MS 541. Sutton and Visser-Fuchs, 'The making of a minor London chronicle', pp. 86–103. Commonplace books traced to London have similar lists: for example, BL, Harley MS 2252, fo. 101 and BL, Lansdowne MS 762, fo. 2v.

[30] Hardman, 'Evidence of readership', p. 15.

[31] On retrieval, Warde bound the manuscript among several sheets of paper. His comments can be found on Bodl, MS Lat. Misc.c.66, fo. i. Warde's mother was Margaret (d. 1637), the daughter and co-heir of William Newton of Pownall (d. 1621). Her husband, John Warde of Monksheath, sold her Pownall inheritance, along with his own estates, in order to buy Capesthorne Hall, Cheshire. Humphrey's manuscript was stored in Capesthorne until it was auctioned at Sotheby's in 1947 and bought by the Bodleian Library.

cles on holding manorial franchises.[32] Like Richard Hill and other compilers, Humphrey is unlikely to have seen his book as one coherent manuscript at the outset, but as a number of independent yet related booklets that at some point were brought together.[33]

This point is illustrated by the watermark evidence. Ralph Hanna has identified fourteen different paper stocks (dating from the 1470s to the 1520s), which were drawn together in such a haphazard way that he has labelled Humphrey's manuscript a 'codicological nightmare'.[34] Hanna sees the origins of the manuscript as the professionally produced medical work (fos 75–90), around which were later gathered two separate manuscripts. One, begun in the late fifteenth century, is a literary miscellany (fos 91–129); the second (fos 1–74) is a heterogeneous collection dating to the early sixteenth century.[35] While this three-fold division has some merit, it under-plays the divisions of fos 1–74: the accounts booklet (24–46) and the courtesy treatises (fos 66–8) were clearly considered separate items before they later came to form part of the miscellany.

While Humphrey compiled his writings in a piecemeal fashion, he did feel the need to order and categorise. This might be expected from a man who worked regularly as a bureaucrat and had the impulse to archive. Some sections have a thematic unity, most easily seen in the accounts booklet (discussed in Chapter 4), the medical miscellany (discussed in Chapter 6) and the literary miscellany. The latter, covering almost a third of the manuscript, has been labelled thus because it comprises the bulk of Humphrey's literature and leisure activities: love lyrics, Middle English poems, literary extracts from Lydgate and Chaucer, prophecies, astrological charts and letter practices. Elsewhere in the manuscript, the impulse to group can be seen on a smaller scale. Some clustering is evident even in the more heterogeneous first sixth of the manuscript: for example, Humphrey placed the obit of Thomas

---

[32] Bodl, MS Lat. Misc.c.66, fo. 4v. While virtually all these additions were made by Humphrey, it is worth noting that one slip of paper was inserted by his son: fo. 27b. See p. 65 n.142 above.
[33] Gillespie, 'Balliol MS 354', pp. 49, 51; Hardman, *The Heege manuscript*, p. 39. Hanna, 'Miscellaneity and vernacularity', pp. 37–8 for discussion of the 'oscillation between the planned and the random' in medieval miscellanies.
[34] Hanna, 'Humphrey Newton, pp. 280–1.
[35] Hence the present sequence of manuscript folios does not reflect the order in which material was obtained and copied. The watermark evidence is laid out in Hanna, 'Humphrey Newton', pp. 280–1. The medical booklet has a single watermark throughout; the literary section has five marks dating to the late fifteenth century; the collection in fos 1–74 comprises eight watermarks, mostly of the early sixteenth century. While the watermarks can offer some guidance to dating, it is clear that Hanna has to rely, at best, on resemblances. For an example where 'closest' watermarks give a very misleading indication of dating see Parker, *The commonplace book*, p. 37.

Fitton and the epitaph of Laurence Lowe among folios containing pardons, a list of ten masses, and prayers to the Virgin.[36]

The imposition of order, at least retrospectively, can be seen further in Humphrey's desire to improve the accessibility of his material. He employed written instructions and cross-references among his accounts and deeds and also in his literary extracts. When he split his extract from Chaucer's *Parson's Tale* over the two sides of folio 128, he wrote under the first section 'on þe todr side be neyth all þe laten be gyn ye þen'.[37] While it could have been a personal reminder, this directive raises the possibility that Humphrey was expecting readers other than himself to use the manuscript. Supporting reasons for suggesting this will be discussed in later sections. Access was additionally helped with the production of contents pages. This was a strategy employed to a much greater and more consistent degree by Richard Hill: he left a few pages near the start of his commonplace book for this purpose, and then copied out a contents list in one sitting.[38] Humphrey's manuscript contains two contents pages, underlining the pre-existence of at least two units before they were brought together into the commonplace book. One, written in a single sitting, lists the contents of twelve folios containing a broad range of items.[39] Most have been lost, but the folios listed as 11 and 12 in the contents page are currently the first two folios of the commonplace book. The missing folios may have been removed or mislaid at a later date, perhaps when it suffered in antiquarian hands. But Humphrey himself had reused and reordered some of the pages, rendering the contents page out of date. One folio (listed in the contents page as folio 2) was later upturned and reused by Humphrey in order to list a series of debts in the 1510s.[40] A second contents page – still *in situ* – begins the literary miscellany and covers items contained in folios 92–129. It was written more incrementally, but it too became out of date. Humphrey underlined its obsolescence by filling the lower third of the page with a series of doodles and letter practices.[41] What the contents page now reveals are the additions and losses to Humphrey's miscellany. The later additions include the Aesop's fable and the Sacred Heart, while the major loss is the booklet(s) containing *De regimine principum* and Lydgate's *Look in the mirror*; it or they perhaps became detached from the manuscript and

---

[36] Bodl, MS Lat. Misc.c.66, fo. 18. Cf. John Colyns's book: Meale, 'The compiler at work', p. 97.
[37] A similar direction can be found on folio 89. For the accounts, see p. 78 above.
[38] Parker, *The commonplace book*, p. 51.
[39] It is now Bodl, MS Lat. Misc.c.66, fo 64ar. The folio contains a watermark that is unique in Humphrey's manuscript and dates from the early sixteenth century: Hanna, 'Humphrey Newton', p. 281.
[40] Now Bodl, MS Lat. Misc.c.66, fo 65. Both folios 64 and 65 have mouse holes in the same place as earlier folios of the commonplace books, indicating that they were at one time at the front of the book.
[41] Ibid., fo. 91. Humphrey's reuse of leaves compare with that of Robert Thornton: Thompson, 'The compiler in action', p. 117.

circulated independently. What both indexes highlight is the shifting nature of Humphrey's writings. They were a mobile, flexible series of units that only later became frozen, partly at Humphrey's death and partly when they were bound together in the seventeenth century.

The nature of its gathering has implications for the book's appearance. Like other commonplace books, Humphrey's manuscript is mostly plain and unadorned.[42] There are very few ruled lines and coloured inks, with some pages as rough and messy as notes can get. They are filled – and that means right down to the bottom line and to each corner – with words informally written, crossed-out, contracted and barely following a straight line. This is seen in several instances in Humphrey's accounts booklet (Plate 2), but can be found throughout the manuscript whenever he spotted a blank space that could be usefully filled with his latest find or observation.[43]

Nevertheless, Humphrey was interested in decorative style and this is most clearly seen in his literary miscellany. It is here that he shows a more creative hand and is more concerned with overall appearance. Margins are employed in a few of the pages containing secular lyrics; his treatise on proportion has both margins and ruled lines; and his hand is often at its neatest. It could never be said that Humphrey's handwriting was uniform. He adopted the common approach of using specific styles for different documents.[44] Some notes were written in a very untidy hand, illustrating the ease rather than the difficulty with which he wielded his pen; he wrote quickly, unthinkingly and therefore illegibly. This either took the form of the small, crabbed writing of the accounts, or the looser, leisurely letters of the prophecy verses. However, elsewhere, and particularly in the literary miscellany, there were occasions where he adopted a very neat hand, such as in the transcription of *Philomena* and *De Caistre's hymn*. In this he compares to Robert Reynes, who wrote his verse entries with great thought and attention, and his accounts, charms and legal documents with the least care.[45]

The literary miscellany is also the section where his signature appears. Humphrey had a well-practised autograph that can still be seen in half a dozen official documents.[46] In a local deed of 1500, fourteen signatures of major landholders of north-eastern Cheshire are recorded, and Humphrey's stands out for the skill and ease with which the letters are formed.[47] Humphrey had a relatively standard autograph for signing deeds: 'Neuton' follows a regular pattern, though he was a little more varied with 'Humfrey'. This

---

[42] Guddat-Figge, *Catalogue of the manuscripts*, p. 25.
[43] Compare with the work of John Colyns who wrote some texts and then went back later, sometimes on more than one occasion, to fill in gaps: Meale, 'The compiler at work', p. 95.
[44] See p. 48 above.
[45] Louis, *The commonplace book of Robert Reynes*, p. 9.
[46] CRO, DDA/1533/1; Legh of Adlington 10/11; JRUL, Egerton 1/2/1/16; JRUL, Jodrell 36, 39; TNA: PRO, C1/411/16.
[47] Legh of Adlington 10/11.

makes the odd exception noteworthy. One wonders whether it was signing his name next to Richard Sutton, sergeant at law, which prompted Humphrey to fashion a large, swooping signature, not unlike that of Sutton's himself.[48] In his commonplace book Humphrey adopted an even more adventurous hand. His signature appears at the end of the *Richard de Caistre's Hymn, Philomena, Secretum secretorum* and an astrological table.[49] In all cases he signs with large, elaborate letters and with a flourish. In the context of widespread anonymity among writers in the fifteenth and early sixteenth centuries, Humphrey seems to have enjoyed writing his name and advertising his dexterity. His actions can be compared to the West Country practitioner Thomas Fayreford in his medical commonplace book, where specific passages and tables compiled by him are indicated by his signature. Peter Jones believes that Fayreford was writing for others; he provided foliation and tables to help readers find information easily, and supplied drawings to texts. Humphrey may have felt a similar impulse to Fayreford, whom Jones describes as trying to 'emulate these authorities', with the prominence of his own name suggesting 'a conscious promotion of his own authorial fame'.[50]

It is certainly the case that Humphrey's flourishes were not confined to his signature, and he introduced the odd embellishment during a number of literary transcriptions. A letter 's' on the fourth line of an extract from the *Parson's Tale* is given an intricate tail; the 't' beginning the recipe to make gold water has a long headstroke; and elaborate ascenders are used on the top lines of two poems, the tract beginning *Qui est carta* and the section on medical recipes. He also copied letters straight from his letter book (the capitals S and B appear in the *Philomena* poem) and not only for literary items. His 1498/9 rental for the Newton estate begins with a large 'R' from the letter book, which Humphrey practiced several times. He never quite mastered it and the 'R' remained very stilted.[51] Nevertheless these are the touches where a sober gentleman showed a more flamboyant side.

His most elaborate letters are the attempts at strapwork, which appear among his letter practices and elsewhere.[52] The capitals A–H were decorated with vegetation, with C and G containing the faces of men and animals. They bear all the hallmarks of being taken from a pattern book designed for a scribe or calligrapher, perhaps even an illuminator. A pertinent example is the sketchbook described by Janet Backhouse, consisting of twenty-three large initials of the alphabet, which are filled with leaf designs and twisted or knotted strapwork. They are of a much higher quality than Humphrey's,

---

[48] JRUL, Jodrell 36.
[49] Bodl, MS Lat. Misc.c.66, fos 98v, 99r, 104v, 106r, 111v and 122r–v. On fo 98v, he wrote 'Domini scripcit carmeni humffridus est sibi nomen'.
[50] Jones, 'Harley MS 2558', p. 44.
[51] Bodl, MS Lat. Misc.c.66, fo. 24r. For the letter book, see pp. 48–9 above
[52] See p. 49 above. Humphrey also practised the letters in his treatise on colour: fo. 128v.

though very similar in design. Given that only Humphrey's copies have survived, the original booklet may well have boasted more sophisticated patterns.[53] Two further initials in Humphrey's manuscript are inhabited. A small boar is drawn into the initial beginning the treatise on proportion. More elaborately, the initial 'O' marking the beginning of an alliterative poem has been enlarged and adorned with page-length decoration.[54] Inside the letter is St Veronica holding her vernicle; foliage descends towards the foot of the page. It is a clear image and one executed with care: Christ's face and halo are visible on the outstretched cloth Veronica holds (Plate 7). Why this image should begin the secular alliterative poetry is not clear, because there is no obvious relationship between picture and text. Humphrey could have been faithful to an original, or the image may have been a personal favourite. A famous indulgence was attached to the image of the vernicle and perhaps Humphrey saw it as an opportunity to augment his pardon collection.[55] If that was the reason, one might have expected it to open the far more appropriate *Richard de Caistre's hymn* written on the previous page; perhaps he had simply been looking for a poem beginning with 'O'.

Humphrey tried his hand at other sketches and he was prone to doodling in free margins and, in one instance, on a whole page. He shared the habit with John Crophill of Wix, who sketched into the margins of his commonplace book *inter alia* a spade, a lady with a spindle, a wheatsheaf, a pickfork, a phallus, a hen, dog and a couple of ploughs.[56] Crophill was an amateur physician servicing a small Essex village, and his crude sketches reflect his rural surroundings. Humphrey's doodles are far less bucolic: he drew the more gentle faces of bushy-haired aristocratic youths, of young maidens, of a monk, of birds such as the eagle and the osprey, and a face of a lion.[57] They were not merely idle doodles, but attempts to improve his artistic skills. He appears to have needed the practice. Humphrey's sketch of a skeleton is the product of someone who is trying to draw with care, but without much flair. He does slightly better with an astrologer holding a sphere – it is rough, but a little more fluid in design. Some images were more practised than others, and one aspiration was to perfect the way cloth folds at the bottom of robes: Humphrey particularly wanted to show a person's back foot as he or she stepped forward. He was a keen, but not a naturally gifted artist.

While most of his manuscript is monochrome, Humphrey was attracted to the use of colour. Like many compilers of commonplace books, it was red ink

---

[53] BL, Sloane MS 1448A: Backhouse, 'An illuminator's sketch book', pp. 3–14; Alexander, *Medieval illuminators:* see figures 215 and 216 for initials that bear similarity to Newton's.
[54] Bodl, MS Lat. Misc.c.66, fos 107, 124r.
[55] Lewis, 'The Veronica', pp. 100–6. For scribes copying not simply the texts, but the layouts too, see O'Rourke, 'Imagining book production', pp. 56–7.
[56] BL, Harley MS 1735, fos 2, 4v, 9v, 10v, 12r and 13r.
[57] For example, Bodl, MS Lat. Misc.c.66, fos 92–3, 95v.

that he mainly employed, either for rubrics, to underline proper nouns or for emphasis. His drawing of the Sacred Heart (Plate 3), for instance, was given greater impact for being coloured in red. While his actual use of colour was limited, Humphrey was evidently keen to use more, because he copied out a series of recipes from a 'Book of scrifure to ley all maner enkis'. Ink recipes, much like medical and culinary recipes, were a common feature of medieval miscellanies, whether as full-length treatises or short items. Presumably Humphrey followed his treatise in order to make the blacks and the reds of his manuscript. More ambitiously, he transcribed recipes for gold and silver inks: 'a sise of gold to ley on a boke', 'a sise to cauch gold', 'to make gold water' and 'how ye shall temper the colors of alummyng'.[58] Was he thinking of illuminating his initials?

While the overall impression of Humphrey's work is not one of a polished anthology, he was nevertheless recording and practising the skills to create such a volume. The margins, bookhand, the initials and the ink endow Humphrey's literary miscellany with some semi-professional touches. As far as is known, Humphrey was only ever hired to write legal documents, but perhaps he aspired to more creative commissions. One limited achievement was the booklet containing *Richard de Caistre's hymn*, *Philomena* and the alliterative poems.[59] Considered thought and effort were put into its presentation: it was very neatly written, had some decoration and contains Humphrey's autograph. It is not too unreasonable to draw a similarity between this quire and the autographed booklets used by scribes for templates and to exhibit their skills. It is possible that Humphrey was copying from a pre-existing booklet and substituting his name for the original scribe. This was the method adopted by the gentleman Robert Thornton in compiling his two anthologies.[60] Alternatively, Humphrey may have been designing his own signed portfolio, advertising his versatility to family, friends and prospective clients.

The poet

Humphrey was no mere copyist, and his proficiency in both English and Latin meant that he had the potential to be creative in his writing; he was someone who thought with his pen. At the simplest level, there were the

---

[58] Bodl, MS Lat. Misc.c.66, fos 123r, 124–128v. 'Sise' or size presumably refers to the wash applied to paper to allow for illumination to take place. Similar recipes were circulating in contemporary Cheshire manuscripts. A miscellany belonging to Vale Royal Abbey, Cheshire, has a good range of ink recipes, as befits its monastic context: Bodl, Ashmole MS 750, fos 145, 168v, 179, 198v. Discussion of ink treatises can be found in Thompson, '*Liber de coloribus illuminatorum sive pictorum*', pp. 280–307, 448.

[59] Bodl, MS Lat. Misc.c.66, fos 105–111.

[60] Keiser, 'Lincoln Cathedral Library', p. 159; Keiser, 'More light on the life', p. 118; Hanna, 'The growth of Robert Thornton's books', p. 61.

brief records of his transactions with his servants and the slightly longer accounts of local genealogies. These would not have stretched his vocabulary, but at least indicate that he could express himself in a variety of ways. A more sustained piece of prose is the Purgatory treatise, and he was seemingly undaunted by the need to write six pages. The narrative has several emendations: spelling changes, eye-slips, and even a few stylistic alterations. Ralph Hanna sees this as the result of transcription errors, Humphrey having problems with an earlier exemplar.[61] Yet altering 'died' to 'decessed' or 'after the color of tawny' to the simpler 'in tawny' might equally reflect a man who searched for the right words to convey a desired meaning.[62]

Humphrey's most well-known contribution to literature is his secular lyrics. He wrote nearly twenty poems in his commonplace book, making it one of the largest collections of medieval secular lyrics written by one person. That Humphrey's identity as a poet is known is of equal significance because there are so few fifteenth-century poets who can be identified.[63] The poems are generally finished versions in the commonplace book, although a number of minor changes were made to the texts, a product of eye-slips and amendments. In a few instances there is an explicit concern for presentation, with the adoption of regular lines and uniform margins; one poem was centred in the page and extenders were applied to the top line; another was written in double columns. There seems to have been some pride in these achievements. But this was not sustained. Several poems were squashed untidily into any available space, including the margins of erstwhile neat poems, and in one case around a failed attempt at drawing a quadrant (Plate 6). It may indicate a time when the maturing Humphrey was less enamoured with his earlier compositions. Secular lyrics in general were not presented with much care and their appearance has been called 'sub-average'.[64]

The content of the lyrics reflected Humphrey's interests and preoccupations. One of the poems shows his fascination with the passing seasons and the zodiac. Beginning with 'frosty' January and Aquarius – its 'fresche tarages vn-to zepherus' – the poem's three verses briefly chart the year until August and Leo.[65] There are some short, fun lyrics. Humphrey has a popinjay say 'Min coloures byn both brizt & shene / And me desires both kynge & qwene / Lords & ladies of gret emprisese / For I am a brid of paradise'.[66] As mentioned in Chapter 6, Humphrey shared a contemporary liking of bird imagery. In another of his poems beginning 'O ye my emprice' (echoing

---

[61] Hanna, 'Humphrey Newton', p. 282.
[62] See pp. 117–18 for further discussion.
[63] The poems have been available in print since 1950, when R.H. Robbins published the majority in 'The poems of Humfrey Newton'. Humphrey did not give titles to his lyrics, as was conventional, and hence Robbins's numbering system has been adopted as an easy means to identify the works.
[64] Boffey, *Manuscripts of English courtly love lyrics*, p. 45.
[65] Bodl, MS Lat. Misc.c.66, fo. 93v (Robbins poem X)
[66] Bodl, MS Lat. Misc.c.66, fo. 95v.

his short lyric) Humphrey describes his lover as a 'precious papyngay of paradice', and as 'tru as a turtill-dove'; a final verse alludes to a sparrowhawk, a thrush and a nightingale.[67]

His favoured compositional style was the courtly love lyric. This highly popular verse form appealed to a significant proportion of gentle society in the fifteenth and sixteenth centuries: over 600 lyrics survive in 100 different manuscripts. The single number attributed to Humphrey is impressive, surpassing that of both Chaucer and Lydgate.[68] His book is one of only a handful of fifteenth-century and early sixteenth-century manuscripts to contain such a large collection of formal secular lyrics. Others include the collections belonging to the gentry families of Findern (Derbyshire) and Armburgh (Warwickshire), and the sixteenth-century gentleman Humphrey Wellys (Staffordshire); an interesting concentration in the Midlands.[69] Humphrey Newton was also fashionable with the technical device he used, adopting the love letterform, a style of poetry at its peak in the first decade of the sixteenth century.[70] Stevens and Green believe the form emerged from conversations of love, and was part of 'the game of love'.[71] Yet the use of the letterform also reflects an increased acquaintance with the written word during the fifteenth century. The layout and vocabulary were based on the writing style, and it was common for the poetry to contain allusions to the form of its composition. In Humphrey's poems, for example, there is found: 'mi hond it qwakis to hold the penne / for whi I write you more and more'; and 'sithen as we may not to geder spek / be writynge we shall oure hertes breke'.[72]

In the Middle Ages creative work was treated as a science with a series of elaborate rules that needed to be learnt; a poet was someone who had mastered a technique and observed the 'fixed and complicated rules of rhetoric'.[73] Criticism of those who had failed to grasp the method was sometimes worked into compositions. Hence one courtly lyric has 'The ynglysch of Chaucere was nat in youre mynd / Ne tullyus termys wyth so gret ellouence / But ye, as vnctures and crabbed of kynde / Rolle hem on a hepe, it semyth by the sentence'.[74] At the same time, disclaimers were made by those

---

[67] Ibid., fo. 94r (Robbins poem XIII).
[68] Boffey, *Manuscripts of English courtly love lyrics*, p. 17.
[69] Harris, 'The origins and make-up'; McNamer, 'Female authors'; Carpenter, *The Armburgh papers*, pp. 58–9, 155–67; Jansen and Jordan (eds) *The Welles anthology*, pp. 22–29 and *passim*.
[70] Camargo, *The Middle English verse epistle*, p. 127.
[71] Stevens, *Music and poetry*, p. 161; Green, *Poets and princepleasers*, p. 118.
[72] Bodl, MS Lat. Misc.c.66, fo. 92v (Robbins poem II), lines 41–2; ibid., fo. 93v (Robbins poem XII), 25–6. Humphrey also expected his lover to communicate with him through writing: 'I was as glad of youre writynge as ever I was of any thynge': ibid., lines 8–9.
[73] Chaytor, *From script to print*, pp. 1, 49–52.
[74] Printed in Robbins (ed.) *Secular lyrics*, no. 209, lines 8–11. The original manuscript is Bodl, Rawlinson poet.36.

amateurs who feared a weak grasp of the rules. Chaucer's Franklin apologised for his inability to speak correctly: 'Have me excused of my rude speche / I lerned nevere rethorik'.[75] Eventually, these disclaimers themselves became one of the technical devices of poetry to convey a sense of modesty and Humphrey incorporated one into his lyrics: 'I conclude here my processe in a breffe space / Because of Retherike termys þat we ar not coth'.[76] Handbooks of creative writing were available from which the practising poet could select a number of conventional phrases to work into his or her compositions. As Walter Ong remarked in reference to several Latin phrase books, a poem could be assembled from epithets or phrases from relevant poetry in much the same way as a child might assemble a structure from a Meccano set. Nevertheless, to become a good poet required more than just a reassembling of phrases; Chaucer's mastery lay in his use of formulae in new and varied contexts.[77]

It is fair to say that Humphrey was no master. Like his letter formation and his sketching, his poetry lacked a creative flair. But as a steward and bureaucrat, adept at using formularies and adjusting written instruments, he was skilled at adapting phrases and the lyrics are competent pieces. Love poetry was a usual choice for the amateur poet because there were many examples available, and it was simple and relatively easy to compose. Julia Boffey's first line index and the poems collected by Robbins and Camargo illustrate the considerable degree of borrowing in love letter poetry.[78] Humphrey's lyrics were filled with conventions. There were acrostic poems spelling the names Humphrey, Ellen, Brian and Margaret; a few poems used the common literary device of addressing lyrics to a mistress 'M'; allusions were made to Venus and to spring, and there were the obligatory references to a lover's physical features. Humphrey's sweetheart is inevitably grey-eyed, red-lipped, cherry-cheeked, fair-faced and fair-haired. Several lines were lifted from other poems – such as the 'go little bill' phrase – and it is possible to compare Humphrey's verses directly with lyrics in other miscellanies, such as the Wellys anthology of neighbouring Staffordshire.[79] One reason for the similarity is the omnipresent influence of Chaucer. Humphrey himself begins one poem with a line virtually straight out of Chaucer's prologue to the *Canterbury Tales*: 'When zepheres eeke with his fresshe tarage' (Humphrey's poem) compares to 'whan Zephirus eek with his swete breeth' (Chaucer's Prologue). Not that Humphrey would have tried to claim originality. They

---

[75] *Canterbury Tales: The Franklin's Prologue*, lines 718–9, p. 178. See also poems in the Armburgh collection: Carpenter, *The Armburgh papers*, p. 158.
[76] Bodl, MS Lat. Misc.c.66, fo. 93r (Robbins poem V), lines 37–40. Compare Gray, 'Middle English courtly lyrics', p. 126.
[77] Brewer, *English Gothic literature*, p. 85; Ong, *Orality and literacy*, p. 22.
[78] Boffey, *Manuscripts of English courtly love lyrics*, Appendix I; Robbins (ed.) *Secular Lyrics*; Camargo, *The Middle English verse epistle*, Appendix I.
[79] See Robbins, 'The poems of Humfrey Newton', pp. 280–1, for specific comparisons.

were conscious borrowings of literary formulae. The acrostic poems were introduced by Humphrey as 'littera amandi et nomen de illa est expressum hic'; above the acrostic 'Brian' poem was written 'alia de homine'. Several verses were bracketed together with the words *mittitur* and *billet*.[80]

The style that Humphrey selected is significant. Courtly literature was 'courtly' in the sense of displaying 'the values of a leisured and cultivated society'. Its central concerns were honour, elegance, wealth and display.[81] The lyrics were based on the premise that falling in love (or at least appearing to) made a man attractive to others. The action took place within the setting of a castle, court or garden, symbolising good breeding; it was never a genre associated with low birth. Humphrey took care to depict himself as the conventional courtly lover. He was love sick; usually unsuccessful in love and wondering whether his lady knew of his pain; he wore black to symbolise his melancholy; and he sent letters and tokens. In carefully describing his lady's beauty, he demonstrated his skill in the language of love. Like knowing hunting terms or armorial bearings, the cultivated gentleman should be capable of speaking or writing appropriate words of love. Humphrey's single line from Ovid containing the famous 'vincit omnis amor' phrase must have been copied with this in mind.[82] In his lyrics, therefore, Humphrey attempted to fashion a refined image of himself.

Nevertheless, despite the use of courtly language and imagery, Stevens describes his lyrics – like those of the Finderns in Derbyshire – as provincial, with Humphrey's efforts 'slightly further from the head of cultural sweetness'.[83] The setting offers supporting evidence. In the four poems that allude to their location, the action takes place in a parish church. In one poem, Humphrey imagines himself hearing mass, another has him attending matins. This is not to say that shows of gentility could not be displayed in a religious building.[84] On one occasion Humphrey presents himself visiting a church on a Friday morning, carrying a sparrowhawk on his hand, and accompanied by a male servant.[85] Yet, according to the *Boke of St Albans*, the sparrowhawk was the bird that a priest was allowed to carry, and it was the common bird of an average citizen. Humphrey did not choose a bird of higher social status, such as the lanner falcon or lancet, birds appropriate for a squire.[86] A church is also evidently not a court, and Humphrey was far

---

[80] Bodl, MS Lat. Misc.c.66, fos 92v, 93v, 94r.
[81] Stevens, *Music and poetry*, pp. 151–5; Green, *Poets and princepleasers*, pp. 109, 114; Kay, 'Courts, clerks and courtly love', p. 92.
[82] Bodl, MS Lat. Misc.c.66, fo. 2v.
[83] Stevens, *Music and Poetry*, p. 224. Gray is a little more impressed, describing Humphrey's lyrics as having an 'attractive awkwardness': 'Middle English courtly lyrics', p. 144.
[84] For example, Gray, 'Middle English courtly lyrics', p. 126.
[85] Bodl, MS Lat. Misc.c.66, fos 93r, 94r–v (Robbins poems VI, XIV, XVI and XVII).
[86] Berners, *The boke of St Albans*. See the list under the subheading 'the naamys of all maner of hawkys & to whom they belong'.

more familiar with the former than the latter. Hence, while his lyrics have the style, they often lack the essence of courtly love.

Humphrey may have tried to boost their courtliness in their delivery. An alternative to reading the lyrics is mentioned in one of Humphrey's poems where, to compensate for his lack of writing skills, he suggests a meeting with his love and 'wyth meloduous tunys I shall meyne with my mouth'.[87] Despite the appearance of another standard phrase, it is the case that many of the surviving courtly lyrics were intended to be sung. It was another important skill expected of a well-bred man, as was the playing of music. When the squires in the household of Edward IV were not talking of the chronicles of kings, they were said to be engaged in 'pypyng, or harpyng, synging, or other actez marciablez, to help ocupy the court and acompany straungers, tyll the tym require of departing'.[88] Humphrey's inclination to play is visible in his drawing and description of how to string a harp (Plate 8). This was the favourite amateur instrument of the day and, until it was replaced by the lute in the 1530s, it was the instrument of choice among English nobility.[89] In Malory's *Morte Darthur*, the young Tristram learnt to play the harp as part of his gentle upbringing, and Humphrey is likely to have wished to enhance his own image, and those of his children, as educated gentlemen.[90] The commonplace book sketch is similar to a gut-strung 'gothic' harp and has twenty strings. Images of comparable instruments can be found in a range of western European manuscripts in the fifteenth and early sixteenth centuries, including the commonplace book of the Ramston family of Essex.[91] Nevertheless, Humphrey's harp does appear small for the time. By the later Middle Ages, twenty-six or twenty-nine strings were more popular and the curve of the arm was more pronounced. It is possible that this older-fashioned model was intended more for didactic than for practical purposes.[92] If so, it is another case of Humphrey learning or teaching how to 'talk' rather than how to 'do'.

The courtly lyric was not the only genre with which Humphrey experimented. Within the conventions of the love lyric, he used phrases of alliteration, and in one verse quite extensively:

---

[87] Bodl, MS Lat. Misc.c.66, fo. 93r (Robbins Poem V), line 40.
[88] Myers (ed.) *The household of Edward IV*, p. 129.
[89] Stevens, *Music and poetry*, p. 277.
[90] Malory, *Works*, p. 232 (lines 5–8).
[91] It is Cambridge, Trinity College MS 0.2.53, fo. 71, as noted in Boffey, *Manuscripts of English courtly love*, p. 101.
[92] Rosenzweig (ed.) *Historische harfen/Historical harps*, pp. 193–7. I am indebted to the harpist William Taylor of Ardival harps for sharing his knowledge on medieval harps, and for offering his opinion on the nature of Humphrey's illustration. The smaller harp is not unusually found in late medieval manuscripts: the written descriptions lagged behind developments to the actual instruments.

> Hit dose comfort to creatures, be Crist and be crede
> To þam þat listonys & lovys of lovers to lerne
> God gif thym space, spekynge, and specily to spede,
> And to bryng thym in to blisse with þat bright burne[93]

What is interesting about the choice of style is its regional significance. In the fourteenth century the so-called 'Alliterative Revival' comprised a number of key works from the North West with a Cheshire man producing the most famous product of that age, *Sir Gawain and the Green Knight*. By the fifteenth century, alliterative poetry had become a more local phenomenon and was confined to the North West Midlands.[94] Strong echoes of the earlier era are found in two poems in Humphrey's commonplace book: a four-stanza work beginning 'On cliffe þat castell so knetered'; the second, an eight-stanza work beginning 'Wyntre that snartely snewes'.[95] Both have a restrictive regional vocabulary, and are written in the typical and intricate pararhyme stanzas of the genre. Neither is particularly courtly. In the second poem the references to the coming spring and to the hunt are there merely to introduce the man's pursuit of a woman. There is no gentle wooing, and he overcomes her in a haystack.

At least in its style, R.H. Robbins thought the parallels between the second poem and *Sir Gawain* were so close that he called the Newton poem a 'Gawain epigone'; in other words, Humphrey had composed the poem in a conscious imitation of the earlier style.[96] It must be emphasised that the evidence in favour of Humphrey's authorship rests mainly on the view that it was written by an amateur. In all other ways the evidence points away from Humphrey. The style, vocabulary and layout are very different from his other works. The poems have a page to themselves, are written in a neat bookhand, are decorated with a large initial containing St Veronica and the Vernicle, and verse rhymes are bracketed together (Plate 7). As noted above, they are also written in a booklet with two other works which are known to be the compositions of others: *Richard de Caistre's Hymn* and *Philomena*. It is clear that Humphrey was setting the work apart from his other poetry, and on these grounds, it seems more likely that he was copying someone else's work, rather than celebrating one of his better attempts. Nevertheless, what it does show is a continued fascination with the alliterative style, and Humphrey's familiarity with a regional literary dialect. While some of the words (such as 'bigge' meaning to build) were still in currency, others would have appeared antiquated in early Tudor Cheshire.

---

[93] Bodl, MS Lat. Misc.c.66, fo. 93r (Robbins poem V), lines 5–8.
[94] Turville-Petre, *The alliterative revival* and his *Alliterative poetry*; Putter, *An introduction to the Gawain poet*, pp. 29, 33–4.
[95] Bodl, MS Lat. Misc.c.66, fo. 106v (Robbins poem XXII). Turville-Petre, *The alliterative revival*, p. 123.
[96] Robbins, 'A Gawain epigone', pp. 361–6.

When he was not checking his marl or presiding over manorial courts, Humphrey composed poetry to fill his leisure time, and it appears to have been something that he enjoyed doing. He took time to craft his poetry and to find the most appropriate word. In his acrostic poem 'Humfrey' he altered the phrase from 'to here me sayn', to 'to here me complayne', and other minor alterations can be seen throughout his lyrics.[97] The right phrase was important and he probably gained some personal satisfaction in perfecting the lyrics. Was it more than just an intellectual exercise? The sincerity lying behind these poems is difficult to gauge. From a twenty-first-century perspective, the lyrics can come across as sickly and clichéd: 'Ye are swetter then the flores to me most swete'.[98] But it is likely to have been less so then, and even clichés can be sincere. As mentioned in Chapter 2, the use of the acrostic for his wife, Ellen, suggests a degree of personal commitment; perhaps it was a love letter. It would be natural for his family to have been both his inspiration and his audience; other poets wrote about their families and localities in their verses. In the Wellys anthology, two poems feature the local acquaintances of the compiler Humphrey Wellys, with one containing several names of inhabitants living in the environs of Ingestre (Staffordshire).[99]

Humphrey was not the first of his family to try his hand at poetry, or to be inspired by his relatives. His great-great grandfather, Richard Newton, had penned a nine-line alliterative verse among papers relating to his son's divorce from Sybil Downes. It was a personal reflection on Sybil's influence on his life:

> Sometime there was in Neuton a hipping hechin
> Hee hadd oxen and kye and corne for the maistrie
> Fatt boars in theyr stye while that they might stand
> Good steedes in his stall well I astande
> Now there is come to this towne a lorde
> Sebott [Sybil] with her loude cry,
> Shee wakens one so early,
> That vndr of the day
> That I noe sleepe may.[100]

This was clearly an occasion piece for the family. It is short and crude, and yet it is stylistically similar to fourteenth-century alliterative verse (seen in the unrhymed lines with four stresses, and the short rhyming lines at the end). Richard's birthplace in the hundred of Macclesfield and his service for Richard II place him within the recognised cultural milieu of *Sir Gawain and*

---

[97] Bodl, MS Lat.Misc.c.66, fo. 95r.
[98] Ibid., fo. 94r (Robbins, poem XIII), line 7.
[99] Wilson, 'Local habitations'.
[100] BL, Add MS 42134A, fo. 20r. *NIMEV*, no. 3189. 'Hippin hechin' means 'limping Richard': Noyes, 'Some notices of the family of Newton', p. 318, n. 9.

the Green Knight.¹⁰¹ His work was hardly in that league, but Richard deserves mention because he is the only identifiable alliterative poet from the fourteenth-century North West. Moreover, this poem indicates that the Newtons were a family who kept lyrics and copied them out over 100 years later.

Nonetheless, the opportunity to display oneself as a poet was in front of a well-chosen audience. Authors of love poetry expected and encouraged others to examine their endeavours.¹⁰² Reading was not a solitary activity, and reading parties were not uncommon in many sections of society. At the higher social levels, such as in the household of Cicely Neville, duchess of York, this might take the form of listening to religious texts during dinner, or, like Edward IV's household esquires, performing lyrics at an after-dinner soirée.¹⁰³ Gentry households, too, provided the location for small-group literary activity, facilitating textual communities. The poetry collection of the Findern family of Derbyshire suggests that the poems were composed by and for members of the Findern household and their friends.¹⁰⁴ In this way, manuscripts and poetry circulated among the gentry through ties of kinship, friendship and patronage.

It would not be surprising if Humphrey had composed his lyrics with a wider, gentle audience in mind, or had been inspired by those he knew. Concerns over presentation and the contents pages may well indicate that Humphrey showed his work to friends and neighbours for their comments and discussion. He certainly had contact with a number of men and their families who were interested in poetry and assisted in its transmission. A survey of the alliterative work from early Tudor England shows that Humphrey was only one of several members of the Cheshire and Lancashire gentry who were enthusiastic for this kind of verse. Among the owners of alliterative works was the Booth family of Dunham Massey, part-holders of the Pownall estate. The name of 'Eesebyt Bothe of Dunham Massey', identified as the wife of Sir George Booth (d. 1531), is found in the margins of the fourteenth-century alliterative poem *St Erkenwald*, which was copied around 1477 into a manuscript also containing *A stanzaic life of Christ* and *The South English Legendary*.¹⁰⁵ The Booths were patrons of the Booth chapel at Eccles church (Lancashire), founded by their cousins the Booths of Barton. It was the chapel's priest, Thomas Bowker, who owned the manuscript in the 1530s and it may well have been donated by Elizabeth Booth.¹⁰⁶ Humphrey

---

101 Bennett, 'Sir Gawain and the Green Knight'; p. 69; Bennett, *Community*, pp. 231–4.
102 Green, *Poets and princepleasers*, p. 118.
103 Armstrong, 'The piety of Cicely, Duchess of York', pp. 79–80; Coleman, *Public reading*, p. 109.
104 Harris, 'The origins and make-up', p. 327; McNamer, 'Female authors'; Scattergood, *Politics*, p. 18; Coss, 'Aspects of cultural diffusion', pp. 42–5; Youngs, 'Cultural networks'.
105 BL, Harley MS 2250, fos 72v–5v. A transcription can be found in Turville-Petre, *Alliterative poetry*, pp. 101–19.
106 Luttrell, 'Three north-west midland manuscripts', pp. 38–42. Bowker witnessed the will of John Booth of Barton in 1526, and appears in the wills of Margaret Hawarden

had cause to meet the Booth family on many occasions. Sir William Booth was one of the feoffees of Thomas Fitton and had helped secure the Pownall inheritance for the Newtons; his son, Sir George Booth, husband of Elizabeth, was a prominent witness in the enfeoffment of lands placed in the marriage jointure of Katherine Mainwaring and William Newton.[107] Moreover, a favoured location for Humphrey's genealogical searches was Dunham Massey, where he perused a 'Remembrance Book' of Robert Booth (d. 1460). It is conceivable that Humphrey also had the time to explore other, more literary items, in the Booth household.[108]

Another supporter of Humphrey's claims to Pownall was Sir John Legh of Baguely, who was married to William Booth's daughter Ellen. This family is of interest because one of their sons, either Richard or Henry, is D.A. Lawton's choice as the writer of the alliterative poem *Scottish Field* (c.1516), which celebrated the military prowess of Cheshire and Lancashire men in the English victory over the Scots at Flodden in 1513.[109] The heroes of this poem were James Stanley (d. 1515) – warden of Manchester College (1485–1506) and bishop of Ely – and his son Sir John Stanley of Handforth, scions of the most powerful family in the region. James makes an appearance with his father, Thomas Stanley, in another Stanley poem called *Lady Bessy*, which dwells on the concerns of Elizabeth of York in the year running up to Bosworth Field. In this he is referred to in his capacity as warden of Manchester College: 'thy son James that young priest/warden of Manchester was made latlye'.[110]

What these examples suggest is a thriving regional literary culture in the early sixteenth century that focused on the Stanley family and Manchester College. The circle can be widened to include others who enjoyed verse.[111] It is James Stanley's grandson Thomas Ireland, for instance, who has been linked with the collection of alliterative romance belonging to the Ireland

---

(dated 1520/1) and her cousin Elizabeth Hurleston (dated 1527/8), both of whom had close connections with the Booth family: Piccope (ed.) *Lancashire and Cheshire Wills*: 1, p. 8; ibid., 2, p. 11. Intriguingly, the preacher at Eccles church in 1551–2 was the scholar and poet Nicholas Grimald, who copied into his notebook the alliterative *Alexander*. Turville-Petre, 'Nicholas Grimald and Alexander A', pp. 180–6.

[107] CRO, DVE 1 MX/10; Bodl, MS Lat. Misc.c.66, fo. 11r; JRUL, Mainwaring 331.
[108] Bodl, MS Lat.Misc.c.66, fos 51r, 70v; Marsh, '"I see by sizt of evidence"', p. 81.
[109] Lawton, 'Scottish Field', p. 44. See pp. 102, 164–5 above.
[110] The main repository for both these and other Stanley poems is the Percy Folio BL, Add MS 27879. Printed copies can be found in Lawton, 'Scottish Field', pp. 42–57; Oakden, 'Scotish Ffeilde', pp. 14–23; Robson, 'The Scottish field', II, pp. 1–28. Internal evidence dates *Lady Bessy* to around 1485, but surviving transcriptions are later in manuscript: BL, Harley MS 367 (dating to c.1560–80) and in print: *Bishop Percy's folio*, III, pp. 318–63; Halliwell (ed.) *Palatine Anthology*, pp. 1–105.
[111] This creativity has been noted before, though with different emphases: Beaumont, *Annals of Warrington*, 2, p. 398; Jones and Underwood, *The king's mother*, p. 151.

family of Hale, Lancashire.[112] Thomas Chetham, gentleman (1490–1546), held his manor of Nuthurst (Lancashire) from Thomas Stanley, earl of Derby, and was bailiff for two of the earl's manors for over twenty years. In the 1530s he copied around 14,000 lines of the fourteenth-century alliterative poem *The Destruction of Troy*, and left it to his son as an heirloom. Nuthurst was a well-read household containing copies of Gower's *Confessio Amantis*, Chaucer's *Canterbury Tales* and a 'Bocas'; the last two had been borrowed from Robert Cliff, who replaced James Stanley as warden of Manchester College (1506–16).[113] It was also a circle with which Humphrey had some familiarity. He was well known to John Stanley of Handforth, the hero of *Scottish Field*: 'that stoute knight, that sterne was of deeds'. Humphrey acted as a bond for Stanley and his wife in 1522, and interviewed Stanley in his Chancery case involving the tithes of Prestbury church. In turn, Stanley witnessed a number of Humphrey's local land deeds. Moreover, in 1518, Humphrey acted alongside John Stanley to convey lands in Dunham Massey to William Booth, which were to finance an obit to commemorate the death of Bishop James Stanley. Given these known connections, it is a pity that Humphrey did not record why, around 1500, he visited Winwick (Lancashire), where Bishop Stanley was rector.[114] Men with whom Humphrey worked, therefore, in the seemingly dry world of land transactions, were also men connected to a range of verse, either as owners or as heroes within it.

Conclusion

With his commonplace book, his poetry, prose and harp, Humphrey presented himself as a cultivated gentleman. It was no façade, for he seems genuinely to have fancied himself as a writer, sketcher and poet. He practised and honed his skills and he added the odd flourish to his letter formation; it suggests a more ostentatious side to this otherwise moderate man. Not everyone would have been able to write and be creative in early Tudor society. It demanded a good level of literacy, dexterity and patience, and Humphrey had all of those. Nevertheless, he never achieved any artistic heights. His calligraphy was painstakingly drawn and his poetry can appear, as Robbins labelled it, 'pedestrian'.[115] This must in part be a product of his personality: a conformist

---

112 Dickens, 'The date of the Ireland manuscript', pp. 62–6; Robson, *Three metrical romances*.
113 Chetham Library, Manchester, MUN.A.7.38; Glasgow University Library, Hunterian MS 388. Luttrell, 'Three north-west midland manuscripts', pp. 41–8. *Cheshire Sheaf*, 3rd ser. XVIII (1921), p. 67. Raines (ed.) *The Rectors of Manchester*, part 1, pp. 44–51.
114 Oakden (ed.) 'Scotish Ffeilde', p. 226; JRUL, Dunham Massey Deeds 1/2/1/16a; JRUL, Bromley Davenport, 'Newton by Mottram', no. 6; TNA: PRO, C1/411/13–16; Bodl, MS Lat. Misc.c.66, fo. 29v; Earwaker, *East Cheshire*, II, p. 246. For the dispute over Prestbury, see p. 132 above.
115 Robbins, 'The poems of Humfrey Newton', p. 279.

and a trusted bureaucrat who liked rules. At the same time, his commonplace book has the 'downmarket' feel of his tomb and window. Without the resources to purchase a number of books or to employ someone else to labour over transcriptions, Humphrey had to make his own work. In so doing he shared the outlook of a growing middling group – Felicity Riddy's 'bourgeois-gentry' – who gathered together literature for themselves and their families.[116] Their commonplace books were reflections of their desire to gather together 'good furniture' to better themselves.

Nevertheless, Humphrey was a man with a finger on the pulse of cultural trends among England's early Tudor elite. He was interested in secular lyrics, love letter poetry and acrostics. As with his reading habits, his creative writing demonstrates the degree of homogeneity in English culture that had occurred by the early sixteenth century. The interesting contrast here is that whereas his reading habits showed no interest in aristocratic romances, preferring moralistic and didactic works, his creative writing habits were more courtly: he penned no religious or moralising verse. In this regard his preferences appear similar to that of the Findern family in Derbyshire, whose manuscript led Felicity Riddy to suggest that 'in fifteenth-century England the taste for courtly lyric and the taste for vernacular romance were not necessarily found together'.[117] At the same time, there was an appreciation of regional literary genres. It partly sprang from Humphrey's firm cultural and linguistic roots in his Cheshire community, but also from a desire to ape the type of literature that was appreciated by his gentry neighbours. The regional, alliterative culture of early Tudor Cheshire was not one maintained merely by oral tradition, but one perpetuated by gentry-owned and gentry-written manuscripts.

---

[116] Riddy, 'Middle English romance', p. 237.
[117] Riddy, *Sir Thomas Malory*, p. 15.

8

Humphrey: The Man and his World

Turning the pages of Humphrey's commonplace book in the filtered light of Duke Humfrey's Reading Room, Bodleian library, draws the reader into a small, intimate world. The fascinating first-person detail can overpower the already faint echoes of 'outside' events, of the major political, constitutional, religious and demographic changes occurring during the Early Tudor period. Humphrey's life in general offers only limited information on this wider world. Whereas the more common problem in researching the late medieval gentry is the dominance of official documents over the personal, in Humphrey's case, the rich material of his manuscript is not always matched by governmental, administrative sources; he has comparatively little public presence. This is largely explained by Humphrey's position at the lower end of the gentry, a level not commonly reachable in the records. What, then, does this rare opportunity and different weighting of evidence tell us about an early Tudor gentleman? In addressing that question, and in drawing together the different facets of Humphrey's identity, this chapter takes its inspiration from Colin Richmond's observation: 'The full individuality of each man and woman cannot be recorded, but some aspects of what distinguished them as well as what they shared can be recovered.'[1]

What type of man was Humphrey Newton? A family man, undoubtedly. He took seriously his role of *paterfamilias* and channelled his energies into protecting the interests of his lineage. He did so by ensuring the continuation of the male line, arranging a good marriage for his heir, keeping the patrimony intact and taking care of his ancestors' souls. He was proud of the name of Newton, foregrounding the tun in his coat of arms, yet his approach was not without concern for the person. There are hints of family affection, notably towards his wife, and he took care over his children's upbringing and the establishment of his sons' livelihood. While we cannot know how harmoniously the members lived together, they certainly worked together, and wider kin – Humphrey's Lowe relatives and his brother-in-law – provided loyal support to the Newtons.

Concern for the lineage was inevitably intertwined with the successful management of the landed estate, the basis of the Newtons' wealth and status. The fortunate survival of Humphrey's accounts reveal a committed

---

[1] Richmond, 'After McFarlane', p. 60.

and energetic landlord. His conscientiousness and industry chimes with what historians are revealing about the enterprising gentry landlords who enthusiastically improved the quality of their holding.[2] Humphrey's significance is in deepening our knowledge of the extent of that enthusiasm in terms of scope and ambition (for instance, the construction of a fulling mill). The energies visible in the accounts are echoed in the strenuous efforts made in relation to the estate's borders. Both his commonplace book and the cartulary lend support to the view that a major motivation for the gentry was the preservation and extension of the estate.[3] Humphrey appears typical in his predatory search for 'chinks in the security of titles' and the competitiveness to recover lands and rights judged to be lost.[4] Thus he ruffled feathers, wrangled more of the Fitton inheritance than his wife was entitled to, and took advantage of widows. His disputes, however, were never as bellicose or disruptive as those of the Paston family or the Armburghs. As befits his status and landholdings, Humphrey's problems were smaller and more localised. They were also not the actions of a newly elevated man, a *parvenu*, but were generated by a family well-established in the area. He clearly infuriated his Newton neighbours, such as the Leghs of Adlington and the Pigots of Butley, but his actions did not cause ructions in the community. Indeed, in securing his tenure at Pownall he had the backing of all significant local landholders. At the same time, he was not vicious or obviously immoral. For a man never meant for the battlefield it is perhaps appropriate that strong-arm tactics were rarely used. In this he not only contrasts with some of the better-known disputants of fifteenth-century England, but with his son, under whom the acrimony over 'Newton' Heath ended in violence and Star Chamber.

Rather, Humphrey's strategy drew on his legal skills and focused on the cut and thrust of the law courts. During Humphrey's lifetime it became increasingly clear through the workings of courts such as Chancery that 'a malefactor need not attack his victim's property physically; he need only wrest it from him by manipulating the instruments pertinent to it'.[5] To this end, Humphrey shared the landholder's passion for preserving family papers and made sure that his title deeds and other relevant documentation were safely recorded and archived. His bureaucratic temperament spilled over into other aspects of his life. He may have depicted himself as a dashing young lover, but it is the more sober, legalistic nature that shines through in most of the commonplace book. His secular lyrics appear to have been constructed very like his legal documents: selecting from a number of key phrases and terms in order to build a case. Humphrey's God similarly balanced accounts – taking note of spiritual credit and debt – and He observed how prayer-charms were formulated and whose names were inserted into the allotted

---

[2] See p. 82 above.
[3] Carpenter, *Locality and Polity*, pp. 244–62, 621.
[4] The phrase is taken from Kirby (ed.) *The Plumpton letters*, p. 4.
[5] Haskett, 'Conscience', p. 162.

spaces. Just as Humphrey knew that a faulty legal clause might lose an estate, so a poorly transcribed charm could lose him spiritual protection.

There was also that impulse to research and to organise. He was a curious man with a mind predisposed to seek out information with an almost magpie-like quality, whether it be from the Chester Exchequer, chained church libraries or 'remembrance books' in gentry households. It was a quality he shared with other commonplace book compilers, such as John Benet, who was described by Gerald and Mary Harriss as 'an assiduous and inquisitive, if credulous, collector of information'.[6] Yet Humphrey's collection encompassed an exceptionally broad range, and it is more fragmentary and note-like than other comparable works. It is fair to say that none of the religious or scientific entries suggest deep learning; he could not be described as an intellectual. Nevertheless, his collection does not signify an antiquarian's interest either. His years of reading legal documents told him that knowledge was power, and this extended to a desire to understand wider aspects of life, particularly the secrets of nature. These might be revealed through birdsong, facial features, hand-markings or even menstruation; prophetic and astrological material provided vital clues to God's will. He was fascinated by words, again not surprising given his legal work: alongside definitions of *ingfangthief* or *homesoken* we see his understanding of sanguine and choleric. Numbers similarly feature prominently in his manuscript. While not on the scale of the extensive calculations contained in William Worcester's itineraries, Humphrey was someone for whom 'life' could be measured.[7] His commonplace book juxtaposes the lengths of marl pits, trees, chapel walls, bricks and a bed next to the length of Christ's wound, Christ's foot and the limits of the heavens. The combination of practicality and a type of 'number mysticism' is further seen in Humphrey's sums and balances: dower payments and servants' wages were totted up alongside pardons and the number of Christ's wounds.[8] All told, in determining such patterns, Humphrey – a court holder, of course – reveals a desire to manage and control his world, a world he saw in holistic terms. He aimed to make his world predictable in uncertain times of disease, land disputes and a new political dynasty.

Humphrey's legal work demanded good literacy skills and he was fully competent in English and Latin, with a working knowledge of law French. That he was an avid reader is no surprise because, by the early Tudor period, we would expect members of the gentry to be owners, even commissioners of books; they were marks of the educated gentleman.[9] This has encouraged

---

[6] Harriss and Harris, 'John Benet's chronicle', p. 171.
[7] Harvey (ed.) *Itineraries*.
[8] For this type of number mysticism and the desire to uncover secrets, see Gurevich, *Categories of medieval culture*, p. 291; Eamon, *Science and the secrets of nature*, pp. 25, 79; Coote, *Prophecy*, p. 41.
[9] Meale, 'The politics of book ownership', p. 103; Ford, 'Private ownership', p. 218; Vale, 'Manuscripts and books', p. 282, and see pp. 143–4, 153–4 above.

a number of investigative studies into the libraries of the gentry in order to gain insight into their thought processes.[10] There are obvious problems to consider when using Humphrey's manuscript for this purpose: the practical hurdles of missing folios and the bitty character of the commonplace book. As K.B. McFarlane warned, 'few of us would care to be judged posthumously by the evidence of our notebooks alone, least of all our prose style'.[11] Nevertheless, in considering what caught Humphrey's eye, the following can be said. His choices are entirely typical of the fashionably eclectic reader of late fifteenth-century England. He was a follower of the new Marian and Christocentric devotions and, in his wider reading material, he was attracted by highly popular texts like the *Brut* chronicle and the *Secretum Secretorum*. His courtly lyrics drew on the *en vogue* love letter form, he enjoyed proverbs and there are references to Arthur and St George. With few entries dating after 1520, however, Humphrey's commonplace book may well have looked old fashioned as Henry VIII's reign progressed. But it had always had a conservative element to it, and there are no continental, or even metropolitan, influences in its pages. Humphrey shows no knowledge of the *devotio moderna*; there are no humanist texts; he knew of Lydgate, not Skelton. As befits his provincial setting, Humphrey was influenced more by regional than European influences, and he shows his Cheshire roots. He read the regional dialect, knew his earls of Chester, and was another member of Lancashire and Cheshire's gentry with a liking for alliterative poetry, not a taste shared with England's aristocracy at large. His otherworld vision was set in one of the region's main towns, Congleton, and his prophecy focused on the destruction of its county town and port, Chester. On the other hand, there is little in Humphrey's notebook that a southern reader would not be able to recognise or, indeed, read: Humphrey was, of course, fully adept at communicating with the courts at Chancery and Star Chamber. His work would appear to support the argument for English culture's growing homogeneity in the sixteenth century, one that shows the natural dominance of the English language in gentry literature. In contrast to early fifteenth-century miscellanies, such as the compilations of Robert Thornton, Humphrey's commonplace book does not dwell on the language or seek to nationalise issues.[12]

Within this England, Humphrey's taste overlapped with several status groups. At its core we can discern a gentle identity. His otherworld vision is interpreted through the eyes of a late medieval gentleman, where the noise of devils is likened to servants; the order of heaven is symbolised by a courtly dance. More importantly, his gentle background is reflected in his choice of moral literature, which emphasised honour, loyalty and social order. These

---

[10] Gross, 'K.B. McFarlane and the determinists', pp. 49–50.
[11] McFarlane, *England*, p. 221.
[12] In this regard, Humphrey exhibits similar feelings to the contemporary writers of MS CUL FF 2.38, who Hardman believes reveal a 'less anxious' view of England: Hardman, 'Compiling the nation', p. 69.

qualities are recognisable from the gentry-owned manuscripts of Thornton and Findern, and in the letter collections of the Stonors, Pastons, Plumptons and Armburghs.[13] While we can identify a distinctive ethical code of the gentry, Humphrey's interests – like the culture of the gentry – was not closed to other influences. This even extends, in a limited way, to the non-literate and lower sections of society, where Humphrey shared a sensory and magical view of religion, and a stress on the visual. He participated in religious practices with his tenants and servants, who bought from the same pardoners and contributed to the same church ales. With the higher, literate, echelons of society, there was a commonality with the literature of the urban elites, particularly in the courtesy and general advice treatises, and Humphrey shared the noble interest in heraldry and hunting manuals. However, the differences are significant. Where his choices departed from the likes of Richard Hill, John Colyns and other metropolitan compilers are in his preferences for courtly love lyrics: mercantile compilers favoured more religious and practical verse.[14] Moreover, and as emphasised throughout this book, war and chivalry did not influence Humphrey's outlook. In his literature, as in his legal service, he illustrates the move away from a military ethos at the end of the Middle Ages to a status vested in landholding and bureaucracy; from the heroic to a preference for the didactic.

While there are reasons to dwell on Humphrey's conformity and conventionality, we should not overlook his bouts of creativity or touches of 'individual' personality. While we know the gentry as an audience for literature, in general there is little evidence that they themselves composed much, although the anonymity of most lyrics means that the picture can never be fully drawn. Humphrey is, therefore, one of the very few poets writing around 1500 whose name is known, and he evidently valued his creations sufficiently to place them among other well-known literature. He also had an eye to presentation, liked to sketch, attempted to play the harp, and was fascinated by magic tricks. He designed his own chapel (however standard it may have been), crafted several signatures, mulled over the design and colours of the Newton shield and, of course, drew together a commonplace book. Humphrey might have been found wanting in the debating chambers of the Inns of Court or university colleges, but he could have joined in admirably on a range of issues at a neighbour's dinner table.

This is how Humphrey appears to the modern researcher, but how was he viewed in his own day? Humphrey himself would have given thought to his reputation. The gentry, as a group, appear preoccupied by concerns for their standing in their 'country'.[15] In seeking those with whom Humphrey spent time, and those who thought him worthy of association, parallels can

---

[13] Radulescu, 'Literature', offers good comparisons.
[14] It was a preference Humphrey shared with other gentry book owners the Finderns and Humphrey Wellys: Jansen and Jordan (eds), *The Welles anthology*, p. 15
[15] Carpenter, *The Armburgh papers*, p. 45.

be drawn with the reconstructed networks of other fifteenth-century gentry such as Simon Fyncham of Fincham, Richard Clervaux of Croft and John Hopton of Blythborough. Their common contacts lay within a small radius of their central estates; their thoughts were on their reputation among tenants and neighbours.[16] Humphrey's estate accounts illustrate the economic interdependence and mutual assistance between a lord and his tenants and servants. Thomas and Christopher Lees (probably husbandmen) sold produce to Humphrey, bought finished goods from his wife, laboured, witnessed deeds and provided the muscle in the defence of Newton estate; Humphrey, in turn, was present at Thomas's wedding, perhaps as guest of honour.[17] Whether such a relationship developed into something that could be called friendship is unknown, but Humphrey did make close ties with men below gentle rank. We met the yeoman, Edward Mottershead of Mottram St Andrew, when Humphrey worked alongside him in the fraternity of Mottram. The two men knew each other for many years and, in addition to Humphrey's brother-in-law and son, Mottershead was explicitly called 'a trusty friend' when he was enfeoffed by Humphrey in a local land transfer. Edward was present during the building of Newton chapel, was on hand to witness several local land deeds for Humphrey, and arbitrated in Humphrey's dispute over Norcliffe mill.[18] His loyalty to the Newtons continued beyond Humphrey's death, as he was the leading witness for the family in the Star Chamber case over 'Newton' heath. Humphrey and Edward would appear to be another example of the close, often affectionate, ties that were established between gentry families and those of minor status. It was perhaps even more significant because there are few cases where the gentry selected non-gentle landholders as feoffees.[19] Nevertheless, Mottershead's status placed limits on his usefulness to Humphrey and he did not have the necessary social weight to be entrusted

---

[16] Maddern, 'Best trusted friends', p. 110; Pollard, 'Richard Clervaux', p. 167; id., *North-eastern England*, p. 113; Richmond, *John Hopton*, ch. 4; Moreton, 'A social gulf?'; Acheson, *A gentry community*, pp. 85–7; Carpenter, 'Gentry and community', p. 355.

[17] Bodl, MS Lat. Misc.c.66, fos 18r, 27ar, 30r, 33r, 35v; JRUL, Bromley Davenport, 'Newton by Mottram', no. 7; TNA: PRO, STAC 2/6/204–8.

[18] TNA: PRO, WALE 29/427; STAC 2/30/86, m. 1r; WALE 29/456; JRUL, 'Bromley Davenport', nos 6 and 8; BL, Add MS 42134A, fo. 2r. Edward Mottershead held a house in the township of Mottram St Andrew, and in the subsidy assessment of 1546 he was assessed on lands worth 40s: TNA: PRO, E179/85/26, m. 2; Earwaker, *East Cheshire* II, p. 355. He and his family's work in county administration centred on minor jury duty and acting as pledges in the Macclesfield hundred courts where their names appear regularly in the rolls: for example, TNA: PRO SC 2/259/5 (in 1498); SC 2/259/8 (1501); SC 2/258/6 (1509). Humphrey appears to have known the wider family well, purchasing meat and grain from Henry and Geoffrey Mottershead and employing several others as labourers and at harvest time: for example, Bodl, MS Lat. Misc.c.66, fos 26av, 27ar, 28r, 29r.

[19] Wright, *Derbyshire gentry*, pp. 143–4, 46; Acheson, *A gentry community*, pp. 83–7; Saul, *Scenes*, pp. 63–4; Richmond, *John Hopton*, p. 166; Pollard, *North-eastern England*, p. 110; Carpenter, 'Gentry and community', p. 353; Maddern, 'Best trusted friends', pp. 100, 106.

with the Pownall estate. Not all friends and acquaintances were equal when it came to land, and Humphrey had to think strategically.

In more weighty matters Humphrey called for assistance from neighbouring gentry. In this, again, he appears typical because micro-studies of the networks of individual landowners and families have revealed the strong mutual support among the gentry in the management of property and the family.[20] He illustrates that interdependence both as legal adviser and court holder, and in the selection of trustees and witnesses in land transfers. Humphrey provides further evidence that feoffees were carefully chosen and not simply drawn from those geographically closest.[21] While Newton was encircled by the resident gentry families of Davenport of Woodford, Legh of Adlington and Pigot of Butley, and they could hardly avoid each other, they rarely looked to each other for assistance. We can presume that their disputes with Humphrey undermined any trust they might have had in one another. Nor were Humphrey's choices dictated by the county boundary. As previous chapters have suggested, Humphrey had few contacts in the western half of Cheshire, and was more likely to seek associations in south Lancashire and west Derbyshire. He remained in close contact with his Derbyshire uncles, and the Newtons had a history of finding spouses outside of Cheshire. Business and perhaps pleasure meant that Humphrey travelled to Winwick and Trafford, his servants went to Doncaster and Manchester, and regular trips to Derbyshire included the fair at Chapel-en-le-Frith. In his excursions to Derbyshire he was following the path of a large number of north-eastern Cheshire families (including his neighbours the Leghs of Adlington) who crossed the river Goyt at Whaley Bridge for business, food, marriage partners and land holdings. One of Humphrey's associates, Nicholas Jodrell of Yeardsley (d. 1528), came from a family who held land in Buxworth and Whaley Bridge (Derbyshire) and Yeardsley, Disley and Kettleshulme (Macclesfield hundred).[22] This is not to say that Humphrey's associations lay over a wide area, they still fell within a twelve- to fifteen-mile radius of his main estates, but land holdings, river valleys and trading links played a greater role than administrative borders.[23]

Humphrey therefore made choices, and he was able to choose well: his feoffees were members of Cheshire's elite and some of the most influential men in North West England. As noted in Chapter 4, the trustees of

---

[20] For example, Pollard, *North-eastern England*, pp. 111–12. Acheson, *A gentry community*, p. 80; Carpenter, 'The Stonor circle'; id., *The Armburgh papers*, p. 52.
[21] Compare Maddern, 'Best trusted friends', p. 111.
[22] It was noted in Chapter 5 that Humphrey acted as witness to Nicholas Jodrell's will. He would also oversee the marriage articles drawn up for the nuptials of Nicholas's son, Roger, and Isabel Sutton: JRUL, Jodrell 36, 38a, 38b, 39; see pp. 110, 178 above. Cameron (ed.) *Place-names of Derbyshire*, XXVII, part 1, p. xxvii. For the connections between Cheshire and Lancashire see Bennett, *Community*.
[23] Similarly, knights and esquires in East Sussex had few social ties with those in the western half of the country: Saul, *Scenes*, p. 61.

his estate and in the jointure for his heir's marriage included Sir Edmund Trafford of Trafford, Lancashire (d. 1513), and his heir Edmund Trafford, esquire (d. 1533), Sir George Booth of Dunham Massey, Sir John Fitton of Gawsworth, William Handforth of Handforth (d. 1513) and John Tatton of Withenshaw. Supporters of Humphrey's right to Pownall included William Davenport of Bramhall (d. 1528) and Sir William Booth of Dunham Massey.[24] He also gained the support of Sir John Stanley of Handforth, son of James Stanley, Bishop of Ely, a tantalising connection of which we know too little. The estates of all these landowners comprised thousands of acres and, in the case of Booth, Trafford and Davenport, stretched across counties. During the early Tudor period they would extend and modernise their halls and improve their parks. Bramhall Hall was redeveloped *c.*1500, and new interior furnishings added to the domestic chapel, while the substantial houses of Trafford and Dunham Massey drew Leland's approval.[25] They were leaders of men who were written into Cheshire's history. Edmund Trafford, esquire, John Fitton and William Handforth fought alongside Sir John Stanley of Handforth in Flodden Field and became immortalised in the 'Stanley' poems generated in the North West during the early Tudor period.[26] Ultimately they were men whose word carried considerable social weight. In 1537, William Ardern petitioned Star Chamber for his dispute with the Booth family to be dealt with in London because George Booth 'be so frendyd withyn the seyd Counte of Chester that your sayd oratore is not of abylyte to nor power to pursue any lawe therfor his remedy'.[27]

With honour among the provincial gentry based on a good reputation, it reflects well on Humphrey that these 'worshipful people' gave him their support and included him in a significant social network.[28] Whether these men could be called friends is less clear. Research on the gentry elsewhere in England has tended simply to accept Nigel Saul's comment that 'if friendship is to be found anywhere, it is to be found surely in the choice of a man's feoffees'.[29] Humphrey did have opportunities to interact with his feoffees and witnesses beyond land transactions. He made visits to Dunham Massey and Trafford where he perused their archives; he purchased oxen, fish and corn from Bramhall Hall; and he was part of a spiritual community that centred on Wilmslow church. The Newton windows were situated among

---

[24] TNA: PRO, CHES 29/211, m. 7; CHES 3/26/8; C1/548/77; JRUL, Mainwaring 331; Bodl, MS Lat. Misc.c.66, fo. 11r.

[25] Thornton, *Cheshire*, p. 30; Earwaker, *East Cheshire*, I, p. 443; Pevsner and Hubbard, *Cheshire*, p. 223; Smith (ed.) *The itinerary of John Leland*, part VII, p. 5.

[26] *Bishop Percy's Folio*, I, pp. 189–92, 286. For John Stanley and Humphrey, see pp. 198–9 above.

[27] Stewart-Brown (ed.) *Lancashire and Cheshire cases in the court of Star Chamber*, part 1, p. 10.

[28] Maddern, 'Honour among the Pastons', p. 360; Keen, *Origins*, p. 105.

[29] Saul, *Scenes*, p. 62.

those financed by the Traffords, Booths and Fittons.[30] What is demonstrably not found, however, is equality and reciprocity: in no surviving documentation do Trafford, Booth, Fitton, Davenport, Handforth or Stanley entrust Humphrey with their properties. Just as Humphrey did not use the trusty Mottershead in his main estate, so these men looked to those of comparable or greater status to help in theirs. Humphrey would return their favour by other means: witnessing smaller deeds or offering legal advice. Bonds between gentry, particularly among feoffees, have often been classed as 'horizontal' ties, but here they reinforce a clear hierarchy among the gentry.[31] Humphrey knew his position, as did his community: he was listed below all of these men in any deeds on which he appeared alongside them.

What mattered to Humphrey was the repositioning of the family in a bid to rise through the ranks of the gentry. His enterprise at Newton, including the new chapel, may have helped; his legal work and seigniorial service certainly contributed; but the single biggest factor was his marriage to a co-heiress, and the estates (more than doubling his acreage) and connections it brought. Success was confirmed in William's marriage into one of the leading knightly families of Cheshire. Socio-economic reasons are the most obvious to determine in cases of social mobility. A study of Humphrey Newton's life illustrates another dimension. The competitive nature of the gentry was channelled through style as well as substance. Image mattered to him, and we can see the lengths to which he went: he made sure his father's tombstone had a place in Prestbury church while he and his son proclaimed their status in the Jesus chapel of Wilmslow church; the Newton shield was designed to display the best impression of the Newton family. In his verses (perhaps with an audience of local gentry in mind), Humphrey presented an image of the archetypal young love-lorn gentleman, of a cultivated man who walked into church with a sparrowhawk in his hand, a servant by his side, whilst thinking of words to describe beauty. At his death, Humphrey's flowing fur-lined robe in his effigy portrayed a man of comfortable means. His commonplace book reveals the works Humphrey collected to help endow his family with the necessary social polish to match and enhance their status. With them, he learnt (and presumably taught) how to serve a banquet, how to string a harp and what might be discussed in polite conversation. Hunting and armorial terms, proverbs and the correct words of love were all key components of gentle language and were 'as important as know-how'.[32] All these actions would have served to distinguish Humphrey from those below him.

To some extent, Humphrey achieved his goal. By the 1520s and probably a decade before, the Newtons appear too substantial for historians to label them parish gentry. Their landholdings extended over 1,000 acres,

---

[30] See pp. 14–15, 73, 120 and 135–6 above.
[31] As also noted by Carpenter, *Locality and polity*, pp. 289–90.
[32] Putter, 'The ways and words', p. 354. Richmond, *The Paston family*, p. 37; Radulescu, *The gentry context*.

their annual income, we must assume, extended to a few tens of pounds. Humphrey was no longer a mere 'gentleman' according to early Tudor society. Cheshire was not subject to the feudal surveys of the 1520s, but Julian Cornwall's calculations of the returns from five English counties would place the Newtons closer to the squirearchy: the median income of land held by a knight was £204 per annum, an esquire £80 and a gentleman £17.[33] Humphrey's changing circumstances can be charted in contemporary documents. During the years when he was merely the lord of Newton, he was exclusively called a gentleman whenever his status was defined. It was a few years after the inheritance of Pownall that a local land deed (1511) assigned him the title 'esquire'.[34] This was a little unusual because the more commonly accepted attribution in the Newton/Pownall area remained 'gentleman' into the early 1520s.[35] However, by that time the Chester Exchequer and royal courts (Chancery and Star Chamber) were uniformly recognising him as an esquire.[36] While it might be a crude guide, in deeds, windows and stone during the 1520s and 30s, Humphrey achieved widespread recognition as *armiger*. Taking this information together, it might be said, using the terminology of early modern studies, that he had succeeded in lifting his family from 'lower' to 'middling' gentry.[37]

Yet, while advancing in some respects, Humphrey's lesser gentry status remained very evident in other aspects of his life. His estates were confined to a small corner of Cheshire and lacked major franchises; he held no key offices and played no obvious role in Cheshire's political community. Similarly, his attempts to demonstrate power culturally may have seemed a little too desperate and served to underline a limited wealth. The personally written manuscript, the fewer dishes in his courtesy treatise, the plain windows and the sandstone tomb in Wilmslow church were not merely 'watered down' nobility,[38] but slightly diluted gentility. Overall, the Newtons advancement is far less impressive than Roger Townshend's rise from yeomen to sergeant at law; unlike John Hopton, Humphrey would not have the pleasure of knowing his heir had become a knight. Rather, Humphrey belongs to the more common modest social risers, whose fortunate marriage moved them up a rank and widened their network. Humphrey took no risks to accelerate

---

[33] Cornwall, 'The early Tudor gentry'.
[34] Legh of Adlington, DLA 69/1/4b.
[35] For example, when he acted as a bond for John Stanley of Handforth (1522): JRUL, Egerton 1/2/1/16.
[36] TNA: PRO, STAC 2/6/205; C1/411/13–16; CHES 5/2 m. 3. This might reflect what Christine Carpenter has seen as the disparity between local and official perceptions of the gentry, or it may simply be an example of what Dorothy Clayton sees as a loose and imprecise use of the term esquire by compilers of palatinate records: Carpenter, *Locality and polity*, p. 74; Clayton, *The administration of the county palatine*, p. 136.
[37] Heal and Holmes, *The gentry*, pp. 13–15
[38] Coss 'An age of deference', p. 41.

their rise, and the Newtons in general were a family who made gradual gains every two or three generations.[39]

In sum, there were various Humphrey Newtons: competitive, communal, conventional, creative. Their relative weight would change with his preoccupations and his age. Perhaps the point to leave this book is the point at which we know him best: the few years either side of 1500. What might explain the commonplace book and the man who wrote it is the conjunction of three orbiting pressures. Large parts of the manuscript were written during his first years at Newton and the run-up to the move to Pownall, a time when the prospect of rising through the ranks seemed close at hand. This may have generated uncertainties, made him a little anxious about his new position and prompted him to reach for the pen; it would explain his interests in the themes of mutability, instability and constancy.[40] The commonplace book was also compiled during a time when his children were growing up. As a responsible father with an eye to the family's future, he would have wanted to provide the proper instruction. The *ABC of Aristotle*, the Aesop's fable, and mirrors of princes were common helpmates in the upbringing of young gentlemen and women, as well as convenient reminders to Humphrey of the terms and information he needed to master. All this took place while Humphrey was in his thirties. He was clearly aware of the significance of the life stage he had entered. It was not unusual to be depicted in effigy in the prime of life, but he had also gathered literature which highlighted the pre-eminence of middle age and outlined the responsibilities that came with it. Here was a man midway through his three score years and ten, where thoughts turned to the second half of that earthly journey. It was an opportunity to contemplate 'worthy fame' and hope that he would be able to die 'whan a man is best of name'.[41] It was an occasion for reflection and action, and Humphrey did both.

---

[39] For comparisons: Carpenter, *Locality and polity*, p. 151 and ch. 4 in general; Maddern, 'Social mobility', pp. 121–2
[40] Riddy, *Sir Thomas Malory*, p. 73.
[41] Bodl, MS Lat. Misc.c.66, fo. 2r and pp. 171–2 above.

APPENDIX 1

Timeline of key events during Humphrey Newton's life 1466–1536

1466 Birth of Humphrey Newton
1469 Rising of Warwick and Clarence against Edward IV
1470 Deposition of Edward IV; Henry VI restored as king
1471 Edward IV returns, defeats the Lancastrians at Barnet and Tewksbury. The deaths of Warwick (Barnet), Edward, Prince of Wales (Tewkesbury) and Henry VI (Tower). Widespread plague
1475 Edward IV's expedition to France. Anglo-French treaty of Picquigny
1476 William Caxton's first printed book in England: *The Canterbury Tales*
1478 Clarence is attainted in parliament; killed in the Tower
1483 Death of Edward IV; accession of Edward V, his deposition and death. Accession of Richard III; rebellion of Henry, duke of Buckingham
1485 Death of Richard III at Bosworth; accession of Henry VII. First outbreak of sweating sickness. Caxton prints *Morte Darthur*
1486 Marriage of Henry VII to Elizabeth of York, daughter of Edward IV
1487 Yorkist rising of Lambert Simnel and its defeat at the battle of Stoke
1490 Marriage of Humphrey Newton to Ellen Fitton
1497 Death of Richard Newton: Humphrey inherits Newton. The Cornish rebellion; Perkin Warbeck captured by Henry VII. John Cabot discovers Newfoundland
1502 Death of Arthur, Prince of Wales and earl of Chester
1506 Death of Thomas Pownall; the Newtons inherit Pownall. City of Chester given county status
1508 Second outbreak of sweating sickness
1509 Death of Henry VII (April); the accession of Henry VIII and his marriage to Catherine of Aragon (June)
1510 John Colet founds St Paul's School, London
1513 Battle of Flodden Field: James IV of Scotland killed.
1515 Thomas Wolsey created cardinal
1517 Foundation of Corpus Christi College, Oxford. Martin Luther's ninety-five theses. Commissioners appointed by Wolsey to inquire into enclosures and depopulation. Sweating sickness
1520 Field of the Cloth of Gold
1521 Burning of Lutheran books in London. Confirmation of the title 'Defender of the faith' for Henry VIII

213

1527 Henry VIII begins proceedings to annul his marriage with Catherine of Aragon
1528 Outbreak of sweating sickness
1529 Meeting of the Reformation parliament
1533 Annulment of the marriage of Catherine of Aragon and Henry VIII; marriage to Anne Boleyn; Act to restrain appeals to Rome
1534 First Act of succession; first Act of Supremacy; Acts abolishing payments to Rome
1535 *Valor ecclesiasticus.* Thomas More and John Fisher executed for refusing to acknowledge Henry as head of the Church in England and take the oath of succession.
1536 Death of Humphrey Newton (March). February-March: second Supremacy Act: King incorporates title of Supreme Head in royal title. First dissolution Act begins the dissolution of lesser religious houses.

APPENDIX 2

Bodleian Library, MS Latin Miscellaneous c.66

This is a full summary of the contents in Humphrey's commonplace book. It will indicate the variety of the entries, and place them in the context of the whole manuscript. It does not provide specific details or references; these can be found in the main text.

A list of contents

Fo. 1	List of Humphrey's Newton ancestors and the births of his children
Fo. 2	List of the kings of England; extract from Chaucer's *Knight's tale*; legal notes; a note on pardon beads; and a line from Ovid (Latin)
Fo. 3	Legal notes and a charm to staunch the blood; extract from Lyndwood's *Provinciale* (Latin); notes on Glastonbury
Fo. 4	Articles on holding manorial courts; a list of masses forming St Gregory's Trental; and a description of a bed at Bradley
Fo. 5	Legal notes; a piece of local doggerel on Wilkin Legh (Latin: unidentifiable); a fish recipe
Fos. 6–8	Legal notes, interspersed with extracts from the *Brut* chronicle (fos 6v–7r); list of the earls of Chester (fo. 7b); instructions on stringing a harp (fo. 8v)
Fo. 9	Biblical extracts from Numbers and Deuteronomy (Latin); notes on the earls of Chester; the measure of the foot of Christ; a local note concerning Richard Newton (d. 1497)
Fo. 10	Legal notes; extract from a letter sent by Adam Mottram (Precentor of Salisbury, late fourteenth century) to John Pigot concerning a local land transfer (Latin)
Fos. 11–13	Legal notes, including definitions of legal terms, and notes on local families
Fos. 14–16	Short descriptive genealogies of local families, plus a charm
Fo. 17	Obit of Thomas Fitton of Pownall (d. 1506); list of pardons; local deed
Fo. 18r	An epitaph of Laurence Lowe; pardon of St Chad, prayer to the Virgin found in a chained book of Newark church (Latin); description of the boundary between Newton and Woodford
Fos. 18v–19r	Notes on the Bollin lordship
Fo. 19v	A letter from Adam Mottram to John Pigot. Refers to the same biblical passages contained in the extract on fo. 10r

Fo. 20	Humphrey's account of the history of Newton
Fos. 21–23	Purgatory treatise: *A vision in a trance* of John Newton (English)
Fos. 24–48	Estate accounts of the Newton estate covering the dates 1498–1506, including: *ABC of Aristotle* (English; fo. 26b) Petition to the king by Richard Newton copied by William Newton, after 1521 (fo. 27b) Bifolium of legal notes (Law French; fos 31b–c) Extact from Middle English *Mirrour of the world* (fo. 34a) Meal-time prayers (Latin; fo. 34b) Charms (fos. 39b, 40b, 41b) Note on Mottram chapel and list of the seven hundreds of Cheshire (fo. 46r) Sketch of a tun (fo. 47r) Two crude circular diagrams of the zodiac (fo. 48v)
Fos. 49–58	Various land deeds, mainly relating to the Fitton estate, but including a note on the manor of Denby (fo. 55r) and the descent of Gawsworth manor (fo. 57r)
Fos. 59–61	Newton accounts, 1519–20
Fo. 62r	List of fifteenth-century battles; units of measurements; and extracts from St Augustine (Latin; unidentified)
Fo. 62v	Recipes; letter of Robert Preston of New College, Oxford (English)
Fo. 63	Rental (1504–5); note concerning the deputy escheator of Chester (1510–11); pedigree of the earls of Chester
Fo. 64ar	Obsolete contents page for the opening folios of common-place book
Fo. 64b	List of Newton tenants and weapons
Fo. 65	A list of debts, early sixteenth century; extract from Mirk's *Festial* (English)
Fos. 66–8	Two Middle English courtesy tracts: *For to serve a lord* and *Feast for a bride*
Fo. 69	Note on the customs of Macclesfield; charm for protection (Latin), probably copied from the document found on fo. 91.
Fo. 70	Local deeds; brief note on the seven ages of the world; descent of the manor of Hawthorn nr. Wilmslow
Fos. 71–3	Fitton inquisitions *post mortem*
Fo. 74	Charm for protection; note on financing a lamp in Prestbury church; extract from *The dicts and sayings of the philosophers* (English)
Fos. 75–90	Medical miscellany, comprising: *De Urinis* (fos 75–83), *Trotula* Version D (fos 83–86), recipes (fos. 87–8), *Mola*

APPENDIX 2: BODLEIAN LIBRARY, MS LATIN MISCELLANEOUS c.66

	Matricis (87b); Middle English urinary (fos 88–9), recipes (fos 89–90)
Fo. 91	Latin charm
Fo. 92r	Contents page for literary miscellany that follows
Fo. 92v	Aesop's fable (Latin; unidentified); courtly love lyrics (English)
Fos. 93–4	Humphrey's courtly love lyrics (English); a quadrant
Fo. 95	Palmistry tract (Latin); drawing practice/doodles
Fos. 96–101r	Letter-writing practice using the parchment book of fos. 112–21
Fo. 101b	Descent of the manor of Newton
Fos. 101–103r	Legal notes, including *Notes on the purchasing of land* attributed to Sir John Fortescue (English)
Fo. 103v	Prophecies (Latin and English)
Fo. 104	Prophecies; petition to the king by Hugh Wiot, yeoman (English)
Fo. 105	Formulary deeds
Fos. 106–7	*Richard de Caistre's Hymn* (English) and two Middle English alliterative poems
Fos. 107r–111	*Philomena* (English)
Fos. 112–21	Parchment book of letter forms and formulary documents
Fo. 122	Astrological tables (Latin)
Fo. 123	Ink recipes; extract from the *Sectretum secretorum* (Middle English)
Fo. 124	Treatise on proportion (Latin)
Fos. 124v–26	Treatise on ink recipes (English)
Fo. 127	List of the books of the Bible and list of service books and prices (Latin). List of shires, towns, and knights' fees in England; list of the four humours; ink recipes; first verse of John Lydgate's *Siege of Thebes*; and extract from Chaucer's *Parson's Tale* (English)
Fo. 128	How to catch rabbits; ink recipes; extract from Chaucer's *Parson's Tale* (cont. from fo. 127)
Fo. 129r	'Magic' recipes and tricks (Latin)
Fo. 129v	the Sacred Heart

Bibliography

Unpublished primary sources

Adlington Hall, Adlington
Legh of Adlington papers

Bodleian Library, Oxford
Ashmole MSS
Dodsworth manuscripts
MS Lat. Misc.c.66
MS Lyell 35
Laud MS 416
Tanner MS 407
Topographical MSS

British Library, London
Additional charters
Additional MSS
Harleian MSS
Royal MS 17 B XLVII
Sloane MSS

Cheshire and Chester Archives and Local Studies, Chester
CR 63	Earwaker collection
ZCR 72	Cotton of Combermere MSS
DAR	Arderne of Alvanley and Harden
DDA	Davenport of Bramhall
DDS	Downes of Shrigley
DDX	Miscellaneous collections
DLE	Leche of Carden
DLT	Leicester-Warren of Tabley
DSS	Shakerley of Hulme and Somerford
DVE	Vernon and Warren
EDT	Tithe maps

Chetham Library, Manchester
Adlington MS
MUN A.3.127
MUN A.6.31
MUN A.7.38

John Rylands University Library, Manchester
Arley charters
Bromley Davenport muniments
Dunham Massey muniments
Egerton of Tatton muniments
English MSS
Jodrell MSS
Latin MS 383
Legh of Lyme muniments
Mainwaring charters
Mainwaring MSS
Ryland Charters
Tatton MSS
Keele University Library, Keele
Legh of Booth Charters
Raymond Richards' Collections
Sneyd Papers

Lancashire Record Office, Preston
DDTr Trafford of Trafford papers
RCHY Hornsby Catholic Mission Papers

Nottingham University Library, Nottingham
Middleton collection

Sheffield Archives, Sheffield
ACM/DD/23

The National Archives, Public Record Office, Kew
Chancery
C1 Early Chancery proceedings

Exchequer
E101 King's Remembrancer, accounts various
E179 King's Remembrancer, subsidy rolls
E301 Court of Augmentations, certificates of colleges, chantries
E315 Court of Augmentations, miscellaneous books

Palatinate of Chester
CHES 1 Chester warrants etc.
CHES 2 Enrolments
CHES 3 Inquisition Post Mortem
CHES 5 Mainprise rolls
CHES 17 Eyre rolls
CHES 24 Gaol files, writs, etc
CHES 25 Indictment rolls
CHES 29 Plea rolls
CHES 31 Fines and recoveries
CHES 34 Quo Warranto Rolls

CHES 37   Warrants of Attorney Rolls
CHES 38   Miscellanea

Palatinate of Lancaster
DL 29   Ministers' Accounts
DL 30   Court Rolls

Prerogative court of Canterbury
PROB 11   Will registers

Special collections
SC 2   Court rolls
SC 6   Ministers' and Receivers' accounts
SC 11   Rentals and surveys
SC 12   Rentals and surveys

Star Chamber
STAC 2   Proceedings Henry VIII
STAC 3   Star Chamber proceedings Edward VI

Wales
WALE 29   Palatinate of Chester, ancient deeds
WALE 30   Palatinate of Chester, ancient deeds

Published primary sources and catalogues

Annual Reports of the deputy keeper of the public records (London, 1840)
Armitage, George J. and J.P. Rylands (eds), *Pedigrees made at the visitation of Cheshire 1613* (*RSLC*, LVIII, 1909)
A Theater of the planetary houres of all dayes of the year (London, 1631, reprinted 1971)
Axon, W.E.A. (ed.), *Nixon's Cheshire prophecies* (Manchester and London, 1873)
Baker J.H. (ed.), *The notebook of Sir John Port* (Selden Society, 102, 1986)
Ballard, J.V. and H. Chalmer Bell (eds), *Lynwood's Provinciale* (London, 1929)
Bannerman, W.B. (ed.), *The visitation of the county of Sussex 1530 and 1633–4* (Harleian Soc., LIII, 1905)
Barnum, Priscilla Heath (ed.), *Dives and pauper*, vol. 1, part 1 (*EETS*, 275, 1976)
Beamont, W. (ed.), *Tracts written in the controversy respecting the legitimacy of Amicia, daughter of Hugh Cyveliock* (*CS*, 3 parts, LXXVIII–LXXX, 1869)
Benson, L.D. (ed.), *The riverside Chaucer* (3rd edn, Oxford, 1988)
Berners, Dame Juliana, *The boke of St Albans* (facsimile of the 1486 edition: Amsterdam, 1969)
Best, Michael R. and Frank H. Brightman (eds), *The book of secrets of Albertus Magnus of the virtues of herbs, stones and certain beasts* (Oxford, 1973)
Bishop Percy's folio manuscript, eds J.W. Hales and F.J. Furnivall (3 vols, London, 1867–8)
Blake, N.F. (ed.), *Caxton's Own Prose* (London, 1973)

Blanchard, I.S.W. (ed.), *Duchy of Lancaster estates in Derbyshire 1485–1540* (Derbyshire Record Society, 3, 1971)
Boyd, W.K., 'Star Chamber proceedings: Henry VIII and Edward VI', *Collections for a History of Staffordshire* (1912), 1–207
Brewer, D.S. and A.E.B. Owen (eds), *The Thornton manuscript (Lincoln Cathedral Ms. 91)* (London, 1975)
Brie, Friedrich W.D. (ed.), *The Brut or the chronicles of England* (EETS, os 136, 1908), part II
Briquet, C.M., *Les filigranes: dictionnaire historique des marques du papier des leur apparition vers 1282 jusqu'en 1600* (4 vols, Geneva, 1907)
Brown, Carleton (ed.), *Religious lyrics of the fifteenth century* (Oxford, 1939)
Brown, Carleton (ed.), *Religious lyrics of the fourteenth century* (2nd edn, Oxford, 1952)
Brownbill, J. (ed.), *Moore manuscripts of Bankhall, Lancashire* (*RSLC*, 67, 1913)
Bühler, C.F. (ed.), *The dicts and sayings of the philosophers* (EETS, os 211, 1941)
Calendar of close rolls (London, 1902–)
Calendar of patent rolls (London, 1901–)
Cameron, K. (ed.), *Place-names of Derbyshire* (Cambridge, 1959)
Campbell, W. (ed.), *Materials for a history of the reign of Henry VII* (2 vols, London, 1873 and 1877)
Carley, J. (ed.), *The chronicle of John of Glastonbury* (Woodbridge, 1985)
Carpenter, Christine (ed.), *Kingsford's Stonor letters and papers, 1290–1483* (Cambridge, 1996)
—— (ed.), *The Armburgh papers. The Brokholes inheritance in Warwickshire, Hertfordshire and Essex c.1417–c.1453* (Woodbridge, 1998)
Christine de Pisan, *The treasure of the city of ladies, or the book of the three virtues*, trans. Sarah Lawson (Harmondsworth, 1985)
Clay, J.W. (ed.), *North country wills* (The Surtees Society, 116, 1908)
Cockayne, Thomas Oswald (ed.), *Leechdoms, wortcunning and starcraft of early England* (London, 1864–5)
Crotch, W.J.B. (ed.), *The prologues and epilogues of William Caxton* (EETS, os 176, 1929)
Davies, G.R.C., *Medieval cartularies of Great Britain: a short catalogue* (London, 1958)
Davis, N. (ed.), *Paston letters and papers of the fifteenth century* (2 vols, Oxford, 1971–6)
D'Evelyn, Charlotte (ed.), *Peter Idley's instructions to his son* (Boston MA and London, 1935)
Dunham, W.H. (ed.), *Lord Hastings' indentured retainers 1461–83* (Transactions of the Connecticut Academy of Arts and Sciences, xxxix, 1955, repr. USA 1970)
Dyboski, Roman (ed.), *Songs, carols and other miscellaneous poems, from the Balliol ms. 354, Richard Hill's commonplace-book* (EETS, es 101, 1907)
Edwards, Robert R. (ed.), *John Lydgate: the siege of Thebes* (Kalamazoo, 2001)
Erasmus, Desiderius, *Praise of folly*, trans Hoyt Hopewell Hudson (Ware, 1998)
Erbe, Theodor (ed.), *Mirk's festial: a collection of homilies by Johannes Mirkus (John Mirk)*, part 1 (EETS, es 96, 1905)
Farrer, William (ed.), *The court rolls of the honor of Clitheroe* (2 vols, London, 1879, 1912)

Fishwick, Henry (ed.), *Pleadings and depositions in the duchy court of Lancaster*, vol. 2, *time of Henry VIII* (*RSLC*, 35, 1897)
Fitzherbert, John, *Booke of husbandrie* (London, 1598; facsimile Netherlands, 1979)
Foster, F.A. (ed.) *The Stanzaic life of Christ* (*EETS*, os 166, 1926)
Fowler, David C., Charles F. Briggs and Paul G. Remley (eds), *The governance of kings and princes: John Trevisa's Middle English translation of the De regimine principum of Aegidius Romanus* (New York, 1997)
Furnivall, F.J. (ed.), *The babees book* (*EETS*, os 32, 1868)
—— (ed.), *Child marriages, and divorces and ratifications etc., in the Diocese of Chester AD. 1561–1566* (*EETS*, os 108, 1897)
Garratt, H.J.H. and C. Rawcliffe (eds), *Derbyshire feet of fines 1323–1546* (Derbyshire Record Society, 9, 1985)
Genet, Jean-Philippe (ed.), *Four English political tracts of the later Middle Ages* (Camden 4th series vol. 18, 1977)
Glauning, O. (ed.), *Lydgate's minor poems: the two Nightingale poems* (*EETS*, es 80, 1900)
Halliwell, J.O. (ed.), *Palatine anthology: a collection of ancient poems and ballads relating to Lancashire and Cheshire* (London, 1850)
Hardman, Phillipa (ed.), *The Heege manuscript: a facsimile of National Library of Scotland MS Advocates 19.3.1* (Leeds, 2000)
Harriss, G.L. and M.A. Harris (ed.), 'John Benet's chronicle for the years 1400–62' (*Camden Miscellany*, 4th ser. XXIV, London, 1972), 151–233
Hartung, A.E., *A manual of writings in the Middle Ages* (vols 3–9, Connecticut 1972–93)
Harvey, John H. (ed.), *Itineraries of William Worcestre* (Oxford, 1969)
Hearnshaw, F.J.C. (eds) *Leet jurisdiction in England* (Southampton Record Society, 1908)
Hilton, R. (ed.), *Ministers' accounts of the Warwickshire estates of the Duke of Clarence, 1479–80* (Dugdale Soc., xxi, Oxford, 1952)
Historical Manuscripts Commission, *Reports on manuscripts in various collections, 2nd report* (London, 1874)
Horstman, C., *Yorkshire writers: Richard Rolle of Hampole, an English Father of the Church and his followers* (2 vols, London, 1896)
Hughes, Paul L. and James F. Larkin (eds) *Tudor royal proclamations, vol 1: the early Tudors (1485–1553)* (New Haven and London, 1964)
Inderwick, F.A. (ed.), *A calendar of the Inner Temple records*, I (London, 1896)
Irvine, W.F. (ed.), *A collection of Lancashire and Cheshire wills* (*RSLC*, XXX, 1896)
—— (ed.) 'List of the eleven deaneries of the diocese of Chester', in *Miscellanies relating to Lancashire and Cheshire* (*RSLC*, XXXIII, 1896), vol. 3
Jack, I. (ed.), *The Grey of Ruthin valor* (Bedfordshire Record Soc., 46, 1965)
Jacob, E.F. (ed.), *The register of Henry Chichele, Archbishop of Canterbury 1414–1443* (Oxford, 1937), vol. 2
Jansen, S. and K.H. Jordan, *The Welles anthology* (New York and London, 1990)
Jeayes, I.H. (ed.), *Descriptive catalogue of Derbyshire charters in public and private libraries and muniment rooms* (London, 1906)
John of Gaunt's Register 1379–83, 1, eds Eleanor C. Lodge and Robert Somerville (Camden Soc., 3rd ser. LVI, 1937)

Kettle, A.J. (ed.), 'A list of families in the archdeaconry of Stafford 1532–3' (*Collection for a History of Staffordshire*, 4th ser. 8, 1976)

Kirby, Joan (ed.), *The Plumpton letters and papers* (Camden Soc., 5th ser. VIII, 1996)

Letters and papers, foreign and domestic, of the reign of Henry VIII, 1509–47, eds J.S. Brewer, J. Gairdner and R.H. Brodie (London, 1862–1910)

Louis, Cameron, *The commonplace book of Robert Reynes of Acle: an edition of Tanner MS 407* (New York and London, 1980)

McCracken, H.N. (ed.), *The minor poems of John Lydgate II: secular poems* (*EETS*, os CXCII, 1934)

Maitland, F.W. and W.P. Baildon (eds), *The court baron* (Selden Soc., IV, 1891)

Malory, Sir Thomas *Works*, ed. Eugène Vinaver (Oxford, 1977)

Manchester Guardian, 13 January 1849

Manly, J.M. and E. Rickert (eds), *The texts of the Canterbury Tales* (Chicago and London, 1940), vol. 1

Manzalaoui, M.A. (ed.), *Secretum secretorum: nine English versions* (*EETS* os 276, 1977)

Mirk, John, *Instructions for parish priests*, ed. Edward Peacock (*EETS*, os 31, 1868)

Morgan, Philip (ed.), *Domesday Book, Cheshire* (Chichester, 1978)

Murray, J.A.H., *The romances and prophesies of Thomas of Erceldoune* (*EETS*, os 61, 1875)

Myers, A.R. (ed.), *The Household of Edward IV: the Black Book and the Ordinance of 1478* (Manchester, 1959)

NIMEV: A new index of Middle English Verse, eds Julia Boffey and A.S.G. Edwards (British Library, London, 2005)

Oakden, J.P., 'Scotish Ffeilde', *Chetham Miscellany* (*CS*, VI, n.s. 94, 1935)

O'Connor. S.J. (ed.), *A Calendar of the Cartularies of John Pyel and Adam Frauncey* (Camden Soc. 5th ser., 2, 1993)

Ogden, M.S. (ed.), *The Liber de diversis medicinis in the Thornton Manuscript (Lincoln Cathedral A.5.2)* (*EETS*, os 207, repr. 1969)

Oschinsky, Dorothea, *Walter of Henley and other treatises on estate management and accounting* (Oxford, 1971)

Piccope, G. (ed.), *Lancashire and Cheshire wills and inventories from the Ecclesiastical Court at Chester*, I (*CS*, LI, 1860)

Prior, O.H. (ed.), *Caxton's Mirrour of the World* (*EETS*, es CX, 1913 for 1912)

Records of the Borough of Nottingham, II: 1399–1485 (London, 1883)

Records of the Borough of Nottingham, III: 1485–1547 (London, 1885)

Register of Edward the Black Prince preserved in the Public Record Office (4 vols, London, HMSO, 1930–33)

Rigg, A.G., *A Glastonbury miscellany of the fifteenth century: a description and index of Trinity College, Cambridge, MS.O.9.38* (London, 1968)

Robbins, R.H., 'The poems of Humfrey Newton, esquire, 1466–1536', *Proceedings of the Modern Language Association of America*, 65 (1950), 249–81

—— (ed.), *Secular lyrics of the fourteenth and fifteenth centuries* (Oxford, 1952)

—— (ed.), *Historical poems of the fourteenth and fifteenth centuries* (Columbia and London, 1959)

Robson, J., *Three metrical romances* (*CS*, ser. 1 XVIII, 1842)

——, 'The Scottish field', *Chetham Miscellany* II (*CS*, XXXVII, 1855)

Rowland, Beryl, *Medieval women's guide to health* (London, 1981)
Rylands, J.P. (ed.), *The visitation of Cheshire, 1580* (Harleian Soc., XVIII, 1882)
Scott, J. (ed.), *The early history of Glastonbury* (Woodbridge, 1981)
Smith, L.T., *A commonplace book of the fifteenth century* (London, 1886)
—— (ed.), *The Itinerary of John Leland in or about the years 1535–1543* (London, 1907–10)
Smith, William and William Webb, *The Vale-Royal of England, or, the county palatine of Chester*, with a foreword by P. Timmis Smith (Congleton, 1990)
Stephenson, Mill, *A list of monumental brasses in Surrey* (Bath, 1970)
Stewart-Brown, Ronald (ed.), *Lancashire and Cheshire cases in the court of Star Chamber*, part 1 (*RSLC*, LXXI, 1916)
Stewart-Brown, R. (ed.), *Chester county court rolls* (*CS*, LXXXIV, 1925)
Swanson, R.N. (ed.), *Catholic England: faith and observance before the reformation* (Manchester, 1993)
Tait, J. (ed.), *The Domesday Survey of Cheshire* (*CS*, ns 75, 1916)
Thompson, John T. (ed.), *Robert Thornton and the London Thornton manuscript: British Library MS Additional 31042* (Cambridge, 1987)
Turville-Petre, Thorlac, *Alliterative poetry of the later Middle Ages* (London, 1989)
Valor ecclesiasticus (6 vols, London, 1810–54)
Ward, H.L.D., *Catalogue of romances in the Department of Manuscripts in the British Museum* (3 vols, London, 1883–1910)
Wedgewood, Josiah C., 'The "Lists and indexes" of records at the Public Record Office', *Collections for a History of Staffordshire*, 3rd ser. (1912), 209–59
Woolgar, C.M. (ed.), *Household accounts from medieval England: Part 1, Introduction, glossary, diet accounts* (Oxford, 1992)
Worcester, William, *The boke of noblesse*, ed. John Gough Nichols (London, Roxburghe Club, 1860)

Secondary sources

Acheson, E.A., *A gentry community: Leicestershire in the fifteenth century c.1422–c.1485* (Cambridge, 1992)
Addy, S.O., *Church and manor: a study in English economic history* (London, 1913)
Alcock, L., *Arthur's Britain* (London, 1971)
Alexander, J.J.G., *Medieval illuminators and their method of work* (New Haven, 1992)
Amos, Mark Addison, '"For manners make man": Bourdieu, de Certeau and the common appropriation of noble manners in the *Book of Courtesy*', in Ashley and Clark (eds) *Medieval conduct*, 23–48
Anon, 'Lancaster jottings V. The New Hall and its owners', *THSLC*, ns 37 (1922), 189–210
Armstrong, C.A.J., 'The piety of Cicely, duchess of York: a study of late medieval culture', in D. Woodruff (ed.) *For Hilaire Belloc* (London, 1942) 73–94
Arnold, John H., *Belief and unbelief in medieval Europe* (London, 2005)
Arthurson, Ian, 'Tuchet, James, seventh Baron Audley (*c*.1463–1497)', *Oxford Dictionary of National Biography* (Oxford University Press, 2004)

Ashley, Katherine and Robert L.A. Clark (eds), *Medieval conduct* (Minneapolis, 2001)

Astill, G.G., 'Social advancement through seignorial service? The case of Simon Pakeman', *Transactions of the Leicestershire Antiquarian Society*, 54 (1978), 14–25

Aston, Margaret, *Faith and fire: popular and unpopular religion, 1350–1600* (London, 1993)

Aston, Michael (ed.), *Medieval fish, fisheries and fishponds* (British Archaeol. Reports, 182, 1988)

D'Avray, D., 'Papal authority and religious sentiment in the late Middle Ages', in D. Wood (ed.) *The church and sovereignty, c.590–1918* (Studies in Church History, subsidia 9, 1991), 398–408

Axon, E., 'The family of Bothe (Booth) and the church in the fifteenth and sixteenth centuries', *Lancashire and Cheshire Antiquarian Society*, 53 (1938), 32–82

Backhouse, Janet, 'An illuminator's sketch book', *British Library Journal* (1975), 3–14

Bainbridge, Virginia, R., *Gilds in the medieval countryside: social and religious change in Cambridgeshire, c.1350–1558* (Woodbridge, 1996)

Bainton, Ronald H., *Here I stand. A life of Martin Luther* (New York, 1950)

Baker, J.H., 'The English legal profession 1450–1550', in W. Prest (ed.) *Lawyers in early modern Europe and America* (London, 1981), 16–41

——, *The common law tradition. Lawyers, books and the law* (London, 2000)

——, 'Common lawyers and the inns of court', in Elizabeth S. Leedham-Green and Teresa Webber (eds) *The Cambridge history of libraries in Britain and Ireland, vol. 1: to 1640* (Cambridge, 2006), 448–60

Bardsley, Sandy, 'Women's work reconsidered: gender and wage differentiation in late medieval England', *Past and Present*, 165 (1999), 3–29

Barron, Caroline M., 'The parish fraternities of medieval London', in C.M. Barron and C. Harper-Bill (eds) *The church in pre-Reformation society* (Woodbridge, 1985), 13–37

——, 'The expansion of education in fifteenth-century London', in John Blair and Brian Golding (eds) *The cloister and the world: essays on medieval history in honour of Barbara Harvey* (Oxford, 1996), 219–45

—— and J. Roscoe, 'The medieval church of St. Andrew's, Holborn', *London Topographical Record*, XXIV (1980), 31–60

Barron, W.R.J. (ed.), *The Arthur of the English: the Arthurian legend in medieval English life and literature* (Cardiff, 1998)

Beamont, W., *Annals of Warrington* (*CS*, os 86 and 87, 1872–3)

Beck, J., *Tudor Cheshire* (Chester, 1969)

Beckwith, Sarah, *Christ's body: identity, culture and society in late medieval writings* (London, 1993)

Bennett, H.S., *Life on the English manor* (Cambridge, 1937)

——, 'Science and information in English writings of the fifteenth century', *Modern Language Review*, 38, no. 1 (1944), 1–8

Bennett, J.M. (ed.), *Women in the medieval countryside: gender, household in Brigstock before the Plague* (Oxford, 1987)

Bennett, M.J., 'Sources and problems in the study of social mobility: Cheshire in the later Middle Ages', *THSLC*, 128 (1979), 59–95

——, 'Sir Gawain and the Green Knight and the literary achievement of the north west midlands: the historical background', *Journal of Medieval History*, 5 (1979), 63–88
——, *Community, class and careerism: Cheshire and Lancashire society in the age of Sir Gawain and the Green Knight* (Cambridge, 1983)
——, *Lambert Simnel and the Battle of Stoke* (Gloucester, 1987)
——, 'Memoir of a yeoman in the service of the House of York, 1452–1461', *The Ricardian*, VIII, 106 (1989), 259–64
——, 'Forms of intellectual life and cultural expression', in Griffiths (Ed.) *The fourteenth and fifteenth centuries*, 117–48
Bindoff, S. (ed.), *The House of Commons, 1509–1558*, III (London, 1982)
Binski, Paul, *Medieval death. Ritual and representation* (London, 1996)
Blair, C., 'Pre-reformation effigies of Cheshire', *TLCAS*, part 1 LX (1948), 117–47; part 2 LXI (1949), 91–120
Blake, J.B., 'Medieval Congleton', in W.B. Stephens (ed.) *The History of Congleton* (Manchester, 1970), 18–44
Boffey, Julia, *Manuscripts of English courtly love lyrics in the later Middle Ages* (Cambridge, 1985)
——, 'Women authors and women's literacy in fourteenth and fifteenth-century England', in Carole M. Meale (ed.) *Women and literature in Britain, 1150–1500* (Cambridge, 1993), 159–82
—— and A.S.G. Edwards, 'Literary texts', in Hellinga and Trapp (eds) *The Cambridge history of the book*, 555–75
—— and J.J. Thompson, 'Anthologies and miscellanies: production and the choice of texts', in Griffiths and Pearsall (eds) *Book production*, 279–315
Booth, P.H.W., *The financial administration of the lordship and county of Chester, 1272–1377* (*CS*, 3rd ser. 28, 1981)
Bossy, J., 'Prayers', *TRHS*, 6th ser. I (1991), 137–50
Brand, Paul, *The origins of the English legal profession* (London, 1992)
——, 'Stewards, bailiffs and the emerging legal profession in later thirteenth-century England', in Ralph Evans (ed.) *Lordship and learning. Studies in memory of Trevor Aston* (Woodbridge, 2004), 139–53
Brewer, Derek, *English Gothic literature* (London, 1983)
Bridbury, A.R., *Economic growth: England in the later Middle Ages* (London, 1962)
——, *Medieval English cloth making: an economic survey* (London, 1982)
Britnell, R.H., 'Production for the market on a small fourteenth-century estate', *Economic History Review*, 2nd ser. XIX (1966), 380–8
——, 'Minor landlords in England and medieval agrarian capitalism', *Past and Present*, LXXXIX (1980), 3–22
——, 'The Pastons and their Norfolk', *Agricultural History Review*, 36, II (1988), 132–44
——, *The closing of the Middle Ages? England, 1471–1529* (Oxford, 1997)
——, *Britain and Ireland 1050–1530: economy and society* (Oxford, 2004)
Brooks, C.W., *Pettifoggers and vipers of the commonwealth: the lower branches of the legal profession in early modern England* (Cambridge, 1986)
Brown, Andrew D., *Popular piety in late medieval England: the Diocese of Salisbury, 1250–1550* (Oxford, 1995)
——, *Church and society in England, 1000–1500* (Basingstoke, 2003)

Bühler, C.F., 'Prayers and charms in certain Middle English scrolls', *Speculum*, 39 (1964), 270–8
Burgess, Clive, '"A fond thing vainly invented": an essay on purgatory and pious motivation in late medieval England', in Wright (ed.) *Parish, church, and people*, 56–84
—— and Eamon Duffy (eds), *The parish in late medieval England* (Donnington, 2006)
Burrow, J.A., *Ages of man: a study in medieval writing and thought* (Oxford, 1986)
Cam, H., 'The community of the vill', in H. Cam *Law-finders and law-makers in medieval England* (London, 1962), 71–84
Camargo, M., *The Middle English verse epistle* (Tübingen, Niemeyer, 1991)
Cameron, K. (ed.), *Place-names of Derbyshire* (English Place-Name Soc., vol. XXVII, part 1, Cambridge, 1959)
Campbell, G.H., 'Chaucer's prophecy in 1586', *Modern Language Notes*, 29, no. 6 (1914), 195–6
Carey, H., 'Devout literate laypeople and the pursuit of the mixed life in later medieval England', *Journal of Religious History*, 14 (1986–7), 361–81
Carey, Hilary M., *Courting disaster: astrology at the English court and university in the Middle Ages* (New York, 1988)
——, 'Astrological medicine and the medieval English folded almanac', *Social History of Medicine*, 17:3 (2004), 345–63
Carley, James P., *Glastonbury Abbey: the holy house of the head of the moors adventurous* (Woodbridge, 1988)
——, 'Arthur in English history', in Barron (ed.) *The Arthur of the English*, 47–57
Carpenter, Christine, 'The fifteenth-century gentry and their estates', in Jones (ed.) *Gentry and lesser nobility*, 36–60
——, 'The religion of the gentry of fifteenth-century England', in Daniel Williams (ed.) *England in the fifteenth century: proceedings of the 1986 Harlaxton symposium* (Woodbridge, 1987), 53–74
——, *Locality and polity: a study of Warwickshire landed society, 1401–99* (Cambridge, 1992)
——, 'Gentry and community in medieval England', *Journal of British Studies*, 33 (1994), 340–80
——, 'Who ruled the Midlands in the later Middle Ages?', *Midland History*, 19 (1994), 1–20
——, 'The Stonor circle in the fifteenth century', in Rowena Archer and Simon Walker (eds) *Rulers and ruled in medieval England* (London, 1995), 175–200
——, *The Wars of the Roses: politics and the constitution in England, c. 1437–1509* (Cambridge, 1997)
——, 'England: the nobility and the gentry', in S.H. Rigby (ed.) *A companion to Britain in the later Middle Ages* (Oxford, 2003), 261–82
——, 'Religion', in Radulescu and Truelove (eds) *Gentry culture*, 134–50
Chaytor, H.J., *From script to print: an introduction to medieval literature* (Cambridge, 1945)
Cherewatuk, K., '"Gentyl audiences" and "grete bokes": chivalric manuals and *Morte Darthur*', *Arthurian Literature*, 15 (1997), 205–16
Cheshire Sheaf (Chester, 1891–1978)

Clanchy, M.T., *From memory to written record, England 1066–1307* (Oxford, 1993)
Clark-Maxwell, W.G., 'Letters of confraternity', *Archaeologia*, 75 (1924–5), 19–60
——, 'Some further letters of confraternity', *Archaeologia*, 79 (1929), 179–216
Clayton, Dorothy, *The administration of the county palatine of Chester 1442–85* (*CS*, 35, 1990)
Clough, C.H. (ed.), *Profession, vocation and culture in later medieval England* (London, 1982)
Coates, B.E., 'The origins and distribution of markets and fairs of medieval Derbyshire', *Derbyshire Archaeological Journal*, 85 (1965), 92–111
Coleman, Janet, *English literature in history, 1350–1400: medieval readers and writers* (London, 1981)
Coleman, Joyce, *Public reading and the reading public in late medieval England and France* (Cambridge, 1996)
Cooper, Nicholas, *Houses of the gentry 1480–1680* (New Haven, 1999)
Coote, Lesley A., 'A language of power: prophecy and public affairs in later medieval England', in Taithe and Thornton (eds) *Prophecy*, 17–30
——, *Prophecy and public affairs in later medieval England* (York, 2000)
Cornwall, J., 'The early Tudor gentry', *Economic History Review*, 2nd ser., XVIII (1965), 456–75
Coss, P.R., 'Aspects of cultural diffusion in medieval England', *Past and Present*, 108 (1985), 35–79
——, 'The formation of the English gentry', *Past and Present*, 147 (1995), 38–64
——, *The origins of the English gentry* (Cambridge, 2003)
——, 'An age of deference', in Horrox and Ormrod (eds) *A social history of England*, 312–73
Crane, Ronald S., 'The vogue of Guy of Warwick from the close of the Middle Ages to the Romantic Revival', *PMLA*, vol. 30 (1915), 125–94
Crane, Susan, *The performance of self. Ritual, clothing and identity during the Hundred Years War* (Philadelphia, 2002)
Cressy, D., *Literacy and the social order: reading and writing in Tudor and Stuart England* (Cambridge, 1980)
Crossley, F.H., *English church monuments AD 1150–1550* (London, 1921)
Cunliffe-Shaw, R., 'Two fifteenth-century kinsmen: John Shaw of Duckinfield, mercer and William Shaw of Heath, Charnock, surgeon', *THSLC*, 110 (1958), 15–30
Daniell, Christopher, *Death and burial in medieval England, 1066–1550* (London, 1997)
Davies, C.S., *A history of Macclesfield* (Manchester, 1961)
Davies, R.R., *The revolt of Owain Glyn Dŵr* (Oxford, 1995)
Denholm-Young, D., *Seignoral administration in England* (Oxford, 1937)
Denton, Jon, 'Image, identity and gentility: the Woodford experience', in Linda Clark (ed.) *The Fifteenth Century*, vol. 5 (Woodbridge, 2005), 1–18
Dickens, B., 'The date of the Ireland manuscript', *Leeds Studies in English*, 11 (1933), 62–6
Dobson, R.B. (ed.), *The church, politics and patronage in the fifteenth century* (Gloucester, 1984)

Dockray, K.R., 'Why did the fifteenth-century English gentry marry?', in Jones (ed.) *Gentry and lesser nobility*, 61–80

Dodgson, J.McN., *The place-names of Cheshire*, part 1 (English Place-Name Soc., XLIV, 1970)

——, 'A library at Pott Chapel (Pott Shrigley, Cheshire) c.1493', *The Library*, 5th ser. XV (1960), 47–53

Dove, Mary, *The perfect age of man's life* (Cambridge, 1986)

Doyle, A.I., 'English books in and out of court from Edward III to Henry VII', in V.J. Scattergood and James W. Sherborne (eds), *English Court Culture in the later Middle Ages* (London, 1983), 163–81

Driver, J.T., 'The Mainwarings of Over Peover: a Cheshire family in the fifteenth and early sixteenth centuries', *Journal of the Chester and North Wales Antiquarian Society*, 57 (1970–1), 27–40

——, *Cheshire in the later Middle Ages, 1399–1540* (Chester, 1971)

Du Boulay, F.R.H., *An age of ambition: English society in the late Middle Ages* (London, 1970)

Duffy, Eamon, *The stripping of the altars* (New Haven and London, 1992)

——, *Marking the hours. English people and their prayers, 1240–1570* (New Haven, 2006)

Dunning, Robert W. (ed.), *Victoria County History of the county off Somerset, vol. VIII: the Poldens and the levels* (Oxford, 2004)

Dyer, Christopher,' A small landowner in the fifteenth century', *Midland History*, 1 (1971), 1–14

——, *Lords and peasants in a changing society: the estates of the bishopric of Worcester, 680–1540* (Cambridge, 1980)

——, *Warwickshire farming, 1349–c.1520: preparations for agricultural revolution* (Oxford, 1981)

——, 'The consumption of fresh-water fish in medieval England', in Aston (ed.) *Fisheries*, 27–38

——, 'The consumer and the market in the later Middle Ages', *Economic History Review*, 2nd ser. 42 (1989), 305–27

——, *Standards of living in the later Middle Ages: social change in England c.1200–1520* (Cambridge, 1989)

——, *Making a living in the Middle Ages: the people of Britain 850–1520* (New Haven, 2002)

——, *An age of transition?: economy and society in England in the later Middle Ages* (Oxford, 2005)

Eamon, William, 'The book of secrets in medieval and early modern science', *Sudhoffs Archive*, 69 (1985), 26–49

——, *Science and the secrets of nature. Books of secrets in medieval and early modern culture* (New Jersey, 1994)

Earwaker, J.P., *East Cheshire* (2 vols, London, 1877, 1880)

Easting, Robert, '"Send thine heart into Purgatory": visionaries of the other world', in Helen Cooper and S. Mapstone (eds) *The long fifteenth century: essays for Douglas Gray* (Oxford, 1997), 185–203

Edwards, A.S.G. and Carole M. Meale, 'The marketing of English books in late medieval England', *The Library*, 6th ser. XV (1993), 95–124

Edwards, A.S.G., 'The transmission and audience of Osbern Bokenham's *Legendys of hooly wummen*', in A.J. Minnis (ed.), *Late-medieval religious texts and their transmission: essays in honour of A.I. Doyle* (Woodbridge, 1994), 157–67

Elton, G.R., *Policy and police* (Cambridge, 1972)

Erler, Mary C., 'Devotional literature', in Hellinga and Trapp (eds) *The Cambridge history of the book*, 495–525

Farmer, D.L., 'Marketing the produce of the countryside, 1200–1500', in Miller (ed.) *The agrarian history of England and Wales*, 324–430

Farnhill, Ken, *Guilds and the parish community in late medieval East Anglia, c. 1470–1550* (Rochester, 2001)

Farrer, William and J. Brownbill, *The Victoria County History of the County of Lancaster*, vol. 4 (London, 1911)

Ferster, Judith, *Fictions of advice: the literature and politics of counsel in late medieval England* (Philadelphia, 1996)

Fleming, P.W., 'Charity, faith and the gentry of Kent, 1422–1529', in A.J. Pollard (ed.) *Property and politics: essays in later medieval English history* (Gloucester, 1984), 36–58

——, 'The "Hautes" and their "circle": culture and the English gentry', in Daniel Williams (ed.) *England in the fifteenth century: proceedings of the 1986 Harlaxton symposium* (Woodbridge, 1987), 85–102

——, 'Household servants of the Yorkist and early Tudor gentry 1460–1560', in Daniel Williams (ed.) *Early Tudor England: proceedings of the 1987 Harlaxton symposium* (Woodbridge, 1989), 19–36

——, *Family and household in medieval England* (London, 2001)

Ford, Judy Ann, *John Mirk's Festial. Orthodoxy, Lollardy and the common people in fourteenth-century England* (Cambridge, 2006)

Ford, Margaret Lane, 'Private ownership of printed books', in Hellinga and Trapp (eds) *The Cambridge history of the book*, 205–28

Foulds, T., 'Medieval cartularies', *Archives*, XVIII (1987), 3–35

Fox, A., 'Prophecies and politics in the reign of Henry VIII', in A. Fox and J. Guy (eds) *Reassessing the Henrician Age* (Oxford, 1986), 77–94

Fox, L., (ed.), *English historical scholarship in the sixteenth and seventeenth centuries* (Dugdale Society, Oxford, 1956)

French, Katherine, L., *The people of the parish: community life in a late medieval English diocese* (Philadelphia, 2001)

Friedrichs, Rhoda L., 'Marriage strategies and younger sons in fifteenth-century England', *Medieval Prosopography*, 4 (1993), 53–69

Fryer, Alfred, *Wilmslow graves and grave thoughts from Wilmslow* (Stockport, 1886)

Gardner, A., *Alabaster tombs of the pre-reformation period in England* (Cambridge, 1940)

Gibson, Gail McMurray, *The theater of devotion: East Anglian drama and society in the late Middle Ages* (Chicago, 1989)

Gill, Miriam, 'Now help St George, oure lady knight … to be strengthe our kyng and England ryght', *TLCAS*, 91 (1997 for 1995), 91–102

Gillespie, Alexandra, 'Balliol MS 354: histories of the book at the end of the Middle Ages', *Poetica*, 60 (2003), 47–63

Girouard, Mark, *Life in the English country house: a social and architectural history* (Harmondsworth, 1980)

Given-Wilson, C., *The English nobility in the later Middle Ages: the fourteenth-century political community* (London, 1987)
Goldberg, P.J.P., 'Female labour, service and marriage in northern towns during the later Middle Ages', *Northern History*, XXII (1986), 18–38
—— (ed.), *Woman is a worthy wight: women in English society c.1200–1500* (Gloucester, 1992)
——, 'Lay book ownership in late medieval York: the evidence of wills', *The Library*, 6th ser. 16 (1994), 181–9
——, 'What was a servant?', in Anne Curry and Elizabeth Matthew (eds) *Concepts and patterns of service in the later Middle Ages* (Woodbridge, 2000), 1–20
——, *Medieval England. A social history 1250–1550* (London, 2004)
Goodich, Michael E., *From birth to old age: the human life cycle in medieval thought, 1250–1350* (Lanham and London, 1989)
Gottfried, R.S., *The Black Death* (London, 1983)
Gougaud, L., *Devotional and ascetic practices in the Middle Ages* (London, 1927)
Graham, H., '"A woman's work ...": labour and gender in the late medieval countryside', in Goldberg (ed.) *Woman is a worthy wight*, 126–48
Gransden, Antonia, 'Antiquarian studies in fifteenth-century England', *Antiquaries Journal*, 60 (1980), 75–97
——, *Historical writing in England, vol. 2: 1307 to the early sixteenth century* (London, 1982)
Gray, D., 'Some notes on middle English charms', in B. Rowland (ed.) *Chaucer and Middle English studies in honour of Rossell Hope Robbins* (London, 1974), 56–71
——, 'Middle English courtly lyrics: Chaucer to Henry VIII', in Thomas G. Duncan (ed.) *A companion to the Middle English lyric* (Cambridge, 2005), 120–49
Green, Monica H., 'Obstetrical and gynaecological texts in Middle English', *Studies in the Age of Chaucer*, 14 (1992), 53–88
Green, R.F., *Poets and princepleasers: literature and the English court in the late Middle Ages* (Toronto, 1980)
Greene, J.P., *Norton Priory* (Cambridge, 1989)
Grenville, Jane, *Medieval housing* (London, 1997)
Griffith, David, 'A portrait of the reader: secular donors and their books in the art of the English parish church', in Kelly and Thompson (eds) *Imagining the book*, 209–36
Griffiths, J. and D. Pearsall (eds), *Book production and publishing in Britain, 1375–1475* (Cambridge, 1989)
Griffiths, R.A., 'Public and private bureaucracies in England and Wales in the fifteenth century', *TRHS*, 5th ser. 30 (1980), 109–30
—— (ed.) *The fourteenth and fifteenth centuries* (Oxford, 2003)
Gross, A.J., 'K.B. McFarlane and the determinists: the fallibilities of English kings, c.1399–c.1520', in R.H. Britnell and A.J. Pollard (eds) *The McFarlane legacy: studies in late medieval politics and society* (Stroud, 1995), 49–75
Guddat-Figge, G., *Catalogue of the manuscripts containing Middle English romances* (Munchen, 1976)
Gunn, S.J., 'Early Tudor dates for the death of Edward V', *Northern History*, XXVIII (1992), 213–16
Gurevich, A.J., *Categories of medieval culture*, trans. G.L. Campbell (London, 1985)

Hadley, D.M., *Death in medieval England. An archaeology* (Stroud, 2001)
Haigh, Christopher, *Reformation and resistance in Tudor Lancashire* (Cambridge, 1975)
Haines, R.M., *Ecclesia Anglicana: studies in the English church of the later Middle Ages* (London and Toronto, 1989)
Hainsworth, D.R., *Stewards, lords and people* (Cambridge, 1992)
Hammond, P.W., *Food and feast in medieval England* (Stroud, 1993)
Hanawalt, B.A., *The ties that bound: peasant families in medieval England* (Oxford, 1986)
Hands, R., *English hawking and hunting in the Boke of St Albans* (Oxford, 1975)
Hanawalt, Barbara A., *Growing up in Medieval London: the experience of childhood in history* (Oxford, 1998)
Hanna III, Ralph, 'Booklets in medieval manuscripts: further considerations', *Studies in Bibliography*, 39 (1986), 100–11
——, 'The growth of Robert Thornton's books', *Studies in Bibliography*, 40 (1987), 51–61
——, 'Miscellaneity and vernacularity: conditions of literary production in late medieval England', in S.G. Nichols and S. Wenzel (eds) *The Whole Book: cultural perspectives on the medieval miscellany* (Ann Arbor, 1996), 37–52
——, 'Humphrey Newton and Bodleian Library MS Lat. misc.c.66', *Medium Aevum*, 69:2 (2000), 279–91
—— and A.S.G. Edwards, 'Rotheley, the De Vere circle, and the Ellesmere Chaucer', *Huntingdon Library Quarterly*, 58 (1996), 11–35
Harding, Vanessa, 'Burial choice and burial location in later medieval London', in Steven Bassett (ed.) *Death in towns: urban responses to the dying and the dead, 100–1600* (London, 1992), 119–35
Hardman, Phillipa, 'Compiling the nation: fifteenth-century miscellany manuscripts', in Helen Cooney (ed.) *Nation, court and culture. New essays on fifteenth-century English poetry* (Dublin, 2001), 50–69
——, 'Evidence of readership in fifteenth-century household miscellanies', *Poetica*, 60 (2003), 15–30
Harris, B.E. (ed.), *Victoria County History of the county of Chester*, vols. II and III (Oxford, 1979–80)
—— and A.T. Thacker (eds), *Victoria County History of the county of Chester*, vol I (Oxford, 1987)
Harris, B.J., *English aristocratic women, 1450–1550* (Oxford, 2002)
Harris, K., 'The origins and make-up of Cambridge University Library MS Ff.I.6', *Transactions of the Cambridge Bibliographical Society*, 8 (1983), 299–333
——, 'Patrons, buyers and owners: the evidence for ownership and the role of book owners in book production and the book trade', in Griffiths and Pearsall (eds) *Book production*, 163–99
Harriss, Gerald S., 'The dimensions of politics', in R.H. Britnell and A.J. Pollard (eds) *The McFarlane legacy: studies in late medieval politics and society* (Stroud, 1995), 1–20
——, *Shaping the nation: England 1360–1461* (Oxford, 2005)
Haskett, Timothy S., 'Conscience, justice and authority in the late medieval English court of Chancery', in Musson (ed.) *Expectations of the law*, 151–64

Hatcher, John, 'England in the aftermath of the Black Death', *Past and Present*, 144 (1994), 3–35
Hatcher, John, 'The great slump of the mid-fifteenth century', in Richard Britnell and John Hatcher (eds), *Progress and problems in Medieval England* (Cambridge, 1996), 237–72
Heal, Felicity, *Hospitality in early modern England* (Oxford, 1990)
—— and Clive Holmes, *The gentry in England and Wales, 1500–1700* (Basingstoke, 1994)
Hellinga, Lotte and J.B. Trapp (eds), *The Cambridge History of the Book in Britain, III: 1400–1557* (Cambridge, 1999)
Hewitt, H.J., *Medieval Cheshire* (Manchester, 1929)
——, *Cheshire under the three Edwards* (Chester, 1967)
——, 'Medical recipes of the seventeenth century', *Archaeological Journal*, 29 (1872), 71–7
Hicks, Michael A., *False, fleeting, perjur'd Clarence: George, duke of Clarence 1449–78* (Gloucester, 1980)
——, 'Four studies in conventional piety', *Southern History*, 13 (1991), 1–21
——, *English political culture in the fifteenth century* (London, 2002)
Higham, N., *The origins of Cheshire* (Manchester, 1993)
Highet, T.P., *The early history of the Davenports of Davenport* (*CS*, 3rd ser. 9, 1960)
Holdsworth, William Searle, *A history of English law* (17 vols, London, 1903–72)
Hilton, R.H., 'Rent and capital formation in feudal society', *2nd conference of economic history*, vol. 2 (2 vols, Paris, 1965)
——, *A medieval society: the west midlands at the end of the thirteenth century* (London, 1965)
——, *The English peasantry in the later Middle Ages* (Oxford, 1975)
Hollingsworth, T.H., 'A demographic study of the British ducal families', in D.V. Glass and D.E.C. Eversley (eds) *Population history: essays in historical demography* (London, 1965), 354–78
Holt, R.A., *The mills of medieval England* (Oxford, 1988)
Horrox, Rosemary, *Richard III: a study in service* (Cambridge, 1989)
——, 'Local and national politics in fifteenth-century England', *Journal of Medieval History*, 18 (1992), 391–403
—— (ed.) *Fifteenth-century attitudes: perceptions of society in late medieval England* (Cambridge, 1994)
—— and W. Mark Ormrod (eds), *A social history of England, 1200–1500* (Cambridge, 2006)
Howell, Cicely, *Land, family and inheritance in transition: Kibworth Harcourt 1280–1700* (Cambridge, 1983)
Hughes, Jonathan, *Pastors and visionaries: religion and secular life in late medieval Yorkshire* (Woodbridge, 1988)
——, 'Stephen Scrope and the circle of Sir John Fastolf: moral and intellectual outlooks', in C. Harper-Bill and R. Harvey (eds) *The ideals of medieval knighthood IV* (Woodbridge, 1992), 109–46
——, *The religious life of Richard III: piety and prayer in the north of England* (Stroud, 1997)
——, *Arthurian myths and alchemy. The kingship of Edward IV* (Stroud, 2002)

Hunt, Alan, *Governance of the consuming passions. A history of sumptuary law* (London, 1996)
Ives, E.W., 'The common lawyers in pre-Reformation England', *TRHS*, 5th ser. 18 (1968), 145–73
——, *The common lawyers of pre-Reformation England* (Cambridge, 1982)
——, 'The common lawyers', in C.H. Clough (ed.) *Profession, vocation, and culture in later medieval England* (Liverpool, 1982), 181–207
Jacob, E.F., 'The Boke of St Albans', *Bulletin of the John Rylands University Library*, 28 (1944), 99–136
James, M.R., 'The Anlaby cartulary', *Yorkshire Archaeological Journal*, 31 (1934), 337–47
James, Mervyn, *Family, lineage and civil society. A study of society, politics and mentality in the Durham region, 1500–1640* (Oxford, 1974)
——, 'English politics and the concept of honour, 1485–1642', *Past and Present*, Supplement 3 (1978)
Jansen, S.L., *Political protests and prophecy under Henry VIII* (Cambridge, 1991)
Jeavons, S.A., *The monumental effigies of Staffordshire, parts I–III* (Oxford, 1955)
Jewell, H.M., *English local administration in the Middle Ages* (Newton Abbot, 1972)
Jones, Douglas, *The church in Chester, 1300–1540* (*CS*, 3rd ser. vol. 7, 1957)
Jones, I.B., 'Popular medical knowledge in fourteenth-century English literature', *Bulletin of the History of Medicine*, 5 (1937), 405–51, 538–88
Jones, M.C.E. (ed.), *Gentry and lesser nobility in late medieval Europe* (Gloucester, 1986)
Jones, Michael K. and M.G. Underwood, *The king's mother: Lady Margaret Beaufort, Countess of Richmond and Derby* (Cambridge, 1992)
Jones, Peter Murray, 'Information and science', in Horrox (ed.) *Fifteenth-century attitudes*, 97–111
——, 'Harley MS 2558: a fifteenth-century medical commonplace book', in Margaret R. Schleissner (ed.) *Manuscript sources of medieval medicine. A book of essays* (New York and London, 1995)
——, 'Thomas Fayreford: an English fifteenth-century medical practitioner', in Roger French *et al.* (eds) *Medicine from the Black Death to the French disease* (Aldershot, 1998), 156–83
——, 'Medicine and Science', in Hellinga and Trapp (eds) *The Cambridge history of the book*, 433–48
Jurkowski, Maureen, 'Lawyers and Lollardy in the early fifteenth century', in Margaret Aston and Colin Richmond (eds) *Lollardy and the gentry in the later Middle Ages* (Stroud, 1997), 155–82
Kamerick, Kathleen, *Popular piety and art in the late Middle Ages. Image worship and idolatry in England 1350–1500* (Basingstoke, 2002)
Kay, Sarah, 'Courts, clerks and courtly love', in Roberta L. Krueger (ed.) *The Cambridge companion to medieval Romance* (Cambridge, 2000)
Keen, Maurice, *Chivalry* (London, 1984)
——, *Origins of the English gentleman* (Stroud, 2002)
——, 'Chivalry', in Radulescu and Truelove (eds) *Gentry culture*, 35–49
Keiser, G.R., 'Lincoln Cathedral Library MS 91', *Studies in Bibliography*, XXXII (1979), 165–77

——, 'More light on the life and milieu of Robert Thornton', *Studies in Bibliography*, 36 (1983), 111–19
——, 'The progress of Purgatory: visions in the after life in late Middle English literature', *Analecta Cartusiana*, CXVII (1987), 72–100
——, 'Practical books for the gentleman', in Hellinga and Trapp (eds) *The Cambridge history of the book*, 470–94
Kelly, C., 'The noble steward and late-feudal lordship', *Huntingdon Library Quarterly*, 49 (1986), 133–48
Kelly, Stephen and John J. Thompson (eds), *Imagining the book* (Turnhout, 2005)
Kermode, J., 'The trade of late medieval Cheshire, 1500–1550', in R.H. Britnell and John Hatcher (eds) *Progress and problems in medieval England: essays in honour of Edward Miller* (Cambridge, 1996), 286–307
Kerridge, E., *Agrarian problems in the sixteenth century and after* (London, 1964)
Kieckhefer, R., *Magic in the Middle Ages* (Cambridge, 1989)
——, 'The specific rationality of medieval magic', *American Historical Review*, 99 (1994), 810–36
Kirby, Joan W., 'A fifteenth-century family, the Plumptons of Plumpton, and their lawyers, 1461–1515', *Northern History*, XXV (1989), 106–19
——, 'A northern knightly family in the waning Middle Ages', *Northern History*, XXXI (1995), 86–107
Kitching, C., 'Church and chapelry in sixteenth-century England', in D. Baker (ed.) *The church in town and countryside* (*Studies in Church History*, 16, 1979), 279–90
Kosminsky, E.A., *Studies in the agrarian history of England in the thirteenth century* (Oxford, 1956)
Kumin, Beat A., *The shaping of a community: the rise and reformation of the English parish, c. 1400–1560* (Brookfield, 1996)
Kussmaul, A.S., *Servants in husbandry in early modern England* (Cambridge, 1981)
Lander, J.R., *Conflict and stability in fifteenth-century England* (London, 1969)
Langdon, John, 'Water-mills and windmills in the West Midlands 1086–1500', *Economic History Review*, 2nd ser. XLIV (1991), 424–44
——, 'Lordship and peasant consumerism in the milling industry of early fourteenth-century England', *Past and Present*, 145 (1994), 3–46
——, *Mills in the medieval economy: England, 1300–1540* (Oxford, 2004)
Laughton, Jane, 'A note on the place-name Mottram St Andrew, Cheshire', *Journal of the English Place-Name Society*, 37 (2005), 32–3
Lawson Lowe, A.E., 'Some account of the family of Lowe, of Alderwasley and Denby in the county of Derby and elsewhere', *Journal of the Derbyshire Archaeological Society*, 3 (1881), 157–76
Lawton, D.A., 'Scottish Field: alliterative verse and Stanley encomium in the Percy folio', *Leeds Studies in English*, ns X (1978), 42–57
Lea, H.C., *A history of auricular confession and indulgences in the Latin Church*, vol. 3 (London, 1896)
Lee, Hermione, *Virginia Woolf* (London, 1996)
Lester, G.A., *Sir John Paston's 'Grete boke'* (Cambridge, 1984)

Lewis, C.P. and A.T. Thacker (eds) *A history of the County of Cheshire*, vol. 5 (Woodbridge, 2002)

Lewis, F., 'The Veronica: image, legend and viewer', in M. Ormerod (ed.) *England in the thirteenth century: proceedings of the 1984 Harlaxton symposium* (Woodbridge, 1985), 100–6

Lewis, P.S., 'Sir John Fastolf's lawsuit over Titchwell 1448–55', *The Historical Journal*, 1 (1958), 1–20

Leycester, Peter, *Historical antiquities* (London, 1673)

Lindberg, D. (ed.), *Science in the Middle Ages* (Chicago and London, 1978)

Lomas, R.A., 'A northern farm at the end of the Middle Ages: Elvethall manor, Durham, 1443/4–1513/14', *Northern History*, 18 (1982), 26–53

Lowe, N., *The Lancashire textile industry in the sixteenth century* (*CS*, 3rd ser. 20, 1972)

Lowry, Martin, 'John Rous and the survival of the Neville circle', *Viator*, 19 (1988), 327–38

Lunt, W.E., *Financial relations of the papacy with England, 1327–1534* (Cambridge, MA, 1962)

Luttrell, C.A., 'Three north-west midland manuscripts', *Neophilologus*, 42 (1958), 38–50

Lyall, R.J., 'Materials: the paper revolution', in Griffiths and Pearsall (eds) *Book production*, 11–29

Lyons, D., *Magna Britannia*, II (London, 1810)

McFarlane, K.B., *The nobility of later medieval England* (Oxford, 1973)

——, *England in the fifteenth century: collected essays* (London, 1981)

McIntosh, Marjorie Keniston, *Autonomy and community: the Royal Manor of Havering, 1200–1500* (Cambridge, 1986)

——, *Working women in English society, 1300–1620* (Cambridge, 2005)

McNamer, S., 'Female authors, provincial setting: the re-versing of courtly love in the Findern manuscript', *Viator*, 22 (1991), 279–310

Maddern, Philippa, 'Honour among the Pastons: gender and integrity in fifteenth-century English provincial society', *Journal of Medieval History*, 14 (1988), 357–71

Maddern, Philippa, *Violence and social order. East Anglia 1422–1442* (Oxford, 1992)

——, '"Best trusted friends": concepts and practices of friendship among fifteenth-century Norfolk gentry', in N. Rogers (ed.) *England in the fifteenth century: proceedings of the 1992 Harlaxton symposium* (Stamford, 1994), 100–17

——, 'Gentility', in Radulescu and Truelove (eds) *Gentry culture*, 18–34

——, 'Social mobility', in Horrox and Ormrod (eds) *A social history of England*, 113–33

Marsh, Deborah, '"I see by sizt of evidence": information gathering in late medieval Cheshire', in Diana Dunn (ed.) *Courts, counties and the capital in the later Middle Ages* (Stroud, 1996), 71–92

Marshall, Peter, 'Fear, Purgatory and polemic in Reformation England', in William G. Naphy and Penny Roberts (eds) *Fear in early modern society* (Manchester, 1997), 150–66

——, *Beliefs and the dead in Reformation England* (Oxford, 2002)

Mason, J.E., *Gentlefolk in the making. Studies in the history of English courtesy literature and related topics from 1531–1774* (Pennsylvania, 1935)

Mate, Mavis, 'Medieval agrarian practices: the determining factors?', *Agricultural History Review*, 33 (1985), 22–31

Matsuda, Takami, *Death and Purgatory in Middle English didactic poetry* (Cambridge, 1997)

Meale, Carole M., 'The compiler at work. John Colyns and BL Harley 2252', in Pearsall (ed.) *Manuscripts and readers*, 82–103

——, 'Patrons, buyers and owners: book production and social status', in Griffiths and Pearsall (eds) *Book production*, 201–38

——, 'The Miracles of Our Lady: context and interpretation', in Derek Pearsall (ed.) *Studies in the Vernon Manuscript* (Cambridge, 1990), 115–36

——, 'The politics of book ownership: the Hopton family and Bodleian Library, Digby MS 185', in Riddy (ed.) *Prestige, authority and power*, 103–31

Mertes, Kate, *The English noble household, 1250–1600: good governance and politic rule* (Oxford, 1988)

Mertes, Kate, 'Aristocracy', in Horrox (ed.) *Fifteenth-century attitudes*, 42–60

Middleton-Stewart, Judith, *Inward purity and outward splendour. Death and remembrance in the deanery of Dunwich, Suffolk, 1370–1547* (Woodbridge, 2001)

Miller, E. (ed.), *The agrarian history of England and Wales, 3: 1348–1500.* (Cambridge, 1991)

Mitchell, R.J., '"Italian nobilita" and the English idea of the gentleman in the fifteenth century', *English Miscellany*, 9 (1958), 23–37

Moorman, John R.H., *Church life in England in the thirteenth century* (Cambridge, 1945)

Moran, J.H., *The growth of English schooling 1340–1548* (Princeton, 1985)

Moreton, C.E., 'A "best bestrustyd frende": a late medieval lawyer and his clients', *Journal of Legal History*, 11 (1990), 183–90

——, 'A social gulf? The upper and lesser gentry of later medieval England', *Journal of Medieval History*, 17 (1991), 255–62

——, 'The "library" of a late fifteenth-century lawyer', *The Library*, 6th ser. 13 (1991), 338–46

——, *The Townshends and their world: gentry, law and the land in Norfolk, c.1450–1551* (Oxford, 1992)

Morgan, D.A.L., 'The individual style of the English gentleman', in Jones (ed.) *The gentry and lesser nobility*, 15–35

Morgan, Philip, *War and society in medieval Cheshire, 1277–1403* (CS, ser. 3, 34, 1987)

——, 'Making the English gentry', in Peter R. Coss and S.D. Lloyd (eds) *Thirteenth century England. Vol. 5: proceedings of the Newcastle on Tyne conference 1993* (Woodbridge, 1995), 21–8

——, 'Of worms and war: 1380–1558', in Peter C. Jupp and Clare Gittings (eds) *Death in England: an illustrated history* (Manchester, 1999), 119–46

——, 'Ranks of society', in Griffiths (ed.) *The fourteenth and fifteenth centuries*, 59–86

Morris, P., 'The small court of the manor of Haywood in the reign of Elizabeth I', *Staffordshire Studies*, II (1989–90), 1–21

Morris, R.H., *Chester in Plantagenet and Tudor Times* (Chester, 1894)

Moss, Amanda, 'A merchant's tale: a London fifteenth-century household miscellany', *Yearbook of English Studies*, 33 (2003), 156–69

Musson, Anthony, *Public order and law enforcement: the local administration of criminal justice, 1294–1350* (Woodbridge, 1996)

——, *Medieval law in context: the growth of legal consciousness from Magna Carta to the Peasants' Revolt* (Manchester, 2001)

—— (ed.), *Expectations of the law in the Middle Ages* (Woodbridge, 2001)

—— and W. Mark Ormrod, *The evolution of English justice: law, politics and society in the fourteenth century* (Basingstoke, 1999)

Mustain, J.K., 'A rural medical practitioner in fifteenth-century England', *Bulletin of the History of Medicine*, 46 (1972), 469–76

Newton, Lady, *The house of Lyme* (London, 1917)

Nicholls, J., *The matter of courtesy and Sir Gawain and the Green Knight* (Cambridge, 1985)

Nichols, Ann Eljenholm, *Seeable signs. The iconography of the seven sacraments 1350–1544* (Woodbridge, 1994)

Noble, T. (ed.), *History and gazetteer of the county of Derby*, II, part I (Derby, 1833)

North, J.D., *Chaucer's universe* (Oxford, 1988)

Noyes, T.H., 'Some notices of the family of Newton, of East Mascells in Lindfield, and Southover Priory, near Lewes; and of Newton and Pownall, in Cheshire', *Sussex Archaeological Collection*, IX (1857), 312–42

Ong, Walter, *Orality and literacy: the technologizing of the word* (London, 1982)

Orme, Nicholas, *English schools in the Middle Ages* (London, 1973)

——, 'Indulgences in the diocese of Exeter 1100–1536', *Transactions of the Devonian Association for the Advancement of Science and the Arts*, 120 (1980), 15–32

——, *From childhood to chivalry; the education of English kings and aristocracy, 1066–1530* (London, 1984)

——, 'Medieval hunting: fact and fancy', in Barbara Hanawalt (ed.) *Chaucer's England: literature in historical context* (Minnesota, 1992), 133–54

——, *Medieval children* (New Haven, 2001)

——, 'Education and recreation', in Radulescu and Truelove (eds) *Gentry culture*, 63–83

——, *Medieval schools. From Roman Britain to Renaissance England* (New Haven, 2006)

——, 'The other parish churches: chapels in late medieval England', in Burgess and Duffy (eds) *The parish in late medieval England*, 78–94

Ormerod, George, *The history of the county palatine and city of Chester*, 2nd edn, rev. and enlarged by Thomas Helsby (3 vols, London, 1882)

Ormrod, W. Mark, *Political life in medieval England, 1300–1450* (London, 1995)

O'Rourke, Jason, 'Imagining book production in fourteenth-century Herefordshire: the scribe of British Library, MS Harley 2253 and his "organizing principles"', in Kelly and Thompson (eds) *Imagining the book*, 45–60

Os, A.B. Van, *Religious visions: the developments of eschatological elements in medieval religious literature* (Amsterdam, 1932)

Os, H.W. Van, *The art of devotion in the late Middle Ages in Europe, 1300–1500*, trans. Michael Hoyle (Princeton, 1994)

Osborne, G.Y., *Sketch of the parish of Prestbury* (Macclesfield, 1840)
Owen, D.H. 'Farming practice and techniques: Wales and the Marches', in Miller (ed.) *The agrarian history of England and Wales*, 238–54
Owen, D.M., *Church and society in medieval Lincolnshire* (Lincoln, 1971)
Oxford Dictionary of National Biography (60 vols, Oxford, 2004)
Pack, R.A., 'A pseudo-Aristotelian chiromancy', *Archives D'Histoire Doctrinale et Litterale du Moyen Age*, 36 (1970 for 1969), 189–241
Page, Sophie, 'Richard Trewythian and the uses of astrology in late medieval England', *Journal of the Warburg and Courtauld Institute*, LXIV (2001), 193–228
Palmer, Robert C., *The county courts of medieval England, 1150–1350* (Princeton, 1982)
Pantin, W.A., 'Instructions for a devout and literate laymen', in J.J. Alexander and M.T. Gibson (eds) *Medieval learning and literature* (Oxford, 1976), 398–422
Parker, David R., *The commonplace book in Tudor London* (Lanham, 1999)
Parkes, M.B., 'Literacy of the laity', reprinted in M.B. Parkes, *Scribes, scripts and readers; studies in the communication, presentation and dissemination of medieval texts* (London, 1991)
Payling, S.J., *Political society in Lancastrian England: the greater gentry in Nottinghamshire* (Oxford, 1991)
——, 'The economics of marriage in late medieval England: the marriage of heiresses', *Economic History Review*, 2nd ser. 54:3 (2001), 413–29
Pearsall, Derek, *John Lydgate* (London, 1970)
—— (ed.), *Manuscripts and readers in fifteenth-century England : the literary implications of manuscript study* (Cambridge, 1983)
——, 'The cultural and social setting', in Boris Ford (ed.) *The Cambridge guide to the arts in Britain, 2: the Middle Ages* (Cambridge, 1988), 2–38
——, 'The whole book: late medieval English manuscript miscellanies and their modern interpreters', in Kelly and Thompson (eds) *Imagining the book*, 17–30
Pearson, Sarah, *The medieval houses of Kent* (London, 1994)
Pederson, O., 'Astronomy', in D. Lindberg (ed.) *Science in the Middle Ages* (Chicago and London, 1978), 303–37
Penn, S.A.C., 'Female wage earners in later fourteenth-century England', *Agricultural History Review*, 35 (1987), 1–14
Perkins, Nicholas, *Hoccleve's Regiment of Princes: counsel and constraint* (Cambridge, 2001)
Pettigrew, T.J., 'Observations upon the extracts from an ancient English medical manuscript in the Royal Library of Stockholm', *Archaeologia*, 30 (1844), 349–418
Pevsner, N. and E. Hubbard, *Cheshire* (London, 1971)
Pfaff, R.W., *New liturgical feasts in later medieval England* (Oxford, 1970)
——, 'The English devotion of St Gregory's trental', *Speculum*, 49 (1974), 75–90
Phillips, Kim M., *Medieval maidens. Young women and gender in England, 1270–1540* (Manchester, 2003)
Plucknett, T.F.T., *The medieval bailiff* (London, 1954)
Pollard, A.J., 'Richard Clervaux of Croft', *Yorkshire Archaeological Journal*, 50 (1978), 151–69

——, *North-eastern England during the Wars of the Roses: lay society, war and politics, 1450–1500* (Oxford, 1990)

Pollock, F. and F.W. Maitland, *The history of the English law* (2 vols, Cambridge, 1911)

Poos, L.R., *A rural society after the Black Death: Essex 1350–1525* (Cambridge, 1991)

Pounds, N.J.G., *A history of the English parish. The culture of religion from Augustine to Victoria* (Cambridge, 2000)

Powell, E., 'Arbitration and the law in the late Middle Ages', *Transactions of the Royal Historical Society*, 33 (1984), 49–67

Price, D.J., 'Precision instruments to 1500', in C. Singer (ed.) *History of technology*, III (Oxford, 1957), 582–619

Pugh, T.B., 'The magnates, knights and gentry, in S.B. Chrimes, C.D. Ross and R.A. Griffiths (eds) *Fifteenth-century England: 1399–1509* (Manchester, 1972), 86–128

Putter, Ad, *An introduction to the Gawain poet* (London, 1996)

——, 'The ways and words of the hunt: notes of *Sir Gawain and the Green Knight*, the *Master of the Game*, *Sir Tristram*, *Pearl* and *Saint Erkenwald*', *The Chaucer Review*, 40:4 (2006), 354–85

Radulescu, Raluca, 'Talkyng of cronycles of kinges and of other polycyez: fifteenth-century miscellanies, the *Brut* and the readership of *le Morte Darthur*', *Arthurian Literature*, XVIII (2001), 125–41

——, *The gentry context for Malory's Morte Darthur* (Cambridge, 2003)

——, 'Literature', in Radulescu and Truelove (eds) *Gentry culture*, 100–18

—— and Alison Truelove (eds), *Gentry culture in late medieval England* (Manchester, 2005)

Raines, F.R. (ed.), *The rectors of Manchester and the wardens of the collegiate church of the town*, I (*CS*, 2nd ser. V, 1885)

Ramsey, N.L., 'Retained legal counsel c.1275–c.1475', *TRHS*, 5th ser. 35 (1985), 95–112

——, 'What was the legal profession?', in Michael A. Hicks (ed.) *Profit, piety and the professions* (Gloucester, 1990), 62–71

Rawcliffe, Carole, *The Staffords, Earls of Stafford and Dukes of Buckingham 1394–1521* (Cambridge, 1978)

——, 'Parliament and the settlement of disputes by arbitration in the later Middle Ages', *Parliament History*, 9 (1990), 316–42

——, *Medicine and society in later medieval England* (Stroud, 1995)

—— and S. Flower, 'English noblemen and their advisers: consultation and collaboration in the later Middle Ages', *Journal of British Studies*, 25 (1986), 157–77

Renaud, Frank, *Contributions towards a history of the ancient parish of Prestbury in Cheshire* (*CS*, XCVII, 1876)

——, 'The family of Foxwist of Foxwist and Duncalf of Foxwist', *TLCAS*, xiii (1895), 43–55

Rhodes, J.T., 'The rosary in sixteenth-century England', *Mount Carmel*, XXXI (1983), 180–91

——, 'Syon Abbey and its religious publications in the sixteenth century', *Journal of Ecclesiastical History*, 44 (1993), 11–25

Richmond, Colin, *John Hopton. A fifteenth-century gentleman* (Cambridge, 1981)
——, 'After McFarlane', *History*, 68 (1983), 46–60
——, 'Religion and the fifteenth-century English gentleman', in Barrie Dobson (ed.) *The church, politics and patronage in the fifteenth century* (Gloucester, 1984) 193–208
——, *The Paston family in the fifteenth century: the first phase* (Cambridge, 1990)
——, 'The English gentry and religion c. 1500' in Christopher Harper-Bill (ed.) *Religious belief and ecclesiastical careers in late Medieval England* (Woodbridge, 1991), 121–50
——, 'Religion', in Horrox (ed.) *Fifteenth-century attitudes*, 183–201
——, *The Paston family in the fifteenth century: Fastolf's will* (Cambridge, 1996)
Riddy, Felicity, *Sir Thomas Malory* (Leiden, 1987)
——, 'Reading for England: Arthurian literature and the national consciousness', *Bibliographical bulletin of the International Arthurian Society*, 43 (1991), 314–32
——, 'Mother knows best: reading social change in a courtesy text', *Speculum*, 71:1 (1996), 66–86
——, *Prestige, authority and power in late medieval manuscripts* (Cambridge, 2000)
——, 'Middle English romance: family, marriage, intimacy', in R.L. Krueger (ed.) *The Cambridge companion to medieval romance* (Cambridge, 2000), 235–52
Ridgeway, M.H., 'Coloured window glass in Cheshire', part II: 1400–1550', *TLCAS*, LX (1949 for 1948), 56–85
Robbins, R.H., 'Private prayers in Middle English verse', *Studies in Philology*, XXXVI (1939), 466–75
——, 'A Gawain epigone', *Modern Language Notes*, 58 (1943), 361–6
——, 'The poems of Humfrey Newton esquire, 1466–1536', *Publications of the modern language association of America*, 65 (1950), 249–81
——, 'Medical manuscripts in Middle English', *Speculum*, 45 (1970), 345–402
Robinson, Pamela R., 'The booklet: a self-contained unit in a composite manuscript', *Codicologica*, 3 (1980), 46–69
Rogers, Nicholas, 'Hic iacet …: the location of monuments in late medieval parish churches', in Burgess and Duffy (eds) *The parish in late medieval England*, 261–81
Rooney, A., *Hunting in Middle English literature* (Cambridge, 1993)
Rosenthal, Joel T., 'The estates and finances of Richard, Duke of York (1411–1460)', *Studies in Medieval and Renaissance History*, II (1965), 115–204
——, 'Medieval longevity: the secular peerage, 1350–1500', *Population Studies*, 27 (1973), 287–93
——, *Patriarchy and families of privilege in fifteenth-century England* (Philadelphia, 1991)
——, 'When did you last see your grandfather?', in Rowena Archer (ed.) *Crown, government and people in the fifteenth century* (Stroud, 1998)
Rosenzweig, Heidrun (ed.), *Historische harfen/Historical harps* (Basel, 1991)
Rosser, Gervase, 'Parochial conformity and voluntary religion', *TRHS*, 6th ser. 1 (1991), 173–89
——, 'Communities of the parish and guild in the later Middle Ages', in Wright (ed.) *Parish, church and people*, 29–55

Rowney, I., 'Arbitration in gentry disputes of the late Middle Ages', *History*, LXVII (1982), 367–78

Rust, Martha Dana, 'The "ABC of Aristotle"', in Daniel T. Kline (ed.) *Medieval literature for children* (New York, 2003), 63–78

Rylands, J.P., 'Impressions of armorial seals of Cheshire gentry by Elias Ashmole in 1663', *THSLC*, ns XXXV (1920 for 1919), 57–82

Saul, Nigel, *Knights and esquires: the Gloucestershire gentry in the fourteenth century* (Oxford, 1981)

——, *Scenes from provincial life: knightly families in Sussex 1280–1400* (Oxford, 1986)

——, 'Chaucer and gentility', in Barbara Hanawalt (ed.) *Chaucer's England: literature in historical context* (Minnesota, 1992), 41–55

——, *Death, art, and memory in medieval England : the Cobham family and their monuments, 1300–1500* (Oxford, 2001)

——, 'The gentry and the parish', in Burgess and Duffy (eds) *The parish in late medieval England*, 243–60

Scarisbrick, J.J., *The Reformation and the English people* (Oxford, 1984)

Scattergood, V.J., *Politics and poetry in the fifteenth century* (London, 1971)

——, 'Fashion and morality in the late Middle Ages', in Daniel Williams (ed.) *England in the fifteenth century: proceedings of the 1986 Harlaxton symposium* (Woodbridge, 1987), 255–72

Schirmer, W.F., *John Lydgate: a study in the culture of the fifteenth century* (London, 1961)

Searle, E., *Lordship and community: Battle Abbey and its banlieu, 1066–1538* (Toronto, 1974)

Siraisi, N.G., *Medieval and early Renaissance medicine* (Chicago, 1990)

Shahar, Shulamith, *Childhood in the Middle Ages*, trans. Chaya Galai (London and New York, 1990)

——, *The fourth estate: a history of women in the Middle Ages*, trans. Chaya Galai (London, 1990)

Sim, Alison, *Food and feast in Tudor England* (Stroud, 1997)

Simpson, A.W.B., 'The legal treatise and legal theory [Littleton's *Tenures* and after]', in E.W. Ives and A.H. Manchester (eds) *Law, litigants and the profession*, R.H.S. Studies in History series, 36 (1983), 11–29

Simpson, W. Sparrow, 'On the measure of the wound in the side of the Redeemer', *Journal of the British Archaeological Association* (1874) 357–74

Singer, D.W., 'Survey of medical manuscripts in the British Isles dating before the sixteenth century', *Proceedings of the Royal Society of Medicine*, XII (1918–19), 96–107

Slack, P., *The impact of the plague in Tudor and Stuart England* (London, 1985)

Smoller, L.A., *History, prophecy and the stars* (Princeton, 1994)

Somerville, R., *History of the duchy of Lancaster, I, 1265–1603* (London, 1953)

Sponsler, Claire, 'Eating lessons: Lydgate's "Dietary" and consumer conduct', in Ashley and Clark (eds) *Medieval conduct*, 1–22

Staniland, Kay, 'Civil costume on brasses', in Jerome Bertram (ed.) *Monumental brasses as art and history* (Stroud, 1996), 40–7

Stephens, W.B. and Norah Fuidge, 'Tudor and Stuart Congleton', in W.B. Stephens (ed.) *The History of Congleton* (Manchester, 1970), 45–81

Stevens, J., *Music and poetry in the early Tudor court* (London, 1961)

Stewart-Brown, R., 'The Cheshire Writs of Quo Warranto in 1499', *English Historical Review*, 49 (1934), 676–84
——, *The sergeants of the peace in medieval England and Wales* (Manchester, 1936)
Stoertz, Fiona Harris, 'Suffering and survival in medieval English childbirth', in Cathy Jorgensen Itnyre (ed.) *Medieval family roles. A book of essays* (New York and London, 1996), 101–20
Stone, David, *Decision-making in medieval agriculture* (Oxford, 2005)
Strohm, Paul, 'Writing and reading', in Horrox and Ormrod (eds) *A social history of England*, 454–72
Sutton, Anne and Livia Visser-Fuchs, 'The making of a minor London chronicle in the household of Sir Thomas Frowyk (died 1485)', *The Ricardian*, X, 126 (1994), 86–103
Sutton, Anne F. and Livia Visser-Fuchs, *Richard III's books: Ideal and reality in the life of a medieval prince* (Stroud, 1997)
Swabey, F., *Medieval gentlewoman: life in a widow's household in the later Middle Ages* (Stroud, 1999)
Swanson, R.N., *Church and society in late medieval England* (Oxford, 1989)
——, *Religion and devotion in Europe, c.1215–c.1515* (Cambridge, 1995)
——, 'Indulgences for prayers for the dead in the diocese of Lincoln in the early fourteenth century', *Journal of Ecclesiastical History*, 52:2 (2001), 197–219
——, 'Indulgences at Norwich cathedral priory in the later Middle Ages: popular piety in the balance sheet', *Historical Research*, 76:191 (2003), 18–29
Sylvester, Dorothy, 'The open fields of Cheshire', *THSLC*, 108 (1957 for 1956), 1–33
——, *The rural landscape of the Welsh borderland* (London, 1969)
Taithe, Bertrand and Tim Thornton (eds), *Prophecy: the power of inspired language in history, 1300–2000* (Stroud, 1997)
Talbert, E.W., 'The notebook of a fifteenth-century practising physician', *Texas Studies in English*, 21 (1942), 5–30
Tanner, Norman P., *The church in late medieval Norwich, 1370–1532* (Toronto, 1984)
Taylor, R., *Political prophecy in England* (New York, 1911)
Tentler, Thomas N., *Sin and confession on the eve of the Reformation* (Princeton, 1977)
Thirsk, J., 'The fashioning of the Tudor–Stuart gentry', *Bulletin of the John Rylands University Library*, 72 (1990), 69–85
Thomas, Keith, *Religion and the decline of magic; studies in popular beliefs in sixteenth- and seventeenth-century England* (London, 1971)
——, 'The meaning of literacy in early modern England', in Gerd Baumann (ed.) *The written word: literacy in transition* (Oxford, 1986), 97–131
Thompson, D.V., '*Liber de coloribus illuminatorum sive pictorum* from Sloane MS 1754', *Speculum*, 1 (1926), 280–307
Thompson, John J., 'The compiler in action: Robert Thornton and the "Thornton romances" in Lincoln Cathedral MS 91', in Pearsall (ed.) *Manuscripts and readers*, 113–24
——, 'Popular reading tastes in Middle English religious and didactic literature', in John Simons (ed.) *From medieval to medievalism* (London, 1992), 82–100

——, 'Authors and audiences', in Barron (ed.) *The Arthur of the English*, 371–95
Thorndike, L., *History of magic and experimental science*, vol. II (New York, 1923)
——, 'Chiromancy in medieval Latin manuscripts', *Speculum*, 40 (1965), 674–706
Thornton, Tim, 'Reshaping the local future: the development and uses of provincial political prophecy, 1300–1900', in Taithe and Thornton (eds) *Prophecy*, 52–67
——, *Cheshire and the Tudor state, 1480–1560* (Woodbridge, 2002)
Thrupp, S., *The merchant class of medieval London* (Ann Arbor, 1962)
Tonkinson, A.M., *Macclesfield in the later fourteenth century: communities of town and forest* (*CS*, 3rd ser. 44, 1999)
Trapp, J.B., 'Literacy, books and readers', in Hellinga and Trapp (eds) *Cambridge history of the book*, 31–46
Truelove, Alison, 'Literacy', in Radulescu and Truelove (eds) *Gentry culture*, 84–99
Turville-Petre, Thorlac, 'Nicholas Grimald and Alexander A', *English Literary Renaissance*, 6 (1976), 180–6
——, *The alliterative revival* (Cambridge, 1977)
Vale, M.G.A., *Piety, charity and literacy among the Yorkshire gentry, 1370–1480*, Borthwick Papers, 50 (1976)
——, 'Manuscripts and books', in Christopher Allmand (ed.) *The new Cambridge medieval history: vol. VII, c.1415–c.1500* (Cambridge, 1998)
Voigts, L.E., 'Scientific and medical books', in Griffiths and Pearsall (eds) *Book production*, 345–402
——, 'Medical prose', in A.S.G. Edwards (ed.) *Middle English prose: a critical guide to major authors and genres* (Rutgers, 1984), 315–35
Walker, Simon, *The Lancastrian affinity, 1361–1399* (Oxford, 1990)
Ward, Jennifer, C., *English noblewomen in the later Middle Ages* (London, 1992)
Watkins, A., 'Landowners and their estates in the Forest of Arden in the 15th century', *Agricultural History Review*, xlv (1997), 18–33
Wheatley, Edward, *Mastering Aesop: medieval education, Chaucer, and his followers* (Gainsville, 2000)
Whiting, R., *The blind devotion of the people* (Cambridge, 1989)
Whittle, Jane, *The development of agrarian capitalism: land and labour in Norfolk, 1440–1580* (Oxford, 2000)
Wilkins, E., *The rose garden game* (London, 1969)
Wilson, Edward, 'Local habitations and names in MS Rawlinson C813 in the Bodleian Library, Oxford', *Review of English Studies*, ns 41 (1990), 12–44
Wilson, K.P., 'The port of Chester in the fifteenth century', *THSLC*, 177 (1965), 1–15
Winchester, A.L., 'The medieval vill in the western Lake District: some problems of definition', *Transactions of the Cumberland and Westmorland Antiquarian and Archaeological Society*, lxxxviii (1978), 55–69
——, 'The castle household and demesne farm at Millom in 1513–14', *Transactions of the Cumberland and Westmorland Antiquarian Society*, 83 (1983), 85–99
——, 'Parish, township and tithing: landscapes of local administration in England before the nineteenth century', *Local Historian*, 27 (1997), 4–7

Winston-Allen, Anne, *Stories of the rose: the making of the rosary in the Middle Ages* (University Park Pa., 1997)

Withrington, John, 'The Arthurian epitaph in Malory's *Morte Darthur*', *Arthurian Literature*, VII (1987), 103–44

Woolgar, C, *The great household in late medieval England* (New Haven, 1999)

Wordsworth, C., 'On some pardons or indulgences preserved in Yorkshire, 1412–1527', *Yorkshire Archaeological Journal*, XVI (1902), 369–423

——, and H. Littlehales, *The old service books of the English Church* (London, 1904)

Wright, S.J. (ed.), *Parish, church and people: local studies in lay religion 1350–1750* (London, 1988)

Wright, Susan M., *Derbyshire gentry in the fifteenth century* (Derbyshire Record Society, VIII, 1983)

Youngs, Deborah, '*A vision in a trance*: a fifteenth-century vision of Purgatory', *Medium Aevum*, LXVII (1998), 212–34

——, 'The Parson's Tale: a newly discovered fragment', *The Chaucer Review*, 34 (1999), 207–16

——, 'Servants and labourers on a late medieval demesne: the case of Newton, Cheshire 1498–1520', *Agricultural History Review*, 47 (1999),145–60

——, 'Estate management, investment and the gentleman landlord in later medieval England', *Historical Research*, 73 (2000), 124–41

——, 'The medieval commonplace book: the example of the commonplace book of Humphrey Newton of Newton and Pownall, Cheshire (1466–1536), *Archives*, xxv, 102 (2000), 58–73

——, 'A spiritual community among Cheshire gentry', in Margaret Aston and Rosemary Horrox (eds) *Much heaving and shoving: late medieval gentry and their concerns* (Lavenham, 2005), 76–87

——, 'Cultural networks', in Radulescu and Truelove (eds) *Gentry culture*, 119–33

——, *The life cycle in Western Europe, c.1300–c.1500* (Manchester, 2006)

Zaleski, C.G., 'St Patrick's purgatory: pilgrimage motifs in a medieval otherworld vision', *Journal of the History of Ideas*, 46 (1985), 467–85

——, *Otherworld journeys: accounts of near-death experiences in medieval and modern times* (New York, 1987)

Zieglar, Philip, *The Black Death* (London, 1969)

Theses

Cavanagh, S., 'A study of books privately owned in England: 1300–1450' (2 vols, PhD thesis, University of Pennsylvania, 1980)

Fleming, P.W., 'The character and private concerns of the gentry of Kent' (PhD thesis, University of Wales Swansea, 1985)

Harrison, C.J., 'The social and economic history of Cannock and Rugeley 1546–1597' (PhD thesis, Keele University, 1974)

Meale, Carole, 'The social and literary contents of a late medieval manuscript. A study of BL Harley 2252 and its owner John Colyns' (DPhil thesis, University of York, 1984)

Rhodes, J.T., 'Private devotions in England on the eve of the Reformation' (PhD thesis, University of Durham, 1974)

Robinson, P.R., 'A study of some aspects of the transmission of English verse texts in late medieval manuscripts' (BLitt thesis, Oxford University, 1972)

Rowney, I.D., 'The Staffordshire political community, 1440–1500' (PhD thesis, Keele University, 1981)

Index

All places listed are in Cheshire (pre-1974 boundary) unless stated.

ABC of Aristotle   27, 151
Acheson, Eric   6, 82
acrostics   24, 192–3, 196
Adlington Hall and estate   15, 36, 38, 87
Aesop's fables   27, 185
Albertus Magnus   115
Alderley   59
Aldford   50, 59
Aleyn, John   80
alliterative poetry   195–99
Altrincham   30, 75
ancestors   13–14, 17, 136
arbitration   52–3, 97
Ardern, Randulph   66
Arderne, John   18
Armburgh family (Warw)   105, 191
arms, coats of   36–7, 135–6
Arthur, King   166–68
Assheton, Thomas   52, 97 n.158
Astbury church: wall painting   109
Astill, Thomas   80
astrology   157–60, 170
Audley   (Staffs)   57–8, 63–4
Augustine, St.   107, 182

Baddesley Clinton (Warw)   75
Baguley   29–30
Barlow, James of Northenden   27, n.85, 28–31, 91
Barlow, Robert   126–7
Barton, Roger, of Irlam (Lancs)   13
Beauchamp, Richard, earl of Warwick   144
Becket, Thomas   162, 166
bede roll   123, 126–7
Bedford, John, duke of   160
Beere, Richard, Abbot of Glastonbury Abbey   167–8
Benet, John   203
Bennett, Laurence   75
Bennett, Michael   6, 8, 42
Bible, books of   45, 107–8
Binski, Paul   138
Bird, John   48

birth,
   aids to   113–14, 156–7
   records of   26
Birtles, John, of Birtles   28–31
Bishop of Coventry and Lichfield, estate of   56–7
Bishop of Worcester, estate of   85
Black Prince, Prince Edward, the   4
Blackwell, Robert   62
Boke of St Albans   37, 172–3, 193
Bollin fee   101, 103–4
Bollin, Lords of   22, 90–1, 136
Bollin river   84, 91–2
Bollington   74
booklets   181–2, 189
books   143, 153–4, 203–4
   conduct (mirrors of princes, 'courtesy' treatises)   107, 147–8, 154, 169–70, 172–4
   of secrets   114–5
Bosworth Field, battle of (1485)   164, 198
Boyd, Thomas, earl of Arran   170
Booth family, of Barton (Lancs)   197
Booth family, of Dunham Massey   101, 137, 178–9, 198, 208–9
Booth, Elizabeth of Dunham Massey   197
Booth, John of Twemlow   183
Booth, George of Dunham Massey (d. 1531)   112, 197–8, 208
Booth, Robert of Dunham Massey (d. 1460)   90, 137 n.145, 198
Booth, William of Dunham Massey   22, 102, 135, 198–9, 208
Boteler, Thomas of Bewsey (Lancs)   32 n.117, 34, 52
Bowker, Thomas   197
Bradley Hall (Lancs)   146
Bramhall Hall and estate   73, 84, 208
Brent, William (of Kent)   146
Brereton family, of Malpas   44
Brome, book of   107–9, 181
   see also Melton, Robert

249

INDEX

Bromley-Davenport family, of Capesthorne 38
Brown family, of Marsh (Derbys) 91
Brown, Nicholas 91–2
Broxton Hundred 72, 100
Brut chronicle 164–5
Bryene, Alice de 151
Buckingham, Edward, duke of 146
Buckingham, Humphrey, duke of 61
burials 16, 136
Burton in Wirral 56
Butley township 76, 93–5, 97–9

Calveley family, of Lea 37
Calveley, George, of Lea (d. 1536) 29, 89, 98, 126–7, 178
Calveley, George, of Lea (d. 1585) 36
Carpenter, Christine 3, 82, 141, 176, 210 n.36
cartularies 4, 182
Casker, John 86
Castletown, Robert (Surrey) 139
Catesby family, of Ashby St Legers (Northants) 149
Caxton, William 157–8, 160, 166, 173–4
charterhouses 119–20
chapel
    Alderwasley (Derbys) 132
    Green chapel, Millington 129
    Lyme (Prestbury parish) 129
    Mottram St Andrew 126–8, 132
    Poynton cum Woodford 133
    Talke (Staffs) 120–1
    See also Newton chapel, Pott Shrigley chapel
Chapel-en-le-Frith (Derbys) 75, 207
chapel of ease 131–2
chaplains 127
Charlemagne prayer 112
charms 112–6
chastity, declaration of 47–8
Chaucer, Alice, duchess of Suffolk 170
Chaucer, Geoffrey 192
    Canterbury Tales 179, 199
        Franklin's Prologue 192
        General Prologue 148, 192
        Knight's Tale 171–2
        Parson's Tale 107, 115, 171, 185, 187
Cheshire
    county administration 65–7
    county court 43, 65–6
    economy 6, 74, 75, 87

marriages 29–30
lawyers 43–4
military history 14
mise 18, 94
visitation of 1580 38
Cheshire acre 71 n.6
Chester
    churches 109, 120–1
    earls of 17, 26, 165–6
    town 65, 112, 164
Chetham, Thomas, of Nuthurst (Lancs) 199
chiromancy 160
Cholmondeley Hall 145
Christine de Pizan 23
Christocentric devotions 108–9, 168
church ales 125–6
church donations 125–6
Church Minshull 101–2, 104
Clare family 137
Clarence, George, duke of 20
Clayton, Dorothy 7, 16, 210 n.36
Clerk, Richard, of Prestbury 90
Clervaux, Richard of Croft (Yorks) 89, 206
Cleyley 89
Cliff, Robert 199
cloth industry 87–8
clothes 28–9, 48–9, 89, 118
    see also Ellen Newton and Humphrey Newton
Coke, Richard 148–9
Coldeaton (Derbys) 20–1
Colshaw 123
Colyns, John 166, 180
commonplace book, definition of 180–1
    lists in 166, 168, 182–3
    see also Brome, John Crophill, John Colyns, Richard Hill, and Robert Reynes
commonplace book of Humphrey Newton 4–5, 179, 181–9, 215–7
    appearance of 186–9
    construction of 183–4
    contents pages 185–6
    decoration 189
    doodles in 20, 188
    literary miscellany 24, 154, 184
    medical miscellany 155–7, 184
    order of 184–5
    sketches in 1, 171
Congleton
    manor of 56, 58, 60, 63

mayor of   57, 117
town of   58–9, 75
cookbooks   150
Coote, Lesley   161
Corbeil, Giles: *De urinis*   155–6
Coss, Peter   143
Counsel   50–1
Court of Augmentations   129–31
Court of Chancery   102–3, 202
court, portmote   59
court procedures   55–6
courts, manorial   55, 59
Crewe, Thomas, of Sond   16–17
Crophill, John, of Wix (Essex)   158, 180, 188
Cross, Thomas, of Norton   1, 85–6
crosses   112, 167–8
Crowther, Gilbert   51
Crowther, Joyce   51, 97
Crux Christi prayer   112, 182

Davenport family, of Bramhall   133, 178
Davenport family, of Davenport   11, 15, 94, 145
Davenport family, of Fulshaw   103–4
Davenport family, of Woodford   71, 92
Davenport, Hugh, of Henbury   18
Davenport, John, of Bramhall   74
Davenport, John, of Wheltrough (d. 1390)   43
Davenport, John, of Woodford   132
Davenport, Robert, of Davenport   96
Davenport, Sybil, of Davenport   11
Davenport, Thomas, of Davenport (fl. 1260–1320)   11
Davenport, Thomas, of Fulshaw   28
Davenport, William, of Bramhall (d. 1528)   53, 66, 102, 208
Davenport, William, of Bramhall (d. 1541)   29–30, 74
David, Humphrey   47
Dean Farm   35, 73, 91–2
Dean Row, Bollin fee   90–1
dedimus potestatum   46, 50, 103
Delamere Forest   163–4
Delamere, Lady Jane of Aldermaston (Berks)   9, 134
Denby (Derbys)   20
Destruction of Troy   199
De Vere, earls of Oxford   144
devotional literature   107–9
Dicts and sayings of the philosophers   174
Dives and Pauper   115

Domes of Urine   156
Doncaster (Yorks)   75
Downes family, of Worth   178–9
Downes, Sybil, of Worth   11, 196
Downes, William, of Worth   11
dowries   29–30, 32
dower   23
Duchy of Lancaster   56, 88
Duffy, Eamon   107, 118
Duncalf, Thomas, of Foxtwist, sergeant at law   43, 45
Duncalf, Thomas, of Foxtwist, steward of Butley   94, 97, 99
Dutton, William of Denbigh   15
Dyer, Christopher   82

Eardswick   101–4
Edington (Somerset)   168
Eccles church (Lancs)   197
Elizabeth of York   198
Elvethall (Durham)   79
Episcopal registers   121–2
Erasmus: *Praise of Folly*   122
Erceldoune, Thomas of, prophesier   163–4
Etchells   59

Fastolf, John   160
Fayreford, Thomas   158, 187
fertility   25
Findern family, of Findern (Derbys)   191, 193, 197, 200
Fitton family, of Gawsworth   66, 101, 178–9
Fitton family, of Pownall   22, 140
Fitton, Edward, of Gawsworth (d. 1510)   18, 29, 101–2
Fitton, Elizabeth, of Pownall   102
Fitton, Laurence, of Gawsworth   22
Fitton, Margaret, of Pownall (d. 1557)   101–3
Fitton, Richard, of Pownall (d. 1436)   125, 135, 154
Fitton, Thomas, of Pownall (d. 1506)   21–3, 66 n.145, 100–1, 102, 103, 123, 135, 140, 184–5
Fitton, William, of Fernleigh (d. 1523)   91
Fitzherbert family monuments   136
Fitzherbert, John, of Norbury (Derbys)   84
Fitzwarren, Lord   45, 57, 60
Fleming, Peter   58, 124

Fleta 60
Flodden Field, battle of (1513)   163, 198, 208
florilegia   181
For to serve a lord   147–51
formulary documents   45, 47–50, 187–8
Fortescue, John   62, 68
   Notes on the purchasing of land   182
Foulshurst, Thomas   63
Foxtwist   84, 92, 96–7
fraternities   120–1, 126–7
Fraternity of St Chad at Lichfield   121
Fraternity of St George at St Peter's Chester   109
Frederick the Wise, Elector of Saxony   121
French, Katherine   125
friendship   19, 31, 206, 208–9
Frowyk, Thomas   166, 183
Fulshaw   103–4
Furnivall, F.J.   148
Fyncham, Simon of Fincham (Norfolk)   206

Gawain and the Green Knight   6, 195–7
gentry   2–3, 7–8, 66, 143–4
   burial practices   136–7
   Cheshire   7, 16, 29–30, 52, 66, 69, 136–7, 145, 178, 199–200
   culture   143–4, 209
   Derbyshire   7, 29, 33, 82
   entrepreneurship   82, 86
   Gloucestershire   7
   Kent   7, 124, 145
   Leicestershire   35 n.131, 82, 104
   Nottinghamshire   7–8
   piety   106, 124–5, 133
   Warwickshire   13, 33, 82, 104
Giles of Rome: *De regimine principum*   169–70, 172, 185
Glastonbury Abbey   166–8, 181
Gloucester, Humphrey, duke of   160
Godley   52
Golbourne Bellow   104
Gower, John: *Confessio Amantis*   199
Grafton   17
Grene, Philip   80
Grey, George, earl of Kent   57, 60
Grey, Lord Henry, of Codnor   20
Grey of Ruthin estates   61–2
Guddat-Figge G.   180
Guy of Warwick   168–9

Hagley (Staffordshire)   95

Handforth   15, 32 n.117
Handforth, William, of Handforth (d. 1513)   32, 135, 208
Handley   21, 104
   church   21
Hanna, Ralph   184, 190
Harding, Vanessa   136
Hardman, Philippa   183
harp   194
Harriss, Gerald   176, 203
Hastings, William, Lord   20, 160
Hawarden of Hawarden family   49
hawking   173
Heal, Felicity   146–7
Herefordshire   48, 121–2
Hill, Richard   26–7, 108, 114–5, 147, 156, 166, 168, 180–1, 184–5
Hockenhall, Richard   49
Holborn, St Andrew's Church   16
Holynshead, William   133
Hoppehall, William (alias Newton)   11, 13
Hopton, John   3, 62, 66, 72, 206, 210
Hopton, Thomasin   24
Hough, James   79–80
Hough, John   79
Hough, William   79–81, 148
household book of Edward IV   144, 172, 194, 197
Hulse, Thomas, of Norbury   59, 178
humours   159–60
hunting   173
Huxley   31, 57, 104
Hyde, Robert, of Norbury (13th century)   96
Hyde, Robert of Norbury (d. 1528)   53

Idley, Peter   24, 81, 172
indulgences, *see* pardons
infant mortality   26–7
ink recipes   189
Inner Temple   43–4
Inns of Court   16, 42–3, 46 n.29, 202
Ireland, Thomas, of Hale (Lancs)   198

Jodrell, Nicholas, of Yeardsley   51, 110, 178, 207
John of Glastonbury   166–7
Jones, Peter   155, 187
Joseph of Arimathea   167–8

Kebell, Thomas   9, 41, 65, 76
Keen, Maurice   14, 36

INDEX

king lists   49–50, 165–6
Knight, Henry of Wilmslow   138
Knutsford   59–60, 75

Lady Bessy   198
Lancashire
  chapels   132
  chantries   127
  monasteries   61
Lanspergius of Cologne (d. 1539)   110
law, expenses and profits of   20–1, 46–8, 63–5
lawyers   41–2
  and literature   68
Leche, John, of Nantwich   178–9
Lees family, of Newton   77–8, 80–1, 88 n.115, 206
Legal
  education   20, 42–4
  notebooks   44–6, 48
  terminology   45, 50
Legh family, of Adlington   71, 73, 92, 103, 133, 173, 178, 207
Legh, Ellen, of Adlington   51, 97–8
Legh, George, of Adlington   66
Legh, John, of Baguley   102, 198
Legh of Lyme family   146
Legh, Sir Philip, of Booth   59–60, 97 n.158, 102, 178
Legh, Sir Piers, of Lyme   52, 138
Legh, Reginald, of Adlington   51, 98
Legh, Robert, of Blakebroke (Derbys)   52–3
Legh, Roger, of Ridge (d. 1506)   52–3, 119, 139
Legh, Thomas, of Adlington   51, 92, 97–8, 132
Leicester, John, of Nether Tabley   42
Leicester, John   67
Leycester, Sir Peter   17
Leland, John   59, 83, 145, 208
libraries   154, 179
London   16, 43, 67–8, 134, 136, 153, 166, 182
Long Dutton church (Surrey)   139
Longinus   111
Lowe, Humphrey, of Denby (Derbys)   19, 21, 102
Lowe, Laurence, of Denby (Derbys)   16, 18–20, 43, 96, 124, 185
Lowe, Ottiwell, of Denby (Derbys)   19–20, 43

Lowe, Thomas, of Alderwasley (Derbys)   19, 132
Lostock (now Lostockfarm Hall)   35
Lydgate, John   170–1
  Look in the Mirror   171, 185
  Siege of Thebes   169–70
Lynwood, William: *Provinciale*   107, 131
lyrics   190–6

Macclesfield   14, 45
  church   119, 139
  forest   73
  hundred and court   65–6, 92, 94
  manor of   90
  mayor of   90, 102
Maddern, Philippa   147
magic tricks   114
Mainwaring family, of Peover   31, 135–6
Mainwaring, Charles, of Croxton   101–2
Mainwaring, James, of Croxton   101–2
Mainwaring, John, of Peover (d. 1515)   32
Mainwaring, Katherine, of Peover   32–3
Malory, Thomas: *Morte Darthur*   166, 172, 194
Manchester (Lancs)   75
Manchester College   198–9
manuscripts
  BL, MS Egerton 1995   173–4
  see also commonplace book
Marian devotions   108, 120, 167–8
masses   112, 123–4, 134
Mass of St Gregory   119, 123–4, 183
Master of the Game   176
meal-times   146–50
medical recipes   155–6
Melton, Robert   180
  See also Brome, book of
memorials (tombs, brasses)   119, 134–40
Mere, John of Mere   178
Mertes, Kate   7, 10, 147
miracle collections   108
Milford Haven (Pembrokeshire)   164
Millom (Cumberland)   80
Mills   64, 85
Milton, Alice, wife of Oliver Newton   16–17, 19, 72
Milton Hall   91
Milton, Morgan   88
Minshull Vernon   31, 101–2
Minshull, William, of Minshull   101–3

INDEX

minstrels 28, 126, 151
Mirk, John: *Festial* 107, 123
Mirrour of the world 157–8
Modus tenendi curiam baronis cum visu franci plegii 55
More, Thomas 68, 122, 153
Moreton, Charles 5, 15
Morgan, Philip 136
Mottram St Andrew 30, 89, 91
    see also chapel, Mottram
Mottram Hall 126
Mottershead, Edward 126–7, 132, 206–7
Mottram, Adam 126

Name of Jesus 113, 115, 119
names 16, 19, 26, 113, 115
nativities 158–9
Needham family 145
Neville, Cicely, duchess of York 144, 197
Newark church (Notts) 108, 179, 182
Newport (Salop) 97
Newton chapel 99–100, 128–33
Newton family, of Mottram-in-Longdendale 37
Newton family, of Newton and Pownall
    burial places 16, 137
    cartulary 4, 96
    coat of arms 33, 36–9, 135–6
    seal 36–7
Newton, Ellen, wife of Humphrey Newton (d. 1536)
    childbirth 25, 113
    clothes 23
    death 39
    heiress 21,100–1, 103, 135–6, 140
    inquisition *post mortem* 100–1, 103
    management of household 24
    marriage 21
    tomb 137–40
Newton estate 11, 71, 95, 104
    accounts 76–8, 82, 181–2, 184
    boundary of 89–92
    cattle 74, 132
    corn mill 85–6, 128
    counters 75
    crops 73, 83
    feoffees of 20, 32 n.117, 207–8
    fish 84–5, 150
    fulling mill 1, 86–8, 92, 128
    harvesters 73, 78–9
    investment 82–88
    labourers 78, 145
    labour services on 72

Lenten purchases 77, 85, 150
markets of 75
marl 83–4
management 76–8
rabbit 75, 149
rentals 71–2, 82–4, 187
rents 72, 86
servants 24, 79–81, 146, 148–9
sheep 30, 74
swan 75, 149
tenants of 72, 94, 97–8
timber 75
tithes 83, 125
wages on 78, 80
Newton, Francis, son of Humphrey Newton 25, 34–5
Newton Hall 71, 145–6, 151
Newton Heath 51, 93–7, 99–100
Newton, Hugh, son of Humphrey Newton 34–5
Newton, Humphrey, of Newton and Pownall (d. 1536)
    ancestors 10–11, 123
    birth 18
    children 25–7, 31–5
    clothes 151–2
    document searches 14–15, 89–90
    dower payments 23, 134
    dowry payments 30–1
    feoffee, acting as 51–2
    handwriting 186–8
    inheritance 71–2, 100–2
    inquisition *post mortem* 71, 98, 100, 128
    jewellery 152
    legal adviser 51–3
    litigation 91–2, 96–7, 102–3
    marriage 21–5
    merchant sign of 88
    poetry 24–5, 190–6
    uncles 19
    scribe 47–8
    signature 49, 186–7
    sisters 18, 28–9, 108
    social advancement 9, 209–10
    social network 207–9
    stewardships 45, 50, 53–6, 62–4, 80
    tomb of 3, 137–40, 152
Newton, Humphrey, son of Humphrey Newton 26, 31, 34–5, 103–4
Newton, Jane (d. 1498) wife of Richard Newton 18

254

INDEX

Newton, John, of Congleton, visionary 117–18, 152
Newton, John, priest 119
Newton, Oliver, of Newton 13, 16–17, 36, 38, 72
Newton, Richard, of Newton (living 1306) 11, 13–14, 76, 196–7
Newton, Richard, of Newton (living 1336–1415) 11, 13–14, 137
Newton, Richard, of Newton (d. 1497) 18–19, 90, 96, 124, 137
Newton, Thomas, of Newton 11, 13, 15, 36
Newton township 89, 93–7, 165
Newton, William, of Pownall, son of Humphrey Newton 4, 26–8, 31–2, 65 n.142, 93, 96, 99, 131, 159, 182, 198
Newton, William, of Pownall (in 1570s) 38, 145–6
Newton, William of Pownall (d. 1621) 40 n.149, 183 n.31
Nixon, Robert, prophesier 163
Norbury church (Derbys) 136
Norcliffe mill 35, 87, 206
Northenden 27 n.85, 28, 29, 30
Norton (Staffs) 57
Nuthurst (Lancs) 199

Olivier de la Marche 10
Oulton 101–2, 104
Ovid 193

pardoners 121–2
pardons 111, 119–23
Parker, David 168, 181
Parkes, Malcolm 153
Paston family 9, 15, 50, 52, 78, 105, 119, 152
Paston, Anne 170
Paston, Edmund 68
Paston, John (d. 1479) 154, 176
Paston, Margaret 24, 136
Paston, William 95, 98
Payling, Simon 8
perfect age 172, 211
Perkynson, Thomas, minstrel 162–3
perpetual lamps 124
Philomena 171–2, 182, 186–7, 189, 195
Pigot family, of Butley 93–4, 96, 173
Pigot, John, of Butley (early 14th century) 43
Pigot, John of Butley (1450s) 96

Pigot, Robert, of Butley (d.1536) 96–7, 99
Pigot, Thomas, of Butley 93
Pigot, William, of Butley 96
pilgrimage 108
plague 16, 89–90, 93, 112, 164–5
Plumpton family, of Plumpton (Yorks) 105
Plumpton, Sir Robert, of Plumpton (d.1507) 62
Pope Innocent VIII 111
Port, John, of Etwall (Derbys) 43–44, 139
Porter's Hall (Essex) 73, 79
Pott Shrigley chapel 74, 129, 154, 179
Pounds, N.J.G. 124–5
Pownall estate 22, 100–2, 104
  feoffees in/of 20, 32 n.117, 102, 207–8
Pownall Hall 38, 133, 145–6
Pownall, John of Pownall 65, 66 n.145
prayers 106–8, 110, 112–3, 135–6, 140, 151
Prestbury church 90, 124–5, 131–2, 137, 199
Prestbury parsonage 73, 132
Preston, Robert 120, 122–3
prophecy 161–4
Prophesies of Rymour, Beid and Marlyng 163–4
proverbs 174
Purgatory 116–24, 135, 140
puture 94

quadrant 159, 190
quo warranto proceedings 59, 65

Radcliff (Lancs) 108
Ramston family (Essex) 194
reading circles 197
Reddich, Robert, of Grappenhall 177
restitution 133–4
Reynes, Robert, of Acle (Norfolk) 107–9, 113, 156, 180, 186
Richard de Caistre's Hymn 109, 186–9, 195
Richard II and Cheshire 14
Richmond, Colin 3, 66, 119
Riddy, Felicity 144, 200
Robbins, R.H. 195, 199
Rode, William, of Congleton 19, 46–7, 60
romance 176

INDEX

rosary 119–20
Rosser, Gervase 131
Ryle, Henry of Wilmslow 133, 135

Sacred Heart 109–10, 185
saints 109
   Benignus 168
   Dunstan 168
   George 109
St Erkenwald 197
Salter, John 44, 97
Saul, Nigel 136, 173
scribes 46, 180–1
Scope v Grosvenor dispute 36
Scottish Field 163, 164 n.110, 198–9
seneschallus curie 54
Secreta mulierum 156
Secreta secretorum 115, 159, 169–70, 176, 187
Seneschaucy 54
service books 129–30
seven ages of the world 158
seven deadly sins 107
sheep farming 74
Shirley, John (d. 1456) 182
Shrewsbury, battle of (1403) 166
signatures 177–8
singing 194
sketchbooks 187–8
Smale, William 92, 148
Smith, William 57
Sneyd, Richard 44, 61–2, 64, 67
Southampton 88
speech, regulation of 172–4, 209
spices 150
Stafford family, dukes of Buckingham 58
Stafford, Humphrey, of Grafton (Worc) 60
Stanford, William 45
Stanley, Edward, Lord Mounteagle (d.1524) 34
Stanley, James, bishop of Ely 164 n.111, 198–9
Stanley, John, of Handforth (d.1527) 132, 198–9, 208
Stanley, John of Etchells (d.1508) 50, 59–60. 64
Stanley literature 163–4, 198, 208
Stanley, Thomas, earl of Derby (d.1504) 164 n.111, 198–9
Stanley, William 67
Star Chamber 46 n.29

Starkey, Ethelreda, daughter of Laurence Starkey 34
Starkey, Humfrey 52, 139
Starkey, Laurence 34
Starkey, Richard, of Stretton 135
statute merchant 59
Statute of Westminster II, 1285 (*de donis conditionalibus*) 49, 93
Statute of Westminster III, 1290 (*Quia Emptores*) 50
steward 41, 54–56, 60–4
Stockport 59–60, 63–4, 75
Stoke Field, battle of (1487) 163
strapwork 49, 187–8
sumptuary legislation 149, 152
Sutton, John 178
Sutton, Richard 43, 44 n.16, 52 n.68, 178, 187
sweating sickness 112
Swettenham, William of Swettenham 66

talismans 112
Tarvin 56–7
Tattenhall 57–8, 60, 64
Tatton family, of Wythenshawe 27 n.85
Tatton, John, of Wythenshawe 51, 178, 208
   William Tatton, of Tatton 29
Thornbury (Glouc) 146
Thornton, Robert of East Newton (Yorks) 107–8, 112, 124, 178, 189, 204
Thornton, Tim 6, 8,9, 46 n.29
Touchet, Lords Audeley 56–7
Touchet, James, 7th Lord Audley 57, 134
Townshend family, of Townshend (Norfolk) 9, 15, 74, 105, 146
Townshend, Eleanor 24
Townshend, Roger (d.1493) 5, 41, 50, 62, 77, 154
Townshend, Roger (d. 1551) 88
township, operation of 93, 95, 98
Trafford family, of Trafford (Lancs) 101, 135, 137, 178–9, 208
Trafford, Edmund, of Trafford, knt (d.1513) 102, 178, 208
Trafford, Edmund, of Trafford, esq (d.1533) 208
Trafford, Henry, rector of Wilmslow 135 n.134, 139–40
Trevisa, John 170
Trewythian, Richard of London 158
Trotula 155–7
Trussell family 57–8

Unsworth, Thomas, chaplain   126–7
urinaries   155–6
Uvedale, William   180

Valor ecclesiasticus   61
Vawdray, Robert   28
Vawdray, Robert of Riddings (d.1576)   30
Vawdray, Thomas   28
Venables, William   67
Verdon family, of Fulshaw   103
Verdon, John (d. 1522)   103
Verdon, Thomas, of Fulshaw   32 n.117, 34, 103
Veronica, St., and the vernicle   109, 188, 195
view of frankpledge   55, 59
Virgin *see* Marian devotion
Vision in a trance   116–19
visions of the otherworld   109, 116–19, 152, 190
Vision of Drythelm   116, 118
Vision of the Monk of Eynsham   117
Vision of Tundale   116

Wales, the Welsh   14–15, 164
Warde, John of Capesthorne   183
Warde, John, of Monksheath   183 n.31
Warmingham   57–8, 60, 63–4
Warren family, of Poynton   59, 178–9
Warren, John, of Poynton   53, 59
Warren, Laurence, of Poynton   59
Webb, William   40
wedding celebrations   28–9, 150–1
Wellys, Humphrey   191–2, 196
wet nurses   25–6
Willot, Griffith   92, 97
Willot, Thomas   99
Willot, William   97
Wilmslow   108
  church   33, 36, 38, 123, 125, 133, 135–40, 208–9
  parish   120
Wilmslow riot   69–70
Wilmslow wakes   126
Winnington, Richard   30
Winwick (Lancs)   199
Wiot, Hugh   47
Wode, Thomas   50
Wolsey, Thomas   46 n.29, 74
Woodford   132–3
Woodville, Anthony, 2nd earl Rivers   174
Woolf, Virginia   1
Worcester, William   41, 68, 167, 169, 203
Worleston   101–2, 104
Worth family, of Titherington   87
Wounds of Christ   109–11
Wrenbury   101–2, 104
writing   177–9, 181
Wyatt, John   79, 85

Zodiac   159